Moral Philosophy

MORAL PHILOSOPHY

*A Systematic Introduction to Normative
Ethics and Meta-ethics*

Richard T. Garner

Bernard Rosen

The Ohio State University

The Macmillan Company, New York

Collier-Macmillan Limited, London

Second Printing, 1972

Three pages of the discussion of the ideal observer theory in Chapter 11 appeared in a paper published in *Philosophy and Phenomenological Research* (XXVII). We are grateful to the editor of that journal for permission to include the material in this book.

Library of Congress catalog card number: 67–18887

THE MACMILLAN COMPANY, NEW YORK
COLLIER-MACMILLAN CANADA, LTD., TORONTO, ONTARIO

Printed in the United States of America

To our parents

Preface

In recent years, philosophers have come to accept a distinction between normative ethics and meta-ethics. Although it is not possible, in practice, to keep the two fields strictly separate, the distinction has been found of great use in sorting out and treating the questions with which moral philosophers deal. This book, therefore, reflects the division. Part One is devoted to the more important normative theories and Part Three deals with questions in meta-ethics. Part Two discusses two problems related to normative ethics: ethical relativism and freedom of the will.

This book is not a mere summary of the views discussed but is an attempt to support views we believe correct and to provide reasons for rejecting views we consider wrong. We have also sometimes found it necessary to distinguish a number of different views that are traditionally classified together. In order to assess any theory, it is important to see as clearly as possible just what is being considered and to know how to support and attack, in a rational way, the theory in question. We have tried, in two ways, to bring the reader to the level at which he can do this for himself: first, we have discussed the defense of theories and the use of simple but essential logical tools; second—and more important—we have attempted, by example, to show the reader how these tools may be employed.

This book can be used as an introduction to moral philosophy, and it is suitable for those who have had no previous exposure to philosophy. Not all the chapters are of equal difficulty, for we have attempted to allow the nature of the subject matter to dictate the depth of our inquiry. The last three chapters are necessarily the most difficult in the book. It would be quite possible, in a short introductory course, to use only the first ten chapters, for Chapter 10 provides a general treatment of some of the material explored in depth in Chapters 11–13. This book can be used with or without additional readings, and—although primarily intended for introductory courses—it would, when accompanied by adequate readings, be useful on a moderately advanced level. The items in the bibliographies are of unequal difficulty and of unequal importance. Unfortunately, sometimes the difficult items are also the important ones. We have taken the liberty of placing stars in front of those articles and works not recommended immediately to beginning students. A star indicates either that the article is nearly inaccessible, too difficult for the beginner, or of interest only to an advanced student. In a few cases we have not placed a star in front of an important work, despite its difficulty. In these cases we feel that the extra work required of a beginner would be justified.

We wish to express our appreciation to our colleagues at The Ohio State University with whom we have discussed many of these topics, and especially to Dr. Paul J. Olscamp and B. R. Nyland. A group of students from the International School of America (1965–66) willingly sacrificed many hours to read and comment on an earlier draft of this book. Concurrently, another group, in Columbus, also read the manuscript. The suggestions that came out of these sessions were of immense value to us and showed us in many cases how to improve the presentation of a particular point.

One person, Miss Kathleen Emmett, not only read the entire draft and made many helpful suggestions, but also assisted in the proofreading, preparation of the final manuscript, and compiled the index. We are especially grateful to her for this. Mrs. Betsy Rosen carefully went over earlier chapters of the manuscript and assisted in the typing and the proofreading.

A detailed, penetrating, and stimulating commentary on an earlier manuscript was provided by Professor Carl Wellman, who pointed out several philosophical mistakes and unclear passages and suggested numerous organizational improvements. This commentary was of the highest quality and proved to be of immense value to us; we are deeply indebted to him. Finally, a research grant from The Ohio State University helped defer the cost of the preparation of the manuscript.

Although it is impossible to separate completely the respective contributions of the two authors, and although each chapter includes numerous comments and suggestions made by both, the basic tasks of organization and writing can be divided in the following way: Rosen—Chapters 1, 5, 8, 9, and 12; Garner—Chapters 3, 4, 6, 7, 10, 11, and 13.

R. T. G.
B. R.
The Ohio State University

Contents

PART TWO   RELATED NONNORMATIVE QUESTIONS

PART THREE   META-ETHICS

PART ONE

Normative Ethics

Theories and Ethical Theories

Moral problems are an unquestioned aspect of everyone's life. Examples of such problems range from the actual and common ("Ought I take this book back to the library?") to the hypothetical and bizarre ("If I could save a hundred lives by pressing a red button which would also cut off the left hand of every tenth philosophy professor, ought I to press the button?"). In this book we shall rarely deal with particular problems for their own sake; we shall, rather, use them as illustrations of how ethical theories may be used to provide very general directions leading to answers for specific questions. One such ethical theory, with which everyone is familiar, is utilitarianism, the view that we all have an obligation to bring about the greatest good for the greatest number of people.

Moral philosophy, then, is a consideration not of specific moral problems, but of general moral theories dealing with a wide range of topics. There are *theories of obligation*, which deal with the question "Which actions are morally right and wrong?," and *theories of value*, which deal with such questions as "What is a morally good man?," "What things are good in themselves?," and "Which desires, intentions, and motives are worthwhile?" In order to gain an understanding of what it is to examine and assess a theory, we shall discuss some scientific theories and then attempt to show how these resemble and differ from theories in ethics. We shall also introduce some techniques which, we believe, are useful in assessing all sorts of theories.

A. Scientific Theories

1. *The Geocentric and the Heliocentric Theories.* In the sixteenth and early seventeenth centuries, a dispute concerning the relative merits of the geocentric and the heliocentric theories was at its high point, engaging some

of the best minds of the time. Copernicus, in 1542, had proposed the heliocentric theory, the theory that the earth moves around the sun. This hypothesis conflicted directly with another—the geocentric theory, according to which the sun and all the other heavenly bodies moved around the earth. At that time this second theory was held by practically all men, educated and uneducated alike.

Those who defended the geocentric theory argued that, if the earth were moving around the sun, then objects would not fall directly under the point from which they were dropped. Another point they made was that if the earth were moving, gigantic winds would be generated. Furthermore they argued that, because the earth must be rotating if it is moving around the sun, the speed of the rotation would generate centrifugal forces so great that the planet would be destroyed. Some geocentricists argued from philosophical principles, such as, "It is the nature of the earth to be in the center of the universe." Others argued from theological premises, such as, "God made the earth as the center of the universe."

Most of these arguments are quite unconvincing today, and are such that even a beginning student in science could reply to them adequately. However, one argument called upon by the supporters of the geocentric theory deserves to be taken more seriously. If the heliocentric theory were correct, they argued, then parallax would have been observed, which it was not.

Parallax is the apparent movement of an observed object against a fixed background; the "movement" results from the movement of the perceiver. For example, if one holds up a finger and observes it first with only one eye open and then only with the other, the finger will seem to move in relation to the fixed background—be it a wall or whatever. The finger does not really move—nor, of course, does the wall; it is the point of observation that moves, from one eye to the other.

Now, if the earth moves around the sun, the geocentricists suggested, a comparison of observations of the fixed stars at two different times of the year would show the sun (which is analogous to the finger) "moving" against the background of the fixed stars (which is analogous to the wall). The fact that parallax could not be discovered seemed to be powerful evidence in favor of the geocentric theory. But in 1838, after advances in the art of building telescopes, parallax *was* observed, and this last argument against the heliocentric theory fell. Since Copernicus published *De Revolutionibus Orbium Caelestium* in 1543, almost three hundred years passed before this final objection was met.

a. THE TWO THEORIES AS COMPETITORS. The geocentric and the heliocentric theories were competitors in that each claimed to be the correct explanation of the movement of the planets and other heavenly bodies. Moreover, both theories "worked," because either could be used to explain the same range of phenomena. Furthermore, either theory, could be used to predict

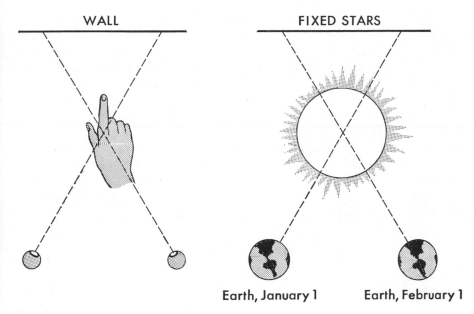

WALL   FIXED STARS

Earth, January 1   Earth, February 1

Examples of Parallax

the future position of any planet and the date of solar and lunar eclipses (the equations and principles of the geocentric theory involved more complex computations than those of the heliocentric theory, but the result was the same).

But although we can now detect parallax, in a sense one could maintain that the geocentric theory is correct. One might say, for example, that the orbit of the fixed stars is odd; that the stars all rotate around the earth in strange paths. This claim will necessitate other changes in the system and lead to a strange physics in which the stars can move faster than the speed of light (for otherwise they would not be able to move so far in such a short time). These facts do not, however, *force* anyone to give up the geocentric theory. In this sense no one is ever forced to give up any theory; any theory can be asserted as long as it is self-consistent. By the same token, one can hold that Mars, or Providence, Rhode Island, is the center of the universe. If one claims that a theory can be "held," in this sense, he is claiming only that the theory is self-consistent. Anyone can construct consistent theories; the difficulty lies in constructing—or selecting—that one theory which is best.

We might ask, however, why the heliocentric theory won any acceptance before parallax was detected. The answer is that the acceptability of a theory does not always depend upon crucial experiments, and when two competing theories "work" in the ways described, other considerations begin to be significant.

b. GENERAL CRITERIA OF ACCEPTABILITY OF THEORIES. Let us set out some of these considerations, and then apply them by comparing two other theories —one will be recognized to be absurd, the other is almost universally accepted.

We shall begin by considering some elementary criteria for the acceptability of scientific theories. Many such criteria have been proposed—some helpful, many not. Some of the helpful criteria are so complex that we, as laymen, could not possibly understand or apply them. Others, less helpful, are such that they distort the question from the very start, suggesting as it were, some particular theory. We shall propose, and then explain, three criteria for the acceptability of scientific theories which suffer from neither of these defects. These criteria should also be of use in the evaluation of theories in other areas, and especially in ethics. A theory ought to be accepted if and only if it meets the following conditions:

1. Serious objections to the theory can be answered adequately.
2. There are good reasons (independent of the statement of the theory itself) in favor of the theory.
3. The theory either fits or explains the range of phenomena better than other competing theories.

Notice that if there are two competing theories in the same area, it is not possible for both theories to meet all three criteria. This is primarily because of Condition 3, for if one theory explains the range of phenomena better than all its competitors it is not possible for any other theory to satisfy this requirement. It is possible, however, that no one theory satisfies Condition 3, in which case it is necessary to wait for further data before deciding which of the competing theories is the most acceptable. It is also possible that no theory perfectly meets all the conditions for acceptability. There might be an objection to a theory, for example, which the theory cannot adequately answer, and there may also be strong objections against all competing theories. In such a situation, we would accept the theory that best fulfills the criteria. (Fortunately, this situation does not arise too often in science or ethics.) Let us now compare two rival theories and attempt to see just how these criteria can be applied.

2. *The Gremlin vs. the Biological Theory of Nourishment.* All of us suppose that food is required for nourishment and the maintenance of life. We also believe that we ingest food, that it is chemically changed by various substances the body produces, and finally absorbed by the billions of cells that make up the human body. This is *the biological theory of nourishment*. In contrast, let us propose what we shall call *the gremlin theory of nourishment*, according to which food has nothing to do with nourishment and the maintenance of life, but that three gremlins found in the stomach radiate *sustinen*, an energy-giving force that nourishes and sustains us.

a. CRITERION 1: DOES THE THEORY ANSWER ADEQUATELY SERIOUS OBJEC-TIONS? In a sense, the gremlin theory "works." It accounts for at least some (and its defenders claim *all*) of the phenomena explained by the biological theory. If we were to argue against a proponent of the gremlin theory, we would probably say something like this "Your claim that there are such beings is contrary to other available evidence. For example, all the evidence we have from physics and biology indicates that these gremlins must be relatively large in order to fulfill their supposed biological tasks, but they apparently do not have mass. This is contrary to evidence available in physics. Moreover, no one has ever observed these beings, so there is no reason for saying that they exist. If these beings were as plentiful as your theory suggests, one would expect that at least some of them would have been observed. Finally, the motivation and origin of these beings is a mystery to us. We have no idea where they come from, nor do we know why they do the things they do."

These are three serious objections to the gremlin theory, and in order for that theory to satisfy the first criterion for the acceptability of theories it would have to answer all of them adequately.

We have, so far, proceeded as though there were no questions to be raised about the first of the criteria—but this is not the case. We have not yet clearly indicated the nature of this criterion, and we have not yet empha-sized the fact that it is not always easy to apply. In order to use this criterion effectively, we must first determine which objections are serious. If someone claims that a theory is to be rejected because it was presented on the day the Yankees won the pennant, or because the man who proposed it is a communist, his objection is not serious. While there can be no general characterization of a serious objection, experts in the field will usually be able to agree as to what constitutes a serious objection to a particular theory. If they cannot, we can appeal to other tests—and, if all of those were to fail, we could construct some other tests.

Of course we shall also find it difficult to specify what 'adequate answer' means, since the sorts of considerations involved in clarifying 'serious' also apply to 'adequate answer'. But, in practice, this does not present a problem, for there is general agreement about what are adequate answers.

b. CRITERION 2: ARE THERE REASONS IN FAVOR OF THE THEORY? Another kind of criticism which we would level against the gremlin theory is that there are no good reasons in favor of it. The mere statement of a theory is no evi-dence for its acceptability. Some evidence other than the theory itself is re-quired. We would not expect that this criterion, viz., that there should be good reasons in favor of the theory, would be violated very often; unfortu-nately it is the one test most often violated by those who have just begun the study of ethics. For example, defenders of psychological egoism (roughly, the view that all men are selfish) often resort to simply reiterating their position or try to deny counterarguments by restating the theory and then pointing out that the criticism is inconsistent with it. This is like claiming that no men are bald and then, upon being shown a bald man, saying that he is not a man because no men are bald. If no other reasons are presented in favor of such theories, we can legitimately claim that Criterion 2 has been violated.

c. CRITERION 3: ARE THERE MORE SUCCESSFUL COMPETITORS? Our last criticism of the gremlin hypothesis is probably the most important. Experience shows that if human beings are denied food they die—an observation that fits the biological theory, but not the gremlin theory. The close similarity of human nourishment with that of one-celled animals (which apparently have no gremlins) is also better explained by the biological theory. The analysis of human tissue and its requirements does not indicate the need for, or the place of, gremlins. Many more reasons which concern the fitting or explaining of phenomena can be presented, and this sort of consideration would be the most effective kind of criticism.

But the advocates of the gremlin theory need not remain silent in the face of these attacks. A gremlin theorist might claim that gremlins are invisible, that they have certain types of motives, and that they are divine beings and so do not have mass. If such a reply is made, however, the theory is so changed that it is more appropriate to say that a new theory is being proposed—one that must be subjected to the criteria described above.

The statement of the third criterion is this: "The theory either fits or explains the range of phenomena better than other competing theories." We must explain the crucial term 'better'. What makes one theory better than its competitors will vary depending on the area under consideration; but generally, one characteristic that makes a theory better is *simplicity*. The heliocentric theory, for example, is a simpler hypothesis than the geocentric theory because it explains the phenomena under consideration with a considerably more compact and manageable set of equations and suppositions. Connected with this is the fact that the heliocentric theory requires far fewer ad hoc additions and explanations. Nothing in the geocentric theory itself would allow us to discover how many epicycles—if any—need be added. These epicycles are added into the system after it is seen that something or other must be done to allow us to predict the orbits of the planets. No such fixing up after the fact is required by the heliocentric theory.

The gremlin theory suffers from the same faults as the geocentric theory. To explain nourishment, digestion, and other related phenomena, this theory needs a set of fantastic principles; and equations, if there were any, would no doubt be as incredible. Since all the replies to objections are based upon ad hoc assumptions, the gremlin theory is in serious trouble as a scientific or empirical hypothesis.

Another characteristic that makes a theory better is *fruitfulness*, as when a theory leads to the discovery of further truths or new theories. The biological theory of nourishment, for example, has led to the notion of a balanced diet and to the treatment of some diseases through modifications of diet. If we discover that a person has rickets, we can prescribe a cure by feeding him food high in Vitamin D, or rich in calcium, or both. The gremlin theory might suggest that he pop another gremlin or two into his mouth, but this is a prescription not easily filled at the corner drugstore.

One general point to be noted concerning the third criterion is that we do not have to say that the phenomena to be explained by the theory actually occur in the world. For example, if one sits on a hillside facing the east before dawn, it certainly seems as though the sun rises over the horizon, moves across the sky, and finally disappears in the west. In this case the sun seems to move and correspondingly the earth seems to stand still, but we do not suppose that the sun moves around the earth. We reject this explanation because we have a better theory. If we accept the theory we must reject what seems to happen and explain the observed phenomenon in a different way. The sun *seems* to move around the earth, we say, but it does not really do so; the earth moves around the sun. The phenomenon is explained by describing why we have the awareness we do even though the earth moves around the sun.

Exercises

Review
1. What is the point of discussing scientific theories?
2. The three criteria of acceptability of theories do not discover correct theories, so of what use are they?
3. Why could the dispute between the geocentric and heliocentric theorists not be resolved simply by "looking"?
4. What care has to be taken with the application of Criterion 3?
5. What features of a theory justify the claim that it has explained the phenomena better than its competitors?

Applications
1. Apply the criteria of acceptability to two competing nonscientific theories and to two competing scientific theories. (It is easier to pick at least one older, clearly discredited scientific theory.)
2. Show that the following claim is unjustified:
   My theory that sleep is simply a trick of our subconscious to keep us from risking ourselves more than we have to in the real world is justified because it suits me.
3. Criticize the following:
   Any actually held theory is as good as any other actually held theory, because no one can, in actual practice, hold a theory that does not work.
4. Apply the criteria of acceptability to the following theories:
   a. I find, upon reflection, that I, Sizer, am the source of all size. The evidence for this is as convincing as it is brief. I have in me an element of sizence, and I am, therefore, the source of all size in the world. The proof of this is

clear. When things move further away from me they shrink, showing that the sizence radiating on them diminishes in proportion to the distance they are from me. When things approach me the radiation becomes stronger, and they therefore grow. I, on the other hand, always remain the same size, and the reason for this is obvious—I am always the same distance from myself.

b. Food is the cause of death, because everyone who eats food sooner or later dies.

5. Construct an absurd (but self-consistent) theory concerning the phenomenon of human birth.

B. Ethical Theories

1. *Acting According to and Acting from.* We believe that conflict among ethical theories can be more fruitfully studied if the three criteria of acceptability are kept in mind. Before we begin an examination of ethical theories, however, we must distinguish two kinds of ethical theory. In order to characterize these two, however, some preliminary clarification is necessary.

Most empirical theories (i.e., theories which can be confirmed by experience), are concerned with discovering laws according to which things behave. We might suppose that the law of gravity (supposing that it is a law) describes how bodies act when they are in certain positions, e.g., unsupported above the surface of the earth. The law accurately predicts that these bodies will fall. Bodies do not fall *because* of the law of gravity, they act *according to* the law, but they do not act *from* it.

All things act according to the law of gravity; that is, the law always describes the way bodies act and can be used to predict how they will interact with other bodies. No individual can "decide" to act according to the law of gravity. Whether or not he knows of the law, whether or not he wishes his behavior to be described by the law, that law is applicable to him and to all humans in the same way that it is applicable to footballs and planets.

Immanuel Kant (1724–1804) made a distinction between acting according to a law and acting from a law which can be brought to bear here. *When a creature can choose whether or not he will act according to a law, then he is capable of acting from a law.* Conversely, when one acts from a law, then one can choose not to act according to the law. To explain how this can be, let us first describe a fanciful but clear case, and then introduce complications as they are required.

2. *Maxims and Laws.* The law of gravity now describes the behavior of objects near the surface of the earth. Men cannot act from the law of gravity for they cannot choose to act other than according to that law. Let us suppose, however, that men acquire the ability to nullify the law, and let us further suppose that one man decides that it is desirable to act according to the law of gravity so that, as a result of that decision, the law of gravity consistently describes his behavior. That man would, unlike us, be acting *from* the law of gravity.

At this point, to avoid conceptual confusion, we require a term other than 'law'. Once again let us borrow a term employed by Kant—'maxim'. A *maxim, in our sense, is a rule of action or conduct which a person chooses or can choose to have describe his behavior.*[1] We can choose, for example, to have the maxim "Never tell a lie" describe our behavior. A maxim is a kind of law, but it is not the same kind, as we have seen, as a law of nature.

a. ETHICAL BEHAVIOR. We can now ask what kind of laws describe ethical human behavior. This is not to ask something about behavior that is morally *right* but to ask something about behavior that is of the sort that can be right *or* wrong. By *ethical behavior* we simply mean behavior which can be said to be morally right or morally wrong, morally praiseworthy or morally blameworthy. What is it that leads people to declare some behavior to be right and other behavior wrong? Anthropologists generally identify "right behavior" as that demanded by the group because of its survival value.[2]

According to William Graham Sumner (1840–1910)

Need was the impelling force. Pleasure and pain, on the one side and the other, were the rude constraints which defined the line on which efforts must proceed. The ability to distinguish between pleasure and pain is the only psychical power which is to be assumed. Thus ways of doing things were selected, which were expedient. They answered the purpose better than other ways, or with less toil and pain. Along the course on which efforts were compelled to go, habit, routine, and skill were developed. The struggle to maintain existence was carried on, not individually, but in groups. Each profited by the other's experience; hence there was concurrence towards that which proved to be most expedient. All at last adopted the same way for the same purpose; hence the ways turned into customs and became mass phenomena. Instincts were developed in connection with them. In this way, folkways arise. The young learn them by tradition, imitation, and authority. The folkways, at a time, provide for all the needs of life then and there. They are uniform, universal in the group, imperative, and invariable.[3]

We can accept one part of Sumner's view. We can suppose that certain ways of doing things helped a particular group of people to survive and that these ways became "universal" and "imperative" in that group. When people act this way social scientists are inclined to apply the term 'law' to descrip-

[1] Whether or not a person can choose and in what sense he can choose are discussed in Chapter 9.

[2] We will take some liberties in order to simplify the discussion. Therefore we do not claim to be presenting a literal description of the rise of morality. However, anthropologists do seem to agree that right behavior had survival value. This is not to say that right behavior is determined by the survival value of an action. There are those who do make this identification, and we shall consider their view in Chapter 11.

[3] William Graham Sumner, *Folkways* (Boston: Ginn and Company, 1906) p. 2.

tions of their behavior.[4] Let us consider two mythical struggling human communities somewhere in northern Africa, about one million years ago. Each small tribe of about thirty-five had to compete with other animals for its food. Neither had fire or any weapon other than the stone ax. Suppose that when one of the members in one group was attacked by a carnivorous animal, the others in the tribe, more often than not, did their best to escape a similar fate. Suppose that if the same circumstances arose in the other tribe, the members, more often than not, would help their fellow tribesman and would, given their numerical advantage, usually succeed in killing or driving off the attacker. The second tribe has a much better chance of surviving than the first, for it is likely that more of its members will live long enough to reproduce. Furthermore, this cooperation would give rise to other kinds of cooperation—e.g., hunting. Given just these two advantages, we can easily see how this kind of behavior would have high survival value.

A tribe that somehow managed to inculcate these same behavior traits in its offspring would also prosper more than a tribe that did not. These traits become behavior patterns according to which the members of the tribe act. The forces causing future members of the tribe to act in the way they do are at first as stringent as (or almost as stringent as) the forces influencing the behavior of any other animal. Animals, while different from rocks, can be said to act according to laws. Human beings can also be said to act according to these primitive customs and folkways. The description of this behavior is a statement of a sociological law. These people do not yet act from the law, they act only according to it. Once again let us quote from Sumner since his view seems still acceptable to most anthropologists today.

The most uncivilized men, both in the food quest and in war, do things which are painful, but which have been found to be expedient. Perhaps these cases teach the sense of social welfare better than those which are pleasurable and favorable to welfare. The former cases call for some intelligent reflection on experience. When this conviction as to the relation to welfare is added to the folkways they are converted into mores, and, by virtue of the philosophical and ethical element added to them, they win utility and importance and become the source of the science and the art of living.[5]

Given this original impetus, man's life then becomes easier; he has more leisure to reflect. With reflection, he can discover the sociological laws according to which he has been acting. Once discovered, these sociological laws can be codified. At this point, it becomes possible for man to act *from* the laws. Perhaps he does so because in so doing he increases his chances of surviving. In short, the laws become maxims.

---

[4] The laws applicable to societies can be said to be laws even though there are several exceptions to them. The contrast between these laws and those of physics is less important than it might seem at first.

[5] *Ibid.*, p. 3.

b. PRESCRIPTIONS. At this point we must make sure that we are not led astray by yet another sense of 'law'. The way we have introduced 'maxim' one can, in some circumstances, choose to have what is a natural law (our example was a sociological law) apply to one. There is another kind of law which one can choose to have describe one's behavior, *viz.*, a civil law. Let us list the various kinds of laws:

1. Physical laws (acted *according to*).
2. Sociological laws (acted *according to*).
3. Maxim (acted *from*).
4. Civil laws (acted *from*).

For example, most cities have laws governing the speed at which automobiles may travel, but the individual driver can stay within the speed limit or exceed it. Such a law *prescribes* behavior—that is, it lays down a rule upon which one is to act.

The rule of behavior we call a *civil law* can also be called a *legal maxim*. Any principle that directs us to act or not to act in a certain way is a maxim. Someone might act from the following maxim: "Always open doors for ladies," but this is not (although it could be) a legal maxim. It is not a moral maxim either, for one who does not follow this maxim is not thought to be a morally wicked man. Moral maxims, like all maxims, prescribe behavior, but they differ from legal maxims, social maxims, and other kinds of maxims. One of the distinguishing features of a primitive morality is that many more maxims are elevated to the status of moral maxims. In some primitive societies there are few actions that do not have some moral significance. The task of stating clearly what is and what is not a moral maxim, of giving criteria for identifying moral maxims, is one of the most difficult tasks in the field of ethics, and we shall not attempt to carry out that task here. We may point out, however, that every reader of this book has at least an intuitive grasp of this distinction. We trust that this intuitive grasp will soon be strengthened, for the nature and status of moral maxims is discussed in many parts of this book.

3. *Two Kinds of Ethical Theory.* Let us now relate this semimythical outline of the rise of ethical codes and their function to our earlier discussion of scientific theories, and distinguish two kinds of ethical theory: empirical ethical theory and philosophical ethical theory.

a. EMPIRICAL ETHICAL THEORY. Let us begin our attempt to specify empirical ethical theories by pointing out some of the differences between a law of physics and a law of sociology (or perhaps of social psychology).[6] The physical law of gravity allows us to predict that a rock will fall if it is un-

---

[6] Roughly, laws of sociology concern large groups of men and laws of social psychology concern the behavior of individuals in large groups.

supported near the surface of the earth. There are no exceptions to this law. Suppose that someone should observe a primitive tribe, and notice that the members of this tribe always come to the aid of a fellow tribesman when he is attacked by carnivorous beasts. This sociological law may well have many exceptions. There are two possible explanations as to why there might be exceptions. First it may be held that some of the laws that describe human behavior are more stringent than others. For example, if S_1 is falling over a cliff and sees S_2 being attacked by a carnivorous beast in a cave half-way down the cliff, he will not come to S_2's aid.[7] One might be able to add conditions concerning the application of the sociological law so that such problems do not arise. If this can be done, we are all in favor of it and the law would be exactly of the same type as a law of physics, but the statement of such a law would then be enormously more complex.

Another exception might arise if S_1 is a coward or has some other psychological disability. In this case, there may be some psychological law that describes S_1 and allows us to explain his behavior. It is enlightening to note there is no rock we know of whose individual nature would be such that, all other things being equal, the rock would not be described by the law of gravity. However, this *is* what happens in societies. Whatever causes S_1 to act the way he does, we are led astray in our prediction. This may arise from our inaccurate formulation of the law, but it may also arise from what some believe is the impossibility of ever formulating any sociological laws that apply to individuals.

When we talk about man's behavior being described by a sociological law, we are talking about a *law* and not a maxim. In order for a man to act *from* maxims, someone, perhaps the man himself, must, in some way, formulate them. A great change takes place when a man ceases acting according to a law and begins acting from a maxim. To understand this change, let us consider two kinds of empirical ethical theorists.

Suppose that the chief of a primitive tribe reads this book and decides that his tribe would benefit from having its moral code become a set of maxims from which his tribesmen act. We can suppose that he believes this will greatly increase their chances of survival. The chief is not suggesting that the members of his tribe change their way of behaving, only that they now base this behavior on the maxims he has discovered. For example, he wants them to continue to help one another when carnivorous beasts attack, but he wants

---

[7] *S* should be read as the name of an individual whose only characteristics (to begin with) are those which he shares with any and every agent. Further on in our discussion, as we present a series of propositions, we shall sometimes assign a letter or a number to each one and then consider the logical relations among these propositions. For the sake of convenience, we shall often refer to these propositions by the letters or numbers we have attached to them. This allows the arguments to be presented in a compact (and sometimes revealing) way.

them to do this not out of instinct or habit, but on the basis of the appropriate maxim. It is not difficult to see how this can fortify behavior which already has survival value.

It is a fact that human beings change things. The chief will undoubtedly bring about a great deal of unrest. His codification, however diligently done, will most likely be incomplete or inaccurate or both. Human behavior is so complex that even today the most sophisticated sociologist's description does not cover all of it or even all of one phase of it. Even if the description were to be complete, it would, no doubt, contain some inaccuracies. But even if the codification were accurate and complete, the chief would bring about many changes. The formulation of maxims will stress many actions the tribesmen would otherwise not think of doing. For example, it becomes more likely that members of the tribe will come to the aid of a fellow tribesman who is attacked by an enemy tribesman.

At least some of the members of the tribe will probably become aware of the difference between what they had been doing and what they are now asked to do. A conflict now arises: Should one now act from maxims or do what one has always done—i.e., act only according to sociological laws? The moral conservative will not want the tribesmen to act from the proposed maxims, but the moral liberal will. Notice, though, that in this situation both are reformers. Once the tribesmen are aware of the maxims they would find it very difficult to go back to their old ways. This is one of the reasons that the moral conservative is a reformer. We can suppose that these two reformers meet to discuss their differences. Their discussion can be based, in part, on what the chief found in his study of the tribe's moral code. However, this study, by itself, cannot provide any resolution of the dispute. If the dispute continues on a rational level, the men cease the descriptive part of their work and will begin to make prescriptive suggestions.

b. PHILOSOPHICAL ETHICAL THEORY. The moral conservative can defend his position by proposing a theory concerning the rise and status of moral maxims. He can propose that the purpose and sole justification for the adoption of maxims lies in their survival value. Let us suppose that the maxims presented are both complete and accurate. The conservative can argue that following the maxims will still lead to behavior different from that of pre-maxim days. His point is that the original behavior, performed according to the sociological laws, has higher survival value than acting from the proposed maxims. These, then, are the moral conservative's reasons for rejecting the proposed maxims. Both moral reformers maintain that the best moral maxims are those that aid survival. Because they have introduced the notion that one set of maxims is better than another, the reformers have become philosophers, engaged in what we call *normative ethics*.

In contrast with the moral conservative, the moral liberal might argue that the proposed maxims, although they lead to different behavior, will increase the chances of survival. He might even suggest some new ways of acting. It is easy to see how the notion of reform can feed itself, and how one kind of change can lead to more radical reform.

The kind of theory held by the moral conservative (and the principle that goes with it) is, we believe, mistaken. It supposes human survival depends on the same factors now as it did in the past. However, man now is the prime causal factor not only in his own survival, but in that of every other thing on earth. To a very large extent, man can bring about whatever he decides is the best environment. Nowadays the question of which is the best among the many ways that man can choose to prosper and survive must be answered independently of the empirical question of which moral codes will best help us to survive in our environment. Given that man is now largely free of his environment, we want to know which of the many available possible futures is best. Now 'best' cannot mean, as the empirical theorists maintain, that which promotes survival. Let us try to clarify what we have claimed above. The moral liberal would say that the conservative supposes that man's environment stands in the same relation to him now as it did when moral codes first arose: that is that relation which existed when man was a creature among many who survived or not depending on how well he could adapt to his environment. This is not so today because man can change his environment in an almost limitless number of ways. Which way man changes his environment is largely up to him. There are, no doubt, many ways in which man could change his environment so that his survival is insured. For example, we could exterminate all other living creatures except certain types of cattle and a few specimens of other animals for zoos. We could develop synthetic foods so that the earth is no longer needed for human sustenance. We could then level the earth and put a green plastic coating on it.

Conversely, we could destroy all our science and technology, and "return to nature."

By the same token, we could prohibit all sexual relations and "grow" all children in test tubes.

Finally, the situation described by George Orwell in *1984* could be brought about.

These worlds which men can bring about are repugnant to us, yet all are now possible and more or less insure the survival of man. If we had to choose which moral code would best help us to survive and if our choice of possible worlds were the ones mentioned, then what the "best" moral code is would depend on which world we picked. We are certain that there are worlds we could create which everyone reading this thinks are better. Since there are alternative possible worlds, some of which are better, the way to find which set of moral maxims can best insure man's survival is not necessarily merely to examine the present environment. Furthermore, suppose it turns out that, in addition to the ways of insuring man's survival mentioned above, there is another way, but one that forces us to travel a somewhat more difficult and uncertain path. There is little doubt that we would all choose the more difficult and uncertain path, as long as it was not incredibly difficult and totally uncertain. One of the main reasons is that such a world would be *morally preferable* to the ones described. It cannot be, then, that what is morally preferable is solely a function of our environment for the environment we choose is, in part, a moral choice or decision.

The best moral code, then, is not what the moral conservative says it is. Corresponding 'best' in 'best moral code,' or accordingly, in 'best ethical theory', or 'best moral maxim' does not mean what such a theorist suggests. Human beings have certain goals and requirements that are a function of man's nature and of the kind of world in which he lives. Philosophical ethical theory, in one of its activities (e.g., normative ethics), is an attempt to express the morally best way for men to live. Such an enterprise may begin with what men do; this is, for the most part, a purely empirical ethical theory. This code, as we saw, is modified and then finally men try to decide what is the best moral code. Often men are not clear about what they wish to do, and they assume that the only legitimate enterprise is some purely "rational" theory which does not take into account the nature of man or his environment. Let us not suppose that what we find human beings to be doing is prescriptive of what they do and let us not suppose that what is prescriptive of human beings is descriptive of them.

Summary and a Look Ahead. Let us now return to our simpler pictures concerning "acting from" and "acting according to." Human beings first act according to what we later call moral codes, that are describable by sociological laws. They then act from those laws—i.e., on moral maxims—but these laws invariably change the behavior of those who act from them. Finally, they change these rules, not on the basis of what their environment is, but on the basis of what they believe is best.

We have now distinguished at least two kinds of thoretical enterprises, empirical and philosophical. One question we have touched upon is the application of the criteria of acceptability of empirical theories to philosophical ethical theories. The first criterion, that serious objections to the theory can be answered adequately, clearly does apply to philosophical ethical theory. Let us only remind the reader once again of the difficulty in specifying what 'serious' and 'adequate' mean. The second criterion, that there be reasons in favor of the theory, also applies, but in a somewhat different fashion. In a sense, all the evidence that is required in ethical theory is available already. We do not need to run any experiments to discover more facts. We usually know what *is* the case; we want to know what *ought to be* the case. Since this is so it is very seldom that reasons of the *sort* that are produced in the physical sciences are produced in ethical theory. There is a kind of evidence which, as we have seen in the dispute between the moral conservative and the moral liberal, can be produced. However, since such reasons as these are peculiarly philosophical, no general characterization of them is possible. The reader should not worry about this at this point because after reading this book, he will know what philosophical arguments and reasons are from direct experience.

The third criterion, that the theory fit or explain the range of phenomena better than other competing theories, is the most important. The crucial term 'better' must, of course, have a slightly different significance than in its application to empirical theories. The notions of fruitfulness and simplicity have a slightly different connotation because the fruitfulness of a philosophical theory is somewhat different from that of a scientific theory. A fruitful ethical theory might lead to the development of better moral maxims or to insights in other philosophical areas, or perhaps to the founding of some new empirical sciences (such as linguistics, whose founding was in part brought about by the work of philosophers).

A theory concerning the best set of moral maxims plus a theory of what has value is called a *normative theory of ethics*. Whether or not we find the best set of moral maxims and discover what has value, let us suppose that it can be found or that we can discover that it cannot be found.

Most philosophers have been aware of the distinctions we have noted, but some have not. We shall try to guide the reader through various ethical theories, keeping two principles in mind as we do so. First, we want to change the philosophers' own views as little as possible. Second, we shall try to show, wherever possible, how the various theories address themselves to the questions we raise and the issues we present.

Philosophical ethical theory is divided into two broad areas that overlap at many places. The first is normative ethics, the purpose of which is to find which moral maxims are best and to discover which things have value. The second is *meta-ethics*, which is not concerned with the attempt to find which moral maxims are best but to discover the nature of moral maxims. Some of the questions in meta-ethics are the following: "Can moral maxims be justified?" "What is the meaning of such terms as 'good', 'bad', 'right', and 'wrong'?" "What is the proper place of general principles in arguments about value, and what relation, if any, do they have to the particular judgments we make, and the particular maxims from which we act?"

Exercises

Review
1. What is the distinction between acting *according to* a maxim and acting *from* a maxim?
2. Why is it a mistake to identify ethical behavior with morally right actions?
3. How could actions that are morally right have survival value?

4. What are the similarities and differences between moral maxims and civil laws?
5. Why would the codification of laws according to which people act so they can act from the corresponding maxims change their behavior patterns?
6. Why cannot 'best' in 'best moral code' mean 'that which promotes survival'?

Applications
1. What kinds of maxims are the following?
   a. Plagiarizing is forbidden.
   b. All men must die.
   c. Love thy neighbor as thyself.
   d. Everyone wants to be "in."
   e. The shortest distance between two points (on a plane surface) is a straight line.
   f. You always hurt the one you love.
   g. The king can move only one space at a time.
2. Criticize the following argument:
   You cannot change human nature, and a moral code is part of human nature. Because this is so, you cannot change anyone's moral code. Normative ethics, therefore, is a waste of time.
3. Present instances of each of the following:
   a. An automobile-driving maxim.
   b. A law of one of the natural sciences.
   c. A sociological law.
   d. A university regulation.
   e. A city or state law.
4. Briefly describe what you believe is the best possible world for human beings. (Orwell's *1984* is the description of one possible world.)
5. What maxims would have to be introduced and what present maxims (of what sort) would have to be changed, in order to bring about the world described in your answer to Question 4?
6. In the following AP news story of September 16, 1966 (written in response to the claim of two astronauts that the earth is round) there is a "defense" of a flat world hypothesis. Evaluate that defense.

   No matter what astronauts Charles Conrad and Richard Gordon said about seeing the earth as a ball, they can't convince Britain's Flat Earth society.

   "Those chaps splashed down in an Atlantic that wasn't revolving as they claimed it was," said Sam Shenton, honorary secretary of the international research society Friday.

   "The Atlantic was down there waiting to receive them," he said in a telephone interview from his home in Dover.

   Shenton's organization has been arguing that the earth is flat despite photographic and visual testimony of American and Soviet spacemen.

   Here is the organization's position as outlined by Shenton:

   "The thing is this. Astronaut Conrad said: 'I will tell you we can't believe it—just out of my left window I could see all the way up to the top of the world—all the way around for 150 degrees including the horizon all the way around.' "

"Now my comment is this. That means to say that astronaut Conrad, at some 800 miles up, has a horizon which is horizontal all the way around for 150 degrees. That means to say that, if he were looking in any other direction . . . that same horizon, level with his eyes, would continue to encircle him."

"Now, we Flat Earthers have always stated, since the early days of balloons and such like adventures into the upper stratosphere, that the horizon is level with the eye of the observer or the camera."

"That means to say that at any height the astronaut is still bounded by land or sea horizon, the great point being that, if the earth were revealed as one complete planet or ball, it would also imply that it was flying through space at 20 miles per second which is 1.5 thousand miles per day, to complete an imaginary orbit around the sun."

"Now if the astronauts had got to land or splashdown in the Atlantic, their very means of landing or splashdown is by parachutes or drags. Therefore, it stands to reason that their Atlantic splashdown is not moving away from under them at over 20 miles per second."

"The Atlantic is there waiting to receive them."

For good measure, Shenton said, "The earth is so much higher than we were ever taught. . . . Why, we're only on the crust of the earth. . . . We have been misguided from childhood."

Any questions? Write Shenton, care of the Flat Earth society, Dover, England.

Normative Ethics and Logic

In Chapter 1 we discussed three criteria for determining the acceptability of ethical and nonethical theories. We concluded that one theory is more acceptable than another if it meets these conditions better, and that the best theory, the theory we are justified in accepting, will be the one which meets them best. They were:

1. Serious objections to the theory can be answered adequately.
2. There are good reasons (independent of the statement of the theory) in favor of the theory.
3. The theory fits or explains the range of phenomena better than other competing theories.

As stated, these criteria were very general, applying both to ethical and nonethical theories. In this chapter we shall attempt to survey, in a very general way, normative ethical theories—theories about which moral maxims are best—i.e., theories about what is right and wrong, and what is good and bad. We shall also attempt to provide the reader with some basic logical tools that will be needed as he joins us in the assessment of theories.

A. Survey of Normative Ethics

Normative ethics can be divided into two parts, one part concerned with judgments of obligation, and dealing solely with the moral assessment of actions, and the other concerned with judgments of value, and dealing with the assessment of persons, motives, and states of affairs.
Normative ethics:

Theory of obligation (e.g., "Jones was wrong to do that").
Theory of value (e.g., "Jones is a bad man").

A judgment of obligation is made when one judges that an action is any one of the following: right, wrong, obligatory, forbidden, permissible, or the like. This list does not claim to be either exhaustive (hence the final clause), nor do we claim that any linguistic or verbal criterion is sufficient for telling when we have produced a judgment of obligation. Nevertheless, it is a start, and the reader should have an intuitive understanding of what it is we are attempting to point out.

One of the many pitfalls is that for every usage of a term in a moral judgment of obligation, there is a usage of that same term in some nonmoral judgment. One can say, "The right thing to do is to marry the girl you have caused to be pregnant" (a moral judgment), or "The right way to build a house is to start with the basement" (a nonmoral judgment). In the first statement, 'right' is used in a moral sense; in the second, it is not. Although it is difficult to present an explicit and foolproof criterion for distinguishing between these two senses, there is little difficulty in handling most cases of actual usage.

Exercises

Applications

1. Distinguish in the following examples, those cases in which 'right' or 'wrong' is being used morally and those in which they are being used nonmorally. If lack of information about the context makes a decision difficult or impossible, describe what further information would influence the classification.
   a. You were right to pay the loan back on time.
   b. Pay the loan right away.
   c. This line in his painting is just right.
   d. What right have you to walk on my flowers?
   e. Your answer was right.
   f. You were right to answer in the way you did.
   g. Turn right at the next corner.
   h. That's the wrong thing to say.
   i. It was wrong to say that.
   j. Killing is wrong.
   k. He said, "You were wrong to kill her."
   l. It is wrong to use cornstarch instead of flour.
   m. This is the wrong time to speak about her illness.
2. Construct sentences in which 'obligatory', 'obligation', 'forbidden' and 'permissible' are used morally. Construct other sentences in which these terms are used nonmorally.

1. Normative Theories of Obligation. A normative theory of obligation usually takes the form "All actions with Properties F, G, and H are right." Or, in terms of maxims, the theory might be stated in the following way:

"The best maxim is 'Do those actions which have *F*, *G*, and *H*.' " On some occasions we are asked to support a particular moral judgment about the rightness or wrongness of a specific action. One of the ways to reply to this request is to appeal to a more general judgment, exemplifying a theory of obligation. Utilitarianism, for example, tells us that the best maxim is "Act in such a way as to maximize the good in the universe." As we shall see, many —though not all—normative theories are committed to the claim that there is always such a general judgment available. Any normative theory of obligation, however, will provide us with grounds, criteria, or directions for justifying particular judgments of rightness and wrongness. Let us examine how this process of justification is sometimes carried out.[1]

Someone might claim, "It is wrong to seduce that girl because she is a virgin and one ought never to seduce the sexually uninitiated." Here one has appealed to a more general maxim ("One ought never to seduce the sexually uninitiated") in order to justify a particular judgment. Both the general and the particular judgments are normative, but one is called upon to support the other.[2] It is possible that one might appeal to further normative judgments in order to support the claim that he ought never to seduce the sexually uninitiated, but at some point this process will stop. Very often the process terminates in a way illustrated by the following argument.

A: You should not seduce that girl.

B: Why not?

A. She is a virgin, and one ought never to seduce the sexually uninitiated.

B: Why ought one never do that?

A: If you do that you will weaken her moral fiber and lead her to promiscuity, which will cause her, ultimately, a great deal of pain.

B: And what does that show?

A: Well, one ought never do anything that will cause anyone pain.

B: Why not?

A: Because pain is evil, and any action that causes evil is wrong.

Here *A* has begun with a particular judgment about a particular action *B* has committed or plans to commit. In order to justify this particular judgment, he resorts to a more general judgment, applying not only to the par-

---

[1] A word about *justification* might be necessary here. If we justify an action, we show that it is right; but we may justify judgments by showing that they are correct. Some judgments claim that certain actions are right and others that certain actions are wrong. In either case, when we justify the judgment, we show that it is correct. To justify a judgment that an action is wrong is not, of course, to justify the action. Also, justification is a different process from deciding what to do, it may or may not come after the action.

[2] As we shall point out later, some theorists would claim that we justify the more general judgment by generalizing from a number of particular ones. Cf. *act deontology*, which is discussed in Chapter 5.

ticular girl in question but also to all girls of a certain condition. He is then forced to say why he believes this more general judgment is correct, and appeals to the consequences of performing such actions. Now a statement of the consequences alone does not satisfy B, for he wants to know what is wrong with actions that have such consequences. The answer is that, given a principle to the effect that one ought never cause pain, B ought not do what he has in mind. B's final question drives A to the most general claim he has so far made, and perhaps to the most general claim he is prepared to make. In A's reply we find, first, his theory of value ("Pain is evil") and his theory of obligation ("Any action which causes evil is wrong"). We have not continued the discussion, but it is at this point that the serious business of moral philosophy begins.

A word may be needed here to clarify the distinction between normative theories of obligation and normative judgments of obligation. Any judgment about the rightness or wrongness of actions, particular or general, is a normative *judgment* of obligation. Some of these judgments, however, are very general, and the people who make them claim that all other normative judgments may be deduced from them. A very general judgment or maxim, such as the one characterizing utilitarianism, is a normative *theory*. Hence a normative theory of obligation is usually stated as a very general normative judgment of obligation. Utilitarianism is one such theory, and another is ethical egoism (see Chapter 3), which claims, roughly speaking, that any action leading to the greatest good of the doer is right, and any that does not is wrong. Another kind of theory of obligation is one holding that all actions with the property of rightness are right. This is not as vacuous as it might seem (see Chapter 5).

a. TELEOLOGICAL AND DEONTOLOGICAL THEORIES. Two broad divisions can be made to help us understand theories of obligation. The first division is that between *teleological* theories of obligation and *deontological* theories of obligation. The former maintains that the moral rightness or wrongness of an action is a function of the good that is produced in the world, and nothing else.[3] Usually a teleologist will claim that the only way a judgment of moral obligation can be justified is by an appeal to the consequences that the action produces or is likely to produce. The utilitarian view is the most frequently encountered teleological theory. According to at least some versions of this

---

[3] Usually a teleologist holds that the rightness or wrongness of an action is a function of the consequences of the particular action being performed, but some teleologists (notably rule utilitarians, see Chapter 4) hold that an action is right if, and only if, it is an instance of a correct rule or maxim, and that a maxim is correct if, and only if, it results in good. This formulation is vague, but it covers many sorts of rule utilitarianism. For the time being, we shall speak of teleologists as though they held that the rightness of an action was a function of the consequences of that action, and the necessary complications will be introduced in their place. The main point, however, is that all teleologists consider consequences and only consequences as determining the moral rightness or wrongness of actions.

view, an action is right if and only if it produces consequences that are better (or at least no worse) than those of any other action possible to the agent.

Deontological theories of obligation hold that things other than (but, perhaps, in addition to) consequences determine which actions are morally right. Some deontologists claim that we must refer to the motive of the agent, or his relation to others, in justifying judgments of obligation. Kant, for example, on one interpretation, holds that an action is justified if the intentions of the doer are good, despite the consequences that might ensue from the action itself.

b. GENERAL AND PARTICULAR CONSIDERATIONS. The second division cuts across that made between teleological and deontological theories and marks the difference between the kinds of considerations thought to be relevant in justifying a judgment. Some judgments of obligation may be justified by general considerations, such as the pleasure or happiness of *all* men, or by something particular, such as the pleasure or happiness of the man performing the action.

Table 1 shows, in relatively simple fashion, the distinctions made in this section and the one preceding. Some of the terms are not yet familiar to the reader, but perhaps their meaning can be inferred from their location on the chart. (The one exception to this is 'hedonism', the name for the theory that the only worthwhile thing is pleasure. This is a theory of value, and, as we shall see in the following sections, it is required to supplement teleological theories of obligation. Theories of value are fully discussed in Chapters 6 and 7.)

2. *Normative Theories of Value.* A judgment of value occurs whenever one judges that something is any of the following, or any variation or synonym of any of the following: good, bad, better, worse, excellent, and so on. Just as there are moral and nonmoral judgments of obligation, so there are moral and nonmoral judgments of value—that is, moral and nonmoral uses of words such as 'good' and 'bad'. (We shall examine this distinction more closely in Chapter 6.)

The nonmoral uses of 'right' in judgments of obligation are of little concern in ethics, but this is not true of nonmoral judgments of value. We shall find (see Chapter 6) that a great deal must be said before we become clear about normative theories of value, but we can anticipate a little here and point out that in the expression "The Cadillac is a good car," 'good' is being used in a nonmoral sense, while in the expression, "Saint Francis was a good man," 'good' is (at least usually) being used in a moral sense.

According to many ethical philosophers, some things have "intrinsic value" —that is, they are "good in themselves." In our discussion of the theory of value, we shall attempt to discover what is meant by this, and we shall consider (in Chapter 7) some of the more important candidates for the role of the one and only one intrinsically valuable thing.

Table 1. Deontological and Teleological Judgments

	Deontological Judgments	Teleological Judgments	
		Egoism	
		Hedonistic	*Nonhedonistic*
The judgment is justified by appealing to particular considerations.	**Act Deontology** — An act is right because it has certain characteristics. (The further claim that all acts which have these characteristics are right is not appealed to, and the characteristics are not limited to the consequences of the action.)	An act is right because it leads to my good (which is to say, it leads to my pleasure).	An act is right because it leads to my good. (Here good is not limited to pleasure.)
		Utilitarianism	
		Hedonistic	*Nonhedonistic*
The judgment is justified by appealing to general considerations.	**Rule Deontology** — An act is right because it is in accordance with a general rule of the form of "All acts which have these characteristics are right." (Again the characteristics are not limited to the consequences.)	An act is right because it leads to the greatest good for a specified group of people (where that group includes more than the person making the judgment); that is to say, it leads to the most pleasure for that group.	An act is right because it leads to the greatest good for a specified group of people (where that group includes more than the person making the judgment), but here considerations other than those of pleasure are relevant to deciding what is good.

Exercises

Review

1. What is the difference between a theory of obligation and a theory of value?
2. What is the relation between a normative judgment and a normative theory?
3. What is the difference between teleological and deontological theories of obligation?
4. If S believes that the rightness or wrongness of an action is partially a function of the motive of the agent, what sort of a theory of obligaion does he hold?
5. Explain the difference between the belief that a judgment is justified by appealing to particular considerations and the belief that it is justified by appealing to general considerations.

Applications

1. Discuss the following passages, pointing out the normative judgments and theories of obligation expressed or implicit in them. Whenever possible, classify the theories held as teleological or deontological, and determine whether general or particular considerations are (or would be) appealed to.
    a. "What custom wills, in all things should we do't." —*Coriolanus*, II, 3.
    b. "I am the measure of all things. I am the center of the world."
    "But there are one or two other people in the world," objected Philip.
    "I speak only for myself. I know them only as they limit my activities. Round each of them too the world turns, and each one for himself is the center of the universe. My right over them extends only as far as my power. What I can do is the only limit of what I may do." —*Of Human Bondage*, Chapter 45.
    c. "There is no independence of law against National Socialism. Say to yourselves at every decision which you make: 'How would the Fuehrer decide in my place?' In every decision ask yourselves: 'Is this decision compatible with the National Socialist conscience of the German people?' Quoted in William L. Shirer, *The Rise and Fall of the Third Reich*, p. 370.
    d. "You will admit," said Albert, "that certain actions are vicious from whatever motive they may occur."
    I shrugged my shoulders and granted him that. "But, my dear fellow," I continued, "even in that case there are exceptions. It is true that thieving is a vice, but does a man who sets out to steal in order to preserve himself and his family from a miserable death by starvation, deserve punishment or sympathy? Who will be the first to cast a stone at the man who sacrifices an unfaithful wife and her worthless seducer to his righteous wraths? Goethe, *The Sorrows of Young Werther*.
2. In your reading, find similar passages in which judgments of obligation are adopted or presupposed.
3. See if you can decide, on the basis of the discussion in the last section, in which of the following sentences 'good' or 'bad' are being used morally and in which they are being used nonmorally.
    a. Ice cream is good.

b. Pleasure is good.

c. His intentions were good.

d. Friendship is good.

e. Democracy is good.

f. He got a good thrashing from his philosophy teacher.

g. Will you get a good grade in this course?

h. This is a good book.

i. A knife is a bad utensil to eat peas with.

j. Bach is a good composer, but he was a better organist.

k. I had bad dreams all year.

l. John is a bad philosopher.

m. John is a bad man.

n. John is a bad man for the job.

o. My motives are usually all bad.

4. In some of the above cases, you probably will not be able to decide how the term is being used. List all the cases of which you are reasonably certain in two columns, moral and nonmoral. Now attempt to discover the factor, if any, that led you to classify these in the way that you did.

5. Discuss the following passages, pointing out the normative theories of value expressed or implicit.

a. What care I that some millions of wretched Israelites died under Pharaoh's lash, or Egypt's sun? It was well that they died that I might have the pyramids to look on, or to fill a musing hour with wonderment. Is there one among us who would exchange them for the lives of the ignominious slaves that died? What care I that the virtue of some sixteen-year-old maid was the price paid for Ingres' *La Source?* That the model died of drink and disease in the hospital is nothing compared with the essential that I should have *La Source,* that exquisite dream of innocence. . . . George Moore, *Confessions of a Young Man.*

b. "Oh, sir, is there no charity or kindness among men!"

"Very little! Is it only much talked about. Why should it be otherwise? People, sensible, no longer oblige others gratis; they have discovered that the pleasures of charity were but the enjoyments of pride. And since pride is a mere illusion, they now seek for more tangible sensations. For instance, they have learned that with a girl like you it is far better to reap all the pleasures love can bring than those very unsatisfying ones of helping her for nothing. The pleasures of sympathy and generosity are not worth even the slightest pleasure of the sense." De Sade, *Justine.*

B. Logical Tools and Techniques

Most men are capable of distinguishing good arguments from bad ones (here, by the way, 'good' and 'bad' are used nonmorally). If someone says, "If utilitarianism is correct I ought to write my aged parent," and then accepts a utilitarian theory of obligation, we would all unhesitatingly agree that this man must admit to an obligation to write to his aged parent. This argument can be symbolized in the following way:

If *U*, then **W**.
U.
Therefore, **W**.

where '*U*' stands for "Utilitarianism is correct" and '**W**' stands for "I ought to write my aged parent." It takes very little logic indeed to notice that any argument of this form is correct, and that anyone who subscribes to the first two statements in the argument (its premises) must subscribe to the third (its conclusion). Logicians have given this argument a name: *modus ponens*. Its general form is:

If *p*, then *q*.
p.
Therefore, q.

There is some disagreement among philosophers as to just what can be used in place of '*p*' and '*q*' in actual arguments in this schema (see Chapter 13). We may note here that any statement whatsoever can replace '*p*' and '*q*', and that we must replace '*p*' and '*q*' consistently. That is, if '*p*' is replaced by "Utilitarianism is correct" in one premise of an argument, that expression must be used in place of all other occurrences of '*p*' in the same argument.

An argument in the form of *modus ponens* must not be confused with another, entirely incorrect, argument. We should be quite suspicious of anyone who argued in the following way: "If utilitarianism is correct, I ought to write my aged parent, and I ought to write my aged parent, so utilitarianism is correct." This argument can be symbolized in the following way:

If *U*, then **W**.
W.
Therefore, U.

Logicians also have a name for this mistake, it is called the *fallacy of affirming the consequent*. The general form of this always mistaken argument is:

If *p*, then *q*.
q.
Therefore, p.

So far we have spoken of arguments being correct and incorrect, but logicians have a special name for the correctness of arguments: *validity*. To the logicians all arguments are either valid (correct) or invalid (incorrect). Logicians tell us that validity in arguments is a formal notion:

To prove the invalidity of any argument it suffices to formulate another argument which: (a) has the same form as the first, and (b) has true premises and a false conclusion. This method is based upon the fact that validity and invalidity are purely *formal* characteristics of arguments, which is to say that any two arguments having the same form are either both valid or both invalid, regardless of any differences in the subject matter with which they are concerned.[4]

Given that this is so, it is possible to discover what it is for an argument to be valid and invalid: "an argument is valid if and only if *the* form of that argument is a valid argument form." [5] Thus the first argument in this section

> If *U*, then W.
> *U*.
> *Therefore*, W.

is a valid argument, because its form is *modus ponens*, which is a valid argument form. The second argument, however,

> If *U*, then W.
> W.
> *Therefore*, *U*.

is an invalid argument, because its form is not a valid argument form.

Two questions arise at this point: What must be done to discover the form of an argument? How do we determine whether or not an argument form is valid? As arguments become more complex a solution to the first problem becomes more difficult; however, for the arguments we shall be considering in this book, no such complicated solution seems to be necessary. In answer, we can say that the form of an argument is that schema which results if we replace the nonlogical expressions in the argument by our variable symbols ('*p*', '*q*' and '*r*'), and retain the logical connectives ('If . . . then . . .', 'and', 'or', 'not') and the structure (two premises followed by a conclusion).

Thus our first argument will have the same form as this one:

> If birds fly, then nests are often out of the reach of cats.
> Birds fly.
> *Therefore*, nests are often out of the reach of cats.

This is revealed more clearly by abbreviating the statements in the argument, making it easier to deal with and stressing its form:

> If *B*, then *N*.
> *B*.
> *Therefore*, *N*.

[4] Irving M. Copi, *Introduction to Logic*, 2nd ed. (New York: The Macmillan Company, 1961), p. 254.
[5] *Ibid.*, p. 256.

Our next problem is to determine whether or not an argument form is valid. Here let us turn to Copi again:

We may define the term "invalid" as applied to argument forms as follows: an argument form is *invalid* if and only if it has a substitution instance with true premisses and a false conclusion.[6]

A quick and easy nontechnical test for determining the validity of any argument, therefore, is the following: Discover its form, and then attempt to find another argument of that form which has obviously true premises and a false conclusion. If you succeed in doing this, you have shown that the original argument is invalid; if not, however, you have not demonstrated its validity, for it is possible, of course, that your inability to discover an analogous argument with true premises and a false conclusion is a result of insufficient diligence. Nevertheless, this technique does provide us with a rudimentary understanding of validity and a method of showing that many arguments are invalid.

An argument, then, is valid if it is such that, if its premises are true, then its conclusion must be true as well. The premises do not have to be true (for there are valid arguments with false premises), but we must be able to say that (true or not) if they were true, then the conclusion would be true also. In other words, the premises of a valid argument provide conclusive reasons for the acceptance of the conclusion—i.e., the conclusion is established by the premises.[7]

Let us consider another valid argument. "If utilitarianism is correct then I ought to write my aged parent, but I have no obligation to write my aged parent, therefore utilitarianism is not correct." When we symbolize this we get

$$\text{If } U, \text{ then } W.$$
$$\text{Not } W.$$
$$\textit{Therefore, } \text{not } U.$$

This is a valid argument. To make its validity clear let us consider another example: "If Dick makes more than $500 a week, he can pay all of his debts, but he cannot pay all of his debts, therefore he does not make more than $500 a week." If anyone should happen to doubt the validity of this argument we could reason with him by saying: "Well, if he does make more than $500 a week, he could pay his debts, but because he can't pay his debts, it is clear

---

[6] *Ibid.*, p. 256.

[7] Note that 'valid' and 'invalid' are terms that are restricted by logicians to arguments. The ordinary use of 'valid' is wider, but we shall not use it. Statements should never be said to be valid or invalid but rather, true or false. Validity, then, is a formal property of arguments, but truth is a nonformal property of statements.

that he doesn't make that much, for if he did make that much he could pay his debts." The general form of this argument is called *modus tollens*:

> If *p*, then *q*.
> Not *q*.
> *Therefore*, not *p*.

Notice that here we have made use of the formal nature of validity once again, for we have attempted to demonstrate the validity of one argument by insisting upon the validity of another argument of the same form. Again let us stress that a valid argument is a substitution instance of a valid argument form. If one argument of a form is valid, then all other arguments of that form are valid, and if one argument of a form is invalid, then all other arguments of that form are invalid.

So far we have considered two valid argument forms, *modus ponens* and *modus tollens*, and one invalid argument form, *affirming the consequent*. We must not, however, confuse *modus tollens* with a similar but invalid argument form:

> If *p*, then *q*.
> Not *p*.
> *Therefore*, not *q*.

This is one of the most commonly accepted invalid argument forms, so it is particularly important to show that this argument form is invalid. One who argues, "If Dick makes more than $500 a week he can pay his debts, but he does not make more than $500, therefore he cannot pay his debts," is arguing incorrectly, for $500 may be sufficient to allow Dick to pay his debts but nothing in the premises implies that quite that much is necessary—$499 a week might do nicely. One more example will help reinforce this point. Suppose it is argued that, "If Buddhism is correct, then we ought to be kind to animals, but Buddhism is not correct, hence it is not the case that we ought to be kind to animals." This would be another instance of the same bad argument. To argue in this way is to commit what logicians call the *fallacy of denying the antecedent*. The conclusion of such an argument may be true, but there is nothing about the truth of the premises that establishes the truth of the conclusion or that entitles us to infer that the conclusion is true.

In the preceding paragraph we spoke of $500 as being *sufficient* to allow Dick to pay his debts, and suggested that perhaps that amount would not be *necessary*. This gives us an introduction to a pair of quite useful notions, for philosophers have found that it is convenient as well as enlightening to speak in terms of necessary and sufficient conditions. The hypothetical statement "If *p*, then *q*" is true if the truth of '*p*' is sufficient for the truth of '*q*', for the two expressions, "The truth of '*p*' is sufficient for the truth of '*q*' " and "If *p*, then *q*," come to the same thing.

For example, let us imagine that S's head has been cut off. We can say "S's head being cut off is sufficient for his death," but it is also possible to express ourselves by saying, "If S's head is cut off, then he will die" (or "If S's head was cut off, then he died").

Notice also that in the example about Dick's wages, we said that, although $500 a week was sufficient for him to be able to pay his debts, such an amount might not be necessary—in other words, another amount may also be sufficient. We say that something is a necessary condition for something else if that second thing could not occur without the first. Thus S's head being cut off is not necessary for his death, for there are many other ways that that end could be brought about.

One final example will help fix this notion. The presence of oxygen is a necessary condition for the occurrence of fire. Fire could not occur unless oxygen were present, but, fortunately, the presence of oxygen is not a sufficient condition. The occurrence of fire, however, is a sufficient condition for the presence of oxygen. This is not to say that the fire "causes" the oxygen, but simply that, if there is fire, we know that oxygen is present as well.

Thus, if x is a sufficient condition for y, then we know that a statement of the form "If x, then y" will be true. If x (think of oxygen) is a necessary condition for y (think of fire), then we know that a statement of the form "If y, then x" will be true. Therefore we can conclude that, if x is a sufficient condition for y, it follows that y is a necessary condition for x. In other words, if fire is a sufficient condition for the presence of oxygen, the presence of oxygen is a necessary condition for fire.[8]

We are now in a position to distinguish between a *sound* argument and a *valid* one. A sound argument is a valid argument with true or acceptable premises. Therefore, we must accept the conclusion of a sound argument.

Given an argument with an objectionable conclusion, there are three possible courses of action. First, one might point out that the argument is invalid, and hence—whether or not the premises are true—it is not necessary to accept the conclusion. Second, one may point out that at least one of the premises is false, and hence—whether or not the argument is valid—it is not necessary to accept the conclusion. Third, and this is of the utmost importance, if one agrees with the premises and the argument is valid, there is no alternative but to accept the conclusion. To refrain from doing so on the basis of doubt about the truth of the premises is always possible and sometimes desirable. But

[8] It is interesting to note that there are different kinds of necessity and sufficiency. Cutting off a man's head is *causally* sufficient for his death—such an action will result in his death, but the fact that a plane figure has three sides is *logically* sufficient for its being a triangle. The fact that a plane figure has three sides does not cause it to be a triangle, except in an unacceptably extended sense of 'cause'. We might notice that the relation between the presence of oxygen and the occurrence of fire is neither strictly causal or logical, although the presence of oxygen, a certain temperature, and flammable material might be thought to be causally sufficient for the occurrence of fire.

once the premises are accepted and the argument is shown to be valid, to reject the conclusion is to abandon utterly and completely any vestige of rationality.

Exercises

Review

1. What is a valid argument?
2. What steps are taken to show that an argument is invalid?
3. Explain the essential differences between the following arguments:
    a. If women are human, then women have souls.
       Women are not human.
       Therefore, women do not have souls.
    b. If women are human, then women have souls.
       Women do not have souls.
       Therefore, women are not human.
4. Explain the difference between x being sufficient for y and x being necessary for y.
5. If one wishes to disagree with the conclusion of what purports to be a valid deductive argument, what can one do to make his disagreement rational?

Applications

1. Discover the form of the following arguments and then classify them as instances of *modus ponens*, and so on. Sometimes, as in real life, premises are left out. In those cases, supply the premise that will make this argument fit one of the forms. Some of these arguments are invalid; when that is the case, attempt to discover what is wrong with them.
    a. If ethics will help us live better lives, it should be taught to everyone, but it ought not be taught to everyone, for it will not help us live better lives.
    b. If Plato is right, then Aristotle is wrong. Therefore Aristotle is wrong, for Plato is clearly right.
    c. Moral philosophy rests upon a mistake, for it attempts to tell us what we ought to do by telling us which things are good.
    d. If democracy is the best form of government, then everyone must be allowed freedom of speech, and everyone must be allowed freedom of speech, so democracy is the best form of government.
    e. If democracy is the best form of government, then everyone must be allowed freedom of speech, and democracy is the best form of government, so everyone must be allowed freedom of speech.
2. One interesting application of necessary and sufficient conditions in ethics occurs in the problem of freedom. It is often suggested that 'ought' implies 'can', which is to say that the ability to do, or to refrain from doing, an action is a necessary condition of the ascription of moral obligation. Assume that this principle is correct and take the following propositions as data:
    a. S has an obligation to pick up his mother from the train station.
    b. S is able to carry out this obligation.
    State the relations between the two propositions in terms of necessary and sufficient conditions.

Someone might argue in the following way:

> If *S* ought to do *A*, then *S* can do *A*.
> *S* ought to do *A*.
> *Therefore, S* can do *A*.

This is an instance of an argument in the form of *modus ponens* but, given slightly different premises, it is also possible to construct another valid argument in the form of *modus tollens*. Try it. Also try to construct invalid arguments using similar premises, and point out, by appealing to analogous arguments, why these arguments are invalid.

Egoism

In the last chapter we divided normative ethics into the theory of value and the theory of obligation. In this and the next two chapters, we shall be discussing the theory of obligation. A theory of obligation, it will be remembered, is called *teleological* if the rightness or wrongness of an action is a function of the consequences of that action; it is called *deontological* if something other than (or as well as) consequences are thought to determine the rightness or wrongness of the action.

It is important to ask a teleologist to be more specific when he speaks of consequences, for a person judging an action may concern himself with those consequences affecting everyone, some limited group, or only himself. For example, if S notices that the consequences *for him* of swindling an aged widow out of her life savings are favorable, he might, on the basis of this, declare that the action is right. His judgment, however, would be different if he began to consider the consequences of that action from the point of view of others, not the least of whom is the widow herself. In the latter case he might notice that the *total* amount of evil is greater than the *total* amount of good, and then he might judge that the action is wrong.

A number of different teleological theories may be distinguished on the basis of the consequences to be taken into account. Someone who maintains that the rightness or wrongness of every action is a function of those consequences affecting only him is called an *ethical egoist*. If, on the other hand, he believes that the consequences affecting others have some bearing on the rightness or wrongness of an action, as well as (or even instead of) just those that affect him, he would be a *utilitarian*.

A. The Distinction Between Ethical and Psychological Egoism

One theory about human nature is often thought to lend some support to the ethical egoist position. This theory, called *psychological egoism*, maintains that all men are selfish, or that the only motive from which anyone acts is self-interest. We might characterize the psychological egoist as claiming that the only motive anyone has in performing a given action is his belief that it will result in more good for him than any other possible action.

A stronger way of expressing this view is often resorted to by the psychological egoist. Instead of saying that men always do, as a matter of fact, act selfishly, the psychological egoist might maintain that actually no one ever *can* act in any other way. We must keep this distinction clearly in mind. At this point, however, the main contrast we wish to draw is between ethical egoism—the view that all men ought to be (or at least have the right to be) selfish—and psychological egoism—the view that all men are (or perhaps must be) selfish.[1]

B. Psychological Egoism

1. *Thomas Hobbes.* Thomas Hobbes (1588–1679) suggests that we call those things which we desire "good" and those things to which we have an aversion "evil." Nothing by itself is either good or evil, but only becomes so when it is desired or detested by someone.[2] Men act, he feels, in order to attain some good (i.e., something they desire) or to avoid some evil (i.e., something to which they have an aversion). He insists that "of the voluntary acts of every man, the object is *some good to himself.*"[3] This is the case, Hobbes claims, with every voluntary action. If someone asks why people give things to other people, Hobbes' unflinching reply is: "No man gives but with intention of good to himself, because gift is voluntary, and of all voluntary acts the object is to every man his own good; . . ."[4] The same is true of joining any group or choosing friends: "We do not therefore by nature seek society for its own sake, but that we may receive some honour or profit from it; . . ."[5]

Here Hobbes seems to be claiming that men always act in order to achieve

[1] According to the table on p. 26, ethical egoism is the teleological view which holds that an action is shown to be right by showing that it leads to the good of a particular person, usually the agent.

[2] Thomas Hobbes, *Leviathan*, ed. Herbert W. Schneider (Indianapolis and New York: The Bobbs Merrill Company, 1958), p. 53.

[3] *Ibid.*, p. 112.

[4] *Ibid.*, p. 125.

[5] Thomas Hobbes, *Philosophical Rudiments Concerning Government and Society*, ed. Sir William Molesworth, Vol. II (London: Bohn, 1841), p. 3.

some good for themselves. In other places, however, he seems to hold the stronger version of psychological egoism, according to which man *cannot* act in any other way:

Among so many dangers therefore, as the natural lusts of men do daily threaten each other withal, to have a care of one's self is so far from being a matter scornfully to be looked upon, that one has neither the power nor wish to have done otherwise. For every man is desirous of what is good for him, and shuns what is evil, but chiefly the chiefest of natural evils, which is death; and this he doth by a certain impulsion of nature, no less than that whereby a stone moves downward.[6]

It is fairly clear that only the stronger version of psychological egoism can be defended, for it would be very odd indeed to hold that, although anyone could act unselfishly, no one ever does. If this were just a generalization about human motivation, anyone who cared to do so could prove it false by acting in a way that went against his own interest. There must be some reason why such a simple refutation is not recognized by the psychological egoist, and that reason must lie in the fact that all psychological egoists hold (or could be quickly forced to hold) the stronger version.

2. Moritz Schlick. The psychological egoists must offer some reasons why their view of human nature and motivation is correct, but it is very difficult to discover any in their writings. Hobbes tends merely to state the view, rather than to present arguments for it. A more recent exponent of psychological egoism, Moritz Schlick (1882–1936), does seem to argue in its support, discussing what he calls *the law of motivation,* according to which anyone choosing between ends always chooses the most pleasant. Stated in this way, the law of motivation involves a hedonist theory of value, but for the time being we can disregard the hedonist aspect of Schlick's theory, and concentrate on the claim that a man will always choose that end which is most pleasant *for him.* The following passage is Schlick's defense of this law of motivation, and hence, of psychological egoism (of the hedonist variety).

In Proof of the Law of Motivation

Having thus become clear regarding the *meaning* of the law, that in the conflict of motives the decision goes to the most pleasant or least unpleasant, we turn now to the question of its *validity.*

I have already remarked that, for the majority of cases of every-day acts of will, its validity is indisputable and obvious. When a child reaches for the largest of several cakes offered it, when I take a walk in the open air instead of going to a faculty meeting, when I reflect whether the destination of a summer's trip shall be the sea or the mountains, when one wavers between a visit to the opera or to a concert, between buying black or brown shoes—then, normally, in all these

---

[6] *Ibid.,* p. 8.

cases and in a thousand similar ones, there is not the shadow of a doubt that the decision is determined by the agreeableness or disagreeableness, by the pleasure quality of the end-in-view, and that it takes place in the described way.

But, in order to pursue the study of ethics, indeed to understand the mechanism of conduct at all, we are little served by a rule that holds good in he majority of cases only; we need a *law*, that is, a description of relationships that fits *all* cases. Now the familiar method always used by science is to ask whether a rule verified in many cases may not itself be a law, that is, actually hold for *all* cases. At any rate, one begins with this assumption and often finds it verified, in that all cases which at first sight seem not to fit the rule are apparent exceptions only, their actual subsumption under the law being hidden by complicated circumstances.

Applying this method to our problem, we express the provisional assumption that the rule governing many cases of motivation may itself be a law, that is, we examine whether or not in *every* case of an act of will the decision be not determined in the direction of the most pleasant, or least unpleasant, motive.

The Law of Motivation in the Case of Sacrifice

At first sight this seems not to be the case at all. It happens that a well-bred child chooses the smallest cake, even though it obviously would "rather have" the largest; and do we not very often find ourselves in the situation of the child and trudge toward a painful, unpleasant goal? Does this not happen whenever we "make a sacrifice?" The fact is, many, if not most, philosophers believe that in such situations the prevailing motive is certainly not the most pleasant, and is often extremely unpleasant. Therefore, they do not consider the law to be universally valid; they deny it represents the law of motivation, and say it is not at all true that a man can desire only that the idea of which possesses relatively greater pleasure for him. They hold that he can desire simply anything, and many of them (including Kant) are of the opinion that although human conduct is determined by pleasant or unpleasant feelings in the described manner in all other cases, this is simply not so in the case of *moral acts*. The latter, according to them, form an exception and are, indeed, defined and distinguished by this fact. Hence we see the extent and importance of our problem, and we cannot be content before learning whether our law of motivation holds only in the limited sphere of the trivial acts of every-day life, or whether it is a true law governing every act of will without exception.

Let us not hesitate to analyze more closely the case of the child who has to choose between its several cakes. If the child takes the smallest in order to leave the larger ones for its companions, one may well consider this to be a "moral" act. Can its behavior really not be explained in terms of the law that the most pleasant end-in-view determines the will? I believe that we must admit that this is very easily done. For how is the state of mind of this child distinguished from that of the other who thoughtlessly takes the largest? We said before that even the child who here decides to make a "sacrifice" would "rather have" a larger piece of cake than a smaller one. But what is the significance of this? Obviously, that under otherwise similar conditions the idea of the larger cake is more pleasant (in the sense previously defined) than is that of the smaller. But conditions here are not the same, since in the mind of the child who renounces, because of his education or natural propensities, certain events are happening which are absent in the other child; and these act so that the original emotional tone of the conflicting ends-in-view is entirely altered. They are events of association by means of which there enter, more or less clearly, into consciousness ideas of pleased or displeased parents, their words of praise or censure, or the ideas of happy or disappointed companions. The strong emotional tones that belong to all these ideas are transmitted to the motive with which they are associated, and completely modify its initial pleasure value. The image of a larger piece of cake is indeed more pleasant than that of a smaller one if both stand side by side unaccompanied by other ideas, but here each is joined by a complex of other ideas together with their feelings, and these feelings are transferred, as experience shows, to those images, even when the ideas to which they originally belonged no longer appear in consciousness. By this process the idea of the lesser good can easily become more pleasant than that of the greater, and the apparently paradoxical decision occurs in complete conformity with our law of motivation. Everyone admits that the act of will could take place as it did only because of certain external influences, for no one believes that a child can choose the smaller cake *merely* because it likes the larger one more. And pedagogical experience teaches us that these influences are of the sort described. Since this suffices to explain the fact completely, we need no further hypothesis. Thus our law of motivation has here been entirely verified; and it is verified in all other cases we may choose to consider. Having dealt with a very simple example, we do well now to turn our attention to those acts of will in which the very highest matters are at stake, and which have from olden times been drawn into the foreground of ethical inquiries. Such are the cases of seemingly-greatest renunciation, or self-sacrifice.

The Law of Motivation in the Case of Heroism

The idea of personal destruction is, in general, one of the most terrifying; not the most terrifying, for there are enough miseries in comparison with which death is felt as a soothing relief. Yet, we observe, in life and history, acts of will whose fatal and miserable consequences are not only inevitable for the performer, but are clearly seen by him to be involved as the goal of his action. The martyr accepts pain and death for the sake of an idea, a friend gives his life or "happiness" for his friend. Can anyone in earnest say of such persons that their decisions are determined by the motives which possess the most pleasant or the least unpleasant emotional tones?

According to my firm conviction, one cannot say anything else if one would tell the truth, for such are the facts. Let us then try to analyze and understand the motive of heroism. The hero acts "for the sake of a cause"; he desires to carry out an idea or realize a definite goal. It is clear that the thought of this goal or that idea dominates his consciousness to such an extent that there is in it hardly room for any other thoughts. At least this holds in the case of inspiration, from which alone an heroic act can arise. It is true that the idea of his own painful destruction is present, but, however burdened with pain it may be in itself, it is inhibited and repressed by the predominant end-in-view, which finally triumphs in an "act of will," in an effort which becomes stronger and sharper the longer and more clearly the thought of the unavoidable catastrophe confronts him. What is the source of the astonishing force of the decisive end-in-view? Whence the power of this affect? Without doubt this is due to *emotion*. Inspiration is the greatest pleasure that can fall to the lot of man. To be inspired by something means to be overcome by the greatest joy in the thought of it. The man who, under the stress of inspiration, decides to help a friend or save another creature from pain and destruction, whatever the cost, finds the thought of this act so profoundly joyful, so overwhelmingly pleasant that, at the moment, the idea of the preservation of his own life and the avoidance of pain cannot compare with it. And he who fights for a cause with such inspiration that he accepts all persecution and insult realizes his idea with such elevated pure joy that neither the thought of his miseries nor their actual pain can prevail aught against it. The notion of giving up his purpose because of pain is, for him, more unpleasant than the pain itself.

Thus the correctness of our law of the will is shown in even the most extreme case, and quite naturally, without any auxiliary hypothesis. It is, in fact, universally true that the will follows the motive which has the greatest degree of pleasant feeling connected with it.[7]

Schlick's position is clear: everyone always chooses the alternative which he believes will bring about the greatest amount of good (i.e., pleasure) *for him*. First, he points out that this is obviously the way men act much of the time; second, by trying to account for difficult cases, he attempts to show that they act in this way all the time. There is no need (and no way) to disagree with his first point, for we all do, very often, act in ways which we believe will maximize the good for ourselves. What is crucial to Schlick's argument, however, is the second point, when he tries to show how such acts as sacrifice, heroism, martyrdom, and the like are really intended to increase the good (i.e., pleasure) of the agent.

The more apparent exceptions Schlick includes under his "law of motivation," the more likely it is that he is actually espousing the stronger version of psychological egoism. In order to claim universality for his law, he would have to show that no one could ever set out deliberately to act in an unselfish fashion. But the arguments he gives are far from adequate for this purpose. He shows that there are many instances of selfish action, and perhaps even that some seemingly altruistic actions must also be treated as selfish; but far from showing that no one ever *can* act unselfishly, he does not even make a clear case for the claim that no one ever *does* act unselfishly. For example, he argues that the hero, faced with the alternative of sacrificing himself or not, will choose the more pleasant alternative—sacrifice—because the emotion attendant upon the thought of such sacrifice is "so profoundly joyful, so overwhelmingly pleasant that, at the moment, the idea of the preservation of

[7] From *Problems of Ethics* by Moritz Schlick, trans. by David Rynin, Dover Publications, Inc., New York, 1939. Reprinted through the permission of the publisher.

his own life and the avoidance of pain cannot compare with it." But even if this should be the case with *some* heroes, there is nothing to justify the claim that it is the case with *all*. Furthermore, if we examine every instance of sacrifice we have made, it is far from clear that we can maintain that considerations of our own good have been crucial in determining our choice of what we shall do *in every case*. There is no doubt that we often act without even thinking of the good that will come to us as a result of what we do.

These remarks seem damaging to the psychological egoist's position, but often he replies that our purportedly unselfish actions are merely instances of self-deception. But this assertion is usually based on nothing more than an adherence to the stronger version of psychological egoism. The psychological egoist begins by claiming that all men act selfishly, and then argues that the counterexamples his critic offers are not really counterexamples. But his only support for this claim is the stronger thesis of psychological egoism, and this amounts to claiming that the alleged counterexamples to psychological egoism are not true counterexamples because psychological egoism is correct— a clear case of begging the question.

Instead of supporting his theory with good reasons (as our second criterion requires) the psychological egoist resorts to a dogmatic reiteration of his thesis. We believe that the counterexamples offered to psychological egoism are serious and cannot be dismissed by a mere reiteration of the theory, and for this reason we believe that the first criterion (the ability to answer serious objections) and the third criterion (the ability to explain the phenomena of experience better than competing theories) also have not been met.

3. *The Subconscious*. Sometimes the psychological egoist resorts to the claim that even though often we can find no conscious intentions in others or ourselves to further our own good, still there must be unconscious or subconscious factors which cause us always to pursue our own good. Without denying the existence of such factors, we may still ask what basis the psychological egoist has for making this claim. At best, this position is unverifiable, for there is no way ever to prove that these forces are *always* operative. To the claim that it cannot be proved that they are *not* always operative, one need only reply that there is no need to prove this, for the burden of proof is on the person who claims that they are, and this proof is not forthcoming. The device of subconscious motivations, it is clear, is simply something seized upon by the psychological egoist to support his theory when all other alternatives fail. It is an ad hoc assumption of the same sort used by the gremlin theorist when he found himself in difficulties.

One further argument should illustrate the inadequacy of resorting to subconscious motivations. It can be pointed out that every possible psychological theory of motivation can be supported by reasoning of this sort. In order to show that this is so let us invent another theory of motivation and call it *psychological utilitarianism*. According to this view, the only reason anyone does anything is that he believes it will ultimately lead to the greatest balance of good over evil for the greatest number of people. Probably nobody actually holds this view, but if we examine carefully the sorts of arguments that the psychological egoist (and especially Schlick) presents, we will find that the same arguments can be presented for psychological utilitarianism. If the fact that people often do not believe they are acting in their own interest is not relevant to a rejection of psychological egoism, why should the fact that people often do not believe they are acting in the interest of the greatest number of people count against psychological utilitarianism? And if this latter fact is relevant against psychological utilitarianism, as it seems to be, then the former fact is relevant against psychological egoism. Because the psychological egoist is allowed to speak of an unconscious (and at least sometimes undetectable) motivation to act in his own interest, the psychological utilitarian should be allowed to speak of an unconscious (and at least sometimes undetectable) motivation to act in the interest of the greatest number.

In terms of the criteria for the acceptability of theories, psychological egoism still has few reasons in favor of it (Criterion 2) and there appear to be facts (the actions of heroes and martyrs and even our own altruistic actions) which other theories of motivation explain more adequately (Criteria 1 and 3). These considerations throw considerable, perhaps even conclusive, doubt upon psychological egoism.

4. *Joseph Butler.* No discussion of psychological egoism would be complete without mentioning Bishop Joseph Butler (1692–1752), who is believed to have refuted this theory once and for all. The best expression of an opinion common to many philosophers is found in C. D. Broad:

> As a psychological theory it [i.e., psychological egoism] was killed by Butler; but it still flourishes, I believe, among bookmakers and smart young business men whose claim to know the world is based on an intimate acquaintance with the shadier side of it. In Butler's day the theory moved in higher social and intellectual circles, and it had to be treated more seriously than any philosopher would trouble to treat it now. This change is very largely the result of Butler's work; he killed the theory so thoroughly that he sometimes seems to the modern reader to be flogging dead horses. Still, all good fallacies go to America when they die, and rise again as the latest discoveries of the local professors. So it will always be useful to have Butler's refutation at hand.[8]

The easiest way to approach Butler's objections to psychological egoism is to begin with his account of the various "parts" of human nature, of which there are four: particular passions and appetites, self-love, benevolence, and conscience.

---

[8] C. D. Broad, *Five Types of Ethical Theory* (Paterson, N.J.: Littlefield, Adams & Co., 1959), p. 55.

Every man hath a general desire of his own happiness; and likewise a variety of particular affections, passions and appetites, to particular external objects. The former proceeds from, or is self-love. . . . The object the former pursues is somewhat internal, our own happiness, enjoyment, satisfaction; whether we have, or have not, a distinct particular perception what it is, or wherein it consists: the objects of the latter are this or that particular external thing, which the affections tend towards, and of which it hath always a particular idea or perception.[9]

Self-love, then, is a principle that leads us to seek our own happiness, and when we seek something else for the sake of our own happiness, we are acting upon the principle of self-love. It is clear that the psychological egoist is claiming, in Butler's terms, that self-love is the primary, or sole, principle of human nature. Butler contrasts this principle with particular affections, passions, and appetites, the objects of which are external. These, he insists, are sought not as a means to happiness but for their own sake.

Benevolence is to society what self-love is to the individual: ". . . if there be any affection in human nature, the object and end of which is the good of another; this is itself benevolence, or the love of another."[10] Conscience, finally, is the principle in man through which "he approves or disapproves his heart, temper, and actions." [11] Conscience, therefore, "tends to restrain men from doing mischief to each other and leads them to do good." [12]

Butler uses these notions to show that it is quite incorrect to say that all of our actions stem from a desire for our own happiness. His point is that, in manifest opposition to what we know will provide our own happiness, we very often act in order to gratify some particular passion, such as the desire for revenge or for power. If we always acted in order to secure our own happiness, we would be much better off than we are, and, in fact, Butler suggests that men do not often enough act from self-love.

Furthermore, he argues, unless we had these particular passions and appetites toward external things, we would never be able to be happy, for "happiness consists in the gratification of particular passions, which supposes the having of them." [13] This shows, therefore, that there are such passions, for if there were not, no one could ever be happy.

That all particular appetites and passions are towards *external things themselves*, distinct from the *pleasure arising from them*, is manifested from hence; that there could not be this pleasure, were it not for that prior suitableness between the object and the passion: there could be no enjoyment or delight for one

[9] Joseph Butler, *Fifteen Sermons upon Human Nature* (London: G. Bell & Sons Ltd., 1958), p. 167.
    [10] *Ibid.*, p. 35.
    [11] *Ibid.*, p. 38.
    [12] *Ibid.*, p. 39.
    [13] *Ibid.*, p. 170.

thing more than another, from eating food more than from swallowing a stone, if there were not an affection or appetite to one thing more than another.[14]

What Butler is arguing, then, is that there are a number of different principles in human nature, two of which are self-love and particular appetites. The psychological egoist claims that all actions are motivated by a desire for happiness, which is to say that self-love is the only principle guiding our actions. But men are sometimes happy, and because happiness consists of the gratification of particular appetites, there must be these particular appetites. But if these particular appetites exist, then self-love is not the only principle of action. Furthermore, men often act in ways other than those designed to provide for their own happiness. Finally, to those who insist that self-love is the only principle operative in man, Butler argues:

If any person can in earnest doubt, whether there be such a thing as good-will in one man towards another . . . let it be observed, that *whether man be thus or otherwise constituted, what is the inward frame in this particular,* is a mere question of fact or natural history, not proveable immediately by reason. It is therefore to be judged of and determined in the same way other facts or matters of natural history are: by appealing to the external senses, or inward perceptions, . . . and lastly, by the testimony of mankind. Now, that there is some degree of benevolence amongst men, may be as strongly and plainly proved in all these ways, as it could possibly be proved. . . .[15]

In effect, Butler is arguing that the claim that self-love is the only principle motivating human action is open to every sort of disproof that any other factual claim is, and that those who continue to deny this are clearly holding a theory for which there is very little evidence, and against which there is more than enough.

Exercises

Review

1. How may different teleological views be distinguished on the basis of the extent of the consequences considered relevant to the rightness or wrongness of the action?
2. What are two possible formulations of psychological egoism and how do they differ?
3. What is the distinction between psychological egoism and ethical egoism?
4. What argument or arguments does Schlick offer in support of psychological egoism?
5. How might one reply to Schlick's arguments?
6. How is the notion of the subconscious brought in by the psychological

[14] *Ibid.*, pp. 167–68.
[15] *Ibid.*, pp. 34–35.

egoist to support his theory, and what reasons are there for believing that this move is not satisfactory?

7. What is the point of introducing the theory called *psychological utilitarianism,* and what is demonstrated by the introduction of that view?

8. How does Butler attempt to refute psychological egoism?

Applications

1. Criticize the following arguments:

   a. Whenever someone does something, he does it to fulfill a psychological need. The most compelling psychological need is avoidance of pain. Thus, whenever anyone does anything, the most compelling motive is his desire to avoid pain.

   b. Whenever S does A, where A is a voluntary act, S does so because he wants to. If S does A because he wants to, then S does A to fulfill his want, then he does A to increase his own good.

2. If you feel that there are any good reasons in favor of the claim that men always act in order to bring about good for themselves, present them.

3. Consider the following statements:

   a. All men are selfish.

   b. Everyone acts to satisfy some desire of his own.

   c. We all look out for ourselves.

   d. Everyone is always concerned to promote his own good.

   e. Everyone does what he wants to.

   Which of the above might be interpreted as expressions of psychological egoism, and which might be true even though psychological egoism is false? Explain in detail the differences between the various formulations.

4. Is it possible to defend the view that all men are actually selfish (in everything that they do) without resorting to the claim that it is not possible for a man to act unselfishly?

5. Arguing as a psychological egoist, attempt to show how the following apparently altruistic acts can be explained on the principles of psychological egoism:

   a. Helping an old lady across the street.

   b. Giving anonymously to charity.

   c. Breaking your own arm to prove to a friend that psychological egoism is false, on the grounds that this action is not one which you believe will lead to your own greatest good.

   d. Allowing yourself to form a habit of drinking, knowing that it will ultimately result in your ruin, and the destruction of your family.

   e. Playing Russian roulette.

   f. Allowing yourself to be crucified to atone for the sins of man.

   Now, examine critically the explanations you have given for these actions, and decide whether or not they are really satisfactory.

6. Arguing as a psychological utilitarian, attempt to show how the following apparently nonaltruistic acts can be explained on the principles of psychological utilitarianism:

   a. Jumping into the last available seat on the bus just as a one-legged old lady is about to sit down in that same seat.

b. Publicizing a charitable gift.
c. Breaking the arm of a friend to prove to the friend that sometimes you do what will not lead to the greatest good for others.
d. Peddling dope.
e. Organizing Russian roulette clubs (without being an active or a rotating member) because you enjoy watching the sport.
f. Informing on your Jewish neighbors in order to be saved from the Nazis (when you yourself are Jewish).

Now examine critically the explanations you have given for these actions, and decide whether or not they are really satisfactory.

C. Ethical Egoism

Philosophers who wish to defend ethical egoism often appeal to psychological egoism. Many seem to believe that some form of ethical egoism follows from psychological egoism. But if ethical egoism depends upon psychological egoism, and if psychological egoism is as unsound as we have suggested that it is, then there is absolutely no reason for holding the ethical view. A theory which is a consequence of an unacceptable theory is not thereby shown to be false, but we are forced to seek support for it from some other quarter.

The main tenet of ethical egoism is that one ought (or has the right) to act in whatever way promotes his own greatest good. There is a distinction, however, between saying that everyone *has the right* to act in his own interest and saying that everyone *ought* to act in his own interest. There is also a difference between claiming that everyone has the right to (or ought to) do that which *is* in his own interest and claiming that everyone has the right to (or ought to) do that which *seems to be* in his own interest. Once these distinctions are noted, we can set forth a number of different formulations of ethical egoism. It is possible that an ethical egoist might hold more than one of these views, but he could not, of course, hold them all, for some are incompatible with others. For example, if we examine the statements below we can see that anyone who holds Statement 1 will also hold Statement 2; but he cannot hold Statement 3 unless he believes that he is never wrong about what is in his own interest.

1. I (and only I) ought, at all times, to act in my own interest.
2. I (and only I) have the right, at all times, to act in my own interest.
3. I (and only I) ought, at all times, to act in the way which appears to me to be in my own interest.
4. I (and only I) have the right, at all times, to act in the way which appears to me to be in my own interest.
5. Everyone ought, at all times, to act in his own interest.
6. Everyone has the right, at all times, to act in his own interest.
7. Everyone ought, at all times, to act in the way which appears to him to be in his own interest.

8. Everyone has the right, at all times, to act in the way which appears to him to be in his own interest.

1. *Objections to Versions 1–4.* Anyone who holds an ethical theory is responsible for offering, upon demand, reasons in support of that theory. What reasons could anyone who held any of the positions represented in 1–4 give to support his view? There seem to be no considerations S could give that would establish, or even begin to establish, the view that he, and only he, has the right (or the obligation) to act in what is (or seems to be) his own interest. If he were asked to defend this claim he would have to give some fact about himself. That is, he would say "I have Characteristic C, and so I am justified in acting in my own interest." But then it would seem to follow that if anyone else had C, he too would be justified in acting in *his* interest, a fact incompatible with any of the versions 1–4.

Suppose that every individual in the universe has one, and only one, absolutely peculiar characteristic, call it B_p (B will stand for the characteristic, and p will identify the individual who has it). S now could keep his egoism by claiming that only one person, himself, would ever fit the rule; but now there is no reason to keep everyone from maintaining the same thing about his own B characteristic. There is never any way to decide which of two egoists each maintaining that he, and only he, has the right (or the obligation) to act in his own interests is correct, and it is obvious that both cannot be correct. Our suspicion, which we have tried to justify by argument, is that neither is correct, for if either is, there is no reason why the other is not also. There does not therefore seem to be very much hope for an ethical egoist who states his position in any of ways 1–4.

2. *Objections to Version 5.* In discussing the version of ethical egoism expressed in Statement 5, we shall appeal to a principle, generally accepted by ethical thinkers, that no one can ever be obliged to do something not within his power. For example, a soldier is not under an obligation to obey the orders of his general if those orders are not conveyed to him—and the general who decides what his orders for the day are and then, without issuing them, begins to court martial people for not obeying them is unjust indeed. The point here is not that the soldier cannot do what the general ordered, it is just that he cannot *obey* the orders if he does not know them. The application of this point to the fifth version of ethical egoism should be obvious. One can be obliged to act in his own interest only when he can reasonably be expected to know what his interest is. It is clear that no one knows, every time he must make a moral decision, exactly which of all possible actions will maximize his own good. It is extremely doubtful that everyone knows, every time he has to make a moral choice, which actions are even good for him. What is clear, and hardly disputable, is that there are cases when, no matter how diligently one attempts to discover what is in his interest, he is doomed to

failure because of the inaccessibility of certain data (the secret plans of his enemies or the unpredictable quirks of his friends). Hence, because no one can always know what is in his interest, no one can always be obliged to act In his own interest. Therefore we suggest that Statement 5 is an indefensible version of ethical egoism.

3. *Interim Review*. As a result of the criticisms offered in the previous two sections, we are left with three versions, or possible interpretations, of ethical egoism. If the arguments against them presented in the following sections are compelling, we shall have to reject ethical egoism altogether unless some new formulation can be given by one of its defenders or the other known ethical theories all fail even more miserably to satisfy our criteria for acceptability.

It is often claimed that the chief (and possibly the only) support for ethical egoism is psychological egoism. However, it is also sometimes claimed that the two are actually incompatible. This divergence of opinion results from the failure to notice carefully enough the different forms that ethical egoism may take. We shall show that psychological egoism, if true, would support Statements 6 and 8, but it is incompatible with Statement 7. However, even if we should show that ethical and psychological egoism are always incompatible, this would neither establish nor refute ethical egoism, for psychological egoism is not true. Thus, anyone who wants to hold Statement 7 must deny psychological egoism, and anyone who wants to hold Statements 6, 7, or 8 must find arguments that are independent of psychological egoism. This fact is often not sufficiently appreciated by those who reason about theories of obligation.

4. *Objections to Version 7*. No one ever has an obligation to do that which it is impossible for him to do, but it seems very peculiar to suggest that if everyone, by "a certain impulsion of nature" always does (or must) act in his own interest, he has an obligation to act in this way. If one has an obligation to do something, then there would seem to be at least the possibility that he could refrain from doing it—otherwise why bother to speak of "obligation" at all? If this point can be accepted, then it is possible to show that psychological egoism (at least in the stronger version) is indeed incompatible with Statement 7. And, of course, if this is the case, it is hardly plausible to suppose that Statement 7 receives any support from the psychological theory. If we reject the principle that one cannot be obliged to do what he cannot refrain from doing, we can allow that 7 is compatible with psychological egoism, but it is still difficult to see how the latter view could lend any support to 7. One could, after all, hardly argue that the reason that we all ought to look after our own interests is that everyone does, all of the time, do exactly that. Thus, with the principle outlined here, Statement 7 is incompatible with psychological egoism; without it, the two positions are compatible, but it is very implausible to maintain that the psychological view lends any support to the ethical view, as defenders of ethical egoism often seem to be claiming.

It is also important to point out that there are serious objections to State-ment 7. Sometimes it appears that a particular course of action is in someone's interest when it actually is not—indeed, the course of action that looks so promising may actually lead to the ruin of the individual who chooses it. Suppose, for example, that S drinks from a bottle labeled 'Cough Medicine' but which actually contains virulent bubonic plague. Are we to admit, with the ethical egoist who holds to Statement 7, that S nevertheless has a moral obligation to perform this action? It is unlikely that very many people would want to grant this.

It might be maintained in defense of Statement 7 that if one is not obliged to act on what he thinks is the case, he cannot be obliged to do anything at all, for all he ever has to go upon is what he believes. There is some plausi-bility in this suggestion, but it will not provide much help for those who hold to Statement 7. Suppose, for example, that S believes it to be in his inter-est to get up early Sunday morning and take a walk. Are we to say that, because of this, he has an obligation (a very strong claim) to take that walk, and that if he elects to stay in bed he is morally blameworthy? This is very unlikely, and when we explore the actual consequence of 7, which seem to be that every time we have an opinion about what will be in our interests, no matter how mistaken it is, and no matter how insignificant the action is, we thereby have a moral obligation, we find that these consequences go very much against the phenomena we must square our theory with. Furthermore, it is appropriate to ask what possible justification could be given for such an extreme view. Unless some pretty strong reasons can be given, which will offset these rather absurd consequences, there is no reason at all for holding to Statement 7.

5. *Objections to Versions 6 and* 8. There is no plausibility in the claim that Statements 6 and 8 are incompatible with psychological egoism and, indeed, these versions of ethical egoism do seem to follow from that psychological view. Thomas Hobbes seems to note this point in the following passage:

> Among so many dangers therefore, as the natural lusts of men do daily threaten each other withal, to have a care of one's self is so far from being a matter scorn-fully to be looked upon, that one has neither the power nor the wish to have done otherwise. For every man is desirous of what is good for him, and shuns what is evil, but chiefly the chiefest of natural evils, which is death; and this he doth by a certain impulsion of nature, no less than that whereby a stone moves downward. It is therefore neither absurd nor reprehensible, neither against the dictates of true reason, for a man to use all his endeavours to preserve and defend his body and the members thereof from death and sorrows. But that which is not contrary to right reason, that all men account to be done justly, and with right.[16]

[16] Hobbes, *Philosophical Rudiments, op. cit.,* 8–9.

Hobbes claims that no one has either the power or the desire to refrain from looking after his own interest. According to Hobbes, man desires what is good for him by "a certain impulsion of nature," and could no more refrain from doing this than a stone could fly upward. It follows from this that it cannot be wrong for a man to act in such a way as to achieve this end. We do not blame the stone which, falling from its place, lands on our head—how, therefore, can we blame the man, whose actions are as necessary as those of the stone, for acting in the way that he does?

Let us first inquire whether psychological egoism supports Statements 6 and 8 with equal strength. Contrary to first appearances, psychological egoism does not support Statement 6 at all. The psychological egoist tells us that everyone does or must act in ways *he believes* to be in his own interest at all times, not that he does or must act in a way that is *in fact* in his own interest. From this it can quickly be seen that only Statement 8 can be thought to follow from psychological egoism, for from the fact that all men do or must act in a way that seems to them at the time to be in their own interest, it does not follow that they do only or can only act in a way that is *in fact* in their own interest. So also it does not follow that they cannot be blamed for acting in their own interest. Thus, even if psychological egoism were correct, it would provide no support for Statement 6. When, however, we look for support for Statement 6, we find none readily available and many plausible counterexamples. For example, suppose that it is to S's interest to refrain from paying his debts, to kill his wife and children, or even to annihilate the citizens of the United States; according to Statement 6, he would have the right to do all these things. Certainly no one who was not blinded by an adherence to ethical egoism would be willing to assert that S did *in fact* have the right to do these things.

Finally, although Statement 8 does seem to follow from psychological egoism, it causes little trouble, for, as we have shown, psychological egoism is an incorrect theory. And, of course, counterexamples for Statement 8, similar to those raised against Statement 7, are even more readily available than counterexamples for Statement 6. If one believes that a certain course of action, disastrous to himself and detrimental to everyone else, is in his interest—can we, in good conscience, affirm that he has the right to pursue it? Little serious thought is required to see that we cannot.

Summary. It should be obvious by now that psychological egoism is not an acceptable theory of motivation, and that ethical egoism is not an acceptable theory of obligation. Both theories fail to meet the criteria for the acceptability of theories: serious objections can be raised against every version of ethical egoism; there are no good reasons supporting any of them; and, finally, according to ethical egoism one is often said to be obliged to do, or to have the right to do, many things which it is quite clear he is not obliged, or does not have the right, to do.

Exercises

Review

1. Explain the differences among the various forms of ethical egoism.
2. Why is it necessary to distinguish so many different forms of ethical egoism?
3. What general objections are there to Versions 1–4 of ethical egoism?
4. How is the principle that no one can ever be obliged to do something not within his power used to criticize Version 5 of ethical egoism?
5. Discuss the relation between psychological egoism and Versions 6, 7, and 8 of ethical egoism.
6. What form of ethical egoism does Thomas Hobbes hold?

Applications

1. Apply the criteria of acceptability to each of the forms of ethical egoism.
2. Would a clever ethical egoist ever argue for his ethical egoism?
3. Are there any situations in which an ethical egoist might argue against his own theory of obligation?
4. Examine this criticism of ethical egoism:

> If ethical egoism is correct, it leads to absurd and contradictory consequences, so it cannot be correct. Suppose that there is a switch in a neutral position, and that
> a. It is to the interest of Jones to turn the switch to the left.
> b. It is to the interest of Smith to turn the switch to the right.
> Then, if ethical egoism is correct, it would be true that
> c. Jones ought to turn the switch to the left.
> d. Smith ought to turn the switch to the right.
> Now it appears that from statement c we can deduce that
> e. The switch ought to be turned to the left.
> And it appears that from statement d we can deduce that
> f. The switch ought to be turned to the right.
> But the conjunction of statements e and f is a contradiction, and any ethical theory that results in a contradiction cannot be correct.

> Is this a good argument? To which, if any, versions of ethical egoism does it apply?

5. Here is another argument, very much like the one above:

> Statements a–d are the same, but from statement c we can derive
> g. Jones can turn the switch to the left.
> And from statement d we can derive
> h. Smith can turn the switch to the right.
> These follow by the "*ought* implies *can*" principle we have already discussed. But then when we conjoin statements g and h we get
> i. Jones can turn the switch to the left and Smith can turn the switch to the right.
> But if Jones turns the switch to the left, Smith cannot turn it to the right, and if Smith turns the switch to the right, Jones cannot turn it to the left. Therefore, statement i cannot be true. But any theory that implies a false statement cannot be correct, so ethical egoism must be wrong.

Is this argument better or worse than the preceding one? How do the two arguments differ—i.e., what significance does their obvious difference have?

6. Criticize the following arguments:

   a. The only reason that anyone has for arguing against ethical egoism is that it is to his interest to to so. If one were to argue that ethical egoism is correct, then many people would act from such a theory. If many people did that, it would be more difficult to maximize one's own good than it was before. Anyone who truly believes that ethical egoism is correct will, therefore, argue that it is incorrect. The number of thoughtful people who believe that ethical egoism is correct is shown by the large percentage of such people who argue against it.

   b. That which is most valuable to a person is that with which he is most careful. A person is most careful with his life, and so a person's life is that which is most valuable to him. Thus, everyone has the right, at all times, to act in the way that appears to him to be in his own interest.

   c. Each person has an obligation to make himself as good as possible. That which makes a person good is that which is to his interest. Therefore, everyone ought, at all times, to act in his own interest.

7. Compare the analysis that Schlick and Butler would give of the following passage:

   "My motive for taking up nursing was chiefly because I had a keen desire to help people who were ill or in serious trouble. I liked doing personal services for them. As quite a young girl I enjoyed visiting the elderly people in our town, and if the opportunity presented itself I would help bathe them, or comb their hair, or clean their false teeth. Once I made so bold as to dress one woman's varicose ulcers. Motive number two was my admiration for the nurse's uniform. . . . I did actual bedside nursing for a number of years and then drifted into Public Health Work. While I always enjoyed the curative phase of nursing while I was doing it, I find now that I like P. H. much better. It seems so much more worth while. I know now that I get more real pleasure in teaching a mother how to control communicable disease in a community than nursing her child through a case of diphtheria which can so easily be prevented these days."

Bibliography *

*BAIER, KURT. *The Moral Point of View*. Ithaca, N.Y.: Cornell University Press, 1958, pp. 188–91. A discussion of a "consistent" form of ethical egoism and an attempt to show that a consistent egoist cannot make moral judgments.

*BROAD, C. D. "Egoism as a Theory of Human Motives," in *Ethics and the His-

* The items in the bibliographies are of unequal difficulty and of unequal importance. Unfortunately, sometimes the difficult items are also the important ones. We have taken the liberty of placing stars in front of those articles and works not recommended immediately to beginning students. A star indicates either that the article is nearly inaccessible, too difficult for the beginner, or of interest only to an advanced student. In a few cases we have not placed a star in front of an important work, despite its difficulty. In these cases we feel that the extra work required of a beginner would be justified.

tory of Philosophy. New York: Humanities Press, 1952, pp. 218–31. A critical discussion of psychological egoism.

*————. in *The Philosophy of G. E. Moore,* ed. P. Schilpp. Evanston, Ill.: Northwestern University Press, 1942, pp. 43–57. An examination of Moore's arguments to the effect that ethical egoism is self-contradictory.

BUTLER, JOSEPH. *Fifteen Sermons upon Human Nature.* London: G. Bell & Sons Ltd., 1958. Especially Sermon xi.

CARRITT, E. F. *Ethical and Political Thinking.* Oxford: The Clarendon Press, 1957, pp. 49–58. A criticism of egoism in its hedonistic form.

HOBBES, THOMAS. *Leviathan: Parts I and II.* Indianapolis and New York: The Bobbs-Merrill Company, Inc., 1958.

————. *Philosophical Rudiments Concerning Government and Society.* London: John Bohn, 1841.

*HOSPERS, JOHN. "Baier and Medlin on Ethical Egoism," *Philosophical Studies,* **12** (1961), 10–16. An argument that a form of egoism called "impersonal egoism," is not inconsistent.

*KADING, DANIEL, and MARTIN KRAMER. "Mr. Hospers' Defense of Impersonal Egoism," *Philosophical Studies,* **15** (1964), 44–46. A reply to Hospers' article, in which it is argued that the impersonal egoist both denies and presupposes utilitarian considerations.

MEDLIN, BRIAN. "Ultimate Principles and Ethical Egoism," *Australasian Journal of Philosophy,* **35** (1957), 111–18. The author distinguishes several forms of ethical egoism and attempts to show that the view is inconsistent, however he seems to presuppose a noncognitivist meta-ethical view. (Cf. Chapters 10 and 13 in this volume.)

*MOORE, G. E. *Principia Ethica.* Cambridge, Mass.: Cambridge University Press, 1959, pp. 96–105. An attempt to show that ethical egoism is self-contradictory.

NIELSEN, KAI. "Egoism in Ethics," *Philosophy and Phenomenological Research,* **19** (1959), 502–10. An examination of psychological and ethical egoism, and the conclusion that there are no good reasons for accepting ethical egoism.

SCHLICK, MORITZ. *Problems of Ethics,* trans. David Rynin. New York: Dover Publications, Inc., 1962. Chapter 2 contains a defense of ethical egoism.

Utilitarianism

Ethical egoism is the view that the only obligation (or right) anyone has is to provide the greatest possible good for himself. Not all teleologists hold this view, for many believe there is an obligation to provide good for other people as well. Of the two teleological theories, this latter view, utilitarianism, has the advantage of being more in line with most people's beliefs about obligation; but it has the disadvantage of being much more difficult to formulate clearly. If it is true that man has an obligation to himself only, then the task of deciding what to do on a given occasion is comparatively simple; but as soon as he admits that he has an obligation toward other people, new and difficult problems arise. For example, does one have an obligation to all other people, or only to some? If the latter, then there is the question of deciding just who those people are. Furthermore, if one recognizes an obligation to a group and then discovers that, as a result of a decision, he must make, some of the group will have to suffer, how does he decide which part must suffer?

A. Two Forms of Utilitarianism: Act Utilitarianism and Rule Utilitarianism

It is customary to distinguish act utilitarianism from rule utilitarianism. The act utilitarian holds that the rightness or wrongness of an action is solely a function of its consequences. The rule utilitarian on the other hand, holds that a particular action is right or wrong if, and only if, it follows or breaks some rule, and that the correctness of the rule (and not the correctness of the action) is a function of the consequences that follow from that rule's being accepted, recognized, followed, or adopted. Different versions differ sharply at this point, for there is obviously a difference between a rule being recognized and one being followed, but we will not worry about these considerations until later.

The difference between the teleologist and the deontologist lies in the fact that the teleologist feels that the rightness of an action or a rule is a function of consequences alone, while the deontologist insists that factors other than, or in addition to, consequences are significant. Suppose, for example, that Poland has just been invaded by Germany. Germany is the more developed country, more advanced and more densely populated. Poland, however, has certain natural resources needed by Germany. An observer might claim that Germany was wrong to undertake the invasion on the grounds that war, in all forms and for any reason, is wrong. Such an appeal to a rule or maxim, apart from any consideration of the consequences, is the mark of at least one sort of *deontologist*. If, on the other hand, the critic attempts to defend this maxim by appealing to the consequences of its adoption, then he would be a *rule utilitarian*. It is possible, however, that the critic (let us suppose he is a German) had argued in the following way: "The invasion was justified because the Germans will be far better off after our quick and inevitable victory. The hardship we suffer as a result of the war will be more than balanced by our future prosperity." This justification is a species of act utilitarianism which we shall identify as *limited act utilitarianism*. We call it *limited* because the only consequences considered are those affecting a limited number of people. (A Pole who condemned the invasion because it brought nothing but hardship to *his* people would also be adopting this normative ethical position.)

A neutral observer might attempt to condemn the invasion because, even though there are more Germans than Poles, the total unhappiness caused to Poles will outweigh the total good coming to the Germans. An appeal to the consequences of an action that takes everyone into consideration, each one counting for one, can be described as *universal act utilitarianism*.[1] This same position would be represented by one who argued that the invasion was justified because, in the long run, most people stood to benefit from it: the Germans, from the availability of the natural resources; the Poles, from the superior discipline and higher technological level of German culture.

B. Act Utilitarianism

A number of views fall under the heading of act utilitarianism. Two have already been suggested: universal act utilitarianism and limited act utilitarianism.

[1] We have classified the universal act utilitarian as one who takes into account all the *people* affected by the action, but one may insist that the good coming to all *sentient beings* is really what matters. If such a way of speaking were adopted, our universal act utilitarian would become a limited utilitarian.

Limited act utilitarianism: S ought to do that which will bring about the greatest amount of good for (the greatest number of) the members of Group G, where Group G is some subclass of the whole human race.

Universal act utilitarianism: S ought to do that which will bring about the greatest amount of good for (the greatest number of) the human race.[2]

These distinctions are just a beginning, though, for they do not allow us to distinguish all of the important kinds of act utilitarianism. Instead of holding that S ought to do that which will *in fact* bring about the greatest amount of good for, say, his race, one might hold that S ought to do that which *he believes* will bring about the greatest amount of good for his race. We can thus distinguish, within limited act utilitarianism, two views: objective limited act utilitarianism, and subjective limited act utilitarianism, respectively. These two versions of utilitarianism can also be found within universal act utilitarianism. This gives us four versions of act utilitarianism:

1. Objective limited act utilitarianism.
2. Subjective limited act utilitarianism.
3. Objective universal act utilitarianism.
4. Subjective universal act utilitarianism.

Exercises

Review
1. What do all theories of ethical egoism and utilitarianism have in common? What differentiates them from one another?
2. What is the distinction between act utilitarianism and rule utilitarianism?
3. What feature is used to distinguish limited act utilitarianism from universal act utilitarianism?
4. What is the difference between objective and subjective forms of utilitarianism?

Applications
1. Describe some situation in which a moral judgment is called for and show how a defender of each of the kinds of act utilitarianism we have distinguished would justify his judgment. Construct your situation so that not all the defenders would make the same judgment.
2. Describe how an objective limited act utilitarian, a subjective limited act utilitarian, an objective universal act utilitarian, and a subjective universal act utilitarian, respectively, would argue for the following moral judgments:
   a. Cheating on examinations is wrong.
   b. Politeness is obligatory.
   c. Everyone has an obligation to vote at election time.
   d. Lying to save the honor of a friend is right.
   e. It is wrong to walk on the grass.

[2] We must include present and future members of the human race or this is just another form of limited act utilitarianism.

1. **Objective Limited Act Utilitarianism.** Objective limited act utilitarianism is the view that an action is right if, and only if, it actually results in the greatest good for the members of a specific group. It is not difficult to see why one might uncritically assume that this view is correct, for people do tend to feel an obligation to do good for other people although they are disinclined to treat all men as equal. Yet there are strong reasons for rejecting this version of act utilitarianism, and few philosophers are willing to defend it.

a. THE OBJECTIVE LIMITED ACT UTILITARIAN CANNOT SELECT HIS GROUP. The most serious problem with this view is that there is really no satisfactory way for the objective limited act utilitarian to select the group he believes ought to be considered in judging an action. The limited act utilitarian believes that it is S's duty to do that which will bring about the greatest good to the members of some particular group (call it G). There are two distinct possibilities here, for S may or may not be a member of this group.

If S is not a member of G, it is difficult to see what reasons anyone could give for saying that he has any obligation to provide good for its members. Suppose S is a Negro, while the characteristic that individuates members of group G is white skin. It would seem that any arguments that could be given to show that S has an obligation to act for the good of the members of G would be no better and no worse than arguments showing that S has an obligation to act for the good of some other group (G'), such as the Orientals, or the Indians.

If S is a member of G, the objective limited act utilitarian's claim is that he has an obligation to that group and to no other. But because everyone is a member of more than one group, how can one establish that S owes his allegiance to Group G, rather than to some other group of which he is a member? As before, it is difficult to see how any argument showing that S has an obligation to G could not be met with an equally strong argument showing that S has an obligation to Group G' or G''. Furthermore, assuming that one wanted to argue that S did have an obligation toward the members of G, no objective limited act utilitarian reasons would be available, for that would nicely beg the question. That is, no one can argue that S's having an obligation to Group G is for the good of some group, for once again there would have to be a reason why S should act in a way that provided good for *that* group. It should also be noticed that no subjective utilitarian justification, no universal utilitarian justification, and no deontological justification can be given for selecting the favored group, for to do so would be to abandon objective limited act utilitarianism for a more basic theory.

b. THERE ARE NUMEROUS COUNTEREXAMPLES TO OBJECTIVE LIMITED ACT UTILITARIANISM. One version of objective limited act utilitarianism maintains that man's obligation is toward his family. But suppose that S is considering giving piano lessons to his daughter and it comes to his attention that there is a little girl next door, with more native musical talent, whose father cannot afford to give her piano lessons. Assume also that S cannot pay for more than one set of lessons. If more good should come to the girl next door than to his daughter from piano lessons, is it S's duty to offer the lessons to his neighbor's child? We think it could be said that it is not his duty to do so, and this would seem to indicate that at least sometimes we would agree with the conclusion of limited act utilitarianism.

Let us consider another case, however. Suppose that S's choice is between piano lessons for his daughter and a life-saving operation for the little girl of his best friend. At this point, most of us would claim that his duty stretches beyond his family and that "familial" limited act utilitarianism must be expanded somewhat. But this suggests that, whatever the group with which one begins, he may be forced to abandon it eventually. If so, it seems impossible to hold that objective limited act utilitarianism is a satisfactory theory of obligation.

Counterexamples of another type may be raised against this view. For example, if S claims to have an obligation toward Group G it is entirely possible that the group may consist of two equal parts, G_1 and G_2. A situation could arise where S has a choice between two actions, where Action A will produce 100 units of good for the members of G_1 and 50 units of evil for the members of G_2, whereas Action B will produce 100 units of good for the members of G_2 and 50 units of evil for the members of G_1. There is no way that S can, on limited act utilitarian principles, decide which action to perform. The limited act utilitarian might reply that this shows only that sometimes it is not possible to make a rational choice between two actions, and since this doesn't happen very often it is nothing to be alarmed about. But this reply is unsatisfactory, for it might be the case that Action A necessitates the death of an innocent child, whereas no such sacrifice is required by Action B. Then we would have to say that, all other things being equal, B is right and A is wrong. However, this judgment cannot be justified by the objective limited act utilitarian. Thus, his position does not adequately account for all moral decisions, and moral judgments must sometimes be made on some other basis.

2. *Objective Universal Act Utilitarianism.* Such considerations would seem to point toward some nonlimited (i.e., universal) form of act utilitarianism, in which it is not necessary to make a selection from all the people in the world. According to objective universal act utilitarianism, man ought to act in such a way as to provide the greatest good for the greatest number of people. Unlike objective limited act utilitarianism, this view has been vigorously defended by a number of important philosophers.

a. JEREMY BENTHAM. Among these philosophers is Jeremy Bentham (1748–1832), who maintains that man has an obligation to provide the greatest good for the greatest number of people, and that pleasure is the only good. Bentham argues that the value of a pleasure or a pain in itself is determined by the following characteristics:

1. Its intensity.
2. Its duration.
3. Its certainty or uncertainty.
4. Its propinquity or remoteness.[3]

The intensity is just the strength of the pleasure or pain, its duration is the length of time it lasts, its certainty is the probability that it will in fact occur, and its propinquity or remoteness is the nearness or distance in time of it. (Apparently a pleasure that will come soon is better than one that is far off, just as one that is sure to come is—all things being equal—to be preferred to one that is not).

In giving a total evaluation of the pleasures for the purpose of evaluating an action, Bentham holds there are two other characteristics of the pleasure or pain to be considered: its fecundity ("the chance it has of being followed by sensations of the *same* kind"), and its purity ("the chance it has of not being followed by sensations of the opposite kind").[4] These considerations allow us to decide the value of an action insofar as it concerns one person alone—that is all that the ethical egoist need concern himself with. But, Bentham adds another consideration: the extent of the pleasure or pain ("that is, the number of persons... who are affected by it").[5] As Bentham puts it:

> Sum up all the values of all the *pleasures* on the one side, and those of all the pains on the other. The balance, if it be on the side of pleasure, will give the *good* tendency of the act upon the whole, with respect to the interests of that *individual* person; if on the side of pain, the *bad* tendency of it upon the whole.
>
> Take an account of the *number* of persons whose interests appear to be concerned; and repeat the above process with respect to each.[6]

It is the action which has the best total consequences that we ought to choose, and for Bentham this is the one that produces the greatest balance of pleasure over pain.[7]

John Stuart Mill (1806–73) was brought up by his father, James Mill, and by Bentham to champion the utilitarian doctrine, but, there is good reason (see Chapter 7) to believe that he abandoned Bentham's "hedonic calculus," or numerical weighing of pleasures and pains, and even hedonism. Furthermore, there is some question as to whether Mill should be classified as an act

[3] Jeremy Bentham, *An Introduction to the Principles of Morals and Legislation* (New York: Hafner, 1948), p. 29.

[4] *Ibid.*, p. 30.

[5] *Ibid.*

[6] *Ibid.*, p. 31.

[7] Bentham's version is clearly hedonistic, but it is easy to see how this theory could be freed from hedonistic implications. One could simply maintain that the action which we ought to perform is the one which produces the greatest amount of good on the whole (where that *good* is not necessarily thought of as *pleasure*).

utilitarian or a rule utilitarian, and J. O. Urmson, a contemporary British philosopher, has defended the latter interpretation.[8] For that reason, we shall not discuss Mill's view here, for if it is an act utilitarian view, it differs from Bentham's essentially about a theory of value, and if it is a rule utilitarian view, it is more properly considered in another place.

b. G. E. MOORE. A view in some respects quite similar to Bentham's has been defended by G. E. Moore (1873–1958), who claimed that "in thus insisting that what is right must mean what produces the best possible results Utilitarianism is fully justified" [9]

That the assertion 'I am morally bound to perform this action' is identical with the assertion 'This action will produce the *greatest possible amount of good* in the Universe' has already been briefly shewn . . . But it is important to insist that this fundamental point is demonstrably certain.[10]

It is "briefly shown" in the following passage:

In short to assert that a certain line of conduct is, at a given time, absolutely right or obligatory, is obviously to assert that more good or less evil will exist in the world, if it be adopted than if anything else is done instead.[11]

The conclusion which Moore draws from this is that

Our 'duty,' therefore, can only be defined as that action, which will cause more good to exist in the Universe than any possible alternative. And what is 'right' or 'morally permissible' only differs from this, as what will *not* cause *less* good than any possible alternative.[12]

Moore was quite aware that, as a consequence of this view "we never have any reason to suppose that an action is our duty: we can never be sure that any action will produce the greatest value possible." [13] Now one way to react to this revelation is to abandon objective act utilitarianism for some view according to which our duty is not to do that which will *actually* produce the greatest amount of good, but rather to do that which we *believe* will produce the greatest amount of good. Moore, however, takes another alternative. He suggests that in order to be safe we follow generally useful rules, and even

[8] J. O. Urmson, "The Interpretation of the Moral Philosophy of J. S. Mill," *The Philosophical Quarterly*, 3 (January 1953), 33–39.

[9] G. E. Moore, *Principia Ethica* (Cambridge: Cambridge University Press, 1959), p. 106. By permission of the publishers.

[10] *Ibid.*, p. 147.

[11] *Ibid.*, p. 25. In passing let us remark that the theory of value which Moore defends is not hedonism, and in this respect at least, his position is considerably different from Bentham's. This difference will be fully discussed in Chapter 7.

[12] *Ibid.*, p. 148.

[13] *Ibid.*, p. 149.

though we will sometimes go wrong in doing this, this will not happen very often.

Since, as I have tried to shew, it is impossible to establish that any kind of action will produce a better total result than its alternative *in all cases*, it follows that in some cases the neglect of an established rule will probably be the best course of action possible. The question then arises: Can the individual ever be justified in assuming that his is one of these exceptional cases? And it seems that this question may be definitely answered in the negative. . . .

It seems, then, that with regard to any rule which is *generally* useful, we may assert that it ought *always* to be observed, not on the ground that in *every* particular case it will be useful, but on the ground that in *any* particular case the probability of its being so is greater than that of our being likely to decide rightly that we have before us an instance of its disutility. In short, though we may be sure that there are cases where the rule should be broken, we can never know which those cases are, and ought, therefore, never to break it.[14]

Now even though Moore advises us, as a matter of policy, to follow rules, he is not, strictly speaking, a rule utilitarian, but an act utilitarian. This is because he insists that the actual rightness or wrongness of an action is determined by its actual consequences rather than by whether or not it is in accordance with a rule that has been found to be useful.[15]

Moore was sensitive, in a way that Bentham was not, to an objection to objective universal act utilitarianism which depends upon the claim that the number of consequences of any given action, being infinite, can never really be determined, and that, therefore, in a particular case one can never know what his duty is. Moore's solution was to suggest that as a matter of policy we follow rules which would lead us in some instances to do what is wrong, but which would be fairly safe guides *on the whole*. Most utilitarians, and most critics of utilitarianism, assume, as did Moore, that the consequences of all actions stretch out into an infinite future. A. C. Ewing has expressed this assumption very clearly:

. . . it may be objected to ideal utilitarianism that its criterion is quite inapplicable because we cannot possibly foresee all the consequences of any action.

[14] *Ibid.*, pp. 162–63.

[15] There is a serious problem of interpretation here, for in the last sentence of the passage quoted from Moore there is the claim that there are cases where the rule should be broken alongside the claim that we *ought never* to break it. Three possibilities of interpretation seem available here: (1) Moore can be treated as a rule utilitarian, but then he should not have said that there are cases where the rule should be broken, for the rule utilitarian does not resort to the principle of utility to test particular cases; (2) Moore can be treated, as we have treated him, as an act utilitarian, in which case the claim that we ought never break the rule must not be taken as a moral *ought*, but simply as prudential advice; or (3) Moore can be treated as simply inconsistent. Of these three possibilities we have chosen (2), but we recognize that this is a matter of interpretation.

For the consequences of an action in the next five minutes will produce other consequences in the following five, and so on for ever or to the end of time.[16]

Ewing has, of course, assumed that because A is a consequence of B, and B is a consequence of C, and C is a consequence of D, it is perfectly legitimate to say that A is also a consequence of D. This assumption, however, can be questioned. Suppose that S kills the milkman; one of the consequences of that action is that the milkman's wife will be a widow, and another is that she will receive damages from S's estate. But if the milkman's children grow up fatherless and turn out badly, and one of them becomes a narcotics addict, and in his quest for money for dope robs a drugstore, and causes that store to close, and as a result of this Mr. Smith is unable to get a copy of the Sunday *Times*, we would not be inclined to say that Mr. Smith's not being able to get a copy of the Sunday *Times* is a consequence of S's killing the milkman, nor would we take that into consideration in judging the rightness or wrongness of S's act. This point is often mentioned in order to avoid the alternative taken by Moore, and it is sometimes called *a ripples-in-the-pond postulate*, for one who makes it is maintaining that the consequences of any given action, like ripples in a pond, tend to dissipate with time.

This assumption plays a large part in the act utilitarianism of the contemporary Australian philosopher, J. J. C. Smart.[17]

c. J. J. C. SMART Smart presents his version of utilitarianism in the following way:

Let us say, then, that the only reason for performing an action A rather than an alternative action B is that doing A will make mankind (or, perhaps, all sentient beings) happier than will doing B.[18]

In meeting the objection that the consequences of any action are infinite, Smart suggests that remote consequences "in the end approximate rapidly to zero like the furthermost ripples on a pond after a stone has been dropped into it." [19] Smart also suggests that such a postulate "seems plausible enough" even though he admits that he does not know how to prove it.[20]

If some such postulate is not adopted, the alternatives for the utilitarian seem clear: (1) He can say (with Moore) that we can never know with certainty what our duty is, and then he will either be forced to say that we must

[16] A. C. Ewing, *Ethics* (New York: The Free Press of Glencoe, 1953), p. 64. By permission of the Macmillan Company. By permission of the English Universities Press, Limited, original publishers.

[17] J. J. C. Smart, *An Outline of a System of Utilitarian Ethics* (Victoria: Melbourne University Press, 1961). Smart, like Bentham, adopts a hedonistic theory of value, but suggests that this is for the sake of exposition, and that his view is compatible with other, nonhedonist theories.

[18] *Ibid.*, p. 20.

[19] *Ibid.*, p. 22.

[20] *Ibid.*, p. 23.

follow generally useful or accepted rules (even though sometimes the rules will lead us to do what is wrong), or that we just never can know what we ought to do. (2) He can abandon objective act utilitarianism and adopt some subjective version of that doctrine, according to which our duty is to do what we *think* will have the best consequences. (3) Or, finally, he can try some form of rule utilitarianism.

3. *Criticisms of Objective Act Utilitarianism.* A. N. Prior has suggested that the notion of the " '*total* consequences' of an action seems to suffer from an incurable incoherence which renders it useless for ethical theory or for any other sort of theory." [21] He argues:

Either determinism is true or it is not. If determinism *is* true then there are not really (though there may seem to be) a number of alternative actions which we could perform on a given occasion; the one action that we can perform is the one that we do perform. Hence whatever we in fact do is the best possible action ... because it is the *only* possible action. ... Suppose that determinism is *not* true. Then there may indeed be a number of alternative actions which we could perform on a given occasion, but none of these actions can be said to have any "total consequences", or to bring about a definite state of the world which is better than any other that might be brought about by other choices. We may presume that other agents are free beside the one who is on the given occasion deciding what he ought to do, and the total future state of the world depends on how these others choose as well as on how the given person chooses. ... [22]

The main point here is that, if determinism is not true, there is no such thing as the total consequences of an action. But Prior also argues that, if determinism is true,

... the succession of situations which follow one another after a given action has been performed is never the result of that action alone, but of that action together with an infinity of other concurrent happenings. It is quite impossible to draw a sharp line and say that everything on one side of it is a consequence of the action, and everything on the other side a consequence of other things; and therefore impossible to arrive at a set of total consequences of the action. [23]

The force of this point is simply that Bentham, Moore, and other act utilitarians are talking nonsense when they speak of evaluating an action on the basis of its total consequences. Unless some way is found to defend act utilitarianism without appealing to the total consequences of an action, that view is quite unacceptable as a theory of obligation. But the problem with the ripples-in-the-pond postulate is that it is difficult to defend and that so far no

[21] A. N. Prior, "Symposium: The Consequences of Actions," *Aristotelian Society Supplement*, **30** (1956), 94.
[22] *Ibid.*, p. 91.
[23] *Ibid.*, p. 94.

way has been provided to put it into application. The objective act utilitarian must explain how one can draw the line betwen those events (which would not have happened if the action being judged had not happened) which are relevant in judging the action, and those which are not. Part of the force of Prior's argument, however, is that it is impossible to draw such a line, and the only reply available to the act utilitarian is the demonstration that such a line can be drawn. No one has yet succeeded in making such a demonstration, which would be an incredibly difficult (if not impossible) undertaking, involving—at the very least—a totally new analysis of the notion of *consequences*. But, as we shall show, even if this difficulty could be met, there would be other quite conclusive objections to universal objective act utilitarianism.

Just as we found a large number of counterexamples to limited objective act utilitarianism (as well as the difficulty in specifying the group), an equally large number of such counterexamples seem to apply to the objective version of that view. The third part of the criterion of acceptability of theories states that any theory must fit or explain the phenomena better than its competitors, and it does not seem possible to remain comfortable with a theory of right and wrong that contradicts many of the considered moral judgments of sensitive and intelligent men.

Assume, for example, that a system of slavery would bring about a slight balance of good over evil in the world. If so, according to objective act utilitarianism, it would be our duty to bring this system into existence. In fact, the list of actions such a theory would have to claim are justified is as horrible as it is long.

1. If killing a hobo by the side of the road will increase the net good in the universe (his life is miserable and we enjoy killing) then it is right and our duty to kill him.

2. If causing one man to suffer terribly will make a large number of men happy, then if their happiness outweighs his suffering, it is our duty to make him suffer.

3. If we would enjoy something more than our neighbor does, and if it is possible to steal it from him without getting caught, and without our feeling any guilt, then it is our duty to steal it.

As Richard B. Brandt has pointed out:

... [Act utilitarianism] implies that if you have employed a boy to mow your lawn and he has finished the job and asks for his pay, you should pay him what you promised only if you cannot find a better use for your money. It implies that when you bring home your monthly pay-check you should use it to support your family and yourself only if it cannot be used more effectively to supply the needs of others. It implies that if your father is ill and has no prospect of good in his life, and maintaining him is a drain on the energy and enjoyments of others, then, if you can end his life without provoking any public scandal or setting a bad example, it is your positive duty to take matters into your own hands and bring his life to a close.[24]

4. *Subjective Universal Act Utilitarianism.* There is a crucial defect in any form of limited utilitarianism: the particular group to be considered in deciding the rightness or wrongness of an action cannot be specified in a satisfactory way. This, plus a number of counterexamples to that view led us to consider a more plausible version of act utilitarianism—objective universal act utilitarianism, perhaps the most widely held of all the versions of act utilitarianism. This view, however, is beset by two serious problems: the impossibility of specifying the total consequences of an action, and numerous damaging counterexamples. Some philosophers, noticing that the first difficulty does not infect subjective varieties of act utilitarianism, but still unhappy with any type of limited utilitarianism, understandably have turned to subjective universal act utilitarianism. Enough has been said about the different kinds of act utilitarianism to make it unnecessary to present an exposition of this view in detail, and so we shall proceed immediately to counterexamples.

There is no reason at all for believing that man always has an obligation to do anything he only *believes* will increase the good in the world. Hitler might have sincerely believed that the world would be better off with only "pure Aryans," yet few people would agree that this belief created an obligation for him to wipe out all non-Aryans by the most efficient (or even the most painless) way possible.

The subjective universal utilitarian might reply, at this point, that only well-founded beliefs create obligations. But if 'well-founded' means 'correct' this position is now indistinguishable from the objective version of universal act utilitarianism. And if 'well founded' does not mean 'correct' but, rather, something like 'reasonable to believe given the information available', there are still difficulties. S might well be a victim of a gigantic plot designed to make him believe that the greatest good in the universe will be brought about if, and only if, he poisons the water supply of New York City. Let us suppose a host of false data is given him which makes his belief extremely reasonable. There is still some difficulty in concluding that he actually has an obligation to perform this act, even though we might agree that he cannot be condemned for doing it.

5. *Some General Objections to Act Utilitarianism.* There are other objections to act utilitarianism that seem to apply to all versions of the theory. No act utilitarian has solved the problem of exactly how the good is to be distributed, and the difficulties involved in such a distribution are brought out by Marcus Singer:

[24] Richard B. Brandt, "Toward a Credible Form of Utilitarianism," *Morality and the Language of Conduct*, ed. Hector-Neri Castañeda and George Nakhnikian (Detroit, Mich.: Wayne State University Press, 1965), pp. 109–10.

. . . I cannot refrain from pointing out a definite ambiguity in the utilitarian standard, which, in view of the seriousness of its consequences, deserves wider recognition than it has in fact received. The utilitarian standard has been stated to be that of conduciveness to the "general happiness" or "the greatest amount of happiness on the whole." But it has also very often, and perhaps even more frequently, been stated to be "the greatest happiness of the greatest number." Now these expressions actually represent different criteria for the interpretation of the utilitarian standard, which may be called, respectively, "the greatest happiness criterion" and "the greatest number criterion," and they are by no means equivalent. In most cases, no doubt, they would coincide, and no distinction would be apparent. But there is no necessity for this. We can easily describe circumstances in which they would conflict. Imagine two acts, *a* and *b*, which are alternatives to each other, and suppose (taking small numbers for convenience, and waiving the point whether such neat and exact calculations can be made) *a* would produce four units of happiness for each of twelve persons, while *b* would produce eight units of happiness for each of eight persons. On the basis of the principle of utility, which ought to be done? It is impossible to say, for the criterion of "utility" is here amgibuous, and it cannot be determined which of the two is the more "useful." On the greatest number criterion, *a* ought to be done, for it produces happiness for a greater number of people. But on the greatest happiness criterion, *b* ought to be done, because it produces, presumably, 64 units of happiness, whereas *a* would produce only 48, and hence it produces a greater amount of happiness on the whole. Now this issue cannot be decided by appeal to the principle of utility. Indeed to plump for one or the other of these two criteria would be essentially arbitrary.

But this is not all. The greatest happiness criterion itself is not free from ambiguity. It can mean either "the greatest *total* amount of happiness" or "the greatest *average* amount of happiness," and one action can produce a greater total amount of happiness, though a smaller average amount, than another. Imagine an action *c*, which will produce a total of fifty units of happiness for five people, an average of ten units apiece, whereas an alternative action *d* would produce a total of 56 units of happiness for a group of seven people, an average of eight units apiece. Which would be right? Indeed, which would be better? Here again the decision would be arbitrary. Certainly no utilitarian reason can be given for saying that one situation would be better than the other. And the ramifications of this sort of thing are practically endless. For a conflict can arise between the greatest average criterion and the greatest number criterion. For example, compare action *c* with action *a*. It follows, then, from the existence of these conflicting criteria, that the principle of utility is not the "first principle of morals," or the "fundamental principle of morality," since some other principle is needed to resolve these conflicts, when they arise. As it stands, it is not even acceptable as a principle, much less as the fundamental one, by ultimate reference to which all questions of morality are to be decided.

It may be thought that the difficulties just noted are purely academic, of the sort that could never arise in practice. This is not true. It is true that the examples selected are artificial, artifically abstract as well as artificially exact. But this does not mean that difficulties of this type could never arise. Such a difficulty could arise in any situation in which one would have to choose between doing something that would benefit a very large number of people each to a very small extent, and doing something that would benefit a relatively small number of people each to a very large extent; and such difficulties are almost always present, though they may not always be recognized, in considering any proposed piece of legislation. I do not say that such issues are undecidable. I say that they are undecidable on the principle of utility.[25]

Another problem facing all act utilitarians is that of explaining the obvious use of rules men make, from day to day, in deciding what to do. Few people ever sit down and calculate the consequences of their actions to the degree required by act utilitarianism; furthermore, if they did so, nobody would ever get anything done, for calculating the consequences of even the most insignificant action is a task of staggering complexity.

Smart attempts to reply to this objection by suggesting that the rules are really rules of thumb and that there is an act utilitarian justification for abiding by them in circumstances where we do not have time enough to calculate the consequences:

Normally he [i.e., the act utilitarian] will act in accordance with them [i.e., rules] when he has no time for considering probable consequences or when the advantages of such a consideration of consequences are likely to be outweighed by the disadvantage of the waste of time involved.[26]

But even if we should succeed in limiting the consequences of an action, there are more than enough immediate and nearby consequences to keep the act utilitarian busy long after the opportunity for performing the action has passed. Thus, a direct calculation of consequences is never practical. Smart suggests that one ought not to consider the probable consequences when the advantages of doing so are likely to be outweighed by the "disadvantages of the waste of time involved," but this suggestion is totally unacceptable, for it implies the impossible—that sometimes one can decide on act utilitarian grounds whether or not to calculate the consequences of a particular action.

For example, let A be the action of deciding whether or not to take a trip after considering the probable consequences of doing so, and let B be the action of deciding without considering the probable consequences. Smart seems to be suggesting that one can decide whether to do A or B on act utilitarian grounds. But no one could do this without knowing the relative value of the consequences likely to follow such actions. And, in order to know this, he would need to know what he would do if he had calculated and what he would do if he had not. In order to know what he would do if he had

[25] From *Generalization in Ethics*, by Marcus Singer. © Copyright 1961 by Marcus Singer. Reprinted by permission of Alfred A. Knopf, Inc. Pp. 197–99.
[26] Smart, *op. cit.*, p. 30.

calculated, he obviously needs to know the consequences of taking the trip—something he can learn only by engaging in the calculation he is trying to decide whether or not to avoid.

Of course it might be possible to suggest that there are good act utilitarian reasons for not calculating when to calculate, but once again one could only provide an act utilitarian justification for not calculating when to calculate whether to do A or B by calculating, and again, one thing he has to know in order to perform this calculation is the probable consequences of doing both. Thus, it seems that Smart has utterly failed to show how the act utilitarian can justify, on act utilitarian grounds, the use of rules of thumb.

Exercises

Review

1. Why is the task of selecting a group important to the limited utilitarian and why is this task difficult or impossible?
2. Discuss some of the counterexamples to objective limited act utilitarianism. Say what a counterexample is and explain why these are counterexamples. If you do not think that they are counterexamples, explain why. Finally, discuss what the existence of counterexamples to a theory shows and why.
3. Discuss the views of one important objective universal act utilitarian.
4. Why must we treat Moore as an act utilitarian even though he advises us to follow generally useful rules?
5. Discuss the claim that the number of consequences to any action is infinite, and its application to objective utilitarian theories.
6. What is the ripples-in-the-pond postulate and what use is made of it by utilitarians?
7. Discuss some of the counterexamples to universal objective act utilitarianism. Explain why these are counterexamples. If you do not think that they are counterexamples, explain why.
8. What difficulties with the objective forms of act utilitarianism might drive one to adopt a subjective type view?
9. Discuss some counterexamples to the subjective forms of act utilitarianism.
10. What is Singer's objection to utilitarianism?
11. Explain the objection sometimes made against act utilitarianism, that the act utilitarian cannot account for the use of rules. Explain Smart's reply to this objection and discuss the criticism of Smart.

Applications

1. If utilitarianism is the view that one ought to provide the greatest good for the greatest number, then everyone ought to have as many children as he can support, for a large population means that there will be more people to be happy, and hence the totality of good in the world is likely to be increased.

   Consider the above claim. Explain it and then criticize it. Try to reformulate or modify it so that it would be more acceptable. Can it be used as a counterexample to any type of utilitarianism?

2. Apply the criteria of acceptability to the various forms of act utilitarianism.
3. What might be meant by a "utilitarian theory of punishment?"

C. Rule Utilitarianism

Arguments and criticisms such as those presented in the last section have led many ethical thinkers to abandon act utilitarianism for rule utilitarianism. One very often does follow rules when he decides what he ought or ought not to do, and rule utilitarianism has the advantage of accounting for this fact. According to the rule utilitarian, the rightness or wrongness of a particular action is a function of the correctness of the rule of which it is an instance. For example, suppose that S is trying to decide whether or not to cheat the government on his income tax return. In order to cheat, he will obviously have to lie, an activity which could conceivably be justified in this particular instance on act utilitarian principles. Let us suppose that this lie will have no bad consequences—S will not be caught, nor will anyone suffer in the least from the fact that government revenue is a hundred dollars less this year. On the other hand, the hundred dollars S saves by lying will give him an opportunity to increase his happiness considerably and, hence, the total balance of good over evil in the world will be slightly increased. Thus, S, on universal act utilitarian grounds, might decide to cheat the government. The rule utilitarian, on the other hand, will suggest that considerations of utility do not apply in particular cases like this. S must act in accordance with some rule, such as "Do not lie," and the correctness of the rule (rather than the particular action) is a function of the consequences of its being adopted.[27]

A number of factors complicate rule utilitarianism. There is, first, an ambiguity surrounding the notion of a rule; for some rule utilitarians think of rules as legal maxims or laws; others, as general nonlegal maxims internalized in individuals; and still others, as conventional practices. But however the notion of a rule is interpreted, there are further complications involving its relation to the principle of utility. Does one use the principle of utility to judge each separate rule, or does one judge entire sets of rules? Furthermore, is it necessary for a utilitarian justification of a rule, or set of rules, that the actual following of the rule or set of rules have the best consequences, or is it enough that the attempt to follow that rule or set of rules has better consequences than an attempt to follow any other rule or set of rules? [28]

Thus rule utilitarians differ among themselves about what sort of a thing a

[27] There is a sense in which the act utilitarian advises us to follow a rule, but this rule ("Do all and only those actions which lead to the greatest good for the greatest number") is not one which is justified by appeal to the principle of utility, for it *is* the principle of utility. Hence our distinction betwen the act utilitarian and the rule utilitarian stands.

[28] In an article we have already mentioned, "Toward a Credible Form of Utilitarianism," Richard B. Brandt presents an interesting and elaborate discussion of these and other complexities in the formulation of an adequate rule-utilitarian position.

rule is, whether it must be adopted, followed, or recognized, and whether one must speak of a particular rule or a whole set of rules. In addition, there are several more basic distinctions among rule utilitarians.

Like act utilitarianism, rule utilitarianism may be universal or limited. It is universal if the justifiability of a rule or set of rules is considered a function of the consequences affecting all mankind, and limited if the rule is justified by its effects on some limited group only. We may also distinguish between a "local" and a "general" form of rule utilitarianism. It is said to be local if it concerns itself only with rules in a certain community, and general if it concerns itself with rules that are thought to apply to all men. Four types of rule utilitarianism may be distinguished on these grounds:

Local limited rule utilitarianism: One ought to do those actions which follow justifiable rules, and a rule is justifiable (in a given community) if, and only if, adherence to it by everyone in that community would bring about the greatest amount of good for the members of that community.

General limited rule utilitarianism: One ought to do those actions which follow justifiable rules, and a rule is justifiable if, and only if, adherence to it by everyone would bring about the greatest amount of good to the members of the community of which he is a part.

Local universal rule utilitarianism: One ought to do those actions which follow justifiable rules, and a rule is justifiable (in a given community) if, and only if, adherence to it by everyone in that community would bring about the greatest amount of good for everyone in the universe.

General universal rule utilitarianism: One ought to do those actions which follow justifiable rules, and a rule is justifiable if, and only if, adherence to it by everyone would bring about the greatest amount of good for everyone in the universe.

These theories have been presented in their objective form, but more positions can be generated by considering their subjective versions. There is, unfortunately, a double possibility of subjectivity here, for it might be suggested that one ought to do those actions which he believes to be in accordance with justifiable rules, or, alternatively, that a justifiable rule is one which the members of the community, for example, believe will provide the greatest amount of good for themselves. These complexities will not be discussed here, but they indicate the fantastically large number of possible rule utilitarian views.

Exercises

Review

1. Both the act utilitarian and the rule utilitarian advise us to follow a rule or rules. What difference between their positions justifies making the act-rule distinction?
2. Discuss some of the factors that complicate the statement of the rule utilitarian position.

3. Examine very carefully the four different formulations of rule utilitarianism listed on p. 71. Clarify the differences among the four positions and describe how each type would justify a particular judgment (and also how it would justify the rule to which it would appeal).

Applications
1. Formulate explicitly the subjective versions of rule utilitarianism, and then, considering the possible complications mentioned on p. 70, discuss a number of different subjective formulations.
2. What are the advantages of rule utilitarianism over act utilitarianism?
3. Read *Utilitarianism*, by John Stuart Mill, and determine whether he was a rule utilitarian or an act utilitarian.
4. Examine the arguments or "proofs" Mill gives of the principle of utility. What is Mill trying to do, and is he successful?

1. General Limited Rule Utilitarianism. According to general limited rule utilitarianism, the least plausible of the four views distinguished, a rule or maxim or law is justified if, and only if, adherence to it by everyone would bring about (or be thought to bring about) the greatest good for the members of a specific community. It would be difficult to show why everyone has an obligation to follow such a rule, and it would be quite natural to ask why one particular group, rather than another, should be the favored choice. The difficulty of answering such a question has already been examined in the discussion of limited act utilitarianism.

2. Local Limited Rule Utilitarianism. This difficulty would seem to lead the rule utilitarian to narrow his requirements for a justifiable rule; and local limited rule utilitarianism is a step in that direction. On this view, a rule or a maxim or a law is justified *in a given community* if, and only if, adherence to it by everyone *in that community* would bring about (or be thought to bring about) the greatest good for the members of that community.

This type of rule utilitarianism seems to be held by Stephen Toulmin.[29] He argues that "so long as one confines onself to a particular moral code, no more general 'reason' can be given for an action than one which relates it to a practice (or principle) within that code." [30] A particular action is right if it is enjoined by a rule of the agent's society. Particular actions cannot be justified by appeal to the principle of utility, which, Toulmin claims, "is appropriate only when discussing whether a social practice should be retained or changed." [31]

If it [an action which is to be evaluated] is an action which is an unambiguous instance of a maxim generally accepted in the community concerned, it will be

---

[29] Stephen Toulmin, *An Examination of the Place of Reason in Ethics* (Cambridge: Cambridge University Press, 1950).
[30] *Ibid.*, p. 148.
[31] *Ibid.*, p. 151.

right just because it *is* an instance of such a maxim; but, if it is an action over which there is a 'conflict of duties' or is it itself a principle (or social practice) as opposed to a particular action, it will be right or wrong according as its consequences are likely to be good or bad.[32]

With the exception of actions that are not governed by rules in a given society or that present a conflict of duties, the only possible justification for a particular action, according to Toulmin, is the fact that it falls under a general rule of the society. Toulmin's position, then, seems to be a clear instance of local limited rule utilitarianism.

When one asks whether this is an objective or a subjective form of rule utilitarianism, a new complication emerges. A view is clearly objective if it makes the rightness or wrongness of an action or a rule a function of the actual consequences, and it is clearly subjective if it makes the rightness or wrongness of an action or a rule a function of what one believes the consequences will be; but how are we to describe a view that depends on the *likelihood* of the goodness or badness of the consequences? It would seem that such a view is not completely objective, for a certain consequence which is likely might, after all, not occur, and one which is quite unlikely may turn up. On the other hand, it is not completely subjective, since it speaks of consequences which are actually likely (as opposed to those which we believe to be likely). A thorough charting of the various differences in these formulations would certainly have to account for this somewhat half-way view—and a thorough consideration of it might well plunge one very deeply into theories of probability, which would be inappropriate here.

The difficulties with local limited rule utilitarianism are not difficult to spot. There may be, within societies, many maxims that ignore the rights and feelings of "outsiders," but is this really justifiable? Suppose, for example, that the members of a very strong society are enjoined to capture and mistreat the members of a weaker society. Suppose also that this course of action, if rigidly adhered to, would be highly advantageous to the members of the stronger society. On Toulmin's view there would be no grounds for objecting to this policy. But an ethical theory must be evaluated partly on the basis of what it permits and forbids, and just as a scientific theory a consequence of which is that there is really no moon after all seriously violates our third criterion for the acceptability of theories, so does an ethical theory which tells us that the members of one society can do anything to the members of another society so long as the first society profits by it. Can anyone say that acceptance of such a maxim by the members of a society is enough to show that actions in accord with that maxim are right?[33] This consideration

[32] *Ibid.*, p. 154.
[33] For a detailed criticism of Toulmin's position, see George Nakhnikian's "An Examination of Toulmin's Analytical Ethics," *The Philosophical Quarterly*, 9 (January 1959), 59–79.

alone indicates the need for a more plausible version of rule utilitarianism, and it is clear now that if such a version is to be found, it will be some kind of universal rule utilitarianism.

3. *Local and General Universal Rule Utilitarianism.* According to the universal versions of rule utilitarianism, it is necessary to consider the consequences, upon everyone, that follow from adherence to the rules. An appropriate definition of rule utilitarianism which seems to fit into this category has been presented by Richard B. Brandt:

> The thesis of rule-utilitarianism may be formulated thus: "It is obligatory over all for an agent to perform an act A if and only if the prescription that it be performed ['Do A!'] follows logically from a complete description of the agent's situation plus ideal prescriptions for his community; and ideal prescriptions for his community are that set of universal imperatives [of the form 'Do A in circumstances C'] containing no proper names, which is (*a*) complete and as economical in distinct imperatives and in concepts as is compatible with completeness, and such that (*b*) a conscientious effort to obey it, by everyone in the agent's community, would have greater net expectable utility than similar efforts to obey any other set of imperatives." [34]

Brandt speaks here of ideal prescriptions *for a community*, and of efforts by *everyone in the agent's community* to obey the prescription, and this classifies this type of rule utilitarianism as local. But in speaking of those efforts having greater net expectable utility, he does not suggest that only the consequences affecting the members of the community be taken into account, and because he does not limit the scope of those consequences, his formulation may be classified as universal. To make this a definition of local *limited* rule utilitarianism, it would be necessary to rewrite (b) to read: "a conscientious effort to obey it, by everyone in the agent's community, would have greater net expectable utility *for the members of that community* than similar efforts to obey any other set of imperatives." [35]

An important similarity between Brandt's definition and Toulmin's position can be found in the fact that Brandt speaks of *greater net expectable*

[34] Richard B. Brandt, *Ethical Theory: The Problems of Normative and Critical Ethics*, © 1959. Reprinted by permission of Prentice-Hall, Inc., Englewood Cliffs, New Jersey.

[35] The definition of rule utilitarianism quoted from Brandt appears in his book (see fn. 34). He has attempted, in a later article (see fn. 28), to provide a more adequate specification of that view, and he makes explicit that the form of rule utilitarianism he favors is indeed local universal rather than local limited rule utilitarianism. There he says, "We should notice, incidentally, that it is *not* suggested that the test be the maximizing of intrinsic good only in the agent's society; such a thesis would promise quite dubious consequences" (p. 135). In both works he clearly adopts a local form: his complete later formulation is "An act is right if and only if it conforms with that learnable set of rules the recognition of which as morally binding—roughtly at the time of the act—by everyone in the society of the agent, except for the retention by individuals of already formed and decided moral convictions, would maximize intrinsic value" (p. 139).

utility while Toulmin speaks of the *likelihood* of the consequences being good or bad. Thus, Brandt's formulation, like Toulmin's, cannot be classified as either purely objective or purely subjective.

One important difference between Brandt's formulation and Toulmin's lies in the greater precision of the former. Toulmin speaks simply of "the consequences" of a social practice, maxim, or principle; he makes no attempt to distinguish among the three or to specify in what respect this maxim is supposed to have consequences. Brandt, on the other hand, suggests that the crucial point is "a conscientious effort to obey" the rule "by everyone in the agent's community." This is to be contrasted both with everyone acknowledging the rule, and with everyone following the rule. Thus, Brandt's definition deals with some of the difficult matters already mentioned (see pp. 55–56).

William K. Frankena's definition of rule utilitarianism gives rise to another sort of view, one which can be classified as objective general universal rule utilitarianism: Here is his definition, although it should be mentioned that this is not a normative position which he accepts:

> Rule-utilitarianism ... adds that we are always to determine our rules by asking which rules will promote the greatest general good for everyone. That is, the question is not which *action* has the greatest utility, but which *rule* has. We should ask, when we are proposing to do something, not "What will happen if I do that in this case?" but "What would happen if everyone were to do that in such cases?" [36]

This formulation is objective because it asks which rule has (actually) the greatest utility; it is general because it asks what would happen if everyone (not just everyone in a given community) were to do what the rule enjoins, and it is universal because the consequences it considers are not restricted to any group.[37]

A difference between Brandt's earlier formulation and Frankena's lies in the fact that Frankena takes the rule utilitarian to be asking what would happen if everyone *actually did* what the rules enjoin, while Brandt asks what would happen if everyone *made a conscientious effort* to follow the rules. The question is not really which is the more accurate formulation of rule utilitarianism, since, as we have seen, there is not one formulation of rule utilitarianism, but many different ones. Our question must be how these different formulations stand up as normative theories.

One interesting point is that Frankena's suggestion seems to lead back to act utilitarianism. Brandt points out that the rule, general conformity with

[36] William K. Frankena, *Ethics* (Englewood Cliffs, N.J.: Prentice-Hall, Inc., © 1963), p. 30. Reprinted by permission of the publisher.

[37] Notice, however, that in his later article (see fn. 35) Brandt moves toward an objective formulation of rule utilitarianism, in that he now speaks about the actual maximization of intrinsic value.

which would have the best consequences, is the rule of act utilitarianism: "Perform an act, among those open to you, which will have at least as good consequences as any other." [38]

The whole point of the preceding remarks has been to focus attention on the point that a role-utilitarianism like Urmson's is different from act-utilitarianism only when it speaks of something like "*recognition* of a rule having the best consequences" instead of something like "*conformity* with a certain rule having the best consequences." [39]

This may be so, in which case a formulation other than that proposed by Frankena is required. But there are other difficulties. First, it has never been fully explained what is meant by a rule. A rule cannot be treated as a law laid down by the civil authorities, for even the most legalistic society does not have enough laws to cover all actions of moral significance. Both Frankena and Brandt seem to treat a rule as a general maxim of the form "Do A!" or possibly "Do A in Circumstance C!" Neither is quite satisfactory though, because the first is too general and the second too vague—just which circumstances are to be mentioned? If we mention enough, each action will fall under a different rule, and if we do not mention enough our rule will result in directions that overlook important differences.

Another problem is that a subjective formulation of rule utilitarianism presents all the difficulties of a subjective type of act utilitarianism. Why should it be one's duty to attempt to follow rules when he only believes the general attempt to follow them will maximize utility any more than it is his duty to perform those specific actions he thinks will maximize utility? On the other hand, if we resort to the objective formulation or to the intermediate formulation, we may never be able to say which set of rules would maximize utility, for we may never be able to tell precisely whether the consequences of adopting, recognizing, or acting from one set of rules are really superior to those of adopting, recognizing, or acting from another set.

But suppose that we could decide what a rule is, and that we know which formulation of rule utilitarianism is preferable, and that we even know the consequences of adopting a number of different sets of consistent rules. Still another quite serious difficulty arises, as is pointed out by William K. Frankena:

To my mind, there is a decisive objection even to rule utilitarianism, one which requires us to adopt some kind of deontological theory after all. The objection consists in an extension of the Butler-Ross line of argument against act utilitarianism, by comparing rules instead of acts. Suppose we have two rules, R1 and R2, which cannot both be made a part of our morality. Suppose further that in the case of

[38] Richard B. Brandt, "Toward a Credible Form of Utilitarianism," *op. cit.*, p. 121.
[39] *Ibid.*, p. 123.

each rule we know the results of everyone's always acting in appropriate situations on that rule (in practice, of course, there would be great difficulties in knowing this) and that when we compute, as best we can, the values of those results, we find that the score is even—in both cases we obtain the same balance of good over evil in the long run for the universe as a whole. Then the rule utilitarian must say that R1 and R2 will serve equally well as principles of right and wrong and there is no basis for choosing between them. But it still may be that they distribute the amount of good realized in different ways: acting on R1 may give all of the good to a relatively small group of people without any merit on their part (to let merit count at this point is already to give up utilitarianism), while acting on R2 may spread the good more equally over a larger part of the population. In this case, it seems to me that we must and would say that R1 is an unjust rule and that R2 is morally preferable. If this is so, we must give up even rule utilitarianism.[40]

A second general objection to rule utilitarianism is that even when a general rule, such as "Do not lie," is justified, exceptional circumstances may arise in which we would all admit that a lie is justified. The rule utilitarian replies to this objection by pointing out that the general rule does not specify the circumstances, or that there are exceptions. The real rule, therefore, is not "Do not lie," but rather "In circumstances of Type C do not lie unless...." As John Rawls says:

... Utilitarians would be inclined to hold that some reliance on people's good sense and some concession to hard cases is necessary. They would hold that a practice is justified by serving the interests of those who take part in it; and as with any set of rules there is understood a background of circumstances under which it is expected to be applied and which need not—indeed which cannot—be fully stated.[41]

The point here is that exceptions are built into every rule, but more important that all the exceptions cannot be stated. This reply, however, is inadequate, for it makes it possible to claim that one never really knows whether or not a rule applies on a given occasion. Suppose, for example, there is a rule R, with exceptions E_1, E_2, E_3.... If the exceptions could be fully stated there would be no difficulty with knowing whether or not the rule applied in a particular case. But if we agree that the exceptions cannot ever be fully stated, no one has any way of knowing whether a particular case falls under one of the unstated exception clauses of R.

It is really no help to suggest that all the exceptions are stated for, as Brandt has recognized, it is important that the set of rules be learnable—and any set of rules complete with all exception clauses would be too fantastically complex to be learnable. In fact, it might not even be stateable.

[40] Frankena, *op. cit.*, p. 33.
[41] John Rawls, "Two Concepts of Rules," *The Philosophical Review*, 54 (January 1955), 17. By permission of the author and *The Philosophical Review*.

Finally, many of the forms of rule utilitarianism are subject to the criticisms leveled against act utilitarianism. In particular, it might be mentioned that the measurement and comparison of quantities of good and, as Frankena points out, the distribution of good, provide as much of a difficulty for the rule utilitarian as for the act utilitarian. It might therefore be well to explore some deontological views, for—although rule utilitarianism offers some advantages over act utilitarianism, and many advantages over egoism, it is still far from being totally satisfactory as a normative theory of obligation.

Exercises

Review

1. State and criticize general limited rule utilitarianism.
2. Why is local limited rule utilitarianism more plausible than general limited rule utilitarianism?
3. Which philosopher seems to hold local limited rule utilitarianism? Describe his normative theory of obligation, and criticize his position.
4. Discuss the differences in the formulations of Brandt and Frankena.
5. Discuss a number of ways to distinguish different sorts of universal rule utilitarianism.
6. Compare the two formulations of rule utilitarianism offered by Brandt, the one offered by Frankena, and the one offered by Toulmin.
7. Discuss the general objections to rule utilitarianism.
8. Why is the notion of a rule with an indefinite number of exception clauses of little or no help in justifying moral judgments?

Applications

1. Examine Nakhnikian's criticism of Toulmin's view (Cf. fn. 33), and discover whether anything further could be said for local limited rule utilitarianism.
2. Consider the four definitions of rule utilitarianism mentioned in Review Exercise 6 above. Apply the criteria of acceptability to them as theories of obligation.
3. How can a utilitarian account for the apparent relevance of the motive someone has in doing an action to that action's rightness or wrongness?
4. How can a utilitarian (of any sort) account for the distribution of goods on the basis of merit? What would the utilitarian have to say about merit raises and bonuses?
5. Is there any relation between utilitarianism and communism, between utilitarianism and democracy?
6. Describe some situation in which a moral judgment is called for and show how a defender of each kind of act utilitarianism, and of a number of different kinds of rule utilitarianism, would react to such a situation. Construct your situation so that not all the defenders would make the same judgment.
7. See if it is possible to construct a situation in which every utilitarian view you can think of would result in the same decision about what ought to be done.

8. Describe a case from your experience in which the amount of good resulting from an action is roughly equally divided between two groups, but in
which more evil accrues to a particular member of one group than to one
of the other. What does such a case show about utilitarianism?

9. It is possible that a view called *negative utilitarianism* might escape some
of the difficulties of ordinary act utilitarianism. According to this view,
man's obligation is not to maximize the good in the universe but rather to
minimize the evil—or although man has no duty to benevolence, he does
have one of nonmalevolence. Distinguish a number of different possible
versions of this view and apply the criteria of acceptability to them.

10. Compare the two formulations of rule utilitarianism offered by Brandt and
discover exactly how, and in what respects, they differ. Given the two different formulations, would it be possible to come up with differing normative
judgments about a particular situation?

11. Set forth the tenets of a theory called *rule egoism*. Is such a theory any
more plausible than the act versions of egoism we considered in Chapter 3?
Does it escape any of the objections raised against ethical egoism in that
chapter?

12. What use can the act deontologist make of the principle of utility?

13. The following is a criticism of utilitarianism offered by the German philosopher, Nietzsche. Read it carefully and then determine whether there are any
good arguments against utilitarianism in it and, if so, whether they apply to
all forms of utilitarianism, or only to some forms of that view.

. . . Observe, for example, the indefatigable, inevitable English utilitarians:
how ponderously, and respectably they stalk on . . . in the footsteps of
Bentham. . . . No new thought, nothing of the nature of a finer turning or
better expression of an old thought, not even a proper history of what has
been previously thought on the subject: an *impossible* literature, taking it
all in all, unless one knows how to leaven it with some mischief. . . . In the
end, they all want *English* morality to be recognised as authoritative,
inasmuch as mankind, or the "general utility," or "the happiness of the
greatest number," —no! the happiness of *England*, will be best served
thereby. They would like, by all means, to convince themselves that the
striving after *English* happiness, I mean after *comfort* and *fashion* (and in
the highest instance, a seat in Parliament), is at the same time the true
path of virtue; in fact, that in so far as there has been virtue in the world
hitherto, it has just consisted in such striving. Not one of those ponderous,
conscience-stricken herding-animals (who undertake to advocate the cause
of egoism as conducive to the general welfare) wants to have any knowledge
or inkling of the facts that the "general welfare" is no ideal, no goal, no
notion that can be at all grasped, but is only a nostrum,—that what is
fair to one *may not* be fair to another, that the requirement of one morality
for all is really a detriment to higher men, in short, that there is a *distinction
of rank* between man and man, and consequently between morality and
morality. They are an unassuming and fundamentally mediocre species of
men, these utilitarian Englishmen, and, as already remarked, in so far as

they are tedious, one cannot think highly enough of their utility. . . .
—Nietzsche, *Beyond Good and Evil.*

Bibliography

AYER, ALFRED J. "The Principle of Utility," in A. J. Ayer, *Philosophical Essays.*
New York: St. Martin's Press, 1955, pp. 250–70. An examination of Bentham's
hedonistic utilitarianism and a consideration of some stock objections.

BENTHAM, JEREMY. *An Introduction to the Principles of Morals and Legislation.*
New York: Hafner, 1948.

*BRANDT, R. B. "Toward a Credible Form of Utilitarianism," in H. Castañeda
and G. Nakhnikian, *Morality and the Language of Conduct.* Detroit, Mich.:
Wayne State University Press, 1963, pp. 107–43. A careful and detailed
consideration of many forms of rule utilitarianism.

*BROAD, C. D. *Five Types of Ethical Theory.* Princeton, N.J.: Littlefield, Adams
& Co., 1959, Chapter 6. A discussion of Sidgwick's theory.

*DUNCAN-JONES, A. "Utilitarianism and Rules," *The Philosophical Quarterly,* 7
(1957), 364–67. Deals with two problems of utilitarianism: the problem of
measuring value and a problem arising from cases where conscious deliberation
between alternative courses of action might be more desirable than mere application of a rule.

EWING, A. C. *Ethics.* New York: The Free Press, 1953, Chapter 3. A brief discussion of utilitarianism in which the standard objections are raised. Most of
the criticism is directed toward the hedonistic varieties. Rather elementary.

*EYORSKY, GERTRUDE. "Utilitarianism and Rules," *Australasian Journal of
Philosophy,* 43 (1965), 225–29. Here it is claimed that "if utilitarians equipped
themselves with a suitably expanded concept of rules, some of the traditional
troubles which have beset their position could be cut down," but also that
"Rawls' notion of rules cannot help the utilitarians in any respect."

*GIBBARD, ALLAN F. "Rule Utilitarianism: Merely an Illusory Alternative,"
Australasian Journal of Philosophy, 43 (1965), 211–20. R. B. Brandt had
attempted to show that a formulation of rule utilitarianism presented by R. F.
Harrod had the same consequences for action as act utilitarianism, and in this
article Gibbard presents counterexamples to Brandt's claim.

*HARE, R. M. *Freedom and Reason.* Oxford: The Clarendon Press, 1963, Chapter
7. A quasi-defense of a kind of rule utilitarianism.

*HARRISON, JONATHAN. "Utilitarianism, Universalization and Our Duty to be
Just," *Aristotelian Society Proceedings,* 53 (1952–3), 105–34. A treatment of
Hume as a rule utilitarian. A comparison of his statement of rule utilitarianism
with that of Harrod, and rule utilitarianism with the rule deontology of Ross.
(Cf. Chapter 5 for a discussion of forms of deontology.)

*HARROD, R. F. "Utilitarianism Revised," *Mind,* 45 (1936), 137–56. A form of
utilitarianism according to which "there are certain acts which when performed
on *n* similar occasions have consequences more than *n* times as great as those
resulting from one performance. And it is in this class of cases that obligations
arise." This is the article criticized by Brandt in "Toward a Credible Form of

Utilitarianism," and discussed by Harrison in "Utilitarianism, Universalization and Our Duty to be Just."

*LANDESMAN, CHARLES. "A Note on Act Utilitarianism," *The Philosophical Review*, 73 (1964), 243–47. A criticism of Smart's position as defended in *An Outline of a System of Utilitarian Ethics*. Landesman argues that Smart cannot account for equitable distribution of goods.

*LYONS, DAVID. *Forms and Limits of Utilitarianism*. Oxford: The Clarendon Press, 1965. A full-length discussion of rule utilitarianism.

*MABBOT, J. D. "Interpretations of Mill's Utilitarianism," *The Philosophical Quarterly*, 6 (1956), 115–20. A discussion of Urmson's article, "The Interpretation of the Moral Philosophy of J. S. Mill," and a criticism of Urmson's interpretation.

*———. "Moral Rules," *Proceedings of the British Academy*, 39 (1953), 97–117. Claims that the only good reason for approving a particular action is that it is a carrying-out of a rule, and that the only good reason for approving a rule is that its general adoption would do good on the whole.

*MARGOLIS, JOSEPH. "Rule Utilitarianism," *Australasian Journal of Philosophy*, 43 (1965), 220–25. An attack on Rawls' claim that only "practices" and not particular acts can be defended on utilitarian grounds. Margolis tries to show that there are cases which can be dealt with by the act utilitarian but not the rule utilitarian and that actually it is "inherently impossible to distinguish rule utilitarianism from act utilitarianism."

*McCLOSKEY, H. G. "An Examination of Restricted Utilitarianism," *The Philosophical Review*, 66 (1957), 466–85. An attack on rule utilitarianism, with criticisms of Urmson's "The Interpretation of the Moral Philosophy of J. S. Mill" and Rawls' "Two Concepts of Rules."

*MELDEN, A. I. "Two Comments about Utilitarianism." *The Philosophical Review*, 60 (1951), 508–24. Argues that utilitarianism fails to account for some of our rights and obligations. Analyzes "experiences" rather than actions.

MILL, JOHN STUART. *Utilitarianism*. Indianapolis and New York: The Bobbs-Merrill Company, 1957.

MOORE, G. E. *Ethics*. New York: Oxford University Press, Inc., 1965. Chapter 1 contains a defense of nonhedonistic act utilitarianism, but Moore insists that his theory differs in many respects from traditional formulations of utilitarianism.

———. *Principia Ethica*. Cambridge: Cambridge University Press, 1959, pp. 146–71. A presentation of non-hedonistic ("ideal") act utilitarianism. 'Right' is defined in terms of 'good'.

*RAWLS, JOHN. "Justice as Fairness," *The Philosophical Review*, 67 (1958), 164–94. Rawls argues that utilitarianism in its classical form cannot account for justice, the fundamental idea of which is fairness.

———. "Two Concepts of Rules," *The Philosophical Review*, 64 (1955), 3–32. An important early defense of rule theories. Distinguishes betwen justifying a practice and justifying a particular action falling under it. Introduces a distinction between summary rules and rules defining a practice.

*ROSS, W. D. *The Right and the Good*. Oxford: The Clarendon Press, Inc., 1930, pp. 16–47. A criticism of ideal utilitarianism.

SHARP, F. C. *Ethics.* New York: Appleton-Century-Crofts, 1928, Chapter 17. A discussion of utilitarians other than Bentham and Mill—e.g., Confucius, Me Ti, Jesus, Cumberland, Sidgwick, Hutcheson, Hume.

*SIDGWICK, HENRY. *The Methods of Ethics.* 7th ed. London: Macmillan and Co. Ltd., 1962. Especially Book iv. Bases utilitarianism on the self-evidence of the principle of utility.

*SINGER, MARCUS. *Generalization in Ethics.* New York: Alfred Knopf, Inc., 1961, Chapter 7. A criticism of both act and rule utilitarianism.

*SMART, J. J. C. "Extreme and Restricted Utilitarianism," *The Philosophical Quarterly,* 6 (1956), 344–54. A defense of act utilitarianism, but 'extreme' and 'restricted' are used in place of the now commonly accepted 'act' and 'rule'. This article is criticized by McCloskey.

———. *An Outline of a System of Utilitarian Ethics.* Victoria: Melbourne University Press, 1961. One of the most recent defenses of act utilitarianism.

*STOUT, A. K. "Suppose Everybody Did the Same," *Australasian Journal of Philosophy,* 32 (1954), 1–29. A discussion of the role of consequences in determining the rightness of an action, and a defense of the claim that an instance of rule-breaking may serve to weaken expectations in others.

TOULMIN, STEPHEN E. *An Examination of the Place of Reason in Ethics.* Cambridge: Cambridge University Press, 1950, Chapter 11.

URMSON, J. O. "The Interpretation of the Moral Philosophy of J. S. Mill," *The Philosophical Quarterly,* 3 (1953), 33–39. One of the first attempts to interpret J. S. Mill as a rule utilitarian.

Deontological Theories

In Chapters 3 and 4 we examined teleological theories concerning judgments of moral obligation. We found that none of them was free from fault, but that some version of utilitarianism best met the criteria of acceptability of ethical theories. Keeping this in mind, let us turn to an examination of deontological theories of obligation. A careful comparison between rule utilitarianism (the best of the teleological theories) and the various forms of deontology should enable us to pick out the best normative ethical theory so far as that is possible without a discussion of the problems of meta-ethics.

The purpose of these theories is, in part, to help us pick out the best moral maxims. Or, to put it another way, these theories concern the justification of judgments about moral obligations. Teleological theorists all maintain that the best moral maxims are those which, when acted from, bring about certain specified consequences (such as pleasure for the greatest possible number of persons). They hold that the way to justify any moral judgment about some Action A is to refer to the consequences of A or the consequences of some rule enjoining A. Deontological theorists hold the opposite position.

All deontologists hold the following thesis: *The rightness (wrongness, obligatoriness, and so on) of an action or the correctness of a rule is not a function solely of the consequences of that action or rule.* Nevertheless, we can distinguish between those deontologists who hold:

1. The rightness (wrongness, obligatoriness, and so on) of an action or the correctness of a rule is a function solely of factors other than the consequences of that action or rule.

and those who hold:

2. The rightness (wrongness, obligatoriness, and so on) of an action or the correctness of a rule is a function of many factors, some of which are or may be the consequences of that action or rule.

We can state 1 less formally by saying that in justifying moral judgments consequences do not count at all. Those who hold Statement 1 are sometimes called *formalists*, and on one interpretation of his work, Immanuel Kant is such a philosopher. The most prominent recent philosopher who holds Statement 2 is W. D. Ross.

The distinction between general and particular considerations in teleological theories applies also to deontological theories. Some philosophers hold that judgments of moral obligation are justified by general considerations (usually a principle or a set of principles); others hold that they are justified by specific considerations (such as the nature of the particular act).

A. Deontology

1. *A Preliminary Statement of Rule Deontology.* All men would agree that, if one judges an action right, wrong, or obligatory, then somehow or other the judgment must be justified by reference to the action. Even if one makes use of a principle, such as the principle of utility, he must still apply the principle to the specific action being justified.[1]

Let us consider the action of giving money to charity, Action A. We can all agree that A has certain characteristics; it is an action of giving money, of giving money to a certain organization, of some person (S) giving to that organization, of the money being earmarked for a certain purpose, and so on. Such descriptions as these may be called *morally neutral*, for they do not contain any terms or phrases of moral significance. What more must be known to permit a justified moral judgment about A? The rule deontologist, who holds that moral judgments are justified in terms of something general, would claim that we must appeal to some principle of the following form: "If any A has Characteristics F, G, and H (where F, G, and H [2] are morally neutral characteristics of the sort mentioned above), then A is right (or wrong, or obligatory)." Given this principle, the rule theorist would continue, we justify our specific judgment, "A is right" by appealing to the fact that A has Characteristics F, G, and H, and to the rule that anything with those characteristics is right. The principle, plus the morally neutral information about the specific action, allows us to conclude that A is right. This, according to the rule deontologist, is the procedure for justification. The teleologist uses this same schema, except that the teleologist holds that all the values of F, G, and H are consequences.

[1] Strictly speaking, the distinction between act and rule deontological theories is not quite the same as that between act and rule utilitarian theories. Act utilitarians insist on the importance of a rule—the principle of utility—and the act deontologist argues that rules are dispensable. It is useful to characterize the two act theories as act theories because it is more true to the literature to do so. If this were a purely systematic work we would have to consider a position which is exactly analogous to act deontology.

[2] At least one of Characteristics F, G, or H may, for the deontologist, refer to something other than consequences.

Put in a schematic way (let us call it Scheme R), the rule deontologist's position is this:

1. If any A has Properties F, G, and H, then A is right (or wrong, or obligatory).
2. This A has Properties F, G, and H.
Therefore, (by *modus ponens*):
3. A is right (or wrong, or obligatory).

For those who hold that moral judgments must be justified by reference to something general the justification of any judgment like 3 is a set of statements such as 1 and 2 (where 1 is always some general statement or principle). For the teleologist, Characteristics F, G, and H will always be some set of consequences and only consequences.[3] The rule deontologist will say that characteristics other than consequences are, or may be, the values of at least one of F, or G, or H.

2. *The Tenets of Act Deontology.* The act deontologist makes the following three claims:

A_1. The procedure for justifying the judgment that A is right (or wrong, or obligatory) need not include Statement 1.

A_2. The judgment that A is right (or wrong, or obligatory) must sometimes be justified by giving Statement 2 as the only evidence.

A_3. Ultimately, statements such as Statement 1 can only be justified by statements such as Statement 3 (and thus Statement 1 need not be part of the ground for Statement 3).

Tenets A_1, A_2, and A_3 are not all required to state the position of act deontology because it is possible to derive both A_1 and A_2 from A_3. However, it is easier to understand the position if we explicitly state all three and explain each.

B. Act Deontology

1. *Thesis A_1 and Its Defense.* What does it mean to assert that the procedure for justifying the judgment that A is right need not include an appeal to a principle? It does not mean that we never do, in fact, appeal to principles, only that we *need* not do so. The act deontologist would agree that principles can be used in moral reasoning to justify judgments, but he would also insist that these principles have a secondary role. E. F. Carritt has the following to say:

I may repeat the decalogue, like the multiplication table, by rote, but when any doubt arises as to the universal validity of a precept I must follow the Socratic method and image, as definitely as may be, *instances* where my moral judgment

[3] Even the ethical egoist's position falls into this pattern, for he would subscribe to the principle that any action which has the characteristic of causing good for him is right.

would work. But if we can judge an instance without general rules, it might seem, as Butler says, that the inquiry after them is merely an occupation, not without some usefulness, for 'men of leisure'. The usefulness suggested is, I suppose, that where the right course is obscure or the passions violent, rules may save the ship. So far as this is so I think that their function is that of a ballast rather than compass.[4]

According to act deontologists such as Carritt, principles of the form of A_1 serve the function of keeping men on "an even keel." When one is angry, for example, it is better to follow a principle he has found in calmer moments to be workable than to trust his moral reasoning.

Another function of rules that the act deontologist can admit and does wish to admit is served by "summary rules"—that is, rules derived from generalizing about similar past cases. The distinction between a summary rule and a rule that "defines a practice" was first drawn by John Rawls in connection with utilitarianism: but one can easily see that the explanation is not dependent upon utilitarianism.

It regards rules in the following way: one supposes that each person decides what he shall do in particular cases by applying the utilitarian principle; one supposes further that different people will decide the same particular case in the same way and that there will be recurrences of cases similar to those previously decided. Thus it will happen that in cases of certain kinds the same decision will be made either by the same person at different times or by different persons at the same time. If a case occurs frequently enough one supposes that a rule is formulated to cover that sort of case. I have called this conception the summary view because rules are pictured as summaries of past decisions arrived at by the *direct* application of the utilitarian principle to particular cases. Rules are regarded as reports that cases of a certain sort have been found on *other* grounds to be properly decided in a certain way (although, of course, they do not *say* this).[5]

Contrasted with this notion of rules is what Rawls calls *the practice conception of rules.*

On this view rules are pictured as defining a practice. Practices are set up for various reasons, but one of them is that in many areas of conduct each person's deciding what to do on utilitarian grounds case by case leads to confusion, and that the attempt to coordinate behavior by trying to foresee how others will act is bound to fail. As an alternative one realizes that what is required is the establishment of a practice, the specification of a new form of activity; and from this one sees that a practice necessarily involves the abdication of full liberty to act on utilitarian and prudential grounds. It is the mark of a practice that being taught how to engage in it involves being instructed in the rules which define it, and that

[4] E. F. Carritt, *The Theory of Morals: An Introduction to Ethical Philosophy* (London: Oxford University Press, 1952), p. 115.

[5] John Rawls, "Two Concepts of Rules," *The Philosophical Review*, 54 (January 1955), 19. By permission of the author and *The Philosophical Review*.

appeal is made to those rules to correct the behavior of those engaged in it. Those engaged in a practice recognize the rules as defining it. The rules cannot be taken as simply describing how those engaged in the practice in fact behave: it is not simply that they act as if they were obeying the rules. Thus it is essential to the notion of a practice that the rules are publicly known and understood as definitive; and it is essential also that the rules of a practice can be taught and can be acted upon to yield a coherent practice. On this conception, then, rules are not generalizations from the decisions of individuals applying the utilitarian principle directly and independently to recurrent particular cases. On the contrary, rules define a practice and are themselves the subject of the utilitarian principle.[6]

An example will help to clarify the distinction between the two kinds of rules and show that the distinction does not just apply within the context of utilitarianism. The rules of chess are not summary rules used to help one play the game; rather, they define the game. One can be said to be playing chess only if one plays according to the rules of chess. It was not that people found themselves playing a game and then codified the rules according to which they were playing; rather, the rules preceded the playing of the game of chess. It is true that changes have been made in the rules of chess, but they were not changed to keep pace with the evolution of chess: the changing of the rules *was* the evolution of the game. When rules stand in this kind of relation to some activity or practice, then the rules define the activity or practice. Such rules are often said to be *constitutive rules,* for they constitute the activity. One who knows and understands the rules of chess knows what chess is.

The rule deontologist claims that the justification of moral judgments ultimately depends upon the appeal not to summary rules but to constitutive rules. That is to say, the practice of morality is defined by the moral rules. The act deontologist, on the other hand, believes that these rules could theoretically be dispensed with (with a great deal of trouble, to be sure) and that there would still be a basis for making moral judgments.[7]

The act deontologist who defends this position about the ultimate dispensability of rules has been criticized in many ways. One point that has been made recently is that act deontology does not allow for the use of rules in teaching—especially in the teaching of children. R. M. Hare propounds such a criticism:

Without principles, most kinds of teaching are impossible, for what is taught is in most cases a principle. In particular, when we learn *to do* something, what we learn is always a principle. Even to learn or to be taught a fact (like the names of

---

[6] *Ibid.,* p. 24.

[7] We have been supposing that the rule deontologists hold a practice conception of rules. Someone might want to claim that the rule deontologists hold the summary conception of rules. If so, they would have no real disagreement with the act deontologist. Furthermore, their insistence on the importance of rules would then become quite mysterious. It is possible that there is another conception of moral rules that is neither a summary nor a practice view, but we are not aware of any such position.

the five rivers of the Punjab) is to learn how to answer a question; it is to learn the principle 'When asked "What are the names of the five rivers of the Punjab?" answer "The Jhelum, the Chenab, &c.".' By this I do not of course mean, that to learn to do anything is to learn to recite by rote some universal imperative sentence. This would involve us in a vicious regress; for learning to recite is a kind of learning, and must have its principles; but in that case we should have to learn to recite the principles of reciting. The point is rather this, that to learn to do anything is never to learn to do an individual act; it is always to learn to do acts of a certain kind in a certain kind of situation; and this is to learn a principle. Thus, in learning to drive, I learn, not to change gear *now*, but to change gear when my engine makes a certain kind of noise. If this were not so, instruction would be of no use at all; for if all an instructor could do were to tell us to change gear *now*, he would have to sit beside us for the rest of our lives in order to tell us just when, on each occasion, to change gear.

Thus without principles we could not learn anything whatever from our elders. This would mean that every generation would have to start from scratch and teach itself, but even if each generation were able to teach itself, it could not do so without principles; for self-teaching, like all other teaching, is the teaching of principles.[8]

Apparently Hare believes the act deontologist cannot account for the need for principles in teaching. However, the act deontologist can reply that only summary rules are required for teaching, and that their use is compatible with his thesis. If Hare accepts the distinction between a summary rule and a constitutive rule, he must claim that summary rules alone are not adequate to account for teaching and learning. It is hard to see, however, what more than a summary rule could be required or what more we have when, to use Hare's example, we learn to change gears.

The reader who has been following the discussion closely probably has another kind of criticism that he wants to raise against the act deontologist. It might be argued that if the act deontologist denies the justification scheme that includes a principle, then when he attempts to justify a judgment such as "A is right," he has simply committed a logical error. The argument that goes from "A has Properties F, G, and H" to "A is right" is as invalid as one that goes from "Bossie is a cow" to "Bossie eats grass." There are two possible replies to this criticism. One can claim that there is a third kind of logic, neither deductive nor inductive, that allows us to make the transition from one to the other.[9] Or one could claim that there is no reason for insisting that the

[8] R. M. Hare, *The Language of Morals* (Oxford: The Clarendon Press, 1952), pp. 60–61. By permission of The Clarendon Press, Oxford.

[9] This notion is discussed in a number of places. Cf. Stuart Hampshire, "Fallacies in Moral Philosophy," *Mind* (1949); Stephen E. Toulmin, *An Examination of the Place of Reason in Ethics* (Cambridge: Cambridge University Press, 1950); J. O. Urmson, "Some Questions Concerning Validity," *Revue internationale de philosophie*, 1953; D. G. Brown, "Evaluative Inference," *Philosophy*, (1955); Stephen E. Toulmin, *The Uses of Argument* (Cambridge, Cambridge University Press, 1958).

justification of a moral judgment must be presented in a deductively valid, or any other kind of valid, argument. The latter position is the alternative taken by the act deontologist.

If the act deontologist is asked how he can say "A is right" on the basis of his knowing "A has F, G, and H," he might give the reply that he "knows directly" that A, which has F, G, and H is right. This position is often called *intuitionism,* and we shall discuss a variety of such theories in our chapter on cognitivistic nondefinism (see Chapter 12). The act deontologist might, however, reply in a different way, for he might claim that we do not *know* that A, which has F, G, and H is right, for to say that we know something implies that that thing is true, whereas normative moral judgments are neither true nor false. He would then suggest that, although we do not know that A is right, we are *justified* in making the judgment that it is, or that our approval, expressed by the words "A is right" is rational, or based upon good reasons. (This is the result of a meta-ethical theory, a species of noncognitivism, to be discussed in Chapter 13.) When these positions are discussed the reader should recall how and why they arose at this point, and take this as further evidence that even though normative ethics and meta-ethics can be separated in theory, it is impossible to do so in practice.

Exercises

Review
1. What distinguishes deontological theories from teleological theories?
2. What are the main divisions among deontologist positions?
3. Describe the role that Scheme R plays in the statement of the tenets of act deontology.
4. What are the crucial differences between a summary rule and a constitutive rule (a rule that defines a practice)?
5. Why is the act deontologist required by his position to deny that there are constitutive moral principles?
6. What is one argument used by the rule deontologist to justify the claim that Scheme R is used in moral reasoning?

Applications
1. List some practices, other than chess, that are defined by a set of rules.
2. List some moral summary rules. Present one counterexample to each one you list.
3. Classify the following as either constitutive or summary rules.
   a. In chess, the king moves one square at a time.
   b. In baseball, three strikes constitute an out.
   c. Crime does not pay.
   d. Always drive to the right.
   e. The way to a man's heart is through his stomach.
   f. The way to a woman's heart is through her vanity.
   g. To draw a plane triangle you have to draw a figure with three sides.

    h. Most rules are summary rules.
4. Below is a list of well-known world figures. For each say whether they hold (or held) a teleological or deontological normative theory of obligation. Justify your answer with facts.
    a. Hitler.
    b. Stalin.
    c. Jesus of Nazareth.
    d. Buddha.
    e. Socrates.

2. *Thesis A₂ and Its Defense.* The defense of A_2 consists in presenting the rule theorist, whether he be a teleologist or a deontologist, with effective counterexamples designed to show that the rule in question is not adequate.

A *single-rule theorist* holds that one rule is adequate for indicating obligation, while a *multiple-rule theorist* holds that at least two rules are required. A single-rule theorist encounters two difficulties. First, his rule will probably not indicate all one's obligations. If his rule is, for example, "Do not steal," how does one account for the obligation (which we all admit) to steal under certain circumstances? The rule may, of course, be made more general, but any increase in generality leads to a decrease in content. The most general type of rule (which would be adequate) is absolutely uninformative since it does not pick out any action for us to perform—e.g., "Always do what is right." [10] Second, the single rule often tells us to do things we would recognize as wrong, or to refrain from doing things we would recognize as obligatory. If, for example, the rule is "Do unto others as you would have them do to you," the masochist would have to injure people whenever possible. If the rule is "Never tell a lie," we will have to refrain from telling a very small lie even when it could save many lives. The single-rule theorist at this point will have either to resort to other rules (to remove the first difficulty), or to exception clauses (to remove the second one). But, exception clauses in rules often cause great difficulty, and the adoption of additional rules is tantamount to the adoption of a multiple-rule theory.

Let us turn to a few general remarks about multiple-rule theories. If there are just a few rules, it is more than likely that they will be unable to deal with all the obligations one should want to recognize. But, as the number of rules, and their likelihood of completeness is increased, economy—a large part of the rule theorists' advantage—suffers. Also, the rules will be stated either with exception clauses or without them. If they have no exception clauses, they will perhaps tell us to do what is wrong or not tell us to do what is obligatory. If, on the other hand, they do have exception clauses, they

---

[10] It can be seen that a teleologist is a single-rule theorist, where the rule refers to the consequences of the action or kind of action.

become subject to the criticism which was leveled against rule utilitarianism.[11]

Another line of reasoning for those who would defend A_2 by attacking rule theories consists in pointing out that when we are considering whether a rule is acceptable or not we must finally do so without the aid of rules. Suppose that a rule is required to justify every judgment of moral obligation. If this were so, then when we present a counterexample to a rule which consists of a judgment of moral obligation (e.g., "it is wrong to shoot people in the leg"), that judgment of obligation would require a rule for its justification. However, if we are correct in suggesting that we can always find counterexamples to any rule or any set of rules, then we shall find an effective counterexample to the rule that is supposed to (and is required to) justify the specific judgment. This would also be true of the rule that would be used to justify the new counterexample. If effective counterexamples could always be found, then it would be impossible to present any counterexamples which consisted of a judgment of obligation which was justified but which, according to the rule being tested, was not justified. We could not do this because we would have no rule to which we could appeal to justify the counterexample. Because we can present such counterexamples, since we have actually done so, then it must be false that every judgment of obligation requires a rule to justify it. This is equivalent to saying that sometimes judgments of obligation are not justified by a rule. If we add that the only thing left to appeal to in justifying the judgment is the action itself, we have the statement of thesis A_2.

The rule deontologist would not admit, of course, that there is an effective counterexample for every rule or principle or set of rules or principles. When we present such a counterexample to any given rule or set of rules, he will try to construct another rule or set of rules to meet the objection. We would then try to construct a new counterexample. It would be unfortunate if the argument between the act and rule deontologists were settled on the basis of who could outlast the other in the construction of counterexamples and rules respectively. One would never know, then, which theory was correct; one would only know that at a given time one theorist was more clever or had more endurance than another.

Fortunately there is another approach that may shed more light on this problem. Let us begin by considering an argument presented by the rule deontologist as a criticism of act deontology and as an attempt to support his own position: Here is W. K. Frankena's way of putting it.

. . . particular moral judgments are not purely particular, as the act-deontologist claims, but implicitly general. For the act-deontologist, "This is what X ought to

---

[11] One interesting attempt to avoid these difficulties is presented by W. D. Ross, when he introduces the notion of a prima facie principle. We shall consider his position on pp. 104–109.

do in situation **Y**" does not entail anything about what **X** or anyone else should do in similar situations. Suppose that I go to Jones for advice about what to do in situation **Y**, and he tells me that I morally ought to do **Z**. Suppose also that I recall that the day before he had maintained that **W** was the right thing for Smith to do in a situation of the same kind. I shall then certainly point this out to Jones and ask him if he is not being inconsistent. Now suppose that Jones does not do anything to show that the two cases are different, but simply says, "No, there is no connection between the two cases. Sure, they are alike, but one was yesterday and involved Smith. Now it's today and you are involved." Surely, this would strike us as an odd response from anyone who purports to be taking the moral point of view. The fact is that when one makes a moral judgment in a particular situation, one implicitly commits oneself to making the same judgment in any similar situation, even if the second situation occurs at a different time or place, or involves another agent. Moral and value predicates are such that if they belong to an action or object, they also belong to any other action or object which has the same properties. If I say I ought to serve my country, I imply that everyone ought to serve his country.

This point is connected with the fact, noted earlier, that particular ethical and value judgments can be supported by reasons. If Jones makes such a judgment, it is appropriate to ask him for his reasons for believing that the act is right or the object good, and to expect an answer such as, "Because you promised to do it" or "Because it gives pleasure." If he answers, "Oh, for no reason whatsoever," we are puzzled and feel that he has misled us by using ethical or value terms at all. Moral and value judgments imply reasons, and reasons cannot apply in a particular case only. If they apply in one case, they apply in all similar cases. Moreover, in order to give a reason in a particular case, one must presuppose a general proposition. If Jones answers your question "Why?" by saying "Because you promised to" or "Because it gives pleasure," he presupposes that it is right to keep promises or that what gives pleasure is good.[12]

If, for example, *S* claims that a particular rock is hard, we can always ask him what his grounds are for making that claim. He will invariably mention some features of the rock—its resistance to touch, its resemblance to other rocks known to be hard, and so on. When *S* has done this, he has set forth criteria for making such judgments. Of course we must all agree that any other rock must be hard if it also has the properties sufficient for judging that *this* rock is hard. The rule theorist concludes that *S* has, in short, presupposed criteria for the hardness of all rocks in his judgment concerning this specific rock.

The rule theorist would now argue that in any specific judgment the characteristics of the thing judged are the basis of the judgment. Therefore, all specific judgments presuppose something general—a criterion, a principle, or a rule. Furthermore, if someone agreed that *x* is *F* by virtue of having *G* and *H*, but denied that a *y* just like *x* (at least in virtue of its possession of *G* and *H*)

---

[12] William K. Frankena, *Ethics* (Englewood Cliffs, N.J.: Prentice-Hall, Inc., © 1963), pp. 22–23. Reprinted by permission of the publisher.

also is *F*, he would be irrational. For example, if someone claims that this ice cream is good because it is cold and chocolate-flavored, he would be committed to saying that any other cold and chocolate-flavored ice cream is also good. He might, of course, suggest that there are other undesirable features about the second batch of ice cream, but these features, the rule theorist may suggest, can be excluded by stipulating other conditions. Finally we shall be saying that any ice cream just like the original batch in all relevant respects must also be good. The rule theorist now concludes that moral judgments are implicitly general because any action like the action being considered (in all relevant respects) is also to be judged in the same way. The act deontologist can argue either that no two cases are alike in all relevant respects, or that to say that an action is, in all relevant respects, like another action judged to be wrong, is already to make a moral judgment. This second reply could also be turned into an argument against the rule utilitarian, for to insist that a particular action, say *S*'s taking candy from a baby, is stealing, or *S*'s firing a rifle at his teacher with dire effects is murder (and thereby falls under a rule), is already to make a moral judgment. The former reply—namely, that no two actions are similar—is hinted at by Aristotle (and adopted by the existentialists of today):

But this is no doubt difficult, and especially in individual cases; for it is not easy to determine both how and with whom and on what provocation and how long one should be angry; for we too sometimes praise those who fall short and call them good-tempered, but sometimes we praise those who get angry and call them manly. The man, however, who deviates little from goodness is not blamed, whether he do so in the direction of the more or of the less, but only the man who deviates more widely; for *he* does not fail to be noticed. But up to what point and to what extent a man must deviate before he becomes blameworthy it is not easy to determine by reasoning, any more than anything else that is perceived by the senses, such things depend on particular facts, and the decision rests with perception. So much, then, is plain, that the intermediate state is in all things to be praised, but that we must incline sometimes towards the excess, sometimes towards the deficiency; for so shall we most easily hit the mean and what is right.[13]

Aristotle believes that no rules derived from reasoning can help us in every specific case—that moral insight is, rather, a matter of perception. When one perceives, say, the color of a ball, one does not, apparently, use any general principle to gain that knowledge. Situations, too, the act deontologist would claim, are specific to such a degree that general rules are useful only when those rules are summary rules.

Sartre seems to take a similar position: He seems to be claiming that values (i.e. rules or principles) are too abstract to determine the particular con-

[13] Aristotle, *Nicomachean Ethics*, trans. W. D. Ross (Oxford: The Clarendon Press, 1925), Book II, Chapter 9, 1109 b 14–27.

crete cases. "No rule of general morality can show you what you ought to do: no signs are vouchsafed in this world." [14] The question here is not whether Sartre adopts act deontology, as he seems to, but whether he adopts it for the reason being discussed, the inherent difference in each particular case. This interpretation is favored by his suggestion that there are no rules available to the man trying to decide what to do, or what is right.

As an example by which you may the better understand this state of abandonment, I will refer to the case of a pupil of mine, who sought me out in the following circumstances. His father was quarreling with his mother and was also inclined to be a "collaborator"; his elder brother had been killed in the German offensive of 1940 and this young man, with a sentiment somewhat primitive but generous, burned to avenge him. His mother was living alone with him, deeply afflicted by the semi-treason of his father and by the death of her eldest son, and her one consolation was in this young man. But he, at this moment, had the choice between going to England to join the Free French Forces or of staying near his mother and helping her to live. He fully realized that this woman lived only for him and that his disappearance—or perhaps his death—would plunge her into despair. He also realized that, concretely and in fact, every action he performed on his mother's behalf would be sure of effect in the sense of aiding her to live, whereas anything he did in order to go and fight would be an ambiguous action which might vanish like water into sand and serve no purpose. For instance, to set out for England he would have to wait indefinitely in a Spanish camp on the way through Spain; or, on arriving in England or in Algiers he might be put into an office to fill up forms. Consequently, he found himself confronted by two very different modes of action; the one concrete, immediate, but directed towards only one individual; and the other an action addressed to an end infinitely greater, a national collectivity, but for that very reason ambiguous—and it might be frustrated on the way. At the same time, he was hesitating between two kinds of morality; on the one side the morality of sympathy, of personal devotion and, on the other side, a morality of wider scope but of more debatable validity. He had to choose between those two. What could help him to choose? Could the Christian doctrine? No. Christian doctrine says: Act with charity, love your neighbor, deny yourself for others, choose the way which is hardest, and so forth. But which is the harder road? To whom does one owe the more brotherly love, the patriot or the mother? Which is the more useful aim, the general one of fighting in and for the whole community, or the precise aim of helping one particular person to live? Who can give an answer to that *a priori*? No one. Nor is it given in any ethical scripture. The Kantian ethic says, Never regard another as a means, but always as an end. Very well; if I remain with my mother, I shall be regarding her as the end and not as a means: but by the same token I am in danger of treating as means those who

[14] Jean-Paul Sartre, "Existentialism is a Humanism," *Existentialism from Dostoevsky to Sartre*, ed. Walter Kaufmann (New York: Meridian Books, 1957), p. 298. Reprinted from Jean-Paul Sartre, *Existentialism is a Humanism*, trans. by Philip Mairet; by permission of Methuen & Co., Ltd., the English publishers. By permission of Les Editions Nagel, original French publishers.

are fighting on my behalf; and the converse is also true, that if I go to the aid of the combatants I shall be treating them as the end at the risk of treating my mother as a means.[15]

3. Thesis A₃ and Its Defense. When we were discussing A_1 and A_2 we were also thereby discussing A_3. When we pointed out that the notion of a counter-example and its acceptability presupposed one's ability to make moral judgments of obligation concerning specific actions without using principles, we were simply stating part of A_3 in another way. If one can make such specific judgments without principles, and if, on the other hand, principles depend for their acceptance on "fitting in" with his specific judgments, then that seems to be evidence that principles depend, in some way, on specific judgments. This is also just another way of saying that principles need not be part of the justification of specific judgments.

A_3 is included because it has been the traditional way of stating act deontology. Also, traditionally, A_1 and A_2 have been the evidence provided for A_3. If there is no more contained in A_3 than is contained in A_1 and A_2, that will not make any act deontologist unhappy.

Exercises

Review
1. Why are extremely general moral rules uninformative?
2. What is an exception clause? What danger does their use involve?
3. What strategy does the act deontologist use to defend A_2?
4. Describe the rule deontologist's argument to establish the claim that all specific judgments presuppose something general, usually a principle.
5. What is the act deontologist's response to the argument mentioned in Review Exercise 4?
6. Describe the features of Sartre's view that classify him as an act deontologist.
7. Why is no new argument needed to defend A_3?

Applications
1. In the paragraph found on p. 91 (that begins with "Another line of . . .") an argument is presented which lends itself to another presentation. Put the argument in the form of *modus ponens* or *modus tollens* arguments, clearly listing those statements that are premises and those that are conclusions.
2. Compare and contrast the arguments used by Aristotle and Sartre to support their positions.
3. Present as complete an argument as you can to show that A_3 of act deontology follows from A_1 and A_2 of that theory.

[15] *Ibid.*, pp. 295–96. One wonders at the compatibility of this interpretation with another view of Sartre's, to the effect that when a man chooses he chooses for all mankind. That is, when he makes a choice he wills the same choice for everybody. If cases are never alike, what point does this declaration have? But if there are relevantly similar cases it would seem that there are rules possible—at least an individual may have his own rules.

C. Rule Deontology

The rule deontologist and the act deontologist have a more bitter dispute with one another than either one has with any teleologist. The position of the rule deontologist has already been outlined in considerable detail, but we will review the major points.

1. *Tenets of Rule Deontology.* The rule theorist's scheme for the justification of judgments presented earlier was the following:

> 1. Any action having F, G, and H is right (or wrong, or obligatory).
> 2. A has F, G, and H.
> *Therefore,*
> 3. A is right (or wrong, or obligatory).

The act deontologist, as we have seen, denies that Statement 1 is part of the justification of moral judgments or is essentially involved in the choice of moral maxims. The rule deontologist believes that the above scheme (Scheme R) is correct. He also believes that at least one of the values of F, G, or H is, or can be, something other than consequences.

We can say that the two tenets of all rule deontologists are:

R1. Scheme R is the general scheme descriptive of legitimate moral reasoning and justification.

R2. At least one of the values of F, G, or H is, or can be, something other than the consequences of A.

2. *Thesis R1 and Its Defense.* We have already discussed Tenet 1 in connection with act deontology, and the arguments the rule deontologist would advance for it. He may claim, with Hare, that principles such as Statement 1 in Scheme R are required for any teaching; or he may claim, with Frankena, that a necessary condition of rationality is agreeing that, because a particular action which has F, G, and H is right, then any other action with F, G, and H is also right. The act deontologist counters the first argument by claiming that summary rules are sufficient to account for teaching, and he counters the second by claiming that, even though one must judge similarly for any relevantly similar case, relevantly similar cases are never encountered in the real world, or alternatively, that the judgment that two cases are relevantly similar is already a moral judgment.

3. *Thesis R2 and Its Defense.* R2 is actually a denial of teleology. Any deontologist (whether he be a rule or an act theorist) would hold R2. The act deontologist would deny that there need be any general principle relating F, G, and H to the rightness of the action they characterize, but he too, when giving reasons, would mention F, G, and H. Both the rule deontologist and

the act deontologist insist that it is possible to appeal to features other than the consequences of an action in order to justify it.

The sort of defense which can be given for R2 is an example designed to show that sometimes consequences are not the only factors relevant to the rightness of actions. If, for example, a person has promised to keep a secret, we would not suggest that he is justified in breaking it if doing so would have slightly better consequences than keeping it. Suppose telling S that his health is bad will increase his good slightly. If there are two people—one who had promised the doctor not to tell S, and the other who had made no such promise—we must sometimes judge them differently for telling S. One of them has broken a promise, and this is often morally relevant. To assert R2 is to hold this, and there seems to be little the teleologist can do to combat this line of reasoning.

We have, so far, characterized the positions of act and rule deontology. We are inclined to believe that some form of act deontology is correct, and best meets the criteria for the acceptability of theories. There are too many facts of moral reasoning (e.g., the use of counterexamples) that conflict with any rule theory. Furthermore, there seem to be serious objections to all teleological views. Now let us consider three important forms of rule deontology. If each of these theories can be shown to have serious difficulties, then there is even more evidence in favor of act deontology.

Table 2.   Deontological Judgments

The judgment is justified by appealing to particular considerations.	*Act Deontology*	
The judgment is justified by appealing to general considerations.	*Rule Deontology*	
	Single	*Multiple*

Exercises

Review

1. What are the tenets of rule deontology? With which would the act deontologist disagree? With which would a teleologist disagree?
2. What is the rule deontologist's strategy in defending R1 and R2?

Applications

1. Describe the use you make of moral rules in your moral reasoning. Are they summary rules or constitutive rules? How did you determine this?

2. Describe an actual moral disagreement that involved a rule. How was it settled?

D. Three Examples of Rule Deontology

1. *Immanuel Kant.* Immanuel Kant is without question one of the most important figures in the history of philosophy, and one of the most difficult to read. Although the following treatment will not fully capture the subtlety of Kant's views, we hope it will be adequate as an illustration of one kind of rule deontology. First, we must familiarize ourselves with some of his technical terms. We have used 'maxim' to mean a rule of action or conduct which a person chooses to describe his behavior. Kant thinks of a maxim as a *rule or law of acting on the basis of what the person acting believes the situation to be.* He contrasts this subjective law with what he calls the *objective law.* The *objective law* is the *rule or law whereby we ought, in fact, to act.*

For example, suppose S believes that milk is harmful to children and so does not give milk to his children. S is here acting from the law, the maxim, "Do not feed a harmful food such as milk to the children." The maxim is based upon the situation as S believes it to be—i.e., that milk is dangerous. However, in this set of circumstances there is something that is true independently of S's beliefs: the objective fact that milk is not harmful to children, but is, on the contrary, beneficial. The objective law corresponding to the maxim is, then, the statement of the law whereby S ought to act regardless of what he believes the situation to be: "Feed health-producing foods such as milk to children." In this case, the maxim that S chooses is not identical with the objective law because S is ignorant of some crucial facts. We can now present Kant's answer to the question "Which actions are right?" or "How do we determine which maxims are best?"

If we ask "Which actions are right?" we are not really asking for a list of all the right actions there are, but rather we are asking for some way to identify right actions. The utilitarian may answer the question "Which actions are right?" by saying "Those which maximize utility," and in doing so he is really telling us how to pick out a right action from a wrong one. That is why, in most contexts, it is possible to interchange the three questions: (1) "Which actions are right?" (2) "How do we determine which moral maxims are best?" and (3) "How does one justify the judgment that an action is right?"

Kant claims that those actions are right whose rule of action (which will be a maxim) is such that:

1. S wills the maxim.
2. S acts from the maxim.
3. The maxim passes the test of the categorical imperative.[16]

[16] It is natural to ask what it is for an action to be wrong. We are less certain of the answer to this than to the question about right actions; but we might say that on Kant's view those actions are wrong whose rule of action is such that 1, 2, and not-3.

When we say that "S wills the maxim," we mean that S has given this maxim to himself rather than having it imposed upon him by some external source. For example, suppose that a child is told by a parent to help a little old lady across the street. The child is acting from the maxim "Always help little old ladies across streets," but the parent, not the child, is the one who legislated or constructed the maxim. If this is so, then no matter what the maxim is and no matter whether conditions (b) and (c) above are met, Kant would claim that such an action has no moral worth. This is not to say that the action is wrong, but that S's action did not, in this instance, have positive moral worth.

When S can choose to have his behavior described by a maxim or a law, then he can be said to be acting from that maxim or law. When a law describes the behavior of S whether S wishes to have it do so or not, then we say that S is only acting according to that law.

The third condition, that the maxim pass the test of the categorical imperative, is the most difficult to explain. Kant believes that the consequences of an action are not only not the sole test of the rightness of that action, but that they are actually irrelevant to the rightness (or wrongness, or obligatoriness) of that action. He believes that the only thing that is good without qualification is the good will of rational creatures:

It is impossible to conceive anything at all in the world, or even out of it, which can be taken as good without qualification, except a *good will*. Intelligence, wit, judgement, and any other *talents* of the mind we may care to name, or courage, resolution, and constancy of purpose, as qualities of *temperament*, are without doubt good and desirable in many respects; but they can also be extremely bad and hurtful when the will is not good which has to make use of these gifts of nature, and which for this reason has the term *'character'* applied to its peculiar quality. It is exactly the same with *gifts of fortune*. Power, wealth, honour, even health and that complete well-being and contentment with one's state which goes by the name of *'happiness'* produces boldness, and as a consequence often over-boldness as well, unless a good will is present by which their influence on the mind —and so too the whole principle of action—may be corrected and adjusted to universal ends; not to mention that a rational and impartial spectator can never feel approval in contemplating the uninterrupted prosperity of a being graced by no touch of a pure and good will, and that consequently a good will seems to constitute the indispensable condition of our very worthiness to be happy.[17]

If consequences and states such as happiness do not count in determining the rightness of actions, what is relevant must be something to do with maxims.

[17] Immanuel Kant, *Groundwork of the Metaphysics of Morals*, trans. by H. J. Paton (London: Hutchinson University Library, 1948), p. 61. By permission of Barnes & Noble, Inc., and Hutchinson Publishing Group, Ltd., publishers.

An action done from duty has its moral worth, *not in the purpose* to be attained by it, but in the maxim in accordance with which it is decided upon; it depends therefore, not on the realization of the object of the action, but solely on the *principle of volition* in accordance with which, irrespective of all objects of the faculty of desire, the action has been performed. That the purposes we may have in our actions, and also their effects considered as ends and motives of the will, can give to actions no unconditioned and moral worth is clear from what has gone before. Where then can this worth be found if we are not to find it in the will's relation to the effect hoped for from the action? It can be found nowhere but *in the principle of the will*, irrespective of the ends which can be brought about by such an action; . . . [18]

What is important, then, is the maxim from which the action has been performed. The test applied to the maxim must be something independent of consequences. Kant next describes the sort of principle we can use to test maxims:

But what kind of law can this be the thought of which, even without regard to the results expected from it, has to determine the will if this is to be called good absolutely and without qualification? Since I have robbed the will of every induce-ment that might arise for it as a consequence of obeying any particular law, nothing is left but the conformity of actions to universal law as such, and this alone must serve the will as its principle. That is to say, I ought never to act except in such a way *that I can also will that my maxim should become a uni-versal law.* Here bare conformity to universal law as such (without having as its base any law prescribing particular actions) is what serves the will as its principle, and must so serve it if duty is not to be everywhere an empty delusion and a chimerical concept. The ordinary reason of mankind also agrees with this com-pletely in its practical judgements and always has the aforesaid principle before its eyes.[19]

Kant presents other formulations of this universal law, which he calls the *categorical imperative*, but he intends that all of them should be equivalent: "I ought never to act except in such a way *that I can also will that my maxim should become a universal law.*" This is the categorical imperative, and now let us see how Kant intends it to work.

Suppose I seek, however, to learn in the quickest way and yet unerringly how to solve the problem 'Does a lying promise accord with duty?' I have then to ask myself 'Should I really be content that my maxim (the maxim of getting out of a difficulty by a false promise) should hold as a universal law (one valid both for myself and others)? And could I really say to myself that everyone may make a false promise if he finds himself in a difficulty from which he can extricate himself in no other way?' I then become aware at once that I can indeed will to

[18] *Ibid.*, pp. 67–68.
[19] *Ibid.*, pp. 69–70.

lie, but I can by no means will a universal law of lying; for by such a law there could properly be no promises at all, since it would be futile to profess a will for future action to others who would not believe my profession or who, if they did so over-hastily, would pay me back in like coin; and consequently my maxim, as soon as it was made a universal law, would be bound to annul itself.

Thus I need no far-reaching ingenuity to find out what I have to do in order to possess a good will. Inexperienced in the course of world affairs and incapable of being prepared for all the chances that happen in it, I ask myself only 'Can you also will that your maxim should become a universal law?' Where you cannot, it is to be rejected, and that not because of a prospective loss to you or even to others, but because it cannot fit as a principle into a possible enactment of universal law.[20]

The categorical imperative, then, is not itself a maxim from which one acts, but a principle or rule that will allow him to test all maxims from which he acts. If one has willed a maxim, and acted from it, and that maxim passes the test of the categorical imperative, then his action is right. Thus, for this third condition to be satisfied, apparently, one must be able consistently to will his action to be a universal law. Kant speaks as though by 'consistently' he means 'without contradiction'. Some laws, when willed universally, would "annul" themselves. If one wishes to lie because he is in a difficult situation, this is justified only if he *can* will that everybody lie when in such a situation. But Kant claims that if everybody did this then soon nobody could do it, because the institution of truthfulness would be "annulled" since there would then be no distinction between lying and telling the truth. Therefore it is not possible to will that everybody lie when in a difficult situation.

Perhaps the institution of lying would, if *universally* practiced, annul itself. But it is hard to see that the institution of lying when in a tight spot, or lying to save a life, would have the same effect. Furthermore, if we consider many of the other things that we believe to be wrong, it is not at all clear why we cannot will them universally, for the universal practice of cheating on philosophy exams, for example, will destroy no institutions. Of course the universal practice of cheating at everything would destroy institutions, but so would most other universal practices, for example, the universal practice of giving money to the poor. Such a practice would lead to A handing his money to poor B, and then B, being wealthy, handing his money to poor A, and on and on.

We have already suggested above that there is something wrong with Kant's principle. He tells us that if Conditions 1–3 are met an action is right, and if an action is right then Conditions 1–3 are met. We have suggested that it is possible that those conditions can be met by wrong actions. Furthermore, we can point out that there are some times when the conditions are met and

---

[20] *Ibid.*, pp. 70–71.

the action is not right or obligatory. Consider the action of getting out on the right side of the bed every morning. This action satisfies Condition 1 because we will it; it satisfies Condition 2 because we act from the relevant maxim, and it seems to satisfy Condition 3 because we can will the maxim to be a universal law. Kant would have to say that it is our duty to do this, but clearly this is not so.

Another counterexample to Kant's view takes advantage of the unspecified nature of the notion of a universal law. Suppose S acts on the maxim "Anyone who has fingerprints with Properties F, G, and H can murder his wife if she leaves the house messy." Let us assume that the maxim passes Kant's first two tests. S wills the maxim and acts from it. S can argue that the action is morally permissible because it does not allow everyone to murder his wife for he, S, is the only one who has fingerprints with Properties F, G, and H. If this is so, then the maxim passes the test of the categorical imperative and S is morally correct in murdering his wife.

There are, for Kant, many moral maxims that are justified, but they are all justified in relation to the categorical imperative. For this reason, we have classified him as a single-rule theorist.

Exercises

Review
1. What is Kant's answer to the question, "Which acts are right?"
2. Describe the process whereby one determines that a maxim has passed the test of the categorical imperative.
3. Describe two important criticisms of Kant's position.

Applications
1. Fit Kant's view into Scheme R.
2. Suppose we amend the categorical imperative so that it reads as follows: I ought never to act except in such a way that I can also will that my maxim should become a universal law and one has no moral obligation to act on maxims whose contrary (or contradictory) can equally well be willed to be a universal law.
   a. Does this allow Kant to escape all the criticisms presented?
   b. Are there any new criticisms that can be made?

2. Ten Categorical Commands. There are many people who believe that the way to determine which actions are right and to discover which maxims are best is to refer to the Bible. A widespread view is that if one follows the Ten Commandments, then he always does what is right and fulfills all his obligations. In short, the best and only maxims that one needs are the Ten Commandments. Let us examine that view as a normative ethical theory of obligation.

a. THE TEN COMMANDMENTS

1. Thou shalt have no other gods before me.

2. Thou shalt not make unto thee a graven image, nor any likeness of anything that is in heaven above, or that is in the earth beneath, or that is in the water under the earth: thou shalt not bow down thyself unto them, nor serve them; for I Jehovah thy God am a jealous God. . . .

3. Thou shalt not take the name of Jehovah thy God in vain. . . .

4. Remember the Sabbath day, to keep it holy.

5. Honor thy father and thy mother. . . .

6. Thou shalt not kill.

7. Thou shalt not commit adultery.

8. Thou shalt not steal.

9. Thou shalt not bear false witness against thy neighbor.

10. Thou shalt not covet thy neighbor's house, thou shalt not covet thy neigbor's wife, nor his manservant, nor his maidservant, nor his ox, nor his ass, nor anything that is thy neighbor's.

b. COUNTEREXAMPLES. It is not difficult to show that it is sometimes not wrong to go contrary to some of the commandments. Suppose that it is necessary for a man to work every day in order to support his family. Such a man could not keep the Sabbath and thus could not keep it holy. Yet no one (except those who are themselves morally perverse) would say that the man did what was wrong.

It is difficult to believe that it is wrong, in wartime, to steal some enemy secret that would bring the war to a swift conclusion. Similarly, if we are impressed into service for the defense of our country from an aggressor nation, it does not seem that we are being immoral in killing enemy soldiers in the course of our duty. Nor would we be judged immoral if we killed, in self-defense, a madman who attacked us.

c. INCONSISTENCIES. In the preceding section we were able to construct counterexamples because we were able to imagine some greater good that would result from our violating the command, or some obligation that overrides the obligation the commandment sets upon us. A much more serious charge is that the commandments are inconsistent in that situations can arise in which it is not possible to obey all the commandments. Suppose, for example, that one must visit his father on his birthday in order to honor him, and it is necessary to travel on the Sabbath to arrive on the right day. Here is an instance where one cannot observe both the Fourth and the Fifth commandments. Imagine, furthermore, that one's father orders him to kill, to commit adultery, to steal, or to bear false witness against some neighbor. To disobey the father is to violate the Fifth Commandment; to obey him is to violate many others.

The natural response to this kind of criticism is that the Commandments are not categorical rules, but only prima facie rules. Let us turn to W. D. Ross, the philosopher who has drawn our attention to prima facie rules.

Exercises

Review
1. Why are the Ten Commandments called *categorical?*
2. Describe how any one counterexample to one principle works to show that the whole theory is mistaken.

Applications
Present real cases, from your own or other's experiences, that show that the Ten Commandments are inadequate because of counterexamples, or inconsistent in the sense described above.

3. W. D. Ross and Prima Facie Duties. An explanation of the term 'prima facie' is provided by Ross:

I suggest *'prima facie* duty' or 'conditional duty' as a brief way of referring to the characteristic (quite distinct from that of being a duty proper) which an act has, in virtue of being of a certain kind (e.g. the keeping of a promise), of being an act which would be a duty proper if it were not at the same time of another kind which is morally significant. Whether an act is a duty proper or actual duty depends on *all* the morally significant kinds it is an instance of. The phrase *'prima facie* duty' must be apologized for, since (1) it suggests that what we are speaking of is a certain kind of duty, whereas it is in fact not a duty, but something related in a special way to duty. Strictly speaking, we want not a phrase in which duty is qualified by an adjective, but a separate noun. (2) *'Prima' facie* suggests that one is speaking only of an appearance which a moral situation presents at first sight, and which may turn out to be illusory; whereas what I am speaking of is an objective fact involved in the nature of the situation, or more strictly in an element of its nature, though not, as duty proper does, arising from its *whole* nature. I can, however, think of no term which fully meets the case. 'Claim' has been suggested by Professor Prichard. The word 'claim' has the advantage of being quite a familiar one in this connexion, and it seems to cover much of the ground. It would be quite natural to say, 'a person to whom I have made a promise has a claim on me'. And also, 'a person whose distress I could relieve (at the cost of breaking the promise) has a claim on me'. But (1) while 'claim' is appropriate from *their* point of view, we want a word to express the corresponding fact from the agent's point of view—the fact of his being subject to claims that can be made against him; and ordinary language provides us with no such correlative to 'claim'. And (2) (what is more important) 'claim' seems inevitably to suggest two persons, one of whom might make a claim on the other; and while this covers the ground of social duty, it is inappropriate in the case of that important part of duty which is the duty of cultivating a certain kind of character in oneself. It would be artificial, I think, and at any rate metaphorical, to say that one's character has a claim on oneself.[21]

[21] W. D. Ross, *The Right and the Good* (Oxford: The Clarendon Press, 1930), pp. 19–20. By permission of The Clarendon Press, Oxford.

We agree with Ross that the notion is understandable even if it is not perfectly clear. Ross puts his explanation in terms of *duty*, and we have put most of our discussion in terms of *right*; so let us put Ross' point in another way and frame it in the context of *right*.

Ross apparently believes that there are exactly six characteristics of acts, each of which is either a positive or a negative factor (depending on whether the characteristic is fulfilled or violated) in an action's being right or wrong. If we can know that Action A has one of the characteristics, and does not have any of the other characteristics negatively, then we can know, without a doubt, that A is right. We cannot usually (Ross believes that we can never) determine with certainty that A is characterized positively by some definite number of those morally relevant characteristics, and not characterized negatively by any others. Therefore, we cannot say without qualification that the act is right, for one of the other characteristics might apply negatively and then we would see that the act is wrong. However, when we do know that at least one of the characteristics applies positively, and do not know of any that apply negatively, we can say that the action is prima facie right.

Let us list those characteristics Ross believes are morally relevant.

(1) Some duties rest on previous acts of my own. These duties seem to include two kinds, (*a*) those resting on a promise or what may fairly be called an implicit promise, such as the implicit undertaking not to tell lies which seems to be implied in the act of entering into conversation (at any rate by civilized men), or of writing books that purport to be history and not fiction. These may be called the duties of fidelity. (*b*) Those resting on a previous wrongful act. These may be called the duties of reparation. (2) Some rest on previous acts of other men, i.e. services done by them to me. These may be loosely described as the duties of gratitude. (3) Some rest on the fact or possibility of a distribution of pleasure or happiness (or of the means thereto) which is not in accordance with the merit of the persons concerned; in such cases there arises a duty to upset or prevent such a distribution. These are the duties of justice. (4) Some rest on the mere fact that there are other beings in the world whose condition we can make better in respect of virtue, or of intelligence, or of pleasure. These are the duties of beneficence. (5) Some rest on the fact that we can improve our own condition in respect of virtue or of intelligence. These are the duties of self-improvement. (6) I think that we should distinguish from (4) the duties that may be summed up under the title of 'not injuring others'. No doubt to injure others is incidentally to fail to do them good; but it seems to me clear that non-maleficence is apprehended as a duty distinct from that of beneficience, and as a duty of a more stringent character.[22]

Let us consider an instance of 1a. Suppose that Johnny makes a promise to his girl friend Franky not to "two-time" her while she is on her spring vacation in Florida. If we now suppose that none of the other sources of obligation are activated either positively or negatively, then we can say that the act of not

[22] *Ibid.*, p. 21.

going out with other girls is a duty (or Johnny's refraining from dating some girl is right). Human beings, though, are limited in their knowledge and it may be that one of the other sources of prima facie duty is open, but that we do not know about it. Even if one of the other sources is open, the act of not going out with another girl is prima facie right, or obligatory.

Let us see what happens when another source becomes relevant. Suppose that Johnny meets a girl who, although the world's most beautiful coed, is desperately unhappy (or so it seems to Johnny). Johnny now reasons in the following way: "If I take this poor unhappy creature to the movies and then we have a friendly drink or two, she will be very much happier; if I do not do this, she will be unhappy. I have, after all, a duty to make the condition of my fellow humans better if it is in my power. In this case, as luck would have it, it is within my power to make this girl happy. Now it is true that I have a prima facie obligation not to take this girl out because of my promise to my girl friend, and yet I also have a prima facie obligation to make this girl happy. It does seem that in this case my obligation to help this poor unfortunate girl is greater than that of keeping my promise, and so I shall only be doing my duty when I take this girl to the movies."

Let us leave Johnny to do his duty. It is to be understood that some readers will be highly critical of Johnny's moral reasoning and would have sympathy with Franky if she suggested that Johnny was doing her wrong, as it were. However that may be, we can see how the prima facie duties can conflict and yet we can see that each can be a prima facie duty. This is not to say that each can be an actul duty, for it is clear that not both can be actual duties, and it may be that neither is. It may even be that something else is Johnny's actual duty, because of the activation of yet another one of the sources of duty.

Although Ross believes that he has found all the principles that embody prima facie duties, he leaves open the possibility that he has left out some principles. This possibility has an important bearing on the production of counterexamples. Suppose we find some action which is a duty to do or not to do (or right or wrong) even though it is not covered by any of the prima facie principles, or the application of one of the principles shows a certain action to be a duty or right when it is not a duty (or a duty not to do) or wrong (or vice versa). If it seems to Ross that the action is a genuine duty, then he can, in good conscience, add the corresponding principle to the list. Ross does not claim any finality for his list and would undoubtedly welcome the addition of further genuine principles. Therefore, we would not expect the production of effective counterexamples of this type.

Having said that, let us hasten to add that counterexamples of this type are available and do have some force. If we can list several such examples and force the increase of the prima facie principles, then we shall have provided evidence that the enterprise of listing all such principles is unworkable and that we do not, in fact, make use of such principles (except as summary rules or rules of thumb) in our moral reasoning.

Let us attend to Principle 4, according to which we have a prima facie duty to "make better" the condition of other beings "in respect of virtue, or of intelligence, or of pleasure." Our doing so would be a prima facie duty, or prima facie right.

It is now possible to connect wires to certain portions of the brain of a rat and, when an electric current is passed through these wires, the rat apparently experiences pleasure. There is every reason to believe that the same thing can be done to human beings. Our hooking some person up to such a device and causing pleasure in the way described is, according to Ross, prima facie right and a prima facie duty. If none of the other principles apply negatively, then our performing this action is actually right or is actually our duty. Let us suppose one more thing: once we put the person in the state of pleasure, we do not let him out. He cannot want to leave, and so he will spend the rest of his life having his pleasure centers stimulated. We shall make sure that all his physiological needs are satisfied and that he will live just as long as he would otherwise.

Let us go through the list of principles and see if any of them apply negatively.

1. We made no promise to our subject either to let him go at a certain time or not to let him go. We may even suppose that we told him he could leave whenever he wanted, and that this condition was acceptable to him. If we also suppose that neither of us had done the other any wrong, then the first principle can be said not to apply either positively or negatively.

2. We can also easily suppose that neither of us has done any service for the other. We can suppose that we met just that day; there are accordingly no duties of gratitude in operation.

3. It is easy to accept the fact that our subject is not being given pleasure that he does not deserve. Because we selected our subject more or less at random, everyone had the chance to gain the pleasure he enjoys. Furthermore, his pleasure is not gained at anyone else's expense, and we shall assume that he has done nothing that would make him undeserving of the pleasure.

4. This is the activated principle.

5. It would seem that we are improving our condition of intelligence by this experiment. If it is difficult to suppose that our store of knowledge has been increased, or that our intelligence has been increased in any way, then we can say that this principle does not apply positively or negatively.

6. Did we injure this man? This last principle is the one most difficult to avoid. If we have injured this man, then it might be claimed that we have activated this principle negatively and that the harm done outweighs the good. It would then be concluded that the action is not only not a duty but actually wrong. To avoid this charge, we can suppose either that the man would have chosen to put himself in the machine (although we did not explain the situation to him and so he did

not choose to have it happen to him), or that we have not done him any harm. The first possibility points up, it seems to us, the reason the action is wrong: we did not let the man choose his own fate. This sort of consideration, however, is not one mentioned in the six principles.

The man is not being harmed physically, so we can say that there is no physical injury being done. It might be said that because we have prevented him from enjoying other goods, such as knowledge and virtue, we have harmed him in a nonphysical way. There are, though, many persons who achieve little or no virtue, and we can suppose our man is one of those. We can easily imagine him to be a person who works at a job requiring little thought, and no thought that is valuable to him or to others. His habit may be to go home after work, watch television, eat, watch television, and then go to sleep. If we put such a man in our machine, we are depriving him of very little in the way of knowledge or virtue.[23]

It would seem, then, that there is some act that is not a duty and is not right which, according to the principles, is a duty and is right. Only one such counterexample is here presented, but it does seem that others of this type can be constructed.

It may be that Ross would accept our counterexample and others like it, and would, consequently, add more prima facie principles. Such a procedure may or may not bring an end to our disputation. But let us propose other kinds of criticism. First we shall propose counterexamples designed to show that sometimes the prima facie principles are not true. That is, sometimes an action falls under one of the principles and either is morally neutral or is to be judged the opposite of what the principle requires. Let us present two such counterexamples. If we activate Principle 5, we have a prima facie duty to improve ourselves in respect of virtue or of intelligence. We must suppose that Ross intends that intelligence be some kind of knowledge, so that if we increase our knowledge we increase our intelligence. If we do not suppose this, then the principle is strange, for we do not have the ability to increase our intellectual potential. Whichever notion of intelligence Ross is discussing, it seems fair to suppose it is one that makes it possible for us to increase our intelligence. The only likely candidate for this role seems to be some kind of knowledge.

It is not difficult to suppose there are many instances in which we do not activate any of the sources of duties except Principle 5, and yet we do not have any duty. For example, we would wager that not one reader of this book has attempted to eat a page of it. If not, they do not know the experience they would have were they to do so. If you, as a reader, decide not to absorb this material fully, and thus not increase your store of knowledge (and intelligence), it would be unfair for someone to judge that you had not fulfilled your

[23] It would seem that a hedonist is committed to saying we did him good. If so, then this case is also a powerful counterexample to most forms of hedonism.

duty to yourself. Similarly, few of us (even in moments of leisure) have torn apart our pillows to find out exactly what the inside of one looks like, though our store of knowledge would thereby increase. Must we, as a consequence of this abstinence, complain about the immorality running rampant in our society?

If we consider Principle 4, which claims that we have a prima facie duty to make better the condition of others in respect of virtue, intelligence and pleasure, more counterexamples of this type can be generated. We do not have a prima facie duty to tell our neighbor intimate details concerning our love life, even though that would increase his knowledge and perhaps even give him some pleasure. In fact, we seem to have a duty not to increase his knowledge or pleasure in this way. That is, Source 4 is activated positively, none of the other sources is activated at all, and yet it is false that we have a prima facie duty to do something; in fact we seem to have a duty not to perform that action.[24]

The counterexample just presented tries to show that an action is not a duty or it is obligatory not to do something just because it is an instance of Principle (4). This is different from trying to show, as we did in the previous section, that there are some actions which are not covered by the principles. It can be seen that the second charge is a much more serious one.

There is another kind of criticism against all rule deontologists: the argument that principles do not save one from making a judgment concerning particular actions (see pp. 85–86). One application of that argument is peculiar to those who hold prima facie principles. Because the principles are prima facie, one must weigh the stringency of each principle that applies to a particular situation, and determine that the principle does apply to the situation. We must, for example, decide that our duty to ourselves is stronger than our duty to starving Indians, and so we do not give away all our money and wealth to Indian relief agencies. This seems to indicate that the obligatoriness of actions is not determined by the principles, but that we use such principles, as Carritt suggests, as guides.

Summary. In Chapters 3–5, we have presented various deontological and teleological theories. We have criticized all of these theories save one—act deontology, which we have defended. Let us now apply the criteria of acceptability to that one theory and see how well it fares.

1. Serious Objections to the Theory Can Be Answered Adequately. In this chapter we raised the most serious criticisms we were aware of and tried to show how they could be answered. If we suppose that we eliminated teleological theories, then we are allowed to conclude that either some form of rule or act deontology is correct. Given this, it was necessary to consider the

---

[24] One may avoid a great deal of dispute concerning this example by supposing that our partners in our love life are all casual. They are persons to whom we owe no great amount of gratitude. We can also suppose that our neighbors won't spread the information.

argument that the act deontologist cannot adequately account for the use of rules. The answer to the charge is, really, the same as the case for Thesis A_1 of act deontology. The act deontologist wishes to claim that the use of summary rules is all that is required for our moral reasoning and that the use of such rules is compatible with the tenets of the position. Although we believe that this reply to this criticism is, at this point, adequate, we shall take up the role of principles in moral reasoning once again in Chapters 12 and 13.

2. THERE ARE GOOD REASONS IN FAVOR OF THE THEORY. Act deontology, it will be recalled, consists of the following three claims:

A1. The procedure for justifying the judgment that A is right (or wrong, or obligatory) need not include a principle (referred to as Statement 1 of Scheme R).

A2. The judgment that A is right (or wrong, or obligatory) must sometimes be justified by giving Statement 2 in Scheme R (A has properties F, G, and H) as the only reason.

A3. Ultimately, statements such as Statement 1 (in Scheme R) can only be justified by statements such as Statement 3 in Scheme R—"A is right (or wrong, or obligatory)".

These claims have been defended in this chapter.

3. THE THEORY FITS OR EXPLAINS THE RANGE OF PHENOMENA BETTER THAN OTHER COMPETING THEORIES. To establish that a theory meets the first two criteria, we mentioned a great many things that constitute the phenomena of our moral life. We discussed the fact that we sometimes justify moral judgments by appeals to something other than consequences. This is a fact of our moral life that the act deontologist, because he is a deontologist, can account for and explain. He can also explain everything the teleologist can explain, for act deontology can maintain that consequences are sometimes to be taken into account, and even that sometimes *only* consequences are to be taken into account. The act deontologist insists that he can account for the fact that we often use rules in our moral reasoning. Furthermore, act deontology best accounts for the fact that often the character of the situation or person must be considered if one is to make a justified judgment. The theory also best explains why we insist on knowing the exact nature of the action under consideration, and why we often change our judgment when we discover that we were mistaken about the facts of the case.

Finally, it can be pointed out that only act deontology can account for the universal acceptance of the procedure of offering counterexamples to normative theories. Our claim is that when a conflict arises between a rule, any rule, and a considered particular judgment, it is, in most cases, the rule that must be changed. We do not judge particular actions by appealing to absolutely unquestionable rules, but rather by appealing to rules that have gradually been formulated by generalizing from particular judgments. It is always possible, given the immense diversity of human activity, that even the best rule will lead us astray, and only the act deontologist can feel comfortable with this fact.

The reader is now advised to review the normative theories of obligation that have been presented and invited to decide for himself, as well as possible at this point, which of them best meets the criteria for acceptability of theories. This is not a matter for personal preference, but for personal decision, in the light of all the arguments which can be advanced for and against a particular view. If the reader has been led to believe, as we are inclined to believe, that the *final* acceptance of a normative theory of obligation depends in part upon the outcome of the discussion of certain meta-ethical issues such as the place of principles in moral reasoning, then we invite him to postpone his final decision concerning the best normative theory until those meta-ethical issues have been fully discussed.

Exercises

Review
1. Describe the important difference between the claim that a principle is a prima facie principle and that it is a categorical principle.
2. What kind of criticism of Ross is most effective?
3. Describe the difference between the two kinds of counterexamples that are proposed against Ross' prima facie principles.

Applications
1. Identify the following as prima facie or categorical principles.
   a. Giving to charity is obligatory.
   b. Do good and avoid evil.
   c. Never start in high gear.
   d. Everyone has an obligation to himself.
2. Suppose the Ten Commandments are prima facie principles, and show how the normative ethical theory of obligation consisting of those principles can be criticized.
3. Describe the normative ethical theory of obligation you believe is best. Apply the criteria of acceptability to it. What further evidence is required to support your theory?
4. Describe a situation in which you made a judgment of moral obligation and present your justification of that judgment. Is there any relation between your justification and what you said in response to the preceding question?
5. Describe a situation in which you made a judgment of nonmoral obligation and present your justification of that judgment. Contrast the justification of this judgment with that given of the moral judgment.
6. Present the supporting reasons of someone who makes a judgment of moral obligation with which you disagree. Show the source of your disagreement (disagreement about the facts, about which normative theory of obligation is correct, and so on). What, besides the judgment itself, would you have to accept in order to agree with the other person?

7. How would you argue with the person described in question 5?
8. Evaluate the argument contained in the following:

Eating, drinking, speaking, writing, thinking, as well as procreation, are all functions with more or less definite purpose. Any use of these functions which is incompatible with their specific end and which cannot be referred to the service of God or man is an unreasonable activity. Because it is unreasonable and incapable of reference to the moral end, such perverted use of a function is always wrong.

Whether or not it is a trivial or a grievous wrong is going to depend upon circumstances and the degree and type of the perversion involved. The sex function holds by its very nature a special and peculiar place. For instance, one may eat or drink at any time without necessarily abusing a human function, for such functions serve bodily nutrition and, unless exercised to excess, food and drink are stored in the body and utilized in due season.

But the function of procreation has as its formal and essential end the production of a new human being who must be cared for throughout infancy, childhood and youth and helped to become independent in early manhood. To exercise the sex function and prevent procreation is an unreasonable abuse of a human function. To procreate a new human individual, without being in a situation to care for and educate one's progeny, is an improper use of the function and a wrong committed against the child.

Therefore *all seeking of sex pleasure outside of normal relations in lawful wedlock is morally wrong.* —T. V. Moore, *Principles of Ethics* (Philadelphia, Lippincott, 1935).

Bibliography

ARISTOTLE. *Nicomachean Ethics*. Trans. W. D. Ross. Oxford: The Clarendon Press, 1925. Probably the most influential act deontologist. Books i–iii should be enough to introduce Aristotle to the new reader.

CARRITT, E. F. *The Theory of Morals*. London: Oxford University Press, 1952. Presentation of act deontology. Chapter 9 is a consideration of Kant's theory. The book contains a defense of act theories.

EWING, A. C. *Ethics*. New York: The Free Press, 1953, Chapters 5 and 6. A clear statement of deontology. The author examines Kant's view in Chapter 5, and ideal utilitarianism and Ross in Chapter 6.

*HARE, R. M. *The Language of Morals*. Oxford: The Clarendon Press, 1952. Chapters 4 and 5 provide a defense of rule theories and an attack on some teleological views.

*KANT, IMMANUEL. *Groundwork of the Metaphysics of Morals*. Trans. H. J. Paton. London: Hutchinson University Library, 1948. A most influential rule deontologist. This work is short but difficult, and the student who reads it is advised to read it all.

*NOWELL–SMITH, P. H. *Ethics*. Baltimore: Penguin Books, Inc., 1954. Chapters 15–17 contain an attack on some deontologists and a partial defense of a rule theory.

*Ross, W. D. *Foundations of Ethics.* Oxford: The Clarendon Press, 1939. Chapters 4–6 contain another statement of Ross' position.

————. *The Right and the Good.* Oxford: The Clarendon Press, 1930. Chapter 2 is a defense of prima facie rule deontology.

*Singer, Marcus G. *Generalization in Ethics.* New York: Alfred Knopf, Inc., 1961. An interesting discussion of Kant's categorical imperative is presented in Chapter 8.

Theories of Value

A. The Normative Question and the Meta-ethical Question

In our discussion of answers to the question "What actions are right?" we found it relatively simple to consider answers to this question without going into detail about the meaning of the word 'right'. Hopefully this will remain true as we consider answers to the question "What things are good?" Yet we must recognize, and comment upon one way of answering this latter question with dazzling, if questionable, ease. One might begin by answering another question: "What does 'good' mean?" One answer to this question is that 'good' means 'pleasant' and, on such a view, the question of what things are good can be dealt with easily: all and only pleasant things are good.[1] We do not feel that this is an adequate way of dealing with the problem, but our discussion will be postponed until Chapter 11, where a number of theories of this type are examined.

B. Intrinsic and Extrinsic Value

Many kinds of things are said to be good, and many sorts of reasons are given for saying that something is good, but philosophers often stress a basic distinction between two kinds of goodness. Sometimes things are said to be good in themselves, good for their own sake, or good apart from what they might lead to, and sometimes things are said to be good not in themselves, but because they are means to, or parts of, other things said to be good in themselves. We say, for example, that money is a good thing—but usually we quickly admit that it is not good in itself but only for the sake of the things which can be purchased with it. These things, in turn, are sometimes

---

[1] A utilitarian might defend his theory of obligation in a similar way, for he might hold that 'right' means 'productive of the greatest good for the greatest number'.

thought to be good as means to other things. But this must stop somewhere, and it is argued that unless something were good without being so because it is a means to something else, the whole enterprise of seeking anything would be pointless. Let us suppose for the moment that some things are intrinsically valuable, or worth seeking as ends in themselves. This kind of goodness is usually contrasted with something called *extrinsic goodness*. We shall use the latter expression here to mean 'good in some way that is not merely intrinsically good'. There are many ways in which a thing may be extrinsically good, and the task before us now is to examine some of them.

A thing may be said to be a good means for bringing about some ends which either is, or is not, good (intrinsically or extrinsically). Thus 'a good means' must be carefully distinguished from 'a means (good or bad) to good'. When something is a good means—that is, an *efficient* producer of something else— we shall say that it is *instrumentally good*, whether or not the end it produces has value.[2] Now a thing may be a good means to things that are intrinsically

[2] This is not a typical use of the notion of 'instrumentally good', for that expression is taken here to mean much the same as 'efficient' or 'effective in the production of something'. Often a thing is said to be instrumentally good only if the end it produces is good, and some think that the end need be intrinsically good and others that it need only be good in *some* way or other. Thus Frankena says, "One may also say that something is good on the ground that it is a *means*, necessary, sufficient, or both, to a good end, as when one says 'It is a good idea to go to the dentist twice a year.' Then it is *extrinsically* or *instrumentally* good, or *good as a means*." *Ethics* (Englewood Cliffs, N.J.: Prentice-Hall, Inc., 1963), p. 65. Ross, too, uses 'instrumental goodness' in this way, for he says that it is a complex notion including "(*a*) the notion of a causal relation between something and something else, and (*b*) the notion of the intrinsic goodness of the effect." *The Right and the Good* (Oxford: The Clarendon Press, 1930), p. 73. G. E. Moore, in speaking of intrinsic value and goodness as a means, says that when someone says that something is good: "They may either assert that this unique property does always attach to the thing in question, or else they may assert only that the thing in question is *a cause or a necessary condition* for the existence of other things to which this unique property does attach." *Principia Ethica* (Cambridge: Cambridge University Press, 1959), p. 21. Finally (though this survey is not complete), C. I. Lewis says, "We may, therefore, say that A *is instrumental to B*, or *useful for* the production of B, without reference to the question of genuine value in B; but we shall say that A has *extrinsic* value, or instrumental *value*, only if B (or some eventual Z to which it may lead) has intrinsic value." *An Analysis of Knowledge and Valuation* (La Salle, Ill.: The Open Court Publishing Company, 1946), p. 385. In contrast to this, we are using 'extrinsically good', or 'extrinsic value', as the complement to 'intrinsic value'—anything which is good in any way other than or in addition to being intrinsically good, shall be said to have extrinsic value. It seems advisable also to make the distinction between a good means, a means to good, and a good means to good, and clearly there is nothing in the ordinary sense of 'a good means' which includes the notion of intrinsic value in what is immediately or eventually brought about. Lewis manages to speak of this by calling means which are nevertheless not means to good 'useful' and Frankena speaks of their utility value, but this doesn't mirror the fact that a good means (to no matter what kind of end) is good *as a means*. Our notion of *beneficial goodness* then, is similar to what is meant by the above writers by 'instrumental goodness', and we diverge from their usage because we feel that it is important to have a sense of 'good' which does not make a good means identical

good (assuming there is such goodness), or to things that are intrinsically bad, or to things that are intrinsically neutral. So also, if the end is intrinsically good, a thing may be a good (efficient) means to that thing, an average means to that thing, or a very poor (but ultimately successful) means to that thing. If something is efficient in the production of another thing (be that latter thing good, bad, or indifferent) it is *instrumentally* good; and if a thing leads (no matter how well or poorly) to something intrinsically good, it is *beneficially good*. By 'instrumentally good', then, we mean 'a good means', and by 'beneficially good' we mean 'a means to good'.

Things may be instrumentally good without being beneficially good—e.g., when they are efficient producers of something not intrinsically good. Bombs, for example, are often said to be good for blowing up cities, but few would classify the destruction of cities as intrinsically good. Or, things may be both instrumentally and beneficially good—e.g., when they are good means (efficient means) in the production of something intrinsically good. Penicillin, for example, is effective in curing of certain diseases. Finally, things may be beneficially good without being instrumentally good—e.g., when they produce intrinsically good things, but inefficiently. A poor teacher who nevertheless taught what was true, for example, would be an inefficient means for the production of knowledge, something often said to be intrinsically good.

There are still other sorts of extrinsic goodness. For example, something may be a part of another thing that is either intrinsically, instrumentally, or beneficially good, in which case the part has *contributive value*. A particular line in a painting may have no intrinsic value, but the painting itself might, and perhaps partly because of that line. Thus not every part of an intrinsically valuable thing has contributive value, but only those which "contribute" to its intrinsic value. It should be clear now why contributive value is different from instrumental value or beneficial value, for the line, for example, would not normally be said to be a *means* to the intrinsic value of the painting.

Exercises

Review

1. What are two alternative ways of saying that a thing is intrinsically good?
2. What is one argument for saying that at least some things must be intrinsically good?
3. What is the difference betwen intrinsic goodness and extrinsic goodness?
4. What is the difference betwen instrumental goodness and beneficial goodness?
5. Why would it be mistaken to say that the lines in an intrinsically valuable painting have instrumental value?

---

with a means to good. Thus, on our account, even if there should be no such thing as intrinsic value, things would still be instrumentally good, and it seems advisable to be able to say this.

Applications
1. Why must teleological theories of obligation be supplemented by a theory of value?
2. List a number of things that are likely candidates for intrinsically valuable things.
3. Assuming that only pleasure is intrinsically good, list a number of things that are beneficially, but not instrumentally, good.
4. Assuming that only pleasure is intrinsically good, list a number of things that are instrumentally, but not beneficially, good.
5. Assuming that only pleasure is intrinsically good, list a number of things that are neither instrumentally nor beneficially good.
6. State explicitly what conditions have to be met by the members of each of the above three lists.
7. What would have to be intrinsically valuable in order to make each of the following both beneficially and instrumentally good?
   a. Fish.   e. Books.
   b. Rocks.   f. Back scratchers.
   c. Guns.   g. Democracy.
   d. Good looks.   h. Communism.
8. Is it possible for something to be intrinsically good, beneficially good, and instrumentally good all at the same time? May a thing be instrumentally good and contributively good at the same time? Examine completely all the other possible combinations, and try to find, where possible, instances of things having the various kinds of goodness.

C. Goodness of a Kind

W. D. Ross distinguishes the "predicative" use of 'good' from its "attributive" use. An expression of the form "X is good" is an instance of the predicative use, while an expression of the form "a good X" is an instance of the attributive use.[3] A few examples will help the reader fix these distinctions firmly in his mind.

Predicative use	Attributive use
Cars are good.	A good car.
Fathers are good.	A good father.
John is good.	A good person.
Apples are good.	A good apple.

It is helpful to notice that a judgment phrased in the attributive form, usually (but not always) conveys the notion of *goodness of a kind.* 'A good X' usually denotes a particularly excellent member of a class. A car is thus a good car because it fulfills the generally accepted criteria for cars better than is expected. According to Ross:

[3] W. D. Ross, *The Right and the Good*, pp. 65 ff. By permission of the Clarendon Press, Oxford.

Within the attributive use of the word we may distinguish (1) its application to persons, and (2) its application to things. In case (1) the root idea expressed by 'good' seems to be that of success or efficiency.... In case (2) there appear to be various elements included in what we mean by 'good'. We seem to mean in the first place (*a*) 'ministering to some particular human interest'.... But there is also here (*b*) the notion that the thing in question is one in which the maker of it has successfully achieved his purpose.... [4]

Ross has much more to say about the attributive use of 'good', but notice that a good X almost always is one that comes up to some standard, and is contrasted with other X's that do not. Even though there are exceptions to this claim, we may use this grammatical distinction to introduce a more important, nongrammatical distinction.

When we turn to the predicative use of 'good' (in "X is good") we find that we are not usually dealing with efficiency, or approximation to a standard; we are not contrasting this X with other X's which fall short of some set of criteria. When we say "X is good," we usually intend to convey the notion of intrinsic value, unless, of course, we add 'for Y' ("Cars are good for the purpose of transportation.") and thereby introduce the notion of instrumental or beneficial goodness.

Suppose we say that a knife is a good carving knife. A good carving knife may be good for many things—removing screws or cutting knots in one's shoelaces—but when it is claimed that it is a good *carving* knife, we must have in mind a rough set of criteria which this knife satisfies. This claim (that a set of fairly conventional criteria are required) is supported by the difficulty we would have in talking about a good earthworm, or a good prime number.[5] No criteria have been suggested for such things (which is not to say that none *could* be suggested and eventually accepted).

Therefore when it is asserted that something is a good X, we are often employing the notion of goodness of a kind. The object is thought to fulfilll rather conventional (and not always arbitrary) criteria. Something may be said to be good in this sense without being instrumentally good or intrinsically good. As J. O. Urmson points out:

If I am asked whether a good apple is good as a means or as an end I should not know how to answer; it is not a real question.[6]

But of course *sometimes* it is a real question, as in "Is that apple good (for impressing the teacher)?" Urmson's point is just that usually this question is not about either intrinsic or instrumental goodness.

---

[4] *Ibid.*, pp. 65–66.

[5] Cf. J. O. Urmson, "On Grading," *Mind*, 69 (April 1950), 145–69. This is reprinted in *Logic and Language*, ed. Anthony Flew (Garden City, N.Y.: Doubleday & Company, Inc., 1965), pp. 381–409.

[6] *Ibid.*, p. 162.

Exercises

Review

1. The distinction betwen the predicative and the attributive use of 'good' is used to introduce another "sort" of goodness. What is this sort of goodness, and how does the above distinction aid in its introduction?
2. Why can we not identify goodness of a kind with intrinsic goodness?
3. Why do we not speak of a good earthworm, or a good hydrogen atom?

Applications

1. Peter Geach has suggested that we can make a distinction between attributive and predicative adjectives on the following basis: "I shall say that in a phrase 'an A B' ('A' being an adjective and 'B' being a noun) 'A' is a (logically) predicative adjective if the predication 'is an A B' splits up logically into a pair of predications 'is a B' and 'is A'; otherwise I shall say that 'A' is a (logically) attributive adjective." Thus 'red' is a logically predicative adjective but 'artificial' is not. Geach then claims that 'good' and 'bad' are always attributive. Compare this way of making the distinction with Ross' and then go on to consider what ramifications the claim that 'good' and 'bad' are always attributive have for the theory of value. It might help to examine Geach's article, which can be found in *Analysis*, **17** (1956), 33–42. Cf. also the replies to Geach's article by R. M. Hare in the same volume of that journal, pp. 103–11, and by Austin Duncan-Jones in an article entitled "Good Things and Good Thieves," in *Analysis*, **26** (March 1966), 113–18.
2. Sometimes, when something is said to be good of a kind there is a corresponding judgment about its instrumental value. For example, a good broom is also a broom that is efficient in doing its job; but often when we say of an X that it is a good X we do not, as Urmson suggests, presuppose or have in mind a judgment of instrumental value as well. Consider a number of judgments of goodness of a kind that do go hand in hand with judgments of instrumental value, and also a number of judgments of goodness of a kind that do not. What explains the difference here?
3. The distinctions we have proposed are still too unsubtle to deal with all the uses of 'good'. Attempt to provide a more adequate classification by considering such expressions as
   a. A good means.
   b. Good for.
   c. Is good to.
   d. Good as.
   e. Does good to.
   f. Good at.
   g. A means to good.
4. Apply the remarks we have made about the different senses of 'good' to 'bad'. Is there such a thing as instrumental badness, intrinsic badness? Is there a notion of badness corresponding to beneficial goodness?
5. Are further distinctions and elaborations needed to deal with questions of

relative value—that is, are there any further problems in dealing with 'better' and 'worse'?

D. Moral and Nonmoral Goodness and Badness

There is another distinction which is independent of, and cuts across, the distinctions just investigated. This is the distinction between what is *morally* good (or bad) and what is *non*morally good (or bad). W. K. Frankena believes that this distinction is partly "a matter of the differences in the objects that are called good and bad."

The sort of things that may be morally good or bad are persons, groups of persons, traits of character, dispositions, emotions, motives, and intentions—in short, persons, groups of persons, and elements of personality. All sorts of things, on the other hand, may be nonmorally good or bad, for example: physical objects like cars and paintings; experiences like pleasure, pain, knowledge, and freedom; and forms of government like democracy. It does not make sense to call most of these things morally good or bad, unless we mean that it is morally right or wrong to pursue them.[7]

The problems raised by this way of making the distinction—and, indeed, by the distinction itself—are great. Exactly what is an element of personality, and why is it that it does not make sense to call certain things morally good or bad? Let us begin by excluding physical objects from the class of morally valuable things. Cars, knives, rocks, and eggs are never either morally good or morally bad. It also seems incorrect to predicate this quality of animals, no matter how much good or harm they do. This provides a clue to the possible factors involved here, for a common feature of animals and inanimate objects is that they are not (or are generally believed not to be) subject to praise and blame, nor are they believed to be in any way responsible for what they do, or for what happens as a result of their being where they are. The rock over which we trip is not wicked, and few of us would be willing to say that the rattlesnake is morally evil.

Pleasure, pain, knowledge, and freedom are cetrainly "human" things, as are motives and intentions, and the question as to why the last two but not the first four can be said to have moral value will naturally arise. One possible answer is that the existence of a pain in the toe, for example, shares with the toe itself the freedom from human control that a motive or an intention does not. We might say, therefore, that only those features of humans which are under their direct conscious control—which they can bring into being by an act of will—can be said to be morally good or morally bad. For example, if some of our intentions are less than could be desired we can alter them ourselves, but this is not the case with feelings such as pain, and we cannot

[7] W. K. Frankena, *Ethics*, pp. 47–48. © 1963. By permission of Prentice-Hall, Inc.

will our knowledge into being either. But this view is not really satisfactory for, like pain and knowledge, emotions are not always under our direct control. Finally, men themselves are said to be morally good or bad, but it makes no sense to speak of Socrates, for example, as willing himself into existence.

There is a further difficulty with this classification, which is that every time we call a man good we do not really intend to say that he is morally good. For example, we may say that Jones is good, and mean that he is good *for* a particular job, or a good salesman, and here there is no question of moral value. Finally, friendship might refer to a *feeling* of friendship, in which case, by the proposed classification, it would not have moral value; or it might refer to a behavior trait, an element of someone's personality, in which case it would have moral value.

On the whole, no satisfactory classification of moral and nonmoral value has been achieved, nor has it been made altogether clear that one is required. The teleologist tells us that an action is right if, and only if, it produces good, but it would seem that no distinction needs to be made here between moral and nonmoral goodness, for should an action result both in pleasure (a nonmoral good) and some set of good feelings (morally good things), both are relevant in a teleological assessment of its rightness. In the same way, if we want to know (*not* as teleologists) which things are good, we want to know about morally good things as well as nonmorally good things, and again, this distinction does not seem to be essential here. It is true that most teleologists have concentrated on nonmoral value, but it is also clear that there is no need for them to do so.

Thus far we have discussed distinctions between intrinsic and extrinsic value, and between moral and nonmoral value. We have fairly clear distinctions within the first set of terms, but the distinction between moral and nonmoral goodness leaves much to be desired. Perhaps though, for our purposes, this will not cause us difficulty. In this chapter we shall attempt to clarify the meanings of claims about intrinsic goodness (or badness), and in the following chapter we shall examine some of the theories about those entities actually said to possess intrinsic value. We shall assume that, if there is a legitimate distinction between moral and nonmoral value, a thing said to be intrinsically good may be so in either the moral or the nonmoral sense. We shall also assume that things said to have nonmoral value and things said to have moral value have equal initial claims upon intrinsic value.

Exercises

Review

1. How does Frankena attempt to make the distinction between moral and nonmoral goodness?

2. What are some problems facing one who attempts to make the distinction in this way?
3. Why is the teleologist interested in nonmoral as well as moral value?
4. What is to be gained by making a distinction betwen moral and nonmoral value?

Applications

1. It is sometimes maintained that actions can be evaluated in two ways— first we can, as teleologists, say that they are either right or wrong, but in addition to this we may also say they have intrinsic value. Consider this claim carefully and think about these possibilities. If actions could be evaluated in this way, would it do away with the need to talk about rightness and wrongness? What grounds might someone give for saying that an action is good, and would this be a case of moral or nonmoral goodness? Is it possible to suggest that although an action may be good it is not right, or that although it is right it is not good?
2. Consider the following list:
    a. Intentions.
    b. Motives.
    c. Ideas.
    d. Feelings.
    e. Desires.
    f. Wants.
    g. Needs.
    h. Dispositions.
    Which of the above would be better classified as morally (as opposed to nonmorally) good? What are your grounds for making the classifications you make?

E. Intrinsic Value

If someone claims that a thing is good as an end, good in itself, or intrinsically good, we can take him to be saying essentially the same thing, and since we may speak of something being intrinsically good *or* bad, we can use the notion of intrinsic value to cover both cases. One might begin a discussion of intrinsic value by asking for a definition of the term, but there are two reasons for not taking that approach here. First, this is a meta-ethical question. Second, perhaps the most important writers who have treated this notion, Moore and Ross, have claimed that a definition of this notion is impossible. At this point, however, it is important to clarify the meta-ethically neutral distinction between intrinsic value and instrumental value, and several related notions.

1. *Aristotle.* Whenever someone says that a thing has intrinsic value, whatever else he might mean, he is clearly making a distinction between things are desirable in themselves and things that are desirable for the sake of something else. Aristotle makes this distinction (although he does not relate it to desirability):

If, then, there is some end of the things we do, which we desire for its own sake (everything else being desired for the sake of this), and if we do not choose everything for the sake of something else (for at that rate the process would go on to infinity, so that our desire would be empty and vain), clearly this must be the good and the chief good.[8]

Two things about this passage deserve special attention. First, Aristotle speaks of what *is* desired rather than of what *ought to be* desired, or is *worthy* of being desired. Second, he speaks of *the good* rather than of *goodness*.

One would think that there is a great difference between saying that something is desired by someone or everyone, and saying that something is desirable, or ought to be desired. To say that someone desires something is simply to make a report about his mental state, whereas to say that something is *worthy* of being desired is quite another thing. It is possible that there are things which no one has ever desired, but which are still worthy of being desired, just as it is possible that there are or have been things which, although unworthy of being desired, are desired by everyone. For example, everyone on both sides of a dispute may desire war, yet it is not at all clear that this fact insures the truth of the claim that war is desirable. It may be evidence that war is desirable, since men often know what is desirable, but it is not conclusive evidence, and there is no logical connection between the two notions. Further, scarcely anyone in the Middle Ages desired a daily bath, yet we can all agree that baths were desirable even then. This point can be made without taking account of the distinction between insrtumental and intrinsic desirability; for even though baths are not thought to be intrinsically desirable, the shift from the desired to the desirable is often made in both areas.

In discussing the good, Aristotle fluctuates between these two notions and finally shifts from the topic of what men do desire to the topic of what is desirable. He begins by defining the good as that which we desire for its own sake, and it seems that this is merely a report of what 'the good' means in Greek. But if it is a report and if the report is correct, we must conclude that Greek is inadequate in this respect and does not make an important distinction between the concepts of *being desired* and *being desirable*. It is, of course, possible that Aristotle's report is incorrect, and it is possible that Aristotle is not giving a report at all but making a recommendation about how 'the good' is to be used. (See the discussion of definitions in Chapter 11.) But if Aristotle is stipulating that 'the good' as used by him shall mean 'that which is desired', we must insist that he can not also stipulate that it shall mean 'that which ought to be desired'. Thus, although we may be willing to accept Aristotle's definition (whatever kind it is) of 'the good'

---

[8] Aristotle, *Nicomachean Ethics*, trans. by W. D. Ross (Oxford: The Clarendon Press, 1925), Book I, Chap. 2, 1094 a 17–22.

as 'that which is desired for its own sake', we cannot by definition allow that notion also to be defined as 'that which ought to be desired'. Yet the fact that Aristotle does shift from one notion to the other, as though they meant the same thing, can be seen from a comparison of the following two passages:

Since there are evidently more than one end, and we choose some of these . . . for the sake of something else, clearly not all ends are final ends; but the chief good is evidently something final.[9]

The chief good, according to Aristotle, is that which we actually choose as final. Now compare this with the following quotation:

Therefore, if there is only one final end, this will be what we are seeking, and if there are more than one, the most final of these will be what we are seeking. Now we call that which is in itself worthy of pursuit more final than that which is worthy of pursuit for the sake of something else, and that which is never desirable for the sake of something else more final than the things which are desirable both in themselves and for the sake of that other thing, and therefore we call final without qualification that which is always desirable in itself and never for the sake of something else.[10]

Here the transition from the desired to the desirable has been made, but not legitimately. There is no reason to believe that whatever is desired by everyone is final in the sense in which Aristotle has now defined 'final'—namely, as desirable in itself.

Aristotle has gone from a notion of the good (that which is desired) to the idea of something being good in itself, good as an end, or intrinsically good. There is no justification for this transition, and no basis is given for the belief that that which everyone seeks is worthy of being sought. Aristotle has changed the subject, and although it may be that the good is (by definition) that which everyone does desire, there is no reason for believing that it is that which everyone ought to desire. Or, if we define the good as that which everyone ought to desire, there is no reason for believing that it is that which everyone does desire. In short, we need to see some reason why everyone *ought* to desire what he *does* desire (or vice versa), and Aristotle gives us none.

When philosophers speak of the good, they may have in mind either the end which all seek (assuming there is one), or the end which everyone ought to seek. Or they may be thinking of the totality of good things. Goodness, on the other hand, is the quality, property, characteristic, or set of characteristics, the possession of which makes something good. Aristotle is more inclined to use the expression 'the good' in either of the former ways, and

[9] *Ibid.*, Book I, Chap. 1097 a 24–28.
[10] *Ibid.*, Book I, Chap. 7, 1097 a 29–37.

Moore, in *Principia Ethica*, is inclined to use the expression to refer to the class of all good things. We are more interested, here, in clarifying the notion of intrinsic goodness. Consequently, it is relatively unimportant to ask what it is that all men seek, or even if there *is* one thing which they all seek; and we are interested here only in what they *ought* to seek. It is, then, the notion *goodness* that concerns us here, and this notion is truly one which moral philosophers have had a very difficult time unraveling.

2. G. E. Moore. Aristotle, although shifting his discussion from the desired to the desirable, does make the distinction between that which is good as an end and that which is good *only* as a means to an end. Moore distinguishes between the good and goodness, and holds that the latter is a property belonging to certain things. He is quite explicit about his beliefs about this property:

'Good', then, if we mean by it the quality which we assert to belong to a thing, when we say that the thing is good, is incapable of any definition, in the most important sense of that word.[11]

Moore believes that some things can be said to be good because of their consequences and others because of their intrinsic nature (no matter what their consequences). If a thing is good in this second way, it is intrinsically good. In other words, Moore holds that there is a simple indefinable property that belongs to some things and not to others, and it is by virtue of the possession of this property (which cannot be defined) that the things are good:

So far as I can see, there is no characteristic whatever which belongs to all things that are intrinsically *good* and only to them—except simply the one that they all *are* intrinsically good and *ought* always to be preferred to *nothing at all*, if we had to choose between an action whose sole effect would be one of them and one which would have no effects whatsoever.[12]

We shall not deal with the claim that there is a definite property of goodness here; it is enough to notice the sharp distinction Moore makes between the two kinds of goodness that such a theory allows.

3. W. D. Ross. A similar if somewhat more elaborately worked out distinction is made by W. D. Ross. Like Moore, Ross believes that there is a distinction between intrinsic goodness and extrinsic goodness. He tells us that "the intrinsically good is best defined as that which is good apart from any of the results it produces." [13] He also claims that "by calling a thing

[11] G. E. Moore, *Principia Ethica* (Cambridge: Cambridge University Press, 1959), p. 9. By permission of the publishers.

[12] G. E. Moore, *Ethics* (New York: Oxford University Press, 1965), p. 106.

[13] Ross, *op. cit.*, p. 68.

intrinsically good we mean that it would be good even if nothing else existed." [14] Such a suggestion naturally leads one to ask what it is for something to be good apart from its consequences and, although both Moore and Ross fail to give a definition of 'good' (in the previous quotations from Ross it is 'intrinsic' that is being defined), Ross makes an interesting attempt to explain the nature of this property. In this, he differs importantly from Moore, who claimed that it is a simple property, logically independent of any other properties. Ross' answer to the question "What is intrinsic goodness?" begins with the "definition" we have already noted: "By calling a thing intrinsically good we mean that it would be good even if nothing else existed." This allows him to assert that goodness must be, as Moore believed, a property predicable of objects, rather than, for example, a relation between two things (such as an object and a mind). There can be no relations other than pure identity if there are not two things to be related. Our question then is, what is the nature of this property? In answering this question, Ross makes a distinction between consequential and fundamental properties:

> The most salient difference [between goodness and yellowness] is that it [goodness] is a quality which anything that has it can have only in virtue of having some other characteristic; as e.g. a conscientious act is good in virtue of being conscientious. This I express later by describing it as a consequential and not a fundamental quality.[15]

Ross insists that there is a difference between intrinsic value (goodness) and most other qualities or properties. He suggests that we consider a rectangle; it has color, a size and a shape; let us also suppose that it has intrinsic value. Ross' point is that the three former properties may vary independently, but that this is not the case with intrinsic value:

> In fact, as a first approximation at any rate, we may say that the difference between goodness or value and such attributes as yellowness is that whereas the latter are *differentiae* (i.e. fundamental or constitutive attributes) of their possessors, the former is a *property* (i.e. a consequential attribute) of them. And in this respect goodness may be compared to the properties that geometry proves to hold good of various types of figure. But if we recognize the affinity, we must also recognize the marked difference between the two cases. (1) In the first place, it is quite arbitrary which of the attributes equilaterality and equiangularity is selected as the differentia of the kind of triangle which in fact possesses both; it is just as proper to say that the relative size of the angles determines the relative length of the sides, as *vice versa*. Value, on the other hand, seems quite definitely to be based on certain other qualities of its possessors, and not the other qualities on the value. In fact the distinction betwen differentia and property as fundamental and consequential attributes respectively is far more appropriate in this

[14] *Ibid.*, p. 75.
[15] *Ibid.*, p. 88.

case than in most of those to which it is applied, since this is one of the comparatively few cases in which one of the attributes is objectively fundamental and the other objectively consequential. We might call value a genuine as opposed to an arbitrarily chosen resultant (or property). (2) Another respect in which value differs from mathematical properties, as well as from certain other resultant properties, is that while mathematical (i.e. spatial, temporal, and numerical) properties follow from part of the intrinsic nature of their possessors, value follows from the *whole* intrinsic nature of its possessors. If a patch of colour is in shape an equilateral triangle, it will be an equiangular triangle, whatever be its size or colour; if it is of a certain colour, it will match certain other patches, whatever be its shape or size; it is of a certain size, it will be equal in size to certain other patches, whatever be its colour or shape. These attributes which are based on some single element in the nature of their possessors may be called parti-resultant properties. In contrast with these, value is a toti-resultant property, based on the whole nature of its possessors. And this is true not only of 'good', the adjective which expresses intrinsic value, but also of 'right' and 'beautiful', which are often classed with it, though 'right' does not stand for a form of value at all, and 'beautiful' does not stand for an intrinsic form of value.[16]

It is fairly clear that Ross feels that the intrinsic value of something follows in some way from its intrinsic nature, that value follows from the *entire* intrinsic nature of the thing, that the relation between the intrinsic value of a thing and its properties is a necessary relation (but not an analytic one), and that it would be inappropriate to say that the intrinsic nature "causes" the intrinsic value. There are serious and important questions which must be asked about these ideas, but they must wait their proper place, which is in the meta-ethical discussion of Ross' views, to be presented in Chapter 12. What is clear here is that Ross does distinguish between intrinisc goodness and the other sorts of goodness mentioned at the beginning of this chapter, and that he takes intrinsic goodness to be a kind of property possessed by certain things.

4. Two Further Alternatives. It is possible, however, to hold that some things are intrinsically good without being committed to either the simple-property view of Moore, or the consequential-property view of Ross; and what is interesting and relevant here is that, even if this alternative is taken, the method of drawing the distinction between intrinsic value and extrinsic value does not differ noticeably from that employed by these two thinkers.

a. DEFINING 'GOOD' IN TERMS OF 'RIGHT'. We have temporarily set aside attempts to define 'good' in terms of such properties as pleasantness. There is, however, a possibility of giving a definition of 'intrinsic value' in normative terms, somewhat as Moore attempted, in his utilitarianism, to define "A is right" in terms of the production of good consequences. If such an attempt were successful, ethics would not be in any sense reduced to some other discipline, but the number of concepts required would be diminished.

[16] *Ibid.*, pp. 121–22.

One attempt at such a definition has been made by A. C. Ewing, who suggests that to say that something is intrinsically good is to say that it ought to be chosen for its own sake, or that at least we have (in Ross' terms) a prima facie obligation to choose it.[17] There are difficulties with this view, many of which are recognized and accounted for by Ewing. For example, it is conceivable that we should want to say that pleasure or works of art are intrinsically good, and Ewing tries to get around saying that we would be morally wrong not to choose pleasure by distinguishing two senses of 'ought'. A thorough treatment of this topic would take us too far into meta-ethics, so we shall not pursue it here—but we have shown that it is possible to speak of intrinsic goodness without taking the expression 'intrinsic value' to be the name of a simple quality (as Moore would have it) or a toti-resultant property (as Ross claims).

b. INTRINSIC VALUE AND JUSTIFIED DESIRINGS. We do not wish to solve normative problems by definition, which is to say that we do not believe that one can identify intrinsic value with pleasure by asserting that the terms 'intrinsically valuable' and 'pleasant' mean the same thing. But there are other, more permissive, analyses of the notion of intrinsic value—more permissive in that the question of what things are intrinsically valuable is left open. This is true if 'intrinsic value' stands for a property, or if it means something like 'ought to be desired', and it is also true for the account of intrinsic value we are now about to discuss.

Richard B. Brandt makes the following suggestion:

> . . . "x is desirable" means "desiring x satisfies all the conditions that would be set, as a general policy, for the endorsement of attitudes governing or appraising choices or actions, by anyone who was intelligent and factually informed and had thought through the problems of the possible different general policies for the endorsement of such attitudes." We might abbreviate all this by saying that "x is desirable" means that "desiring x is justified." [18]

This definition of "X is desirable" is thought to be relevant to a discussion of intrinsic value, for Brandt claims that to say that something is a good thing is "nearly if not quite the same as to say" that it is a desirable thing.[19] Next he gives a definition of 'intrinsically desirable', one which should by now seem quite familiar to us:

> To say that something is intrinsically desirable is to say that it is desirable, taken just for itself, viewed abstractly, and in particular, viewed without respect to any consequences its existence will or may produce.[20]

[17] A. C. Ewing, *The Definition of Good* (New York: The Macmillan Company, 1947), pp. 145–85.

[18] Richard B. Brandt, *Ethical Theory* (Englewood Cliffs, N.J.: Prentice-Hall, Inc., © 1959), p. 302. By permission of the publisher.

[19] *Ibid.*, p. 301.

[20] *Ibid.*, p. 302.

Thus according to Brandt, 'intrinsic' is to be understood much as Moore and Ross understand it, but, unlike them, Brandt does not accept the view that either rightness or goodness is a property of objects. He offers his view as a "quasi-naturalist" position, and as we shall see in Chapter 11, his position has much in common with the so-called "ideal-observer theory." But if we concentrate upon the abbreviation of his definition of "X is desirable," more light may be thrown upon possible alternative treatments of intrinsic value. To say that "X is desirable," one need not say it is desired, but simply that *if* it is desired, that desire is justified.

As an example of something that may be said to be intrinsically desirable, Brandt mentions "a child who is swinging, in a rapturous state of enjoyment," and suggests that this state of mind (although possibly valuable for its effects) is something "worthwhile for itself alone." [21] It is easy to supply similar examples, and they all have an initial plausibility. But as we shall now see, such a position has not always been acceptable to philosophers.

5. Denials of Intrinsic Value. Some philosophers, either because of an inability to accept standard accounts of intrinsic value, or because of theories which tend in different directions, have suggested that although things may be valuable or desirable, nothing is *intrinsically* valuable or desirable. That is, they have maintained that anything said to be good can only be instrumentally good.

a. JOHN DEWEY. One attempted explanation of the notion of intrinsic value is in terms of the distinctions between ends and means—or the distinction between that which is valuable as a means to something else and that which is valuable without being a means to anything. Dewey attempts to break down this distinction, and insists that there is no such thing as a final end, one which can be worthwhile in itself, or intrinsically good.

Means are means; they are intermediates, middle terms. To grasp this fact is to have done with the ordinary dualism of means and ends. The "end" is merely a series of acts viewed at a remote stage; and a means is merely the series viewed at an earlier one.

The first or earliest means is the most important *end* to discover.

Means and ends are two names for the same reality. The terms denote not a division in reality but a distinction in judgment.

Having an end or aim is thus a characteristic of *present* activity. It is the means by which an activity becomes adapted when otherwise it would be blind and disorderly, or by which it gets meaning when otherwise it would be mechanical. In a strict sense an end-in-view is a *means* in present action; present action is not a means to a remote end. Men do not shoot because targets exist, but they set up targets in order that throwing and shooting may be more effective and significant.

[21] *Ibid.*, p. 303.

Not *the* end—in the singular—justifies the means; for there is no such thing as the single all-important end.[22]

Let us examine these quotations and attempt to see just what Dewey's position is on the matter of intrinsic value.

One who claims that some things are intrinsically good is inclined to say that these things are good or desirable even if they should have no consequences, and even if they and they alone should exist in the world. Dewey is strongly opposed to such a view, and would hold that anything with no consequences would have no value, that a thing can have value only in relation to human beings. More important, all value, for Dewey, is instrumental. The difference between means and ends, therefore, is really a distinction between two kinds of means, immediate and remote.

A short analysis of Dewey's theory of human behavior will make this notion more intelligible. He holds that all conscious or cognitive experience begins in conflict.

... reflection appears as the dominant trait of a situation when there is something seriously the matter, some trouble, due to active discordance, dissentiency, conflict among the factors of a prior non-intellectual experience; when, in the phraseology of the essays, a situation becomes tensional.[23]

It is possible to divide cognitive experience into three stages. In the first stage conflict arises, brute experience becomes tensional, habitual actions are blocked. The second stage is reflection, culminating in the suggestion of a hypothesis. Here one seeks immediate means to overcome the conflict. In the third stage, the hypothesis is tested in experience. This stage requires overt action. Choice is, for Dewey, "hitting in imagination upon an object which furnishes an adequate stimulus to the recovery of overt actions." [24] The important thing to discover, that which gets us going again, is the immediate means. An end in view is a means to present action. If the end is too remote or abstract it will not be effective.

Dewey seems to be saying that this is an accurate description of human behavior. Ultimate ends, things good in themselves, are worthless in action; they take on value only when that value is instrumental. But it is still possible to raise a number of potentially embarrassing questions here. Just because an end is remote, has it no relation to action? But even if this is so, how does this show that that "end" has no value? It certainly cannot be maintained that a remote (even ultimate) end would have intrinsic value only if it led to action,

[22] John Dewey, *Human Nature and Conduct* (New York: The Modern Library, 1930), pp. 34, 35, 36, 226, 229.
[23] John Dewey, *Essays in Experimental Logic* (New York: Dover Publications, Inc., 1916), p. 11.
[24] John Dewey, *Human Nature and Conduct, op. cit.*, p. 192.

for this would be raising action itself to some absolute value. Dewey some-times seems to be doing just that:

> Good consists in the meaning that is experienced to belong to an activity when conflict and entanglement of various incompatible impulses and habits terminate in a unified orderly release in action.[25]

It might, of course, be replied here that action, too, is only instrumentally good, but good for what? The answer can only be "further action," but why would one act at all under these circumstances? We suggest that, for all Dewey's denials of intrinsic value, he, too, holds that at least one thing, resolution of conflict, is worthwhile in itself. If he does not, then he is forced to the absurd position of holding that it is valuable only as a means to further resolutions, and so on *ad infinitum*.

b. RECENT "CONTEXTUALISTS." Many philosophers have been influenced by Dewey's thought, and several attempts have been made to do away with the notion of intrinsic value on Deweyan grounds. In effect, these positions are not much different from Dewey's, but the mode of exposition is sometimes clearer.

Abraham Kaplan, suggests that, for the pragmatist, a value judgment is always conditional:

> It is not that there are no qualifications, but that the qualifications are not brought into question. They are not problematic in the context of *that* valuation, but that is very different from saying that there is nothing that ever *could* be problematic. In every valuation, as a matter of principle, *all* our values are at stake.[26]

Kaplan sees this as a view that "circumstances alter cases" and suggests that any value can be questioned, but that not all values can be questioned at the same time. When one of our values *is* questioned, it is necessary only to show that it is instrumental in the production of other valuable things.

R. B. Brandt, in characterizing this view, says that the contextualist sug-gests that we look at ethical problems in context. If we would do this and thereby become aware of

> ... when and under what conditions practical problems arise, we would notice that we *always do have ethical premises available* for the assessment of any ethical principle about which we may have serious question.[27]

Thus, the contextualist argues that when it is questioned whether or not A is good, it is possible to prove that it is by showing that it leads to B, C, and

[25] *Ibid.*, p. 210.
[26] Abraham Kaplan, *The New World of Philosophy* (New York: Random House, 1961), p. 38.
[27] Brandt, *op. cit.*, p. 41.

D. If we want to know whether *B* is good, it is possible to prove that it is by showing what it leads to *A, C,* and *D.*

In an article on Dewey's ethical theory, Sidney Hook, a leading American philosopher of the pragmatist school, expounds and attempts to defend Dewey's claim that all values are instrumental.[28] He suggests that, whenever we are puzzled about the value of anything, it is always in a situation which involves choice. (This in itself does not seem correct—surely one can attempt for the sake of information, or simple curiosity, to assess the relative values of things.) More important, he claims:

> ... whenever we are mature enough to make a decision or even begin to be puzzled, we never start *de novo* or from scratch. We carry with us a heavily funded memory of things previously discovered to be valuable, ends or goods to which we feel committed as prima facie validities. The list will not be the same for everybody or for any one all the time, but it will contain values like health, friendship, security, knowledge, art, amusement in their plural forms.[29]

Any of these "values" may be questioned, but never all at once, and so we find that each of them—being instrumental to something else which is, in this context, unquestioned—has value.

In order to assess the contextualist theory of value, it will be necessary to review again the distinction between a theory of value and a theory of obligation. A theory of obligation is a theory about which actions are right and wrong, and a theory of value is a theory about which things (other than actions) are good and bad. There are very general teleological theories of obligation, usually stated in the form of rules—either very general rules, such as the principle of utility, or more specific ones, such as those held by the rule deontologists. No rules, however, are completely inviolate and free from exceptions, and on some occasions we may find that our rules do not tell us the right thing to do, in which case we alter the rules to accord with the particular judgment we have made. We then admit that our rules are summary rules and that this is one of the occasions upon which they do not apply. This is the position of act deontology, and the position we have defended in Chapter 5.

It might seem required, therefore, that we adopt a similar theory of value, and that we treat such claims as "pleasure is intrinsically good" as merely summary rules, and that this is really to adopt the contextualist position. But this is not so. It is perfectly compatible with act deontology to say that pleasure, and other things too, are intrinsically good, and that they remain so no matter what their consequences. This is not, for the act deontologist, or

[28] Sidney Hook, "The Desirable and Emotive in Dewey's Ethics," in *John Dewey: Philosopher of Science and Freedom,* ed. Sidney Hook (New York: The Dial Press, 1950), pp. 194–216.
[29] *Ibid.,* p. 197.

for any other thinker to say that these things always ought to be chosen. Pleasure of any sort, according to Bentham, is valuable, but he recognized that under certain conditions (when it is followed by a greater quantity of pain), we ought not choose it. The total situation therefore, composed of pleasure (which is intrinsically good) and the following pain (which is intrinsically evil), may have a negative balance. For Bentham, and for many others, situations are not pure, but composed of many elements, some of which are intrinsically good and some of which are not. The best situation is that which has the greatest balance of good over evil and, as a teleologist, Bentham claimed that this is the situation that should be chosen.

Thus, we can recognize that "circumstances alter cases" and at the same time admit things have intrinsic value. Any state of affairs can be questioned, but the values of its ingredients (pleasure, pain, knowledge, and so on) are not necessarily questionable. The need to examine the context of an evaluation does not lead necessarily to contextualism, and the fact that something of intrinsic value may be set in a total situation which is bad "on the whole" does not detract from its value.

It would seem, therefore, that much of the motivation for adopting a contextualist theory is misguided. One can quite well admit that "circumstances alter cases" and that any particular judgment about value "on the whole" may be subject to revision, without stipulating that evaluation of the ingredients also be subject to revision. Also, the necessity for recognizing the prima facie nature of moral rules for action does not mean that judgments of intrinsic value are also prima facie, even if we would like to say that our estimation of the total value of a whole is prima facie.

Yet these considerations are not sufficient to throw doubt on the contextualist's claim that all values are instrumental. His main argument, it seems, is to try to show that the phenomena of everyday judgments of value can be explained without recourse to the notion of intrinsic value. If he is correct, his theory is considerably more simple than one which recognizes intrinsic value, and for that reason it probably explains the phenomena better. But does the contextualist succeed in explaining the phenomena? He argues that, whenever we make a particular judgment of value, we prize something because it is a good means for achieving something else. This something else, however, also has value—but, according to the contextualist, that value too is instrumental. Thus, at any given moment, we accept a number of things as valuable, and we can show that other things are valuable by showing that these other things are means to the things we accept as valuable. If we wish to question one of our other accepted values, this is also possible, and it will be proved to be valuable if it can be shown to be a means to other things we accept as valuable.

The disturbing feature of this theory is that it really never explains why anything is desirable—i.e., worthy of being desired. The contextualist seems to live in a world of tools, but rather peculiar tools, for they make only other tools to make other tools, and so on. Dewey implied that "toolmaking" was itself worthwhile. But is it intrinsically worthwhile? If so, intrinsic value becomes a factor again. If "toolmaking" is only instrumentally valuable, what is it valuable for? The inevitable and unsatisfying answer is that it is valuable because it allows us to make more tools.

Let us put this objection another way. Suppose that there are just two kinds of thing in the world: A's and B's. Suppose, further, that A's are instrumental to bringing about B's, and vice versa. We probably will not question the value of both A's and B's at the same time, but it would not be convincing to argue that A's are good because they are of value in bringing about B's, and then to argue that B's are good because they are useful in the production of A's. Why should anyone bother producing either? Now it should be clear that the situation does not alter just because actual circumstances are more diverse. No matter how many kinds of thing there are in the world, unless some are thought to have value in themselves, none would be worth seeking.

Dewey attempted to avoid this difficulty by making activity itself a value, but that is to affirm what he is trying to deny. However, without such an alternative, there really is no point in doing anything. It does not seem therefore, that contextualism can explain why anything has value—why anything is worthy of being chosen.

6. Are There Intrinsic Values? Let us attempt to see how well the theory that something is intrinsically valuable stands up under the criteria for acceptability of theories. The first criterion was that serious objections to the theory can be answered adequately. One objection to the theory is that there is no such thing as intrinsic value because the admission of intrinsic values creates fixed and stable ends and denies any possibility of growth or progressive action. This is implied in Dewey's denial of intrinsic value, but the objection is misguided. If someone claims that happiness is intrinsically valuable (but agrees that there are conditions under which it is less valuable than something else, and does not hold a teleological theory of obligation), he does not seem to be arguing for fixed and stable ends in just the way Dewey supposed, for the ways of achieving happiness are indefinitely diverse, and there may be much debate over how it is to be attained, and much progress in the means of relieving suffering.

Another objection to the view that there are things with intrinsic value is that the notion of intrinsic value cannot be formulated. The worth of this objection cannot be decided upon without a thorough treatment of meta-ethical questions, but we can point out that there are many different formulations of what it is for something to have intrinsic value. Furthermore, this objection would, at least, have to crticize a number of important and distinct formulations. We are aware of no such undertaking.

The second criterion was that there be good reasons in favor of the theory.

Part of the difficulty in providing good reasons for the theory of intrinsic value is that, stated in this general way, the theory is empty. Any argument that was designed to show that pleasure, happiness, knowledge, and so on had intrinsic value would also have the force of showing that something with intrinsic value exists. For this reason, the best sort of argument for claiming that there is something with intrinsic value would be one to the effect that some particular thing has intrinsic value. We shall examine several arguments of this nature in Chapter 7.

The third criterion is that the theory either fits or explains the range of phenomena better than other competing theories. The only other competing theories here are contextualism and nihilism (the claim that nothing has value). Given that all or most men prize things, that they believe that some things remain good no matter what else happens, it is hard to see how the nihilist can explain this universal error. It is also hard to see how the contextualist can (without presupposing an intrinsic value) argue that instrumental value alone is sufficient to account for man's prizings and endeavors.

Finally, it would seem that, unless intrinsic value is assumed, pleasure is no better than pain, ignorance no better than knowledge. If one could establish two competing sets of "values," one consisting of all the things men have always prized, and the other consisting of things they have always shunned, and if it could further be shown that all the members of both classes were instrumentally good in the production of other members in their class, there would be no way to choose between sets. That is, suppose Class A consists of health, knowledge, pleasure, enjoyment, courage, industry, and so on and that Class B consists of disease, ignorance, pain, boredom, cowardice, slothfulness, and so on. A reasonably good case could be made for the claim that all the members of Class A were instrumentally good in the production of the other members of that class, and that all the members of Class B were instrumentally good in the production of the other members of that class. Now it is a fact that we would choose Class A, but the contextualist could not justify that choice. That is why his theory is mistaken.

There seem, therefore, to be no conclusive arguments against intrinsic value, and many arguments for it, depending upon what is thought to have intrinsic value. Furthermore, the hypothesis that such a thing exists is consistent with our preferred normative theory of obligation as well as with the phenomena of experience. Finally, a theory that denies the existence of intrinsic value will find it difficult to explain why anything is valuable in any sense, and it will be open to the objections already cited. It is likely, therefore, that some things are intrinsically valuable, and the question to be answered in the next chapter is "What?"

Exercises

Review

1. Evaluate Aristotle's claim that the good is what all men desire.
2. List a number of different ways in which philosophers have distinguished between *the good* and *goodness*.
3. What advantages are there in speaking about goodness rather than about the good?
4. What, according to Moore, is it that makes a thing intrinsically good?
5. What is the difference between the conceptions of intrinsic goodness held by Ross and by Moore?
6. Why would it be inconsistent for Ross to claim that goodness is a relation between an object and a mind?
7. Explain Ross' distinction between a consequential property and a fundamental property. What are his reasons for saying that goodness is a consequential property?
8. What is Ewing's suggestion for a normative definition of 'good'? How is this similar to Moore's definition of 'right'?
9. How can Brandt maintain that a thing is intrinsically valuable without also holding that intrinsic value is a property of an object?
10. According to Dewey, what is the difference between means and ends?
11. Why does Dewey feel that there is no such thing as intrinsic value? In what way might this be incompatible with the position he holds about the resolution of conflict?
12. Explain the tenets of the view called *contextualism*. What objections were raised to that view?

Applications

1. Aristotle speaks of *the good* rather than *goodness*. What theories about the notion of goodness are compatible with Aristotle's account of the good?
2. Finish the following dialogue (or carry it out reasonably far) as though you were speaking for (a) Aristotle, (b) Moore, (c) Dewey, (d) Beardsley, (e) yourself.
   A: I want to get up early.
   B: Why?
   A: So I can get to work on time.
   B: Why do you want to get to work on time?
   A: So I won't be fired.
   B: Why don't you want to be fired?
   A: Because if I'm fired I won't get paid each month.
3. Certain objections were raised to Dewey's theory. Are the same, or similar, objections relevant against Hook? If not, are other objections available?
4. Apply the criteria of acceptability to contextualism.
5. A version of contextualism is also presented in an article by Monroe Beardsley, "Intrinsic Value," *Philosophy and Phenomenological Research*, **26** (1965), 1–17, as well as in his book *Aesthetics* (New York and Burlingame: Harcourt, Brace & World, Inc., 1958), pp. 541–43 and Chap.

xii. Examine these passages and determine whether contextualism receives any further support from them.
6. Consider and discuss the following argument, entertained by a character in John Barth's *Floating Opera:*
    I. Nothing has intrinsic value. Things assume value only in terms of certain ends.
    II. The reasons for which people attribute value to things are always ultimately arbitrary. That is, the ends in terms of which things assume value are themselves ultimately irrational.
    III. There is, therefore, no ultimate "reason" for valuing anything.
    IV. Living is action in some form. There is no reason for action in any form.
    V. There is, then, no "reason" for living (or for suicide).

Bibliography

*BAYLIS, C. A. "Grading, Values, and Choice," *Mind*, **67** (1958), 485–501. A modification of the theory of Lewis. According to Baylis the existence of a pro-attitude is evidence for intrinsic value. This article is discussed in Beardsley and in Taylor, pp. 21 ff.

*BEARDSLEY, MONROE. "Intrinsic Value," *Philosophy and Phenomenological Research*, **26** (1965), 1–17. Beardsley claims that there are no good arguments showing that there is intrinsic value and attempts to give an argument against that notion. He is indebted to Dewey.

*BROAD, C. D. "G. E. Moore's Latest Published Views on Ethics," *Mind*, **70** (1961), 435–57.

DEWEY, JOHN. *Human Nature and Conduct*. New York: The Modern Library, 1930. A denial of ultimate ends and intrinsic values.

*DUNCAN-JONES, AUSTIN. "Good Things and Good Thieves," *Analysis*, **26** (1966), 113–8. A criticism of Geach's article.

———. "Intrinsic Value: Some Comments on the Work of G. E. Moore," *Philosophy*, **33** (1958), 240–73.

EWING, A. C. *The Definition of Good*. New York: The Macmillan Company, 1947, pp. 112–8 and 145–85. Ewing distinguishes many senses of 'good' and 'bad' and defines 'good' in terms of 'ought'.

FRANKENA, W. K. *Ethics*. Englewood Cliffs, N.J.: Prentice-Hall, Inc., 1963. Especially pp. 63–7, where Frankena distinguishes many uses of 'good'.

*GEACH, P. T. "Good and Evil," *Analysis*, **17** (1957), 33–42.

*HALL, EVERETT W. *What is Value?* New York: The Humanities Press, Inc., 1952. An attempt to "analyze value, to try to find out what it is."

*HARE, R. M. "Geach: Good and Evil," *Analysis*, **17** (1957), 103–11. A reply to Geach's article: "Good and Evil."

*HOOK, SIDNEY. "The Desirable and Emotive in John Dewey's Ethics," in *John Dewey: Philosopher of Science and Freedom*, ed. Sidney Hook. New York: The Dial Press, 1950, pp. 194–216.

*LEPLEY, RAY (ed.). *The Language of Value*. New York: Columbia University Press, 1957. A group of essays concerned with the "semantic or linguistic aspects of value theory." There are comments and responses to each essay.

——— (ed.). *Value: A Cooperative Inquiry*. New York: Columbia University Press, 1949. Essays on value. Cf. espccially Essay 1: "Reflection on Dewey's Questions about Value," by H. D. Aiken; and Essay 4: "Intrinsic Good: Its Definition and Referent," by A. Campbell Garnett. Criticisms and rejoinders follow the articles.

*Lewis, Clarence Irving. *An Analysis of Knowledge and Valuation*. La Salle, Ill.: The Open Court Publishing Company, 1946. Chapters 11 and 12 contain a discussion of intrinsic and extrinsic value.

Moore, G. E. *Ethics*. New York: Oxford University Press, Inc., 1965. Chapter 7 contains a discussion of intrinsic value.

*———. *Philosophical Studies*. London: Routledge & Kegan Paul, Ltd., 1922. Chapter 8: "The Conception of Intrinsic Value."

———. *Principia Ethica*. Cambridge: Cambridge University Press, 1959.

*Parker, Dewitt. *The Philosophy of Value*. Ann Arbor, Mich.: University of Michigan Press, 1957. Intrinsic value is identified with the satisfaction of desire but is expressed in volitional statements.

*Pepper, Stephen C. *A Digest of Purposive Values*. Berkeley and Los Angeles, Calif.: University of California Press, 1947. A study in general value-theory. Indebted to Perry.

*———. *The Sources of Value*. Berkeley and Los Angeles, Calif.: University of California Press, 1958.

*Perry, Ralph Barton. *General Theory of Value*. New York: Longmans, Green and Company, 1926.

*———. *Realms of Value*. Cambridge, Mass.: Harvard University Press, 1954. Value is defined in terms of interest.

Ross, W. D. *The Right and the Good*. Oxford: The Clarendon Press, 1930, Chapters 3 and 4.

Stevenson, C. L. *Ethics and Language*. New Haven, Conn.: Yale University Press, 1944, Chapter 8. Stevenson gives a noncognitivist definition of "X is intrinsically good," and discusses whether moralists can concentrate solely on judgments about ends. Influenced by Dewey.

Taylor, Paul W. *Normative Discourse*. Englewood Cliffs, N.J.: Prentice-Hall, Inc., 1961, Chapter 12. Taylor suggests nine ways of classifying values. Cf. also pp. 19–32, where the notions of intrinsic and extrinsic value are discussed.

Urmson, J. O. "On Grading," *Mind*, 59 (1950), 145–69. Urmson discusses the possibility that 'good' is a "grading label" applicable in many different types of contexts, but with different "criteria of application" in each.

*Von Wright, G. H. *The Varieties of Goodness*. London: Routledge & Kegan Paul, Ltd., 1963. The author distinguishes many kinds of goodness other than intrinsic and instrumental.

7

What Is Good?

If the conclusions of Chapter 6 are sound, then although a case has been made for the existence of intrinsic value, nothing has yet been said to help in a determination of what things or kinds of thing have intrinsic value. There are several different kinds of answers to this question, and there seem to be two ways to classify them. The most obvious dividing line between the two is one drawn between those thinkers who claim that one, and only one, thing (or kind of thing) has intrinsic value and those who claim that more than one thing (or kind of thing) does. We shall call the former *value monists* and the latter *value pluralists*, or *monists* and *pluralists*. There are also those who believe that the only sorts of thing that can have intrinsic value are elements of experience, and others who maintain that other things may also have intrinsic value. The former will be called *mentalists*; the latter, *nonmentalists*.

Most value monists are hedonists, maintaining that pleasure is the only thing with intrinsic value—and this, of course, classifies them as mentalists as well. But a value monist may also be a nonmentalist, holding, for example, that not pleasure but power or freedom is the only thing with intrinsic value. A value pluralist may maintain or deny that pleasure is intrinsically valuable; but if he holds that pleasure is intrinsically valuable, he must add that other things are also intrinsically valuable.

A. General Examination of Monistic Answers

Let us survey in a general way a number of monistic answers to the question "What things are intrinsically valuable?"

1. *Happiness.* It is often claimed that happiness is the only thing with intrinsic value. Aristotle, one of the first philosophers to make this claim, asks, "What is the highest of all goods achievable by action?":

Verbally there is very general agreement; for both the general run of men and people of superior refinement say that it is happiness, and identify living well and doing well with being happy; but with regard to what happiness is they differ, and the many do not give the same account as the wise. For the former think it is some plain and obvious thing, like pleasure, wealth or honour, . . .[1]

He then raises the question of the identification of pleasure with happiness, and (since most philosophers are more inclined to classify themselves among the wise than among the many) rejects such an answer. His reluctance to identify happiness with pleasure has not always been shared, even by the wise. John Stuart Mill, for example, makes it quite clear that he considers the two notions identical.

By happiness is intended pleasure and the absence of pain; and by unhappiness, pain, and the privation of pleasure.[2]

'Happiness' and 'pleasure' however, obviously do not ordinarily mean the same thing. As Aristotle pointed out long ago, 'happiness' signifies something long-standing and relatively stable.[3] Pleasure, on the other hand, usually comes in brief spells. The word 'happiness' in Greek is sometimes translated 'well-being', a translation which brings out the difference between pleasure and happiness; for the expression 'well-being' conveys something of what we intend to convey by the English word 'happiness'.

There are further differences between happiness and pleasure. For example, it may not be possible to be happy without feeling pleasure from time to time; there are certainly occasions when one would say that he is happy and yet deny that he feels any pleasure. Also, it is possible to feel pleasure (perhaps with the company of people you do not respect) and not to be happy.

Aristotle was of the opinion that happiness consists of the disposition to perform virtuous actions, and because this disposition is an element of a person's mental life, this view seems to be mentalistic.[4] But if happiness is interpreted in this way, the claim that everyone does seek this and only this and the claim that this is the only thing worth seeking for its own sake are both patently false.

If we interpret 'happiness' in some other way, perhaps by an elaboration on the expression 'well-being', then the claim that it is the only good gains some plausibility, but there are still serious problems. It is difficult to see how

---

[1] Aristotle, *Nicomachean Ethics*, trans. W. D. Ross (Oxford: The Clarendon Press, 1925), Book I, Chap. 4, 1095 a 16–23.

[2] John Stuart Mill, *Utilitarianism* (Indianapolis, New York: The Library of Liberal Arts Press, Inc., 1957), p. 10.

[3] Aristotle, *op. cit.*, Book I, Chapters 8–11.

[4] There is more to Aristotle's definition than this, and admittedly this needs expansion, but perhaps it will do for our purposes here.

anyone could defend the view that happiness is all anyone ever seeks, in view of the way that people behave. But aside from this, one will claim either that one seeks happiness only for oneself, or for oneself and others, or only for others. The last claim is obviously false, and the claims that one is always seeking happiness either for oneself or for others are nearly as obviously so.[5]

The more interesting claim is that happiness is the only thing worth seeking because it is the only thing that is intrinsically good. We may attack this view by adapting one of Plato's arguments used by Aristotle himself to prove that pleasure is not the only thing that is intrinsically good. Plato argues that although the addition of pleasure to any good (e.g., justice or temperance) makes it more desirable, this fails to establish that pleasure is the only good for every good is more worthy of choice along with another good than alone.[6] He then argues that "nothing else, any more than pleasure, can be the good if it is made more desirable by the addition of any of the things that are good in themselves."[7] If something is not made more desirable by the addition of something else, then that must be the good. But clearly happiness, in Aristotle's sense or in any other sense, would be made more desirable by the addition of any number of things—for example, pleasure or knowledge. It would seem, therefore, that happiness, even though it might be a good, is not *the* good, and that the value monist who argues that it is ignores fairly obvious and pervasive facts of our experience.

2. *Pleasure*. The hedonist holds the view that pleasure is the only thing that is intrinsically good. This treatment will be brief because hedonism is treated thoroughly later in this chapter. Here we shall merely point out what the hedonist maintains and mention one preliminary counter-argument to the view. The hedonist makes three claims:[8]

1. Pleasure is intrinsically good.
2. Nothing other than pleasure is intrinsically good.
3. Of two quantities of pleasure, the greater has more intrinsic value than the lesser.

The counter-argument is the one employed against the view that happiness is the only thing that is intrinsically good.[9] Hedonism is most often coupled

[5] Cf. the refutation of psychological egoism in Chapter 3. Psychological egoism gains no plausibility when coupled with this theory of value.

[6] Cf. Plato. *Philebus* 60 b–e.

[7] Aristotle, *Op. cit.*, Book X, Chap. 2, 1172 b 33–35.

[8] It can be noticed here that any value monist would make similar claims about that thing which he chooses to put forward as the only intrinsically valuable thing.

[9] One who proposes an argument of this sort against a value monist of any kind might be accused of merely begging the question. If S claims that X and X alone is good, he could only be refuted by this argument if the addition of some Y would make X more desirable. But his claim is that no Y is intrinsically good, hence no Y could be found the addition of which to X would make X more valuable. One can only suggest that here the

with egoism or utilitarianism to provide a complete normative teleological theory (hedonistic egoism or hedonistic utilitarianism), but just as we considered the theories of obligation separately in earlier chapters, we will consider the hedonistic theory in isolation. (See pp. 146–57.)

3. Good Will. It is possible to interpret Kant's view as a monistic theory of value. Kant claims that the only thing that is good *without qualification* is a good will:

> It is impossible to conceive anything at all in the world, or even out of it, which can be taken as good without qualification, except a *good will*. Intelligence, wit, judgement, and any other *talents* of the mind we may care to name, or courage, resolution, and constancy of purpose, as qualities of *temperament*, are without doubt good and desirable in many respects; but they can also be extremely bad and hurtful when the will is not good which has to make use of these gifts of nature, this will is entirely lacking in power to carry out its intentions; if by its quality. It is exactly the same with *gifts of fortune*. Power, wealth, honour, even health and that complete well-being and contentment with one's state which goes by the name of '*happiness*', produce boldness, and as a consequence often over-boldness as well, unless a good will is present by which their influence on the mind —and so too the whole principle of action—may be corrected and adjusted to universal ends; not to mention that a rational and impartial spectator can never feel approval in contemplating the uninterrupted prosperity of a being graced by no touch of a pure and good will, and that consequently a good will seems to constitute the indispensable condition of our very worthiness to be happy.
>
> A good will is not good because of what it effects or accomplishes—because of its fitness for attaining some proposed end: it is good through its willing alone—that is, good in itself. Considered in itself it is to be esteemed beyond comparison as far higher than anything it could ever bring about merely in order to favour some inclination or, if you like, the sum total of inclinations. Even if, by some special disfavour of destiny or by the niggardly endowment of step-motherly nature, this will is entirely lacking in power to carry out its intentions; if by its utmost effort it still accomplishes nothing, and only good will is left (not, admittedly, as a mere wish, but as the straining of every means so far as they are in our control); even then it would still shine like a jewel for its own sake as something which has its full value in itself.[10]

It is easy to see how a monistic interpretation may be put upon these passages by identifying the notion of being good without qualification with

---

matter lies open to inspection, and that we trust that inspection will reveal that (at least for happiness and pleasure) this is not the case. As we pointed out in Chapter 1, a theory must account for all the facts. It certainly seems that the addition of elements to either a pleasurable or a happy state might increase their value. If this is false it is up to the thinker who proposes one of these as the only valuable thing to show that it is false.

[10] Immanuel Kant, *Groundwork of the Metaphysics of Morals*, trans. H. J. Paton (London: Hutchinson University Library, 1948), pp. 61–62. By permission of Barnes & Noble, Inc., publisher. By permission of Hutchinson Publishing Group, Ltd., publishers.

that of being intrinsically good. Kant claims that the good will "is good through its willing alone—that is, good in itself." In Chapter 6 we had some trouble arriving at a satisfactory explanation of intrinsic value, but it seemed that the notion could be understood to imply at least two things: if a thing is intrinsically good, it would remain so even if it were the only thing in the universe, and it remains good no matter what its consequences are. Kant explicitly states that the good will has the first of these characteristics. He also claims that it remains good no matter what its consequences, and, furthermore, that a good will is the only thing which—if added to another good thing—is capable of preventing that other thing from being bad and hurtful. This, of course, presupposes that such things as power, wealth, honor, health, and happiness are bad if they have evil or hurtful consequences. But this must mean that Kant cannot claim that these are intrinsically good. He also feels that pleasure, honor, health, and so on, are not good if they are possessed by a person without a good will. He says that uninterrupted prosperity, for example, would not be approved by an impartial spectator if it were not graced by a good will. This is to suggest that a necessary condition of the goodness of these things is that they be possessed by a person with a good will. Again, it seems that we are justified in concluding that, for Kant, the only intrinsically good thing is a good will.

Many objections can be raised against this view. Kant is claiming three things: (1) only a good will has intrinsic value, (2) a good will is the only thing which when added to another thing is capable of preventing that thing from being bad and hurtful. It is not quite clear whether he is also claiming that the addition of a good will is always sufficient to ward off evil consequences, but some of the phrases in the passage quoted above suggest that. Finally (3) he is claiming that things which are ordinarily good are not so if possessed by someone who lacks a good will.

Against the first point we can employ the familiar antimonistic argument. Also it is hard to see why a good will which has been rendered completely impotent by circumstances should be preferred to a collection of other goods accompanied by a will which is neither good nor bad, or often good but sometimes bad. Yet Kant's theory would force us always to choose the good will.

Against the second point it can be argued that the addition of a good will is sometimes not sufficient to ward off evil consequences, and that other goods sometimes do more to improve the total intrinsic value of a situation. Knowledge, and a rigid adherence to the oath of Hippocrates, would seem to be preferable in the operating room to a good will alone. Also, a good will added to knowledge sometimes will not prevent that knowledge from being harmful if courage is lacking. For example, a medical student who would like to save a traffic accident victim by performing an emergency operation, may—through cowardice—fail to do so.

Kant could reply here that a good will contains all of the needed things—
no will is good unless it is accompanied by knowledge, courage, and so on.
But to attempt to account for these difficulties in this way is to pack so much
into the notion of a good will that that notion loses all descriptive content and
to be guilty of making ad hoc additions to the specification of a good will.

We can argue against Claim 3 in two ways. First we can point out that the
fact that bad consequences follow from the application of a bad will to, say,
knowledge, does not, in itself, show that the knowledge is bad or not intrinsically good. It is compatible with the fact that knowledge is intrinsically good
that a combination of knowledge and a bad will is bad. If this is not so, then
we can also show that a good will is bad by showing that a good will plus ignorance can lead to evil consequences. Because we want to avoid the latter
conclusion (for, among other things, we do not want to beg the question
against Kant), we shall also have to say that the former conclusion cannot be
drawn.

Another way of criticizing this last point would be to present a counterexample. What would be required is a circumstance in which S has a bad
will, but also in which one of the goods which Kant is willing to acknowledge
is present, and, finally, in which the total situation is good. Let us suppose
that S is a tyrant who treats his subjects cruelly, and that the main reason for
his acting in this way is that he does not have a good will. Let us suppose that
one day one of his ministers gives him a book of poetry to read, and that the
tyrant reads the book and is, as a consequence, happy for the whole day. Let
us even add that the tyrant does not deserve any good that he achieves or
enjoys. These conditions do not make it bad for the tyrant to have the happiness that he does. We might even argue, although we need not do so, that
the experience the tyrant has is valuable because it will lead him to be a better
ruler. If that were so, we might even argue that we have an obligation to
make the tyrant happy. It is not difficult to see that the same sort of counter
example can be constructed for the other goods that Kant lists.

We may conclude that, if Kant identifies being intrinsically good with
being good without qualification, there is really no adequate defense of his
value monism, and rather strong antimonist arguments against it.

4. *Other Candidates*. It is much more difficult to maintain that a thing is
the only intrinsically good thing than to maintain that it is one intrinsically
good thing among others. A number of other possibilities for the sole intrinsic
good have been advanced, which would be defended and criticized in much
the same way as the monistic theories we have considered. Nietzsche has
often been mentioned as holding that power is the only thing with intrinsic
value. A number of early twentieth-century philosophical idealists claimed that
"*self-realization*" is the only intrinsically good thing. Apparently they believed
that a man must develop those elements of himself which can be developed,
and that such a development is the only thing of value. Theologians have

often claimed that God is the only good, and to suggest this may be to suggest that God is the only proper object of men's love and desire.

The number of candidates for the one intrinsically good thing are multiplied considerably by the ambiguity of the term 'happiness'. What *we* mean by happiness is far from what Aristotle meant by it, and even if we agreed with Aristotle in saying that happiness is the only intrinsically good thing, the agreement would be merely verbal. If we allow each different view of happiness to count as a distinct theory of value, then we have many more monistic theories than we seemed to have at first. Aristotle, the Stoics, and Augustine all claimed that happiness is the only thing intrinsically good, but whereas by 'happiness' Aristotle meant something like 'habitual virtuous actions of the soul', and the Stoics meant 'virtue' (which they sometimes defined as 'living according to nature', Augustine meant 'communion with, or possession of, God'.

In general, to refute a monistic theory of value, it is usually sufficient to employ some version of the argument used by Plato, Aristotle, and many others. It runs like this: "You say A is the only intrinsically good thing, but would not a world in which only A existed be less preferable than a world in which A was combined with some B?" Suppose A is knowledge. The argument, then, would run that, although knowledge is good and its existence is desirable, the existence of knowledge accompanied by pleasure is even more desirable. This is the standard pluralist argument against the value monists, and it is a reasonably good one. It would seem, then, that if it makes sense to claim that anything at all is intrinsically good, more than one thing must be so.

Exercises

Review

1. Make a chart illustrating the combinations of value monism and pluralism with mentalism and nonmentalism. Give an illustration of each view.
2. How does Aristotle agree with John Stuart Mill about what the good is, and how does he differ?
3. Discuss the differences in ordinary English between the meanings of 'happiness' and 'pleasure'.
4. What is the antimonist argument used by Plato and adapted by Aristotle? In this chapter it was also used against Aristotle. How was this done?
5. What are the three tenets of hedonism?
6. What, for Kant, is the relation between being good without qualification and being intrinsically good? What arguments were raised against his view?
7. What are some other candidates for the one thing with intrinsic value?

Applications

1. Make a list of things that might be considered to be intrinsically good. What sort of arguments might be offered for, and against, the candidates you suggest? Does the difference in candidate in any way alter the argument? If so, how?

2. List a number of possible definitions of 'happiness' and evaluate them. (One way to expand your list is to look in a good dictionary.)

B. Pleasure Again—Hedonism

Before we accept the pluralist conclusion, let us turn to the most popular monistic theory of value—hedonism. We have already characterized hedonism as maintaining three propositions:

1. Pleasure is intrinsically good.
2. Nothing other than pleasure is intrinsically good.
3. Of two quantities of pleasure, the greater has more intrinsic value than the lesser.[11]

1. *Pleasure and Pain.* In order to consider the acceptability of hedonism as a normative theory of value it will be necessary to begin with a consideration of what is meant by 'pleasure', and its customary contrasting term, 'pain'.

a. EPICURUS. This early Greek thinker, from whom the name 'epicureanism' has been (somewhat unjustly) taken, suggests that pleasure is simply the absence of pain:

When we say, then, that pleasure is the end and aim, we do not mean the pleasures of the prodigal or the pleasures of sensuality, as we are understood to do by some through ignorance, prejudice, or willful misrepresentation. By pleasure we mean the absence of pain in the body and of trouble in the soul.[12]

And again:

The magnitude of pleasure reaches its limit in the removal of all pain. When pleasure is present, so long as it is uninterrupted, there is no pain either of body or of mind or of both together.

Pleasure in the flesh admits no increase when once the pain of want has been removed; after that it only admits of variation.[13]

Here the definition of 'pleasure' is dependent upon that of 'pain', which was believed to need no definition. Pleasure is a neutral state in which the pains of the body and the desires or wants of the soul have been conquered. There

---

[11] Sometimes the hedonist says that pleasure is intrinsically good and pain is intrinsically evil, that only these two things are good and evil, and that the goodness and evilness of a thing is a function of the quantity of pleasure and pain it produces, but we shall not explicitly introduce the notion of pain here. The topic of pain, and its relation to pleasure will be dealt with in the following section.

[12] From a letter of Epicurus quoted by Diogenes Laertius in *Lives of Eminent Philosophers*, reprinted in Richard B. Brandt, *Value and Obligation* (New York and Burlingame: Harcourt, Brace & World, Inc., 1961), p. 24.

[13] *Ibid.*, pp. 25–26.

certainly may be such a state, but to suggest that there is nothing more to pleasure than this is to contradict common experience.

b. HENRY SIDGWICK. Henry Sidgwick (sometimes described as one of the most able and careful of all moral thinkers) dismisses Epicurus' view on just these grounds: "This doctrine is opposed to common sense and common experience." [14] Here is Sidgwick's own definition of 'pleasure':

> I propose therefore to define Pleasure . . . as a feeling which, when experienced by intelligent beings, is at least implicitly apprehended as desirable or—in cases of comparison—preferable.[15]

The difficulties with this definition are serious and somewhat subtle. The definition is both too narrow and too broad—that is, it allows us to call some things pleasure which are not, but it also prevents us from calling many things pleasure which are. It is possible that Sidgwick does not mean to tell us how the word 'pleasure' is used, but to propose that we adopt this definition. If the definition is a stipulation rather than a report of actual usage, the criticisms we are about to make will not apply, but we will be justified in asking why we should accept such a definition, especially one that differs from the ordinary sense of the word. Our main argument against accepting this as a stipulation to revise our language is that it would leave us without a word to serve the purpose that 'pleasure' now does.

First, Sidgwick's definition is too broad—that is, it allows us to say that certain experiences are experiences of pleasure when they are not really so. Suppose that pleasure is a "feeling which is implicitly apprehended as desirable," then there are many feelings which are so apprehended but which we would never ordinarily identify as feelings of pleasure. For example, someone may desire (and find desirable) the feeling of mild hunger or thirst, or the feeling of expectation before a race, yet it is difficult to see how these can be said to be pleasure or feelings of pleasure. It may be suggested that they are all pleasurable, but this suggests, at least, that pleasure itself is not some specific feeling. Our first objection, therefore, is that, if pleasure is what Sidgwick says it is, many feelings not now identified with pleasure would have to be so identified.

It will not help to say that all these feelings are pleasurable, because to say that a feeling is pleasurable is, in a way, to deny that it is a feeling *of* pleasure, and to suggest that it is some other kind of feeling which has the quality of being pleasurable. This is not really paradoxical, for, analogously, feelings vary in intensity, but it is not usually thought that an intensely painful feeling is "a feeling of intenseness" plus "a feeling of pain."

[14] Henry Sidgwick, *The Methods of Ethics* (7th ed., London: The Macmillan Co., Ltd., 1962), p. 125.
[15] *Ibid.*, p. 127.

Another objection to Sidgwick's definition is that it is too narrow. If pleasure is a feeling, it is not always apprehended as desirable or preferable. We often pass up pleasures for other satisfactions, which is to say that we do *not* prefer them on every occasion, even though we might well admit that they would still be pleasures (or at least pleasurable). Of course it might be replied here that it is only necessary that they be apprehended as "implicitly" desirable or preferable, but it is far from clear what the force of this 'implicitly' is at this point.

c. GILBERT RYLE. A more radical criticism of Sidgwick's definition of pleasure might begin from the not implausible claim that pleasure is not a feeling at all. Such a view has been defended by Gilbert Ryle, a contemporary British philosopher. Ryle argues that one of the main differences between pleasure and feelings (such as pain) is that, whereas pain is localizable and datable, pleasure is not:

> Now though we are, in effect, told by this kind of theory that the role of the concept of *pleasure* is the precise counterpart of the role of the concept of *pain*, as that of *north* is the counterpart of that of *south*, there are insuperable objections to playing them as proper counterparts. We are ready to say that some things hurt us, while others please or delight us; and ready to say that some things give us pain, while others give us pleasure. But we fight shy of saying, for example, that two minutes ago I had a pain, and one minute ago I had a pleasure; or that while my headache was the effect of eye-strain, my pleasure was the effect of a joke or of the smell of a rose. We can tell the doctor where it hurts and whether it is a throbbing, a stabbing or a burning pain; but we cannot tell him, nor does he ask, where it pleases us, or whether it is a pulsating or a steady pleasure. Most of the questions which can be asked about aches, tickles and other sensations or feelings cannot be asked about our likings and dislikings, our enjoyings and detestings. In a word, pleasure is not a sensation at all, and therefore not a sensation on one scale with an ache or twinge.[16]

Ryle's two main points are that we do not locate pleasures temporally and that we do not locate them in specific places in our bodies. If this is true, then pleasure differs from pain in two important respects.

But, as Ryle recognizes, caution is needed here. Let us distinguish *sensation words*, or words that describe a definite localizable sensation (a *pain* in the neck, for example), from *quality words*, or words that predicate some quality of something (the twinge was *severe*). There is no sensation of severeness; rather, 'severe' qualifies the sensation. In this language then, Ryle might be thought to be saying that whereas 'pain' and its cognates refer to sensations, 'pleasure' and its cognates describe qualities of other sensations. Thus the correct locution would be 'a pleasurable twinge' not 'a twinge of pleasure'.

There are difficulties with putting matters in this way though, for 'painful',

---

[16] Gilbert Ryle, *Dilemmas* (Cambridge: Cambridge University Press, 1960), pp. 57–58.

at least, is sometimes used as a quality word; as in 'a painful meeting'. A difference between pleasure and pain, however, can still be found, for it can be argued that 'pain', 'painful', and so on, can operate as sensation words *or* quality words, but 'pleasure', 'pleasurable', and so on can operate only as quality words. If this is so, there is still an important difference between the uses of the two expressions, and it is still incorrect to treat pain as simply a negative quantity of pleasure.

The relevance of Ryle's point will be seen when we come to examine the standard formulations of hedonism, for almost all of them treat pleasure as though it were on a par with pain. Sidgwick, for example, states:

> It will be convenient for the most part to speak of pleasure only, assuming that pain may be regarded as the negative quantity of pleasure, and that accordingly any statements made with respect to pleasure may be at once applied, by obvious changes of phrase, to pain.[17]

It is just this assumption that Ryle is calling into question, and it is easy to see that, if Ryle is correct, some new statement of hedonism is called for.

2. *Arguments for Hedonism.* To attack hedonism it is not necessary to question its first tenet; for a nonhedonist can subscribe to it. The hedonist must be most concerned with the defense of his second and third tenets. We will now show how the hedonist attempts to carry this defense out.

a. PSYCHOLOGICAL HEDONISM. The view that a man always seeks good for himself is thought by some to support the view that he either has the right to do so, or that he ought to do so (see Chapter 3). But we are not interested here in considering views as to what someone ought to do or what someone has the right to do, but rather with questions as to what has intrinsic value. Ethical hedonism maintains that the only thing of value is pleasure, and the related psychological view would be that pleasure is the only thing anyone really values for itself. Like ethical hedonism, psychological hedonism has three tenets:

1. Pleasure is desired as an end.
2. Nothing other than pleasure is ever desired as an end.
3. Of two quantities of pleasure, the greater is always desired in preference to the lesser.

Now if psychological hedonism provides any support for ethical hedonism it will most likely be true that each tenet of psychological hedonism supports the corresponding tenet of ethical hedonism. John Stuart Mill is frequently quoted as one who attempts to support ethical hedonism by appealing to psychological hedonism. This interpretation of Mill is based primarily on the following statement:

[17] Sidgwick, *op. cit.*, p. 125.

The only proof capable of being given that an object is visible is that people actually see it. The only proof that a sound is audible is that people hear it; and so of the other sources of our experience. In like manner, I apprehend, the sole evidence it is possible to produce that anything is desirable is that people do actually desire it. If the end which the utilitarian doctrine proposes to itself were not, in theory and in practice, acknowledged to be an end, nothing could ever convince any person that it was so. No reason can be given why the general happiness is desirable, except that each person, so far as he believes it to be attainable, desires his own happiness. This, however, being a fact, we have not only all the proof which the case admits of, but all which it is possible to require, that happiness is a good, that each person's happiness is a good to that person, and the general happiness, therefore, a good to the aggregate of all persons.[18]

This is, at best, however, only a defense of Tenet 1 of hedonism, making use of the corresponding principle of psychological hedonism. As Mill correctly points out, this does not prove that happiness is the only valuable thing: "To do that, it would seem, by the same rule, necessary to show, not only that people desire happiness, but that they never desire anything else." [19]

Mill does seem to suggest that Tenet 2 of ethical hedonism can be proved by appealing to Tenet 2 of psychological hedonism. His argument that happiness is the only thing that people *actually* desire begins by an apparently contradictory admission:

Now it is palpable that they do desire things which, in common language, are decidedly distinguished from happiness. They desire, for example, virtue and the absence of vice no less really than pleasure and the absence of pain.[20]

This would be no problem as long as it were admitted that virtue is desired only as a means to a more ultimate end—namely, happiness. But Mill makes an even greater concession. He grants that it is possible to desire virtue for itself:

Virtue, according to the utilitarian doctrine, is not naturally and originally part of the end, but it is capable of becoming so; and in those who love it disinterestedly it has become so, and is desired and cherished, not as a means to happiness, but as a part of their happiness.[21]

Nor does Mill deny that even money is "in many cases desired in and for itself." [22]

---

[18] Mill, *op. cit.*, pp. 44–45. Note that Mill admittedly uses 'happiness' as a synonym for 'pleasure'.

[19] *Ibid.*, p. 45.

[20] *Ibid.*, p. 45.

[21] *Ibid.*, p. 46.

[22] *Ibid.*

Mill seems to be under the impression that it is possible to say all this and still hold Tenet 2. Money and virtue are not desired for themselves as money or virtue, but rather as pleasure or happiness. This means that the miser, like everyone else, desires only pleasure or happiness—only he comes to identify money with pleasure or happiness, or at least to suppose that it is a part of pleasure or happiness. Mill's revised conclusion, then, is that men desire nothing which is not either happiness (i.e., pleasure), a means to it, or a part of it, and in this sense, Mill does subscribe to Tenet 2 of psychological hedonism.

Let us turn to Mill's proof of the corresponding claims of ethical hedonism. He uses the term 'desirable' and we shall continue to interpret this as 'worthy of being desired'. One of the best known criticisms of Mill's "proof" of ethical hedonism is that he commits what seems to be a very simple linguistic error:

> Well, the fallacy in this step is so obvious that it is quite wonderful how Mill failed to see it. The fact is that 'desirable' does not mean 'able to be desired' as 'visible' means 'able to be seen'. The desirable means simply what *ought* to be desired or *deserves* to be desired; just as the detestable means not what can be but what ought to be detested and the damnable what deserves to be damned.[23]

Now Moore is quite correct in pointing out that there is an important difference between the meaning of 'visible' and the meaning of 'desirable'. But it might be suggested that Mill was aware of this and that, although he took the fact of a thing's being seen as a "proof" that it is visible, he only took the fact that a thing is desired as "evidence for" its desirability. In that case the psychological premise would not "prove" the ethical one, but, again, because people are at least sometimes correct in what they desire, it does seem to be evidence for it. Furthermore, if no one ever desired happiness, but always something else, that would be strong evidence that it was not desirable.

When we look closely at what Mill actually says, we discover that he explicitly declares that

> Questions of ultimate ends are not amenable to direct proof. Whatever can be proved to be good must be so by being shown to be a means to something admitted to being good without proof. . . . Considerations may be presented capable of determining the intellect either to give or withhold its assent to the doctrine; and this is equivalent to proof.[24]

Now it is unlikely that Mill should have forgotten the weaker sense of 'proof' he pointed out in the beginning of his book. However, if we keep this in mind

[23] G. E. Moore, *Principia Ethica* (Cambridge: Cambridge University Press, 1959), p. 67. By permission of the publishers.

[24] Mill, *op. cit.*, p. 7.

when we examine his argument, we will not be so inclined (as Moore was) to demand a proof with strict logical cogency. What we must admit, and what Mill must admit, too, is that he has not proved, in any strict sense, that only pleasure is intrinsically good.

Suppose that Mill is right, that pleasure is the only thing originally desired for itself. If that were true, then it would seem odd to claim that other things were intrinsically valuable. It would, of course, be possible that there are other intrinsically valuable things not yet recognized as such, but it would be unlikely that in all this time every one of them should have been missed, desired only as a means to pleasure, or desired because they were mistaken for pleasure. To that degree therefore we can agree that Tenet 2 of psychological hedonism, if correct, provides some evidence for Tenet 2 of ethical hedonism.

However, it is possible to question Tenet 2 of psychological hedonism, and thereby question the support for Tenet 2 of ethical hedonism. One can deny that pleasure is the only thing that anyone ever desires as an end in itself, and one can argue that, although Mill is correct in suggesting that people desire things other than pleasure, he is not correct in suggesting that this is because these things are mistaken for pleasure. It is possible to ask of Mill what reasons he has for believing that any given thing desired for itself is actually mistaken for pleasure. It is hard to see how he can defend this claim without appealing to the principles of psychological hedonism itself.

There is another argument which can be used to show that Tenet 2 of psychological hedonism is false. Suppose that one is approached by an enthusiastic experimental psychologist who has invented a "pleasure machine," a coffin-like box in which one lies motionless and receives from bottles all the food required for life and from wires attached to the brain continuous "pleasure stimuli." Although this machine will exclude all stimuli other than those of pure pleasure, few people would be content to commit themselves to spending the rest of their lives in such a box. But if Tenet 2 of psychological hedonism were true, people would jump at such an opportunity. What this example shows, therefore, is not that people do not desire pleasure at all, but that they desire other things as well, and that—given a choice—almost everyone would choose a mixed diet of pleasure and other things. If this is true, and there is much empirical evidence for believing it is, then Tenet 2 of psychological hedonism is false.

It is not enough for the psychological or the ethical hedonist to hold Tenets 1 and 2; he must also subscribe to Tenet 3, the claim that the amount of pleasure is always proportional to the amount of desire (the psychological view) and to the desirability (the ethical view). It does not seem that this claim was held by Mill, and so there are good reasons for doubting whether he can be considered to be a psychological or an ethical hedonist in the full sense. His disagreement with Jeremy Bentham over this point is one of the famous disagreements in the history of ethics. Bentham subscribed to all three tenets of psychological and ethical hedonism, although it is not clear that he used the one as support for the other. He is usually called *a quantitative hedonist,* which is to say that he believes that the quantity of pleasure is the only determining factor in its value. He is often quoted as having said: "Quantity of pleasure being equal, pushpin is as good as poetry." Mill could not accept this, however, and argued:

It is quite compatible with the principle of utility to recognize the fact that some kinds of pleasure are more desirable and more valuable than others. It would be absurd that, while in estimating all other things quality is considered as well as quantity, the estimation of pleasures should be supposed to depend on quantity alone.[25]

Here Mill is explicitly denying Tenet 3 of ethical hedonism. His claims come to this: everyone desires pleasure and really no one desires anything else, and this fact lends some support to the claim that only pleasure is desirable. But in denying Tenet 3 of psychological and ethical hedonism, he seems to be claiming that people do not always desire the greater pleasure over the lesser, and that the greater pleasure is not always more desirable. For Bentham, the desiredness and the desirability of anything are directly proportional to the quantity of pleasure it provides, and Mill objects to both of these claims.

It is sometimes suggested, and not unplausibly, that although Mill is correct in his denial of Tenet 3, Bentham alone is consistent. This is to suggest that there is an inconsistency in accepting Tenet 2 and denying Tenet 3. If two things vary in their desirability, there must be some factor (not itself without value) that makes the difference. If so, and if pleasure alone is valuable, only an addition of pleasure could bring about an increase in the value of anything. Bentham accepts this but Mill does not, and therefore Mill is sometimes criticized as being inconsistent. But Mill is not without an answer to the question of why some pleasures are more desirable than others:

Of two pleasures, if there be one to which all or almost all who have experience of both give a decided preference, irrespective of any feeling of moral obligation to prefer it, that is the more desirable pleasure.[26]

But this really tells us no more than *how to determine* whether one pleasure is more desirable than another. Mill does not tell us what is responsible for the greater desirability of the one, nor is it easy to see how, given his acceptance of Tenet 2, he could. This entire argument rests upon the claim that it is not possible that the value of a thing could be altered by the alteration of one of its valueless elements. But we shall not attempt to resolve this difficult issue here, for Tenet 3 of psychological hedonism (and Tenet 3 of ethical hedonism) may be criticized from another direction.

[25] *Ibid.,* p. 12.
[26] *Ibid.*

G. E. Moore has argued in the following way:

Is it true that one whole will be intrinsically better than another, whenever and only when it contains more pleasure, no matter what the two may be like in other respects? It seems to me almost impossible that any one, who fully realizes the consequences of such a view, can possibly hold that it *is* true. It involves our saying, for instance, that a world in which absolutely nothing except pleasure existed—no knowledge, no love, no enjoyment of beauty, no moral qualities—must yet be intrinsically better—better worth creating—provided only the total quantity of pleasure in it were the least bit greater, than one in which all these things existed *as well as* pleasure. It involves our saying that, even if the total quantity of pleasure in each was exactly equal, yet the fact that all the beings in the one possessed in addition knowledge of many different kinds and a full appreciation of all that was beautiful or worthy of love in their world, whereas *none* of the beings in the other possessed any of these things, would give us no reason whatever for preferring the former to the latter. It involves our saying that, for instance, the state of mind of a drunkard, when he is intensely pleased with breaking crockery, is just as valuable, in itself—just as well worth having, as that of a man who is fully realizing all that is exquisite in the tragedy of King Lear, provided only the mere quantity of pleasure in both cases is the same. Such instances might be multiplied indefinitely, and it seems to me that they constitute a *reductio ad absurdum* of the view that intrinsic value is always in proportion to quantity of pleasure.[27]

Here Moore seems to be arguing that, not only would no reasonable person choose the more pleasurable whole when other goods are lacking, but also that there are differences of value even when the amount of pleasure in two wholes is the same, and this argument has much force.

b. AN ANALYTIC ARGUMENT FOR ETHICAL HEDONISM. Bentham does not seem to use psychological hedonism to support ethical hedonism, although he subscribes to both views. He seems to feel that ethical hedonism is true by definition. That is, he seems to believe that "X is good" just means "X is pleasant." Consider the following passage:

Now, pleasure is in *itself* a good: nay, even setting aside immunity from pain, the only good: pain is in itself an evil; and indeed, without exception, the only evil; or else the words good and evil have no meaning.[28]

This is a clear case of a naturalistic theory of the meaning of 'good', and since we shall show that naturalism is not acceptable (see Chapter 11) we shall not take the time to criticize this definition in any detail at this point. Let us merely point out that we are inclined to agree with Mill that some pleasures

[27] G. E. Moore, *Ethics*, p. 102.
[28] Jeremy Bentham, *Introduction to the Principles of Morals and Legislation* (New York: Hafner, 1948), p. 102.

can be worse than others even though they are greater, or that some lesser pleasures are preferable to some greater ones. If this is true, then 'pleasure' cannot mean 'good', for then 'more pleasurable' would mean 'better'.

3. *A Serious Difficulty for Hedonists.* If one should ask the hedonist how he can speak accurately about the comparative amounts of pleasures and pains, no satisfactory answer is likely to be forthcoming. Obviously, many people find listening to Bach more pleasurable than watching football games, but they might find it difficult to say just *how much* more pleasurable the former experience is. It is sometimes suggested, rather humorously, that a unit of pleasure called a *hedon* be provided to make the computation easier. This suggestion has the advantage of showing how pointless it is to set up any exact scale. What, it might be asked, is the standard hedon? Perhaps the amount of pleasure a normal person would feel during a twenty-second immersion in a tub of 100° water after standing naked in a rainstorm for five minutes (where the rain has an average temperature of 50°)? But it is clear that this specification, or any other, raises many problems. It presupposes the ability to talk about and measure quantities of pleasure in a normal person, the ability to apply the unit consistently to everyone, and the ability to arrive at some reliable means of comparing different quantities of pleasure of different people. Anything like an accurate "pleasure scale" is doomed to failure. As Sidgwick points out:

> The first and most fundamental assumption, involved not only in the empirical method of Egoistic Hedonism, but in the very conception of 'Greatest Happiness' as an end of action, is the commensurability of Pleasures and Pains. By this I mean that we must assume the pleasures sought and the pains shunned to have determinate quantitative relations to each other; for otherwise they cannot be conceived as possible elements of a total which we are to seek to make as great as possible.[29]

The importance of being able to measure and compare pleasures and pains is unquestionable if pleasure is to be the sole good, and pain the sole evil, and if things are to be said to be better or worse as they lead to more pleasure or more pain.

We can introduce a preliminary doubt about the possibility of measuring and comparing pleasures and pains by recalling Ryle's point to the effect that they are not the same kinds of things at all. Thus, if there are no pleasures, in the sense that there are pains, it is quite impossible to say that a certain amount of pleasure is greater than a certain amount of pain. Shall we say, then, that all these estimations of pleasure are subjective guesses, without any objective justification? It would seem that an acceptance of Ryle's point would lead to this conclusion, but it is not clear that such a conclusion can be avoided even if Ryle is not correct.

[29] Sidgwick, *op. cit.*, p. 123.

Jeremy Bentham, at least, seemed to feel that precision in this area could be attained. He argues that the factors that decide the values of a pleasure or a pain can be determined:

> To a person considered *by himself*, the value of a pleasure or pain considered *by itself*, will be greater or less, according to the four following circumstances:
> 1. Its *intensity*.
> 2. Its *duration*.
> 3. Its *certainty* or *uncertainty*.
> 4. Its *propinquity* or *remoteness*.
> These are the circumstances which are to be considered in estimating a pleasure or a pain considered each of them by itself. But when the value of any pleasure or pain is considered for the purpose of estimating the tendency of any *act* by which it is produced, there are two other circumstances to be taken into account; these are,
> 5. Its *fecundity*, or the chance it has of being followed by sensations of the *same* kind: that is, pleasures, if it be a pleasure: pains, if it be a pain.
> 6. Its *purity*, or the chance it has of *not* being followed by sensations of the *opposite* kind: that is, pains, if it be a pleasure: pleasures, if it be a pain.
> These two last, however, are in strictness scarcely to be deemed properties of the pleasures or the pain itself; they are not, therefore, in strictness to be deemed properties only of the act, or other event, by which such pleasure or pain has been produced; and accordingly are only to be taken into the account of the tendency of such act or such event.[30]

For Bentham to be interpreted as a purely quantitative hedonist, it is necessary that he maintain—among other things—that the value of a pleasure or a pain is strictly a function of its quantity. But by his suggestion that the value of a pleasure or a pain is partly determined by its certainty or its propinquity, he seems to be introducing a new element which endangers his purely hedonistic approach. A pleasure (if there be such a thing) or a pain is not more of a pleasure or a pain for its being more certain or for its being nearer in time. Thus, although intensity and duration would seem to be relevant in estimating the value of a pleasure or a pain, certainty and propinquity would seem to be of no more importance for an assessment of the value of a pleasure than fecundity or purity, or even quality. The only relevant factors in judging the value of a pleasure or a pain on pure quantitative hedonist grounds are those that have something to do with its amount—the longer a pleasure lasts, and the greater its intensity, the more there is.

The important question, therefore, is whether we can accurately measure and compare the intensity and duration of pleasures and pains. Henry Sidgwick expresses grave doubts about this possibility:

> It may still be maintained (1) that this comparison as ordinarily made is both occasional and very rough, and that it can never be extended as systematic Hedon-

[30] Bentham, *op. cit.*, pp. 29–30.

ism requires, nor applied, with any accuracy, to all possible states however differing in quality; and (2) that as commonly practised it is liable to illusion, of which we can never measure the precise amount, while we are continually forced to recognise its existence.[31]

Later he confesses:

Now for my own part, when I reflect on my pleasures and pains, and endeavour to compare them in respect of intensity, it is only to a very limited extent that I can obtain clear and definite results from such comparisons, even taking each separately in its simplest form:—whether the comparison is made at the moment of experiencing one of the pleasures, or between two states of consciousness recalled in imagination.[32]

He points out that this is true even when the pleasures are the same in kind, and that the situation becomes even more doubtful when the feelings differ in kind. Next he argues that "if these judgments are not clear and definite, still less are they consistent." That is, not only does one man's estimate as to the quantity of pleasure and pain differ from another's but the same man's estimates are likely to vary at different times. Thus, there are strong reasons for doubting that each of our pleasures and pains has an exact quantity. Even if it has, there are reasons for believing that we do not (and often could not) measure it accurately, or compare one with another.

4. A *Final Argument Against Hedonism*. The pluralist will argue that, although pleasure is a good, it is not the only good. According to the monist, if X is valuable, then anything of which X is a part is valuable because of its presence, and anything which leads to X is valuable (has beneficial value) just because it leads to X. But, in estimating the values of wholes, we sometimes want to say that two wholes containing the same amount of X differ in value because of the presence of Y. Now it may not be plausible to suggest that every single factor, the presence of which increases the intrinsic value of a whole, is itself intrinsically valuable, but it hardly seems more plausible to suggest that no element which brings about a change of value in a whole has any intrinsic value in itself. The obvious alternative here is to deny that any single thing has a monopoly on intrinsic value, and that is, of course, the alternative taken by the pluralist.

Exercises

Review

1. What is Epicurus' view of pleasure and pain?
2. How is Sidgwick's definition of 'pleasure' criticized?

[31] Sidgwick, *op. cit.*, p. 140.
[32] *Ibid.*, pp. 142–43.

3. Ryle argues that pleasure and pain are not proper counterparts. What does he mean by this assertion? How is it relevant in a discussion of hedonism?
4. Why can a nonhedonist subscribe to the view that pleasure is intrinsically good?
5. What is the difference between psychological hedonism and ethical hedonism?
6. What is Mill's proof of his theory of value? What is Moore's criticism of that proof?
7. Mill makes a distinction between quantities of pleasure and qualities of pleasure. What reasons are there for thinking that this may make him no longer a hedonist?
8. What is the analytic argument for hedonism?
9. How does Bentham propose we measure and compare pleasures and pains? What are the difficulties connected with this?

Applications
1. Why would it be wrong to call Epicurus a hedonist in the modern sense of that term?
2. Does Moore have a good argument against Mill?
3. Read R. MacNaughton, "A Metrical Conception of Happiness," *Philosophy and Phenomenological Research*, 14 (1954), 172–83. How far toward solving the problems of the measurement and comparison of pleasure and pains does this article take us?
4. Is there any necessary relation between ethical hedonism and ethical egoism? That is, is it possible to be a nonegoistic hedonist? Is it possible to be a non-hedonistic egoist? Describe one possible version of each view.
5. Consider the following argument:
   Pleasures and pains cannot be measured and compared because they are quantities such that each is over before the other is begun.
6. Explain the tenets of hedonistic egoism and of hedonistic utilitarianism. (Hint: you should have more than two sets of tenets here.)

C. Pluralist Theories

The chief support for ethical hedonism has been psychological hedonism, but there are good reasons for being dubious about the correctness of the main tenets of the latter view, and questions about how much support it would offer to ethical hedonism even if it were true. There are also serious problems in comparing and measuring pleasures, exceeded only by those one encounters when he attempts to compare and measure pleasures and pains. We have also presented a general argument against monistic theories of value, and specific arguments against hedonism. We seem justified, therefore, in attempting to see whether a pluralistic theory of value might be more successful in escaping objections, and in meeting the criteria of acceptability of theories.

1. *Ideal Utilitarianism: Moore and Rashdall.* The most succinct characterization of the view called *ideal utilitarianism* (which is contrasted with hedonistic utilitarianism) is given by Hastings Rashdall:

This view of Ethics, which combines the utilitarian principle that Ethics must be teleological with a non-hedonistic view of the ethical end, I propose to call Ideal Utilitarianism. According to this view, actions are right or wrong according as they tend to produce for all mankind an ideal end or good, which includes, but is not limited to, pleasure.[33]

According to the ideal utilitarians, then, although pleasure can be said to be intrinsically good, other things are also intrinsically good.

The most important exponent of this view is G. E. Moore. We have already examined the utilitarian aspect of this view and it is now time to examine the theory of value contained in his theory. In the last chapter of *Principia Ethica*, Moore tells us that he will attempt to answer the fundamental question of ethics: "What things are goods or ends in themselves?" [34] A few pages later, he makes it clear that he is dealing with the question "What things have intrinsic value, and in what degrees?" [35]

The method Moore proposes to use in discovering the answer to this question is a consequence of his meta-ethical theory. He believes that goodness is a property of things, just as yellowness is, and the only problem is to determine which things have this property, and to what degree:

In order to arrive at a correct decision on the first part of this question, it is necessary to consider what things are such that, if they existed *by themselves*, in absolute isolation, we should yet judge their existence to be good; and, in order to decide upon the relative *degrees* of value of different things, we must similarly consider what comparative value seems to attach to the isolated existence of each.[36]

This "method of isolation" is made plausible by the claim that a thing either has the property of goodness or it does not, much in the way that a thing has a specific size, shape, or color (see Chapter 12). In indicating some of the things he claims are intrinsically good, Moore begins by suggesting:

By far the most valuable things, which we know or can imagine, are certain states of consciousness, which may be roughly described as the pleasures of human intercourse and the enjoyment of beautiful objects. No one, probably, who has asked himself the question, has ever doubted that personal affection and the appreciation of what is beautiful in Art or Nature, are good in themselves; nor, if we consider strictly what things are worth having *purely for their own sakes*, does it appear probable that any one will think that anything else has *nearly* so great a value as the things which are included under these two heads.[37]

[33] Hastings Rashdall, *Theory of Good and Evil* (London: Oxford University Press, 1924), Vol. I, p. 184.

[34] Moore, *Principia Ethica*, p. 184.

[35] *Ibid.*, p. 187.

[36] *Ibid.*

[37] *Ibid.*, pp. 188–89.

Although Moore admits that things which are not states of contemplation may have some intrinsic value, he holds that they possess it only to a small degree. Thus, although a beautiful object may be worthwhile in itself, a whole that includes both the object and the contemplation of it is of far greater intrinsic value. At one point Moore even defines *the beautiful* as "that of which the admiring contemplation is good in itself." [38] This clearly places Moore among those who deny a purely mentalistic theory of value.

When asked what reasons he can give for saying that these things are good in themselves, Moore appeals to his intuition and invites his critics to apply honestly and sincerely the method of isolation. His assumption seems to be that, unless a person is blind to value (somewhat as a color blind person is blind to certain colors) agreement can be reached in this way.

2. *The Pluralism of Ross.* Although Moore is reasonably explicit about his method, his catalog of intrinsically valuable things is far from clear. W. D. Ross is more satisfactory on this point. Ross claims that four things are intrinsically good: virtue, pleasure, the allocation of pleasure to the virtuous, and knowledge (and, in a less degree, right opinion).[39] Let us see what Ross has to say about each of these.

The first thing for which I would claim that it is intrinsically good is virtuous disposition and action, i.e. action, or disposition to act, from any one of certain motives, of which at all events the most notable are the desire to do one's duty, the desire to bring into being something that is good, and the desire to give pleasure or save pain to others. It seems clear that we regard all such actions and dispositions as having value in themselves apart from any consequences.[40]

Ross argues for this by appealing to the traditional antimonist argument. He proposes that we consider two equally pleasant universes—one containing all virtuous people, the other containing nothing but vicious ones—and see that they would not really be equal in intrinsic value. It seems, however, that Ross really feels arguments are unnecessary, for he suggests that these considerations are raised only "to bring before us in a vivid way what is really self-evident, that virtue is a good apart from its consequences." [41]

Next, Ross suggests that pleasure is always good in itself, although he adds that the whole of pleasure-experienced-by-an-undeserving-or-bad-person is not intrinsically good:

If we look at the matter thus, I think we can agree that the fact that a sentient being is in a state of pleasure is always in itself good, and the fact that a sentient

[38] *Ibid.*, p. 201.
[39] W. D. Ross, *The Right and the Good* (Oxford: The Clarendon Press, 1930), p. 140. By permission of The Clarendon Press, Oxford.
[40] *Ibid.*, p. 134.
[41] *Ibid.*, p. 135.

being is in a state of pain always in itself bad, when this fact is not an element in a more complex fact having some other characteristic relevant to goodness or badness. . . .

The two characteristics that may interfere with its being good are (*a*) that of being contrary to desert, and (*b*) that of being a state which is the realization of a bad disposition.[42]

This consideration leads us to the third thing that is thought by Ross to be intrinsically good: "the allocation of pleasure to the virtuous." The reasons Ross believes this must be recognized to have intrinsic value have already been hinted at, but a familiar argument is given to establish this point:

If we compare two imaginary states of the universe, alike in the total amounts of virtue and vice and of pleasure and pain present in the two, but in one of which the virtuous were all happy and the vicious miserable, while in the other the virtuous were miserable and the vicious happy, very few people would hesitate to say that the first was a much better state of the universe than the second. It would seem then that, besides virtue and pleasure, we must recognize (3), as a third independent good, the apportionment of pleasure and pain to the virtuous and the vicious respectively.[43]

This line of argument is initially convincing, but it is easy to see how it may lead to a proliferation of intrinsic goods. Ross lists only four intrinsic goods, but it is difficult, once the correctness of this way of arguing is admitted, to see how it is possible to keep from adding an indefinite number of other good things. This same argument is used by Ross to show that knowledge or right opinion is among the things that have intrinsic value.

Both Ross and Moore believe that we can directly perceive the intrinsic value of wholes or their elements. This view is often criticized on the grounds that there is no way to determine which of two conflicting reports is correct, but this argument (see Chapter 12), though frequently encountered, has less plausibility than is often thought. It is not necessary to hold that we know directly that a thing has intrinsic value in order to be justified in claiming that it does (see Chapter 6). A noncognitivist might well say that, when one claims that something has intrinsic value, he is expressing a favorable attitude toward that thing, and that he has this attitude independently of the consequences the thing has. The problem for the noncognitivist, then, is to go further and show that the expression of this attitude is justified or justifiable. There does not seem to be any a priori reason for claiming either that thinkers like Ross and Moore cannot agree about what is intrinsically valuable, or that noncognitivists cannot hold any of the monistic or pluralistic theories we have considered in this discussion.

[42] *Ibid.*, pp. 137, 138.
[43] *Ibid.*, p. 138.

3. *Toward a Pluralistic Theory of Value*. Our discussion thus far has led us to the conclusion that there are a number of things with intrinsic value, but we have not attempted to provide a list of them. Such an attempt would take us too deeply into quite specific normative problems, and would also involve considerations of cases too specific for our general discussion.

Our conclusions have not been altogether negative, however, for we are inclined to believe that pleasure is one of the intrinsically valuable things, and to accept Ross' catalog of intrinsic goods. There are probably other things of intrinsic value, though we have left this an open question which the reader must decide for himself. One conclusion that should be avoided is that if pleasure *is* intrinsically valuable, all pleasures are of equal value. In determining the value of a particular pleasure, or of a whole of which pleasure is one element, other factors must be taken into account. Thus the assessment of the value of a complex whole is a complicated matter, calling for much discernment and thought. We believe it is not unlike the assessment of the rightness of an action, for each actual case in which one must make a decision about the intrinsic value of the entire state of affairs involves many factors.

Exercises

Review
1. What is meant by 'ideal utilitarianism'?
2. What sorts of things does Ross feel are intrinsically good?

Applications
1. What theory of value do you hold? Defend it against the possible objections that have occurred to you in reading Chapters 6 and 7.
2. How would you go about refuting someone who maintained that everything is intrinsically good?
3. Analyze and criticize the following argument from Sidgwick (*op. cit.*, p. 40). What does it claim to show and what does it show?

> There is, however, one view of the feelings which prompt to voluntary action, which is sometimes thought to cut short all controversy as to the principles on which such action ought to be regulated. I mean the view that volition is always determined by pleasures or pains actual or prospective. This doctrine—which I may distinguish as Psychological Hedonism—is often connected and not seldom confounded with the method of Ethics which I have called Egoistic Hedonism; and no doubt it seems at first sight a natural inference that if one end of action—my own pleasure or absence of pain—is definitely determined for me by unvarying psychological laws, a different end cannot be prescribed for me by Reason.
>
> Reflection, however, shows that this inference involves the unwarranted assumption that a man's pleasure and pain are determined independently of his moral judgments: whereas it is manifestly possible that our prospect of pleasure resulting from any course of conduct may largely depend on our conception of it as right or otherwise: and in fact the psychological theory

above mentioned would require us to suppose that this is normally the case
with conscientious persons, who habitually act in accordance with their moral
convictions.

4. Countries can sometimes be instructively thought of as individuals, and as
such they can be said to act in morally relevant ways. They perform certain
actions or bring about certain situations (a high tariff, a state of war, and
so on), and often it is claimed that these actions are morally right, and
that the situations brought about are of more value than other situations.
For each of the following countries, choose some actions they are often said
to have done, or some situations they are said to have brought about, and
then try to decide what theory of value and theory of obligation their actions
seem to presuppose, whether those actions are right, and whether the situation brought about is indeed better than the possible alternative situations.
   a. The United States
   b. Great Britain
   c. France
   d. The Soviet Union
   e. Cuba
   f. Communist China
   g. Portugal

Bibliography

ARISTOTLE. *Nicomachean Ethics*. Trans. W. D. Ross. Oxford: The Clarendon
Press, 1925, Books i, ii, and x. Aristotle claims that the good is happiness,
which he claims is an activity of the soul. Chapter 10 contains a criticism of
hedonism.

BENTHAM, JEREMY. *Introduction to the Principles of Morals and Legislation*.
New York: Hafner Publishing Co., 1948, Chapters 1–4. This is the classical
presentation of quantitative hedonistic utilitarianism.

*BRANDT, R. B. *Ethical Theory*. Englewood Cliffs, N.J.: Prentice-Hall, Inc., 1959,
Chapters 12 and 13.

*KANT, IMMANUEL. *Groundwork of the Metaphysics of Morals*. Trans. by H. J.
Paton. London: Hutchinson University Library, 1948. Kant claims that a
"good will" is the only thing good without qualification.

*McNAUGHTON, R. "A Metrical Conception of Happiness," *Philosophy and
Phenomenological Research*, 15 (1954), 172–83. An attempt to outline a concept of happiness with special emphasis on the problem of measurement.

MILL, JOHN STUART. *Utilitarianism*. Indianapolis and New York: The Library of
Liberal Arts Press, Inc., 1957.

MOORE, G. E. *Ethics*. New York: Oxford University Press, Inc., 1965, pp. 150–
54. This work contains a rejection of hedonism and a defense of pluralism.

*———. *Principia Ethica*. Cambridge: Cambridge University Press, 1959. A
criticism of hedonism is found on pp. 59–95 and in Chapter 6 there is a presentation and defense of a pluralistic theory of value.

*PENELHUM, TERENCE. "The Logic of Pleasure," *Philosophy and Phenomeno-
logical Research*, 15 (1954), 172–83. This article contains a criticism of Ryle's

The Concept of Mind and a defense of the claim that pleasure is an event, not a disposition.

PLATO, *Philebus*. An examination of pleasure as the sole good for man. Plato adopts a pluralistic theory of value.

*RASHDALL, H. *Theory of Good and Evil*. London: Oxford University Press, 1924.

Ross, W. D. *The Right and the Good*. Oxford: The Clarendon Press, 1930, Chapter 5. Ross defends a pluralistic theory of value.

*RYLE, G., and W. B. GALLIE. "Pleasure" (a symposium), *The Aristotelian Society Supplementary Volume*, 28 (1954), 135–64. A discussion of pleasure as a species of "paying attention" rather than as a sensation.

*SIDGWICK, HENRY. *The Methods of Ethics*. 7th ed. London: Macmillan & Co., Ltd., 1962, Book ii, Chapter 3. Sidgwick discusses measurement and comparison of pleasures and pains. Book iii, Chapter 4 he adopts a form of hedonistic utilitarianism.

PART TWO

Related
Nonnormative Questions

Relativism

In searching for the best normative theory, we are obviously assuming that there *is* one—or, at least, that some are better than others. In speaking of the conditions under which it is correct or justifiable to praise or blame someone for his actions, we are assuming, or so it seems, that they had some control over them. But both assumptions have been denied by serious and important thinkers, and it seems appropriate now to put them to the test. Therefore, we shall examine the claim that moral judgments are relative, that there is really no way to objectively evaluate or assess them. If this is true, then the practice of making moral judgments of obligation or of value would be undermined. We shall also examine the question of freedom (see Chapter 9). If man does not have free will, then we cannot expect anyone to act in any way other than he does, nor are we justified in saying that he is morally responsible for what he does.

There are two ways to approach these positions. One way is to examine the independent arguments for and against relativism and freedom, and that is what we shall be doing in this chapter and the one to follow. But another way to approach the problem of relativism, for example, is to show that some normative theories are indeed better than others. Similarly, if we can give fairly strong reasons for claiming that, under certain circumstances, we *are* justified in praising or blaming someone for what he has done, this would be strong evidence against determinism. This is what we have been doing in the last several chapters, and what we shall continue to do when we begin our discussion of meta-ethics.

A. Two Views and Their Relation

1. *Cultural Relativism.* The first view we shall examine is one usually called *cultural relativism*—the view that people in different cultures make different moral judgments of the same action or thing. Another view which

almost always accompanies this view is the belief that the cause of the differing judgments is the fact that those who make them live in different cultures. It is interesting to note that cultural relativism is an empirical view that could be confirmed or refuted by a survey. Such a survey might consist of describing some action to people in different cultures or societies and then observing if their moral judgments are the same or different.

It is common knowledge that some cultures forbid the taking of life, while others approve of killing for revenge; that some cultures condemn nudity, while others lack even an understanding of the function of clothing. It is possible to agree that often, if not always, the reason for the differences has to do with the facts of daily existence: nudity has never been prized in the Arctic, nor extreme modesty in the sweltering jungle.[1]

The thesis of cultural relativism, then, can be stated in this way: *In different cultures the same action or thing, or the same kind of action or thing often is judged differently, and the cause of this divergence is that the people who make the judgments come from different cultures.* The term 'often' is included because, of course, sometimes people in differing cultures make the same moral judgment concerning an action or a thing. We shall not attempt to guess the percentage of times that judgments will differ about any action, but only suppose that sometimes they do. Stated in this way there seems to be little to object to in the thesis of cultural relativism, and abundant evidence for this view can be found in any textbook on anthropology.

2. *Ethical Relativism.* Ethical relativism is not a thesis about differences of judgment, but about the correctness of differing judgments. It contains all the claims made in the thesis of cultural relativism plus a claim concerning correctness or truth. The thesis of ethical relativism is this: (a) the thesis of cultural relativism and (b) *In each of the respective cultures the judgments made by the members of that culture are correct.* Let us explain part (b) at greater length. Suppose, for example, that there are two cultures, C_1 and C_2, in which some individual or group of individuals judge A (either a specific action or a kind of action that calls for a moral judgment). Suppose that, in C_1, A is judged to be morally right and that, in C_2, A is judged not to be morally right. We can even suppose that the judgment "A is right" is made in C_1 and "A is wrong" is made in C_2.[2] According to the thesis of ethical relativism, both of these judgments can be correct: "A is right" is justified or

[1] In a discussion of cultural relativism, R. B. Brandt suggests that the thesis should be interpreted as maintaining that different peoples or groups differ in their "basic moral axioms," but we do not adopt such an approach because there are great difficulties in making clear the notion of a moral axiom. Furthermore, if moral axioms are (as they seem to be) constitutive rules, this way of putting the issue supposes the correctness of some kind of rule theory. Although we admit that many philosophers hold such a position, it is not obviously correct, and we have argued that it is mistaken.

[2] The reader will understand that we could have considered any moral judgment here. For example, we could replace "A is right" with "X is good."

correct in C_1, and "A is wrong" is justified or correct in C_2. Let us consider A to be a kind of action—namely, that of eating one's captured enemies. Suppose that C_1 is a cannibal culture and that C_2 is our own culture. The majority of the members of C_1 judge A to be right and the majority of the members of C_2 judge it to be wrong.[3] So far we have only illustrated the thesis of *cultural* relativism. The *ethical* relativist would claim that a member of C_1, living in his own culture and judging that A is right, would be judging truly or correctly, and that a member of C_2, living in his own culture and judging that Λ is wrong, would also be making a correct moral judgment.[4]

It is by no means difficult to find serious students of society making the transition from cultural to ethical relativism. Consider the following example:

We cannot possibly understand the actions of other groups if we analyze them in terms of *our* motives and values; we must interpret their behavior in the light of *their* motives, habits, and values if we are to understand them. Consider, for example, the administration of justice in the far North. The Canadian Mounties are occasionally called to go into the arctic region to apprehend Eskimos who have committed a murder. This action in terms of our culture is a crime, and the individual has violated the mores. In the culture of many Eskimo tribes, however, the killing may have been justified, since their mores demand that a man avenge an injury committed upon a kinsman. This type of revenge is not considered unruly or deviant but is the only honorable kind of action which a respectable member of the society could take. We would condemn the man who takes the law into his own hands and seeks revenge, while they would condemn the man

[3] It is of course possible that there are some members of each culture who would agree with members of the other culture. It is for this reason that we must add some qualification about "the majority." This clearly does not make any difference in the philosophical issue. The only time there would be any difficulty would be when the percentage of those in each society agreeing and disagreeing was about the same. But such cases are not common and we need not go into them in a discussion at this point.

[4] We must ask whether, e.g., a member of C_1, while living in C_2, who judged that A is right is judging truly or not. The most consistent reply here seems to be that, if he is really living there (rather than visiting), he is not. It is only when he returns to his own culture, that his judgment becomes correct again. The line where one's moral judgments can change their correctness is that point where the influence of one's culture ends. This is a strange proposition, but it is difficult to see how the ethical relativist can avoid such a reply. Another phenomenon which we shall not pursue at length is what the ethical relativist would say about intercultural moral judgments. Suppose S_2, who is a member of C_2, judges that S_1's action of eating his captured enemy *in* C_2 is wrong. The ethical relativist can say that S_2 is narrow-minded, a provincial type who does not appreciate the full diversity of human existence. He might also say that S_2 can correctly make the judgment about S_1 in C_2 but not in C_1. The former response is a value judgment which, one must suppose, the ethical relativist believes is, at most, justified in his own culture. We might note that such an outlook concerning S_2's judgment is not approved of or held by the majority of men in any culture we are aware of. If the ethical relativist's position with respect to value judgments is correct, then his value judgment concerning S_2 is not correct. It would seem then that only the latter position is open to the ethical relativist. This conclusion, however, does not seem to be crucial to any important philosophic issue.

who has so little courage and group loyalty as to allow his kinsman to go unavenged.

Few culture traits are so disturbing to most Americans as the primitive practice of head hunting—an apparently useless and bloodthirsty pastime. However, this trait nearly everywhere has a fairly complex meaning. The Marindese of New Guinea, a quite gentle and affectionate people, hunted heads in order to provide names for their children [Van der Kroef, 1952]. Since they firmly believed that the only way a child could get a name and a separate identity was to take it from a living person, they hunted heads from neighboring tribes. A Marindese husband had a moral obligation to have one or two head names on hand, in case he was presented with a child. Thus head hunting, like any other important trait, was deeply integrated into a total cultural system within which it was moral and necessary.

These illustrations show what we mean by cultural relativism—*that the function and meaning of a trait are relative to its cultural setting.* A trait is neither good nor bad in itself. It is good or bad only with reference to the culture in which it is to function. Fur clothing is good in the arctic, but not in the tropics. Premarital pregnancy is bad in our society, where the mores condemn it and where there are no comfortable arrangements for the care of illegitimate children; premarital pregnancy is good in a society such as that of the Bontocs of the Philippines, who consider a woman more marriageable when her fertility has been established, and who have a set of customs and values which make a secure place for the children. Adolescent girls in the United States are advised that they will improve their marital bargaining power by remaining chaste until marriage. Adolescent girls in New Guinea are given the opposite advice, and in each setting the advice is probably correct. The rugged individualism and peasant thrift of early America would produce great unemployment if they were widely practiced in our present mass-production economy. From such examples we see that *any cultural trait is socially "good" if it operates harmoniously within its cultural setting to attain the goals which the people are seeking.* This is a workable, non-ethnocentric test of the goodness or badness of a culture trait.

The concept of cultural relativism does not mean that all customs are equally valuable nor does it imply that no customs are harmful. Some patterns of behavior may be injurious in any milieu, but even such patterns serve some purpose in the culture, and the society will suffer unless a substitute is provided.

Sociologists are sometimes accused of undermining morality with their concept of cultural relativism, and their claim that almost "everything's right somewhere." If right and wrong are merely social conventions, say our critics, one might as well do whatever he wishes. This is a total misunderstanding. It is approximately true that "everything's right somewhere"—but not everywhere. The central point in cultural relativism is that in a particular cultural setting, certain traits are right because they work well in that setting, while others traits are wrong because they would clash painfully with parts of that cuture. This is but another way of saying that a culture is integrated, and that its various elements must harmonize passably if the culture is to function efficiently in serving human purposes.[5]

[5] From *Sociology* by Paul B. Horton and Chester L. Hunt. Copyright 1964, by McGraw-Hill, Inc. Used by permission. Pp. 86–88.

The claim that we would certainly make a different judgment about the Eskimo avenger than would his tribesmen, or even his enemies, is simply a reiteration of cultural relativism, and cannot be denied. It is also possible to understand why the Marindese feel an urgency to hunt heads. Here it is merely stressed that the different evaluations are caused by the different cultural backgrounds. But then there is an astounding transition to ethical relativism: "A trait is neither good nor bad in itself. It is good or bad only with reference to the culture in which it is to function." But nothing in the passage justifies this conclusion. Although it is possible to admit that "fur clothing is good in the arctic, but not in the tropics," it is another thing to claim that killing is good in the North but not here, or that torture was good in Spain during the Inquisition but not in New York City. The conclusion drawn from this is that "any cultural trait is socially 'good' if it operates harmoniously within its cultural setting to attain the goals which the people are seeking." Although the adjective 'socially' is added here, and 'good' is placed in quotes, both of these devices are dropped in the following sentence. It is that view we propose to examine (and reject).

There are many variations and complications of the view we are discussing (see footnote 4). One set of complications concerns the specification of the object of moral judgment. It might be held that it is never true that the same A is judged differently by members of different cultures because when A occurs in C_1 it is A_1, and when it occurs in C_2 it is A_2. When S_1 (a member of C_1) judges that A_1 (performed in C_1) is right, and S_2 (a member of C_2) judges that A_2 (performed in C_2) is not right, the ethical relativist can say that they are not disagreeing about A, because they are judging different actions—A_1 and A_2, respectively. The action of a Marindese killing a man in the Marindese culture because he believes that only in that way can his child get a name and identity, is different from a man in New York killing his neighbor because he believes that the neighbor insulted him. There is something to this claim, but not as much as the ethical relativist maintains.

The motives, beliefs, and settings of an action are important in determining its moral worth. If S_1, a surgeon, cuts open a man's stomach to eliminate a diseased appendix, this action is certainly morally right. But if S_2, a shoemaker, cuts open a man's stomach to eliminate a rival for the woman he loves, this action is morally wrong—even though S_2 will lose face in his subculture if he does not win the woman.

We can say that S_1 and S_2 have performed the same kind of action which is right in one case, wrong in the other. The ethical relativist might want to claim that all moral judgments, even of the same kind of action, are justified by the social context. Although we certainly agree that the justification of a judgment sometimes depends on the social context, we cannot agree that it always does.

Many persons who believe that certain actions are necessary to accomplish certain ends are mistaken. The man who believes he must kill in order to secure a name and identity for his child is wrong. This latter judgment is a judgment based on what is known about human beings, their personality and development. If someone believes that to secure an identity you must get it from someone else he is wrong. He is wrong in New York and he is wrong in New Guinea. He is wrong if he is a New Yorker and he is wrong if he is a New Guinean. The fact that a man believes that an action is required does not actually make it required. If the whole society believes that the action is required, then the whole society is mistaken. We might, in some circumstances, excuse people because they could not know better, but we can still say that the action is wrong. We shall not argue that in every instance in which a man does an act which we judge to be wrong he *has* performed an action which is wrong. All that has to be shown is that it is wrong in some cases, and it is wrong regardless of the culture of the person or the culture in which the action occurs. In many parts of the world in the past, and in a few today, slavery existed or exists. When someone today keeps human beings as slaves to increase his wealth or further his own good in some way, then his action is wrong. Arab slave traders may have been approved of by their neighbors, but that does not excuse them. Someone might say that it *does* excuse them on the grounds that ethical relativism is correct, but this is clearly question begging. These examples do not beg the question because they appeal to part of the phenomena which are to be analyzed. If they are not legitimate then those who claim they are not must provide evidence.

To make it more plausible that there are judgments the correctness of which apparently does not depend on the culture in which they are made, let us list a few more kinds of actions that are wrong in most instances.

1. Being cruel to a loved one.
2. Betraying a friend.
3. Killing a business rival.
4. Treating a human being as a means to an end of one's own.
5. Failing to relieve suffering when it is within one's power to do so.
6. Doing to one's neighbor what he would not want the neighbor to do to him.

As far as we are concerned, this list is a set of summary rules concerning kinds of actions. We have defended act deontology as the best normative theory of obligation and, if we are right, this is the only sort of rule one can have. We are not, then, saying that always, and in all circumstances, it is wrong to do these things. We are saying that these are fairly reliable rules, and that their reliability is not a function of the society.

Both the man in New York who killed his neighbor because he believed that the neighbor insulted him, and the Marindese who killed because he believed this was the only way to obtain a name and identity for his child have performed a kind of action—killing. However, the mere fact that these two people live in different cultures does not seem to be relevant, as the ethical relativist seems to be maintaining, to the rightness or wrongness of their actions. Suppose that we take two instances of the same *kind* of killing, say ones resulting from anger following an insult to one's virility, in both New York and New Guinea. It is difficult to see how, if we allow all other things to remain equal, the ethical relativist could hold that one was right and the other wrong—yet that seems to be the conclusion to which he is bound. It is, of course, possible that two cases of killing following this kind of insult may be judged differently, that one may be right and the other wrong; but the fact that the two killers live in different cultures is almost certainly not the crucial difference. That fact (as well as any other) *might* be relevant, although it is difficult to see how it could be.

In order to appreciate the claim of ethical relativism, let us contrast the supposed relativity of morality with the nonrelativity of some other areas of human concern. For example, even today people in different cultures judge the shape of the same object differently. There are some primitive societies in which the majority of the members judge that the earth is flat, whereas in modern societies, the members believe it is spherical.

In spite of this disagreement, no one would suppose that in the different cultures the different judgments are true. If the primitive culture is C_1 and the modern one is C_2, no rational person believes that "the earth is flat" is true in C_1 and "the earth is not flat but is rather spherical" is true in C_2. The earth cannot be both flat and spherical—it may be neither but it is logically impossible that it should be both. This point is a simple consequence of elementary geometry and can be established to everyone's satisfaction.

There is no theory of "shape relativity" analogous to the theory of ethical relativity. Some may wish to claim that, in C_1, "it is true for them" that the earth is flat whereas, in C_2 "it is true for us" that the earth is spherical. This, however, solves no problems and is, at best, misleading. The expression "it is true for them" in this context seems to mean neither more nor less than "they believe it is true."

If the interpretation we suggest is correct, it can be shown that no problem has been solved by introducing the expression "it is true for them." We would all agree that some people believe the earth is flat, but it is one thing to *believe* the earth is flat and another for it to *be* flat. We are considering the truth or justifiability of the belief, *not* the fact that people have it. It is a mistake to suppose that all beliefs are true or that a proposition becomes true simply because someone believes it.

Suppose, for example, that the United States and Canada decide to build a bridge from Nova Scotia to England. This would be a tremendous undertaking and would cost, let us suppose, $100 billion. Suppose, though, that for only $10 million we can cause the vast majority of people to believe that such a bridge already exists: we can create a "Bridge Authority" that will sponsor television and radio programs and urge everyone to drive to Europe this summer; we can print newspaper stories describing trips taken across the bridge, and so on. But, however many people believe there is such a bridge, this will not make it easier to drive across the Atlantic Ocean. In short, believing does not make it so. One would not suspect that anyone would hold the principle "If S believes p is true, then p is true" (or "S's belief that p is true is sufficient for the truth of p"), but this false principle has probably proved to be the philosophical undoing of more students than any other false principle in philosophy.

It is easy to see why the introduction of the expression "it is true for them," where it is equivalent to "they believe it is true," can solve no problems. What people believe may or may not be true, but its truth rarely depends upon the belief. We say "rarely" because, as William James has pointed out, sometimes a belief in one's ability to perform some task is an aid to the accomplishment of that task. If, for example, S believes that he can swim across a certain river, his chances of doing so may be enhanced, because his belief gives him the added strength he needs for the task. But, under most circumstances, belief does not have this effect. No matter how firmly S believes he can swim across the Atlantic Ocean, he will not be able to do so.[6]

Exercises

Review

1. Describe the difference between cultural and ethical relativism.
2. How is cultural relativism established?
3. How do those who wish to assert ethical relativism usually argue their position?
4. What positive evidence is there against ethical relativism?
5. Show how the mistaken principle "If S believes p is true, then p is true" enters the controversy.

Applications

1. Describe the arguments most often used, in your experience, to establish ethical relativism. Evaluate those arguments.
2. What are some reasons for denying that physics is relative to the culture in which one lives?
3. Evaluate the following argument:

> Every culture in the past believed it had the truth concerning almost everything. However, most of the things that men believed in the past turned out to be false. So, we should not say that what we believe is true, only that it is true for us. The latter is the only claim that anyone is ever justified in making.

[6] One might say that it is social usefulness that makes moral traits and judgments acceptable. (Horton and Hunt seem to hold this view.) It is a simple matter to construct the same type of example applying to *usefulness* as was used above to apply to *belief*.

3. *The Relation of Cultural Relativism and Ethical Relativism.* We are prepared to grant that cultural relativism is correct. Most ethical relativists believe that cultural relativism supports their view. Similarly, psychological egoism was thought to support ethical egoism, but we found that the former was not only unacceptable, but it failed to give any support to most forms of ethical egoism. In this instance, at least, cultural relativism is correct, and the only question is whether or not it supports ethical relativism.

a. SIMPLE ENTAILMENT. Suppose someone claims that the correctness of cultural relativism logically entails the correctness of ethical relativism, much as the correctness of the heliocentric theory logically entails the correctness of the view that there is a sun or that the sun is the center of the solar system.

To say that one proposition entails another one is simply to say that, if the first proposition is true, it is impossible for the second to be false. Thus the claim that some S is P entails the claim that some P is S, and the premises of a valid argument (such as *modus ponens*) entail the argument's conclusion. It is easy to see that cultural relativism does not entail ethical relativism in any simple sense. If it did, it would be possible to argue in the following way:

P: In different cultures, C_1 and C_2, Action A is judged differently with respect to its moral worth.

C: Therefore, in C_1 the judgment "A is ———" is correct, whereas in C_2 the judgment "A is not ———" is correct. (Here the blanks are filled in with some moral term such as 'right', 'wrong', 'good', or 'bad'.)

In the first place, it is obvious that the Premise P does not by itself entail the conclusion C, any more than "S is big," entails "S is strong." What we need is some intermediate proposition such as "If anyone is big, then he is strong." Then this claim, plus the claim that S is big, does entail the conclusion. Likewise, to get from P to C, we need an intermediate claim to the effect that if P then C. Do we have such a claim? Only if the thesis of ethical relativism is true. But we cannot prove that this thesis is true by going from P to C because we cannot get from P to C unless the thesis is true. Once again, if we can go from P to C by simple entailment then ethical relativism is true. But the best we can do is go from P and "If P then C" to C by simple entailment. But this does not prove ethical relativism, since the claim "If P then C" presupposes the correctness of ethical relativism. It is not, of course, surprising that if one assumes that ethical relativism is true, it is possible to construct an "argument" showing it is true, but we need not take such an attempt seriously.

It might be suggested that we have a more general form of "If P, then C," but a moment's consideration will show that we do not. We cannot go from "Culture C_1 believes proposition p and culture C_2 believes proposition not-p," to the claim that p is true in C_1 and not-p is true in C_2, because as we have shown, in most cases the belief in a proposition (e.g., "The earth is flat") is irrelevant in the determination of its truth or falsity. If ethical relativism is correct, then, there must be some other way of showing it to be so, for it is clear that ethical relativism is not entailed by cultural relativism.

b. EVIDENTIAL RELATION. Adherents to ethical relativism can claim that cultural relativism does not entail, but rather, is evidence for, ethical relativism. This claim is interesting, but somewhat unclear, for we are never told what kind of evidence is being provided. Furthermore, if one considers the relation between the cultural relativism of shape judgments and the relativity of the truth of those judgments, then that relation seems to be the same as the one between cultural relativism and ethical relativism. That is, however, one specifies the relation between cultural and ethical relativism so that the former supports the latter, this kind of relation applies equally well to shape judgments. It is a most unfortunate theory which allows us to conclude that the shape of the earth is relative to one's culture, but that is, apparently, the position in which the ethical relativist finds himself.

c. GENERAL CRITICISM OF THESE ARGUMENTS. There is a common flaw with both the ways that cultural relativism may be thought to support ethical relativism: it is possible to construct an analogous argument proving, for example, that the validity of the belief in the flatness of the earth also varies from culture to culture, but few people would accept such a conclusion; therefore, few people can accept the general argument that leads to it and, finally, the claim that cultural relativism supports ethical relativism. Those who can are those who believe that the shape of the world varies from culture to culture, and hardly need to be taken seriously in a rational discussion.

At this point, defenders of ethical relativism are likely to lose patience with philosophers, and argue in the following way: "You are comparing two kinds of things, value judgments and judgments about the shape of the world. These judgments are completely different in nature, and yet your criticism of ethical relativism's appeal to cultural relativism for support rests on the assumption that they are similar. This means that your analogy is misleading and that what is true about shape judgments and how they do not vary from culture to culture shows nothing about the invariance of value judgments."

It is clear how one could be led to make such a claim, but it is also clear that it is not justified. The ethical relativist needs an argument to show that moral judgments are unlike other judgments, such as shape judgments, in that they are relative. We have used neutral logical tools to show that the arguments presented do not support their conclusions, that they are invalid. It does no good to assert that moral judgments are different from, say, shape judgments because that was the point that was going to be established. What we demand are some reasons to establish ethical relativism, and until these reasons are forthcoming, the ethical relativist complains without justification.

4. *Two Arguments.* We shall now present two of the arguments most commonly used in support of ethical relativism.

a. From Varying Beliefs. Often someone will argue in the following way:

Premise 1: Tribe X believes that Action A is right.
Premise 2: Tribe Y believes that Action A is wrong.
Conclusion: Therefore, what is right and wrong is relative to one's tribe.

In the premises, we could substitute "X is good" or any other moral judgment, and then the conclusion would be changed, depending on the moral judgment. It is not difficult to determine that Premises 1 and 2 are another way of stating cultural relativism, and that the conclusion is another way of stating ethical relativism. Therefore, we can use the already developed strategy of presenting another argument of the same form, with true premises and a false conclusion, to show that the original argument is invalid:

Premise 1′: Tribe X believes the earth is roughly spherical.
Premise 2′: Tribe Y believes the earth is not roughly spherical (but rather is disk-shaped).
Conclusion: Therefore, the shape of the earth is relative to one's tribe.

If the conclusion of the first argument follows from Premises 1 and 2, then the conclusion of the second argument follows from Premises 1′ and 2′. Because the conclusion of the second argument does not follow from Premises 1′ and 2′ we can conclude, by *modus tollens*, that the conclusion of the first argument does not follow from Premises 1 and 2.

b. The Cause of a Belief. Another argument for ethical relativism is represented by the following:

P: The cause of S's belief that A is right is ———.
C: Therefore the truth of "A is right" is relative to ———.

We may supply 'S's society or culture', 'S's parents', or 'S's church' to fill in the two blanks. We fill the blank in the premise and the blank in the conclusion with the same thing. Also, to stress the perfect generality of this sort of argument, any value judgment may be supplied in place of "A is right."

The procedure for criticizing this argument is the same. We shall present, in the same form, an argument which everyone recognizes to be bad. If the first argument is good, the second must be good also. But since the second argument is not good, neither is the first.

P′: The cause of S's belief that the earth is roughly spherical is ———.
C′: The truth of "The earth is roughly spherical" is relative to ———.

To generalize: any factual belief can be substituted for the belief that the earth is spherical, and the blank can be filled in with such things as 'his trust in his geography teacher'. But it is absurd, of course, to suggest that the truth of a claim about the shape of the earth is relative to a student's trust in his geography teacher. This shows that P' is true and that C' is false, which is sufficient to show that arguments of this form are invalid. But if arguments of this form are invalid, the first argument is also invalid.

These, then, are two arguments often used as a defense of ethical relativism. But, because they are invalid, they can establish nothing. So far the theory of ethical relativism has fared quite badly; there are no reasons in its favor and there are reasons against it.

Exercises

Review

1. What is one important difference and one important similarity between the relationship of cultural relativism and ethical relativism, on the one hand, and the relationship of psychological egoism and ethical egoism, on the other?
2. What is the reason for denying that cultural relativism entails ethical relativism?
3. Describe the general method used to show that cultural relativism does not support ethical relativism.
4. Which is the most plausible argument in favor of ethical relativism? What is the criticism of that view?

Applications

1. If you know of another argument to establish ethical relativism, present it and evaluate it. (If the argument involves a relationship between cultural relativism and ethical relativism, show why it is not one of the arguments already examined.)
2. Evaluate the following argument:

    If tribe X uses an herb to cure colds, and it works, then we can say that it is true in Tribe X that the herb cures colds. Similarly, if, in Tribe X, they use slaves to till their fertile fields and they justify this on the grounds that it is morally preferable for slaves to work than members of their tribe, then (because a slave society works for Tribe X) we can say that it is true in Tribe X that slavery is morally acceptable.
3. Evaluate the following claim:

    The arguments in the preceding section are not acceptable because they all claim that moral knowledge is like scientific knowledge or some other kind of objective knowledge. However, this is just the point that the authors are attempting to establish; thus, they are begging the question.

B. Another Argument

1. *The Most Reasonable Hypothesis.* There are those who argue for ethical relativism in a different way. They point out that moral judgments concerning the same action or thing differ not only between two cultures but among almost all cultures. These people claim that cultural relativism, as stated, is correct but incomplete. In each culture, a different set of moral maxims is thought to be best, and these maxims usually conflict with one another. American morality is different from Indian morality, and both are different from Arabian morality. Given this difference, it is an unwarranted presumption on our part that our morality is the only "correct" morality. All the people in the various cultures are sincere and there are as many intelligent people living in Saudi Arabia or India as in the United States. The hypothesis that best explains the disagreement about which moral maxims are best is ethical relativism.

2. Reply. The history of science is full of instances of disagreement among sincere intelligent men. The shape of the earth has been disputed by members of different cultures. In modern times scientists have disagreed concerning the existence of caloric fluid, a substance that was supposed to be the cause of fire, and ether (a subtle medium through which light was thought to travel). It was a long time before the germ theory of disease was accepted, and in many cultures diseases are still believed to be the result of evil spirits.

If cultural relativism, plus the observation that there are many cultures that disagree concerning which moral maxims are best, is sufficient for establishing ethical relativism, then we can similarly establish medical relativism and physical relativism, for the arguments said to establish ethical relativism have exact analogues in those fields. Because relativism analogous to ethical relativism is a false doctrine in these areas, the argument that purports to establish ethical relativism must be rejected.

Ethical relativists overlook the fact that there has been disagreement in almost every area of human inquiry. There has been tremendous and continuing disagreement in physics, for example, and yet there are few physical relativists. We say that someone, or perhaps everyone, is mistaken when there is such disagreement. Sometimes it is even said that no one has yet discovered what is correct in physics and that perhaps no one ever will. This kind of explanation of disagreement can be applied to the phenomenon of cultural relativism. It might be that this area of human investigation, like every other area of human investigation, is one in which we have not yet discovered what is correct, or in which there is not yet widespread agreement on what is correct. In short, the explanation of cultural relativism can be of the same type as the explanation of the corresponding physical relativism.

3. Objectivity. Once again we have rejected an argument because another argument of the same form produces obviously false conclusions. This last argument is less formal than those examined earlier, but it has the same kind of defect and must, accordingly, be repudiated. The arguments presented in this discussion in favor of ethical relativism are, as far as we know, the main arguments proposed to establish that position; and they all fail. Yet, one must wonder why this view is so widespread, especially among college students.

There are, we believe, two reasons for this. First, students come to believe that it is "unscientific" to hold any position other than ethical relativism. They believe this because the distinction and relation between cultural relativism and ethical relativism is not made sufficiently clear in those areas of study concerning cultural relativism. Also, they believe that, if one denies ethical relativism, one is committed to "an absolute," and absolutes are "bad" things.

Second, and more important for our purposes, philosophers have presented some reasons that seem to throw doubt on the *objectivity* of moral judgments. Many people are inclined to believe that moral judgments, unlike scientific judgments, are "a matter of taste." They believe that the status of moral judgments is radically different from that of scientific judgments. They often believe, falsely, that the way to express this difference is through ethical relativism. Now that ethical relativism has been shown to be seriously lacking as a theory, it is time to point out that those who believe there is a great difference between moral and factual judgments will be served best by noncognitivism. This theory has often been accused of having consequences similar to those of ethical relativism, but this is a conclusion repudiated by its leading exponents, and justifiably so (see Chapter 13).

Summary. We have distinguished between cultural and ethical relativism. The former view concerns the fact of moral disagreement in different cultures and traces the source of such disagreement to the different cultures involved. Ethical relativism is a thesis concerning the truth or correctness of moral judgments; it claims that the same action can be correctly or justifiably judged, in contrary or contradictory ways, in different cultures. Various attempts to establish some connection between the two theses were examined. All were found to be ineffective, and most were invalid as well. We then attempted to explain why there is a fairly widespread belief in ethical relativism. To all of these explanations we might add that the belief in ethical relativism is no doubt the result of cultural influences.

Exercises

Review

1. What is the most reasonable hypothesis argument? How is it criticized?
2. Why is it that one is not committed to the claim that moral judgments have the same status as scientific judgments when one denies ethical relativism?

Applications

1. What, in your opinion, accounts for the widespread popularity of ethical relativism? What misunderstandings are involved in that kind (or those kinds) of reason (or reasons)?
2. Evaluate the following claim:

   If we reject ethical relativism, then we are opening the door to intolerance.

We are saying that one nation has the right to impose its values on other nations that it judges to be wicked. One would think that moral progress consists of the opposite view—of tolerance.

3. What arguments can be generated from the following, and how can it be evaluated:

If we do not let other societies live the way they want, they will not let us live the way we want.

Bibliography

BENEDICT, R. *Patterns of Culture*. New York: Houghton Mifflin Company, 1934. Cultural relativism is vividly presented, and ethical relativism espoused.

*BRANDT, RICHARD B. *Ethical Theory*. Englewood Cliffs, N.J.: Prentice-Hall, Inc., 1959, Chapter 11. A thorough treatment of all aspects of the problem; unfortunately couched in terms of "moral axioms." (See fn. 1 on p. 168.)

———. *Hopi Ethics: A Theoretical Analysis*. Chicago: University of Chicago Press, 1954, pp. 87–90. The author makes distinctions that, in part, are the same as the ones made in this work in the context of a sophisticated discussion of ethical and cultural relativism. The author attempts to determine whether any facts about the Hopi support ethical relativism and is on the whole inclined to think that such facts do not support ethical relativism.

FRANKENA, WILLIAM K. *Ethics*. Englewood Cliffs, N.J.: Prentice-Hall, Inc., 1963, pp. 92–94. A brief explanation of the difference between cultural and ethical relativism.

GARNETT, A. C. "Relativism and Absolutism in Ethics," *Ethics*, 54 (1943–44), 186–99. Garnett argues that while the good is relative, the right is absolute.

*HENSON, RICHARD G. "Ethical Relativism and a Paradox About Meaning," *The Philosophical Quarterly*, 11 (1961), 245–55. A criticism of a definition of 'ethical relativism' given by Brandt in *Hopi Ethics*.

KLUCKHOHN, CLYDE. "Ethical Relativity: Sic et Non," *The Journal of Philosophy*, 52 (1955), 663–77. Part of a symposium on ethical relativity. The author argues that discoveries of psychology, psychiatry, sociology, and anthropology, plus the regularities in the human situation make the position of radical ethical relativism untenable, but he still allows possibility of a limited form of ethical relativism.

*LADD, J. *The Structure of a Moral Code*. Cambridge, Mass.: Harvard University Press, 1957. An investigation of Navaho ethics and ethical beliefs. See especially pp. 322–28; a defense of the claim, "The particular situation in which the agent finds himself determines to some extent what he ought to do."

*NORTHROP, F. S. C. "Ethical Relativism in the Light of Recent Legal Science," *The Journal of Philosophy*, 52 (1955), 649–62. Part of a symposium on ethical relativity. Northrop discusses three theories of law: the thesis of natural law, the law of the land, and the "living law," and argues that the last must be judged according to the first.

PLATO. *Gorgias*. An argument against ethical relativism.

*SCHMIDT, PAUL F. "Some Criticisms of Cultural Relativism," *The Journal of Philosophy*, 52 (1955), 780–91. Author uses 'cultural relativism' to mean what we mean by 'ethical relativism', so this article is a criticism of ethical relativism. He points out many confusions, mistakes, and ambiguities in the relativist position.

SUMNER, W. C. *Folkways*. Boston: Ginn and Company, 1934. An influential relativist.

*TAYLOR, PAUL W. "Four Types of Ethical Relativism," *The Philosophical Review*, **63** (1954), 500–16. Taylor distinguishes and criticizes four types of ethical relativism.

WELLMAN, CARL. "The Ethical Implications of Cultural Relativity," *The Journal of Philosophy*, **60** (1963), 169–84. A clear defense of the claim, "By themselves the facts of cultural relativity do not imply anything for ethics."

WESTERMARCK, E. *Ethical Relativity*. New York: Harcourt, Brace & World, Inc., 1932. A clear statement of the ethical relativist's view.

CHAPTER

9

Freedom

A theory of obligation is intended to provide a theoretical foundation for the assessment of the rightness of actions of individuals, while a theory of value concerns the evaluation of the individuals themselves plus their desires, motives, intentions, as well as some of the consequences of their actions.[1] We might say that a philosopher who presents a theory of obligation—for example, a utilitarian—attempts to provide the normative conditions for an action's being right or wrong, or for a person's being praiseworthy or blameworthy for what he does. A normative judgment is justified when it satisfies the conditions described by some justified normative theory. For example, if S can prove that utilitarianism is justified, and that his action of burning his draft card in protest against militarism leads to the greatest good for the greatest number, then the judgment that he did what was right is correct. The theory of obligation, in this case, describes the normative condition of the correctness of the judgment.

A correct normative theory allows us to determine which judgments are correct—even judgments about the moral correctness of making or uttering incorrect judgments. Sometimes we are morally justified in making incorrect judgments, and some of the incorrect judgments that we are justified in making are themselves moral judgments. We would all agree that we are justified in merely uttering a false statement when our cause is just and we wish to mislead the enemy. We may say that our main forces are at one place when they are at another, or we may say that the leader of our country is a wicked man in order to mislead the enemy as to our loyalty. In the first case we

[1] As we have pointed out, a theory of value is needed to supplement any teleological theory of obligation; but there are some things which philosophers have thought to have *moral* value. These are (with the exception of some of the consequences of actions) the things listed above, but the reader is reminded that a general theory of value is wider than this list indicates.

would be morally justified in saying what is false, and in the second in uttering a moral judgment which we believe to be incorrect.

It is easy to construct examples to show that we are sometimes justified in uttering incorrect moral judgments (whether or not we know them to be correct). Suppose that the father of a cowardly soldier is dying and we, who witnessed the death of his son, are present. The father does not believe that his son is a coward—and, if he did, his last moments of life would be a terrible agony of shame and regret. If we say that what the son did in battle—*viz.*, hid instead of holding his position—was morally right, the father will believe us and not suffer. If we say what his son did was wrong the father will suffer and then die (at the same time he would have if we had said nothing or the opposite). If we suppose that our uttering of this judgment will have no other morally relevant effects, then we can safely say that we would be morally justified in saying that the son did what was right. However, we would know that we had lied.[2]

Thus, one can be morally justified in uttering moral judgments that are not correct. Uttering a moral judgment is an action performed by human beings, and the moral justifiability of that action is to be treated in the same way as the moral justifiability of any other action.[3]

There are also some nonnormative conditions that must be met before we can make a correct moral judgment. For example, the judgment that S was wrong to do A would not be correct unless S actually did A. It might be that someone is morally justified in uttering the judgment that S's doing A was wrong, but it would not be a correct judgment. It is not necessary to include conditions of correctness in a normative theory of obligation, and usually it is not done because such conditions are not really part of normative ethics. Another important condition for the correctness of some normative judgments of obligation is that the person involved in the action be free. If S were not,

---

[2] The justification of the uttering of the above judgment is not dependent upon any particular normative theory of obligation.

[3] In some cases, a person is morally justified not only in *uttering* an incorrect judgment. but in *making* an incorrect moral judgment. Let us suppose that the cowardly soldier has a wife and three children. It is not fantastic also to suppose that the wife will not be able to raise her three children well unless she believes that her husband was not a coward, and that he did what was morally right when he fled. When we consider that the future well-being of the three children, as well as the mother, depends upon her believing that moral judgment to be correct, it does seem that there is a greater obligation to her children than to truth.

The woman, whatever her evidence, can be said to be morally justified in making the judgment that her husband's action was, itself, morally justified. If we were teleologists we might say that there is greater good to be gained from her believing the incorrect judgment about her husband than there is to be gained from her believing the contrary. Such a woman, on any normative theory, is not only morally justified in uttering the judgment, but also in making it.

in some sense, free to do A, then the judgment that he is blameworthy for having done A would not be correct.[4]

A. The Positions

1. *Some Necessary Conditions for Making a Correct Judgment of Moral Obligation.* There are two conditions that most philosophers would agree are necessary for the correctness of judgments of obligation:

1. S was able to do A.
2. S did A knowingly.

It seems to be a necessary condition of making a correct judgment of obligation that one be able correctly to assign moral praise or blame to the agent. Some philosophers seem to hold that to attribute moral praise to S for doing A is the same thing as to judge that the action of doing A is right. Certainly there is at least a close connection between the two. Because there is this connection, and because most authors who have written about freedom have used the language of praise or blame, we shall also avail ourselves of that mode of speech on occasion.

No correct moral judgment concerning any action of any agent, S, can be made without Condition 1 being true of S, because no blame can correctly accrue to S for not doing A if he could not possibly do A, and no justified praise for A's happening can come to S if he is incapable of doing anything to bring A about. We can say that when such a condition as (1) is necessary before a correct moral judgment can be made, it is a necessary condition for the correctness of such a judgment. For example, suppose that A is the action of saving the life of a small child about to dart in front of a car, by the pushing of a horn button. Imagine that S is sitting in his car but tied to the steering wheel by sturdy piano wires which prevent him from moving his hands to the horn button and sounding the horn. In such circumstances it would be incorrect (though not always morally blameworthy) to blame S for not sounding the horn.

Condition 2—"S did A knowingly"—is also necessary. It means that S did cause A, and that he knew that he was doing so. For example, suppose that

---

[4] Philosophers sometimes distinguish between an *action* and an *act* in a way which is here relevant. It is said that an action is the happening (the movement of the arm striking the little boy, the striking, and so on) *plus* the fact of the agency of the person doing the act. The act is the action without the inclusion of the intentions, desires, feelings, and so on of the person performing. If we use act in this restricted sense, then we can say that acts are good or bad independently of the person doing or not doing the act; freely or not. We are here concerned, though, with the actions of persons, not just acts. This is a problem concerning judgments of obligation, not judgments of value.

S teaches ethics in a rundown classroom scheduled for demolition. S does not know that dynamite charges have already been placed, to be set off by a button on the floor near the blackboard. One day, while pacing back and forth during his lecture, he steps on the button and his classroom is transformed into a pile of rubble. But it would be grossly unfair, and incorrect, to say that S is to be blamed for this catastrophe, or that he has violated any obligation. Nor would we be justified in saying that S is a bad or evil man.[5]

2. **A Problem Concerning Teleological Theories.** There is a problem concerning teleological theories, and especially utilitarianism, which must be discussed before we go on. There is reason to suppose that, if utilitarianism is a correct normative theory, one can make correct moral judgments about men's actions even though men are not free.

Utilitarianism is not one position, but many. However, for the purposes of this discussion we can consider a simple version of that view. Let us say that "A is right" means that "A brings about the greatest amount of good for the greatest number of persons." The second phrase is a general statement of the principle of utility. All moral terms, for most utilitarians, are defined by means of the principle of utility or by means of terms that are themselves defined by means of the principle of utility. Someone might claim, for example, that "S is morally praiseworthy for doing A" means "S's doing A is right." Because 'right' is defined by means of the principle of utility, 'morally praiseworthy' is not a moral notion independent of the principle of utility. (If it were, the utilitarian might find himself a deontologist.) Similarly, "S is morally responsible for doing A" can probably be rendered as "S knowingly brought about A, and a moral judgment (either positive or negative) concerning S's doing A can be correctly made." In the latter expression there occurs the notion of a correct moral judgment and, for the utilitarian, this is to be determined by the principle of utility. Once again we can see that the utilitarian would bring in the principle of utility to explain a seemingly independent moral notion.[6]

If (1) the above line of reasoning is correct, and (2) the greatest good for the greatest number can be brought about independently of the freedom of the agent, and (3) utilitarianism is correct, then (4) freedom is not a necessary condition of correct moral judgments. Some will say that Statements 1–3 are not sufficient evidence for Statement 4 because utilitarians such as Mill do say that men must be free in order for them to be responsible, and to allow correct judgments of right and wrong, praise and blame. Nevertheless, utilitarians seem to believe that freedom from external restraint is all that is

---

[5] Sometimes, of course, we would say that people are responsible for knowing things like where they must walk to avoid setting the charges off, but this does not seem to be one of those cases—especially if, as we can suppose, S had no good reason for even believing that there were charges set.

[6] Some have argued that the principle of justice is independent of the principle of utility. If so, then the above discussion will have to be modified.

necessary to allow correct moral judgments. Someone is free to do A, Mill says, when he is not physically restrained from doing A.

An examination of this kind of view independently of utilitarianism is justified because we have already shown that utilitarianism is an inadequate normative theory of obligation. It may be that we are mistaken in that claim, but if so the problem of freedom can be restated in utilitarian terms.

In order to show that Statement 2 is true, we must first point out that 'freedom' in Statement 2 does not merely mean 'lack of restraint'. This use is one that will be partially justified in what follows and fully in the course of this chapter. We can all admit that lack of restraint is a necessary condition for correctly saying that S brought about A. Suppose A consists of S's handing a pail of grain to a starving Indian, but that A comes about because someone else is pushing S's hand. We may say, along with the utilitarian, that S did not bring about the greatest good for the greatest number, (supposing that to be the effect of the giving) but that someone or something else did so. Suppose, though, that S is under the influence of drugs which make it impossible for him not to obey the commands of a person behind him who says, "Give the grain!" S knows what he is doing, but he does not have the ability to do otherwise. Under these circumstances, it would seem that the utilitarian is committed to saying that S did A freely. In a clear sense, however, S is not free at all. Yet, in spite of his not being free, he can bring about the greatest good for the greatest number. If this is so, then we have shown that Statement 2 is correct.

Under these circumstances, we can correctly judge that S's action is praiseworthy only if we suppose some theory such as utilitarianism. If we do suppose that utilitarianism is correct, then we can say that the action is right and that S is praiseworthy for what he did. All that is needed is lack of restraint, plus fulfillment of the principle of utility, for a correct moral judgment. Furthermore, this seems to be true no matter what moral terms one uses within a utilitarian context because it seems that other moral terms are defined either directly or indirectly by means of the principle of utility. In short, once we suppose the truth of Statements 1–3 it would seem that freedom is not required to make correct moral judgments—i.e., Statement 4.

We have argued that utilitarianism (and all other teleological theories) are inadequate. If we are correct in this we can proceed. If we are not correct, then perhaps the utilitarian solution to the problem of freedom must be accepted, and the discussion of this point can be viewed as a philosophical exercise.

3. *The Sufficient Conditions for Making a Correct Judgment of Moral Obligation.* Conditions 1 and 2 are recognized by most philosophers as necessary conditions for the correctness of judgments of obligation, or the correct assignment of praise or blame, but these conditions are not sufficient. For example, suppose that S comes home early from work one day because he has just been fired, and he finds his wife *Se* in the arms of the man who has been given *S*'s job. *Se* laughs at *S* when he tells her of his plight, and informs him that she is leaving him. His rival, who is drinking his twelve-year-old Scotch and wearing his favorite smoking jacket, throws the remains of his drink in *S*'s face. At this moment, *S* flies into a blind rage and strangles his antagonist.

The prosecutor may argue that *S* was able to do the strangling, and that when he did it he intended to bring about just the condition that resulted. *S* was certainly able to strangle the dead man, for he did it. When he brought about the death of the man through strangling he did it knowingly in that the act of his arms moving toward the man, his hands closing around the poor fellow's throat and squeezing was a willed act, not one that had some external cause or motive power. *S* intended, at that moment, to strangle the victim. But if the prosecutor rests his case at this point, the defense has a very good chance of winning.

The defense can argue that, under these circumstances, given the nature of human beings and that of *S* in particular, it was not humanly possible for *S* to forebear from inflicting harm. Given the passions that were aroused in *S*, he could not have done otherwise. In a court of law, this kind of defense is sometimes effective. We shall suggest that *S* is not *morally* to blame if we can indeed show that he could not have done otherwise; that there were not many possible actions open to *S*, but only the one. (If the reader is not persuaded, he is invited to add as many more similar conditions as will finally lead him to say that *S* is not to blame for what he did, or that the judgment that what *S* did was wrong is not correct.)

If Conditions 1 and 2 are necessary for the correctness of moral judgments, but not sufficient, what further condition or conditions must be added? The kinds of answers that have been given can be divided into two main groups: the conditional, and the nonconditional.

Conditional: 3a. If *S* had chosen otherwise, or if his character and desires had been different, then *S* could have done otherwise.[7]

Nonconditional: 3b. *S* could have done otherwise.[8]

If we hold that Conditions 1, 2, and 3a are jointly sufficient for making a correct moral judgment, we can say that the described case does not meet the three conditions. We can say that, given *S*'s state, his action was not

---

[7] G. E. Moore, *Ethics* (New York: Oxford University Press, 1965). In this book, on pp. 85–86, Moore says, "Our theory holds that, provided a man could have done something else, *if* he had chosen, that is sufficient to entitle us to say that his action really is either right or wrong."

[8] C. A. Campbell, "Is 'Free Will' a Pseudo-Problem?" *Mind*, 60 (1951), 441–465.

performed on the basis of some choice, but on the basis of passion. Given that we apply these conditions to human beings, the desires that S had in those conditions could have been only to do some kind of harm to his rival. If his desires had been different he might have beaten the man to death with a poker, or poured brandy on him and set him aflame, or—if he were outweighed—he may have shot his adversary. The description of the case would then become more complex, but that is no reason for rejecting this kind of explanation.

If we hold that Conditions 1, 2, and 3b are jointly sufficient for making a correct moral judgment, we should say simply that, given the situation, S could not have done otherwise and he is, therefore, not to be praised or blamed for what he did. The judgment that what he did was morally wrong is not correct.

There is a great difference between the two versions of Conditions 3—a difference which gives rise to a number of competing positions on the issue of freedom. But before these positions can be stated fully, another set of distinctions must be drawn.

4. The Positions. Let us present two rival theses—the thesis of determinism (TD) and the thesis of indeterminism (TI):

The thesis of determinism: For every event, E_1, there occurs another event or set of events, E_2, which precedes E_1 and is causally sufficient for E_1.

The thesis of indeterminism: For some event (or events), E_1, there does not occur an event or set of events, E_2, which precedes E_1, and is causally sufficient for E_1.

The thesis of determinism is simply a precise way of saying that every event has a cause. Similarly, the thesis of indeterminism is simply a precise way of saying that some events are uncaused.

In order to distinguish the rival positions on the issue of freedom, we can make use of three premises:

Premise 1: If TD, then all human actions (events performed by human beings) are preceded by other events which are causally sufficient for them. (We might have said this by saying that all human acts are determined. Let us use the letters *HAD* to symbolize the consequent of this proposition.)
The first premise will read, "If TD, then *HAD*."

Premise 2: If *HAD*, then it is causally impossible for a person to do any action other than the one he did. The consequent of this proposition might be expressed "No one can do other than he did," or *CDO*.
The second premise will read, "If *HAD*, then *CDO*."

Premise 3: If *CDO*, then one is never correct in judging that anyone's action is morally right or wrong, or that anyone is to be praised or blamed for what he does. (Let us use the letters *NCJ* to stand for the consequent of this statement—the claim that no correct judgments of the type described can be made.) The final premise will read, "If *CDO*, then *NCJ*."

So far no argument has been presented, but merely some of the premises of an argument. We shall see how these premises, combined with others, lead to the positions we wish to consider. Notice that, if someone asserts Premise 1, he is asserting neither *TD* nor *NCJ*, but only that *if TD, then NCJ*. By the same token if one asserts, "If it rains then I'll stay at home," he is not aserting that it is (or will be) raining, nor that he will stay at home, but merely the hypothetical proposition that *if* it rains *then* he will stay at home.

The hard determinist asserts *TD* and then, by *modus ponens*, concludes *HAD*, *CDO*, and finally *NCJ*. The answer that the hard determinist gives to our original question is that under no conditions are we ever able to make a correct moral judgment concerning *S* or *A*.

From the fact that human beings do not ultimately shape their own character, I said, it *follows* that they are never morally responsible. . . . I mean "follow" or "imply" in the same sense as, or in a sense closely akin to, that in which the conclusion of a valid syllogism follows from the premises.[9]

Paul Edwards, the author of the passage quoted, believes that there are always *causes* beyond a person's control that shape his character. If *TD* is correct, there are strong reasons for believing Edwards. If a person does not shape his own character, and all his actions proceed from that character, the person is not ever responsible for anything that he does.

The soft determinist denies the truth of Premise 1 or Premise 3, or both. He thinks that either *TD* is not sufficient for *HAD*—and, hence, that Premise 1 is false and/or that *CDO* is not sufficient for *NCJ*, and, hence, that Premise 3 is false. The soft determinist also claims that Conditions 1, 2, and 3a are the nonnormative conditions sufficient for making correct moral judgments of obligation.

The libertarian will attempt to prove that *NCJ* is false and that *CJ* is true and then, by *modus tollens*, deduce that *CDO* is false as well. (This means that he accepts all three premises but claims that *S* could have done otherwise.) Then, because *CDO* is false, he can, by *modus tollens* and Premise 2, conclude the falsity of *HAD*. Finally, the falsity of *HAD* and the truth of Premise 1 lead him to assert the falsity of *TD*. (The libertarian, though, presents a separate argument to show that *TD* is false.) The libertarian denies *NCJ*—that is, he asserts that we are sometimes correct when

[9] Paul Edwards, "Hard and Soft Determinism," in *Determinism and Freedom*, ed. Sydney Hook (New York: Crowell-Collier Publishing Company, 1958), p. 125.

we make moral judgments about people or actions. The hard determinist answers that no moral judgments are ever correct, and the soft determinist maintains that moral judgments are correct when and only when Conditions 1, 2, and 3a are met. The libertarian says that Conditions 1, 2, and 3b are the necessary and sufficient nonnormative conditions for the correctness of moral judgments.

Let us state the thesis of libertarianism:

The thesis of libertarianism: For some human actions, E_1, there does not occur an event, or set of events, E_2, which precedes E_1, and is causally sufficient for E_1, and yet E_1 is the result of a choice of the doer of E_1.

B. A Closer Look at the Three Positions

1. Soft Determinism. The soft determinist answers the question "Under what conditions are we justified in judging that S's doing A is morally right (or wrong, or obligatory)?" by listing Conditions 1 ,2, and 3a.

1. *S* is able to do *A*.
2. *S* knowingly brought *A* about.
3. If *S* had chosen otherwise, or if his character and desires had been different, then *S* could have done otherwise.

a. EVIDENCE IN FAVOR OF SOFT DETERMINISM. If we deny the thesis of determinism, the soft determinist argues, then we are denying one of the necessary conditions of moral responsibility. Presented below are two such views:

If a man's choice were indetermined, it would be theoretically unpredictable. The man himself could not have foreseen his choice, nor could he have taken any steps to prevent it. It would have sprung not from his personality, but from nothing at all. He would still be a "victim," not of determining circumstances, but of *chance*. What room is there here for an ethical judgment? [10]

We can speak of motives only in a causal context; thus it becomes clear how very much of the concept of responsibility rests upon that of causation, that is, upon the regularity of volitional decisions. In fact if we should conceive of a decision as utterly without any cause (this would in all strictness be the indeterministic presupposition) then the act would be entirely a matter of *chance*, for chance is identical with the absence of a cause; there is no other opposite of causality. Could we under such conditions, make the agent responsible? Certainly not. Imagine a man, always calm, peaceful and blameless, who suddenly falls

[10] C. L. Stevenson, *Ethics and Language* (New Haven: Yale University Press, 1944), p. 313. By permission of the publisher.

upon and begins to beat a stranger. He is held and questioned regarding the motive of his actions, to which he answers, in his opinion truthfully, as we assume: "There was no motive for my behavior. Try as I may I can discover no reason. My volition was without any cause—I desired to do so, and there is simply nothing else to be said about it." We should shake our heads and call him insane, because we have to believe that there was a cause, and lacking any other we must assume some mental disturbance as the only cause remaining; but certainly no one would hold him to be responsible.[11]

The above argument can be put in the following way: In order for us correctly to judge that S is morally responsible for some action, S must not only have brought that action about, but he must also have done it knowingly.[12] According to the thesis of indeterminism, we must say that a free action is preceded by nothing causally sufficient for it. But the notion of an action being preceded by nothing is quite puzzling. Suppose, for example, that a teacher discovers his hand picking up a pistol left on the lectern by the lecturer in a preceding firearms class. If his hand is not under his control and his finger squeezes the trigger and students begin to fall from bullet wounds, we cannot truly say that the teacher is to blame for what happened. Any sudden, unexpected, unpredictable action which does not "come from" the agent is not, according to the soft determinist, something for which the individual can be held morally responsible. This is, in fact, one of the main arguments of the soft determinist, and it can also be used by the hard determinist against the libertarian. On the whole, the argument seems to be quite a strong one: there must be some connection between the individual and his action (other than his performing it) before he can be held responsible for it.

[11] From *Problems of Ethics* by Moritz Schlick, trans. by David Rynin, Dover Publications, Inc., New York, 1939. Reprinted through the permission of the publisher. Pp. 156–57.

[12] It must be admitted that sometimes it is correct to judge that S was wrong to bring about A even when he did not do so knowingly. This might occur when we can justly hold that S had an obligation to know that A would be the result of what he did do. Suppose, for example, that a man takes his children for a long ride in mountainous country, a worn tire blows and the resulting accident causes the death of his two children. We might say that he did not knowingly cause the death of his two children, but even so we would be justified in saying that he is morally responsible for their deaths. Even if he did not know that the tire was worn, we can still blame him for driving on it, for in certain circumstances a man has an obligation to take reasonable precautions against such occurrences. The principle which would cover this is that a man has an obligation to know whatever is required (so long as the requirement is reasonable) in order to fulfill (other) obligations that he has.

Given the above line of reasoning, we can restate Condition 2 so that it is in line with this truth. (2'): S did A knowingly or he would have done so had he fulfilled his obligations with respect to doing A (call them A') where A' is a necessary condition of doing A. It may seem to the serious student that we are including normative considerations here (where none belong). However, for A' we can give the list of nonnormative conditions which are necessary before we can make a normative judgment about A.

b. Arriving at Soft Determinism. If one accepts the thesis of determinism and yet denies the conclusion that we are never morally justified in praising or blaming a person for his actions, he must deny at least one of the basic premises:

1. If *TD* then *HAD*.
2. If *HAD* then *CDO*.
3. If *CDO* then *NCJ*.

If one affirms *TD*, it takes but little logic to see that *NCJ* follows. If one want to assert *TD* and deny *NCJ*, one of the three premises will have to be shown to be false.

The soft determinist finds himself in exactly this position: sometimes he attempts to deny Premise 1, sometimes Premise 3, and sometimes both. Premise 3 might be expressed in the following way: "If it is causally impossible for anyone ever to do any action other than the one he does, one is never correct in judging that another's action is morally right or wrong, or that anyone is to be praised or blamed for what he does." It is this thesis, then, that the soft determinist denies. He says that even though there may be an action which is the only one a person could have done, still we can say correctly that his doing that action is morally right or wrong or that he is to be praised or blamed for what he does.

Now it is possible to express *CDO* in another way. The soft determinist says that *CDO* expresses the claim that a person's actions are the causal result of his personality and desires. Given the kind of person S is, it is not possible, in a given set of circumstances, that S do anything other than A. Surely, the soft determinist would add, it would be strange to hold S responsiblie for that which did not proceed from his personality and character —which, in effect, did not come from him at all. Another soft determinist, John Stuart Mill, makes this point in a very straightforward manner:

> . . . given the motives which are present to an individual's mind, and given likewise the character and disposition of the individual, the manner in which he will act might be unerringly inferred; that if we knew the person thoroughly, and knew all the inducements which are acting upon him, we could foretell his conduct with as much certainty as we can predict any physical event. This proposition I take to be a mere interpretation of universal experience, a statement in words of what everyone is internally convinced of. No one who believed that he knew thoroughly the circumstances of any case and the characters of the different persons concerned, would hesitate to foretell how all of them would act. Whatever degree of doubt he may in fact feel, arises from the uncertainty whether he really knows the circumstances, or the character of some one or other of the persons, with the degree of accuracy required; but by no means from thinking that if he did know these things, there could be any uncertainty what the conduct would be. Nor does this full assurance conflict in the smallest degree with what is called our

feeling of freedom. We do not feel ourselves the less free, because those to whom we are intimately known are well assured how we shall will to act in a particular case. We often, on the contrary, regard the doubt what our conduct will be, as a mark of ignorance of our characters and sometimes even resent it as an imputation.[13]

Given the above interpretation of *CDO*, it would seem that Premise 3 is clearly false. After all, are we to say that no one should be blamed for his actions—actions he performs because he is the person he is? If a man could do otherwise, where this means acting contrary to his personality, character, and desires, then we *would* refrain from making a moral judgment, for then the man himself is not acting.

c. The Argument Against Soft Determinism. The libertarian, the hard determinist, and the soft determinist all agree that the basic premises, when supplemented by the assertion of *TD* or the denial of *NCJ*, result in a valid argument. The soft determinist claims, however, that at least one premise (usually Premise 3) is false, while the libertarian and the hard determinist claim that all the premises are true. The way to attack the soft determinist, therefore, is to argue for the truth of all the premises. We shall here argue only for the truth of Premise 3, for it is the one most often attacked. (Similar arguments can be constructed, however, for Premises 1 and 2.)

The soft determinist's assertion of Condition 3a involves the notion of internal causation. Certainly, the soft determinist says, our actions are caused, but Condition 3a specifies that only when the cause is internal, is the action the performer's. However, internal causes seem to be no less causes for their being internal. For example, suppose that *S* is given a posthypnotic suggestion to strangle anyone who argues against ethical egoism. Having dispatched his deontologist roommate, *S* becomes fully aware of his horrible deed. However, we can save *S* from moral (and legal) condemnation by getting a confession from his other roommate, a psychology major, to the effect that he had hypnotized *S* and given him the posthypnotic command.

Hence, even though the causes seem to be internal, we would not correctly judge that the action is wrong, or blame *S*. Now, if *TD* is correct (as the soft determinist admits), there are causes operating within each of us that are no less compelling than this hypnotic suggestion. (Especially if a person is to be compared with a computer, or a machine, as is often done, it is quite difficult to see how he is to be blamed for what he does.) Hence this ploy of the soft determinist fails to answer the objection to his claim that Premise 3 is false, and until further evidence is presented we must grant that Premise 3 is true, and that soft determinism is thereby shown to be unacceptable.

[13] John Stuart Mill, *A System of Logic, Ratiocinative and Inductive: Being a Connected View of the Principles of Evidence and the Methods of Scientific Investigation* (New York: Harper & Row, Publishers, 1874), Book VI, Chap. 2, pp. 581–82.

d. "S Could Have Done Otherwise." In the face of mounting criticism, the soft determinist is likely to argue that all that is required for a person to be free from compulsion is for it to be true that, if he had chosen otherwise or if his character and desires had been different, he could have done otherwise. But *can* a man choose otherwise? Unless he can, both the hard determinist and libertarian would argue, he is not free. Furthermore, if *TD* is true, there is little reason for believing that a man can choose otherwise, and so this argument does not help the soft determinist. This reply is one that is frequently used by the libertarian, especially by C. A. Campbell:

We saw that there is no real question whether A who told a lie could have acted otherwise *if* he had chosen otherwise. But there is a very real question, at least for any person who approaches the question of moral responsibility at a tolerably advanced level of reflexion, about whether A could have *chosen* otherwise. Such a person will doubtless be acquainted with the claims advanced in some quarters that causal law operates universally: or/and with the theories of some philosophies that the universe is throughout the expression of a single supreme principle; or/and with the doctrines of some theologians that the world is created, sustained and governed by an Omniscient and Omnipotent Being. Very understandably such world-views awaken in him doubts about the validity of his first, easy instinctive assumption that there are genuinely open possibilities before a man at the moment of moral choice. It thus becomes for him a real question whether a man could have chosen otherwise than he actually did, and, in consequence, whether man's moral responsibility is really defensible. For how can a man be morally responsible, he asks himself, if his choices, like all other events in the universe, could not have been otherwise than they in fact were? It is precisely against the background of world-views such as these that for reflective people the problem of moral responsibility normally arises.

Furthermore, to the man who has attained this level of reflexion, it will in *no* class of cases be a sufficient condition of moral responsibility for an act that one could have acted otherwise *if* one had chosen otherwise—not even in these cases where there *was* some possibility of the operation of 'external constraint'. In these cases he will indeed expressly recognize freedom from external constraint as a *necessary condition*, but not as a *sufficient* condition. For he will be aware that, even granted *this* freedom, it is still conceivable that the agent had no freedom to choose otherwise than he did, and he will therefore require that the latter sort of freedom be added if moral responsibility for the act is to be established.[14]

Let us present what we should expect to find if Campbell is correct: a counterexample to the soft determinist's claim that Conditions 1, 2, and 3a are the three nonnormative conditions that must be met before we can make a correct moral judgment about S or his actions. Let us consider the three conditions in terms of the story about the man who strangled his roommate.

---

[14] Campbell, *op. cit.*, pp. 455–56.

1. *S* was able to strangle his roommate.
2. *S* strangled his roommate knowingly. (Let us suppose that he was also given the posthypnotic suggestion to be perfectly aware of everything that he did.)
3a. If *S* had chosen otherwise, or if his character and desires had been different, then *S* could have done otherwise. (He certainly would not have strangled his roommate if he had chosen not to be subject to the hypnotic command. Of course, what we want to know is whether he could have chosen that.)

S has met all the conditions which the soft determinist claims he must meet before he can be correctly held responsible for his actions, yet one cannot justifiably claim that *S* can be held responsible. This satisfies all the criteria for a good counterexample, and seems to be quite damaging to the soft determinist's position.

Thus, the soft determinist claims that the Conditions 1, 2, and 3a are the only nonmoral conditions that must be met before a judgment about a person's actions can be correct. However, there seems to be good reason for supposing that this is not so. The positive arguments of the soft determinist lack force, and there are convincing counterexamples to his position. Furthermore, the sort of consideration that Campbell raises has a great deal of weight. Both the libertarian and the hard determinist would agree that the soft determinist is not their most formidable rival.

Exercises

Review

1. Describe a circumstance in which it would be justifiable to make an incorrect nonmoral judgment. Also describe a circumstance in which it would be justifiable to make an incorrect moral judgment.
2. What are the two conditions most philosophers think are necessary for the making of a correct judgment of praise or blame?
3. Why, if utilitarianism is an acceptable theory, can correct moral judgments be made about men's actions, even though men are not free?
4. What are the reasons for believing that Conditions 1 and 2 are not necessary and sufficient for the making of a correct moral judgment?
5. Describe the difference between Conditions 3a and 3b.
6. State the position of the soft determinist. How does he argue for his case, and what are the objections to his position?

Applications

1. Describe an action from your own experience in which Conditions 1–3a are met, and yet the person performing the action is not morally responsible.
2. Show, in a precise way, how the (correct) claim that natural laws are descriptive rather than prescriptive has led some philosophers to the position of soft determinism.

2. Hard Determinism. It is now time to examine the hard determinist's answer.

a. THE HARD DETERMINIST'S ANSWER. Both the hard determinist and the libertarian agree that the three premises from which each wishes to draw his own conclusion are true. Their disagreement is over which premise is to be added to those three premises to complete the argument. The hard determinist asserts *TD*, which allows him to conclude *HAD*. Given *HAD*, he can conclude, also by *modus ponens*, *CDO*, and finally *NCJ*. The assertion of *NCJ* allows him to assert that under *no* circumstances are we correct in judging that *S*'s doing *A* is morally right (or wrong, or obligatory) or that *S* is to be praised or blamed for what he does.

This answer is contrary to what seems to be true. However, if hard determinism meets the criteria of acceptability of theories better than its rival, we would be justified in asserting that answer. The crucial aspect of the hard deterministic position is the thesis of determinism. If this is established, and the truth of the premises is shown, then hard determinism is correct, no matter how little we should like to admit it.

b. THE EVIDENCE FOR THE THESIS OF DETERMINISM. In our daily existence, we constantly encounter verifications of the thesis of determinism. Whenever some event occurs, we are almost invariably either directly or indirectly aware of its cause. If a sound of squealing tires is heard the car which caused that sound can usually be seen also. When we are not directly aware of the cause of an event, we can usually infer its existence and nature from our previous knowledge of the causes of such events. If we perceive an artificial satellite we infer that someone launched it. If we find the level in the bottle of gin diminished, we can infer that someone has been at it. If someone suggests that the gin might have simply disappeared, we would not know what to make of this suggestion. We would insist that things do not simply disappear and that there is always a cause for such things as empty or nearly empty gin bottles. Hence, in our experience, the hard determinist concludes, there is ample evidence for *TD*, and to suppose that human behavior or choice is an exception is no better than to suppose that everything has a cause except the disappearance of gin from the gin bottle.

All types of scientific research suppose that the events being studied have causes. Without this assumption, there would be no sense at all in carrying out any experiments or proposing theories. Furthermore, when the thesis of determinism is supposed there is always great success in scientific work. When it is not supposed, science stagnates.

It has always been believed by some that many areas of human experience are not described by the thesis of determinism. This thesis was, at various times, believed not to be applicable to the movement of bodies on earth, the motion of the planets, the stars, living animals, and, finally men. Area after area, however, has come within the sphere of the thesis of determinism. The hard determinist might point out that, although it is often claimed that human actions are not causal consequences of other states (that they are not strictly determined) in the light of past scientific successes, this is a very weak claim.

We have discovered, in the last three hundred years, a vast number of facts about human beings. We have discovered the nature of the circulatory and respiratory systems, the function of every important organ in the body, the explanation of locomotion, the nature and causes of many diseases, and the methods of preventing and curing most human ailments. The science of psychology attempts to find the causes of behavior, and psychologists have indeed explained much of human behavior.

If we list the past success of scientists in explaining the nature of human beings and the partial success of psychologists in explaining human behavior, there is good evidence for supposing that all human behavior will, one day, be explainable by scientific laws. Given that scientific laws are deterministic, it seems to be the case that the thesis of determinism applies to human actions just as much as it applies to anything else. If we do not suppose this, we must give some other evidence to show that human actions are different from all other human phenomena—different in that they alone are not describable by the thesis of determinism.

Hard determinists often view human beings as wax tablets onto which their elders impress whatever they wish. Each of us is molded by our teachers and environment so that what we feel and do is solely a function of these influences.

Mores are taught to the young, not as a set of practical expedients but as a set of sacred absolutes. Wherever the mores are firmly established, obedience is automatic. When fully internalized by the individual, the mores control behavior by making it psychologically very difficult for him to commit the forbidden act. For example, we do not refrain from eating our children or our enemies because of an intellectual decision that cannibalism is impractical or wasteful, but because the idea of cannibalism is so repellent to us that the thought of eating human flesh never seriously occurs to us. Most of us would be unable to eat human flesh even if we tried to do so. Mores function by making their violation emotionally impossible. In a society with a clearly defined, firmly implanted set of mores, there is very little personal misconduct.[15]

This argument is very simple. Each of us has a certain nature and finds himself in a certain environment. Given what "goes into" us, that is, how our environment affects us and the mores that we are taught, what "comes out" is causally necessitated. We might go even further and say that, according to this argument, human beings are simply very complex thinking machines that are "programmed" by their environment and training. A computer does not have any choice as to what information it supplies, and similarly, neither

[15] From *Sociology* by Paul B. Horton and Chester L. Hunt. Copyright 1964 by McGraw-Hill, Inc. Used by permission. P. 60.

do human beings. They cannot do many of those things that have been forbidden. On the other hand, if they do something, then that, too, is just a result of prior influences.

Exercises

Review
   1. What is the relation betwen hard determinism and the thesis of determinism?
   2. What reasons are there for *TD*?

Applications
   1. Describe an action from your own experience that seems to call for a moral judgment, and show how the hard determinist would analyze the situation to show that the judgment is not correct.
   2. If you know of any further arguments to support *TD*, present them.
   3. Present and evaluate some reasons to support the following claim. "If everyone were a hard determinist our entire social structure would change."

3. Libertarianism. Let us set aside, for a moment, the hard determinist's positive arguments, and see how the libertarian argues for his position. The libertarian argues for *CJ* (that is, the denial of *NCJ*) and then, by *modus tollens*, concludes not-*CDO*. Not-*CDO* allows us to conclude not-*HAD* (again by *modus tollens*) and, finally, not-*HAD* allows us to use *modus tollens* once more in deriving not *TD*. The libertarian also presents arguments independent of the assertion *CJ* for supposing not-*TD*.

One can see that the libertarian and the hard determinist start from different ends of the argument. The libertarian must defend his assertion *CJ* and also provide an answer to the question "What nonnormative conditions must be met before a normative judgment about a person or his actions can be correct?" Although an answer to this question follows naturally from the hard determinist's position, this is not true of the libertarian's position. We shall be interested, in what follows, in seing what sort of answer the libertarian has for this most important question, but let us begin by examining the libertarian's case for *CJ*.

   a. THE CASE FOR *CJ*. The case for *CJ* is short and not unconvincing. It is a fact of human existence that moral judgments concerning men and their actions are made. We seem to be totally justified in making some, but not all, of these judgments. Whatever the analysis or explanation of this phenomenon, it is something that cannot be denied. If it seems to be true that correct moral judgments are sometimes made, and there is no reason for supposing that what seems true is not, then that is a good reason for holding *CJ*.

It is easy to see that the libertarian must say something about the hard determinist's case for *TD*. If the libertarian says nothing, the hard determinist will have the advantage; but insofar as the case of the libertarian is strengthened, that of the hard determinist is weakened. First, however, we must present the libertarian's answer to our main question.

b. THE LIBERTARIAN'S ANSWER. The libertarian replaces Condition 3a of the soft determinist with Condition 3b: "S could have done otherwise." The problem is now to explain Condition 3b so as to clarify the libertarian's answer: "When Conditions 1, 2, and 3b are satisfied, then S is justified in judging that something is good or right." The libertarian can explain Condition 3b in the following way: "To say that S could have done otherwise is to say that A is the result of S's choice." This explanation forces us to distinguish between reasons and causes. Without going into a detailed analysis of the notion of causation, we can say that a cause is the sort of thing that is sufficient for some other event. It is not really helpful to say that some events are causally sufficient for other events, but it is perhaps the least misleading thing that can be said here. We can speculate that causal connections are the subject matter of most, if not all, scientific laws, but it is impossible to pursue such speculation here.

One thing that is relevant for our purposes is the fact that, if E_1 is the cause of E_2, then given E_1, E_2 will occur. E_2 always occurs when E_1 occurs unless another cause intervenes. If a man's drinking poison causes his death, then whenever a man drinks poison that man dies.

Reasons are different from causes in many respects. First, men can act *from* reasons, but not *from* causes (see Chapter 1). If we tell S that a good reason for helping a little old lady cross the street is that she always gives people who do this ten dollars, S might act from the appropriate maxim. But, the libertarian claims, it is up to S whether or not he acts from this maxim. This is not so with causes. We do not choose to die when our heads are cut off; it is not, in those circumstances, within our power to live.

In making this distinction between reasons and causes, the libertarian is not begging the question against the hard determinist. The hard determinist would, of course, claim that all reasons (or at least all "effective" reasons) are causes; that there are no reasons of the sort the libertarian supposes. Whether or not there are depends on the correctness of the theories, not upon the notions required to explain them. The libertarian introduces the notions of acting from a reason which may or may not have any instances. If the libertarian is correct, there are such instances; if the hard determinist is correct, there are no such instances. Whether there are or are not such instances is not, however, a function of the meaningfulness of the notion.

c. THE ATTACK ON *TD*. If his prima facie case is to have any weight, the libertarian must attack the hard determinist's case for *TD*. First, the libertarian would admit that deterministic descriptions apply to many, and indeed, most events in our lives, but he denies that it applies in *all* cases. The hard determinist has not established that claim, the libertarian would continue, and he will attempt to provide evidence that shows that *that* claim (and thus *TD*) is false. In the scientific sphere, there are at least two instances when *TD* is not only not presupposed, but is actually denied. The first instance of a denial of *TD* which we shall present is drawn from physics:

As an example we take the law of causality. Kant says that whenever we observe an event we assume that there is a foregoing event from which the other event must follow according to some rule. This is, as Kant states, the basis of all scientific work. In this discussion it is not important whether or not we can always find the foregoing event from which the other one followed. Actually we can find it in many cases. But even if we cannot, nothing can prevent us from asking what this foregoing event might have been and to look for it. Therefore, the law of causality is reduced to the method of scientific research; it is the condition which makes science possible. Since we actually apply this method, the law of causality is "a priori" and is not derived from experience.

Is this true in atomic physics? Let us consider a radium atom, which can emit an α-particle. The time for the emission of the α-particle cannot be predicted. We can only say that in the average the emission will take place in about two thousand years. Therefore, when we observe the emission we do not actually look for a foregoing event from which the emission must according to a rule follow. Logically it would be quite possible to look for such a foregoing event, and we need not be discouraged by the fact that hitherto none has been found. But why has the scientific method actually changed in this very fundamental question since Kant?

Two possible answers can be given to that question. The one is: We have been convinced by experience that the laws of quantum theory are correct and, if they are, we know that a foregoing event as cause for the emission at a given time cannot be found. The other answer is: We know the foregoing event, but not quite accurately. We know the forces in the atomic nucleus that are responsible for the emission of the α-particle. But this knowledge contains the uncertainty which is brought about by the interaction betwen the nucleus and the rest of the world. If we wanted to know why the α-particle was emitted at that particular time we would have to know the microscopic structure of the whole world including ourselves, and that is impossible. Therefore, Kant's arguments for the a priori character of the law of causality no longer apply.[16]

The libertarian would here stress that the uncertainty principle is not being brought up because human choice is thought by him to be like the movement of α-particles. It is brought up because it demonstrates that it is impossible to assert *TD*. If *TD* is denied, the way is cleared for his position.

The second example from science is F. Hoyle's cosmological theory of continuous creation.[17] This theory is not so widely accepted as Heisenberg's

---

[16] Werner Heisenberg, *Physics and Philosophy* (New York: Harper & Row, Publishers, 1958), pp. 89–90.

[17] Pp. 121–22. *The Nature of the Universe* by Fred Hoyle. Copyright 1950 by Fred Hoyle. Reprinted by permission of Harper & Row, Publishers. By permission of Basil Blackwell & Mott, Ltd.

uncertainty principle, but it is considered as a strong candidate for an acceptable theory.

Although I think there is no doubt that every galaxy we observe to be receding from us will in about 10,000,000,000 years have passed entirely beyond the limit of vision of an observer in our Galaxy, yet I think that such an observer would still be able to see about the same number of galaxies as we do now. By this I mean that new galaxies will have condensed out of the background material at just about the rate necessary to compensate for those that are being lost as a consequence of their passing beyond our observable universe. At first sight it might be thought that this could not go on indefinitely because the material forming the background would ultimately become exhausted. The reason why this is not so, is that new material appears to compensate for the background material that is constantly being condensed into galaxies. This is perhaps the most surprising of all the conceptions of the New Cosmology. For I find myself forced to assume that the nature of the Universe requires continuous creation—the perpetual bringing into being of new background material.[18]

Hoyle then explains the "origin" of this new material:

The most obvious question to ask about continuous creation is this: Where does the created material come from? It does not come from anywhere. Material simply appears—it is created. At one time the various atoms composing the material do not exist, and at a later time they do. This may seem a very strange idea and I agree that it is, but in science it does not matter how strange an idea may seem so long as it works—that is to say, so long as the idea can be expressed in a precise form and so long as its consequences are found to be in agreement with observation. Some people have argued that continuous creation introduces a new assumption into science—and a very startling assumption at that. Now I do not agree that continuous creation is an additional assumption. It is certainly a new hypothesis, but it only replaces a hypothesis that lies concealed in the older theories, which assume, as I have said before, that the whole of the matter in the Universe was created in one big bang at a particular time in the remote past. On scientific grounds this big bang assumption is much the less palatable of the two. For it is an irrational process that cannot be described in scientific terms. Continuous creation, on the other hand, can be represented by precise mathematical equations whose consequences can be worked out and compared with observation. On philosophical grounds too I cannot see any good reason for preferring the big bang idea. Indeed it seems to me in the philosophical sense to be a distinctly unsatisfactory notion, since it puts the basic assumption out of sight where it can never be challenged by a direct appeal to observation.[19]

Once again, the point is not that choosing is like continuous creation, but that a respectable theory may deny *TD* without thereby disgracing itself. It would seem to follow that *TD* is not a necessary condition even for a scientific

[18] *Ibid.*, pp. 121–22.
[19] *Ibid.*, pp. 123–24.

theory, and the ethical thinker who denies *TD* would feel some comfort from this fact.[20]

d. The Hard Determinist's Rejoinder. The hard determinist must, of course, reply to the libertarian's attack. He begins by admitting that *TD* does not apply in all areas. However, he would continue, there is evidence that it describes human beings. The areas in which *TD* does not apply are microphysical, whereas on the macrophysical level—the level on which human beings exist—*TD* does apply. The evidence for this claim is almost identical with the evidence already presented. Practically all the phenomena concerning human beings have been shown to fall under *TD*; the only questionable area is that of choice. Because all these other areas fall under *TD*, he argues, it is reasonable to suppose that this last one does also.

Furthermore, the libertarian's explanation of choice and its relation to action is quite mysterious. If hard determinism is correct, the problem of choice does not arise for there are no choices of the sort the libertarian assumes.

e. One Last Comment. The libertarian might argue that the history of psychology as a science is notorious for the lack of laws of human behavior. It is a praiseworthy thing, he would continue, for a man to have faith that such laws will be discovered, but one would think that fifty years of failures would be good evidence that, in this area, the type of laws found in physiology do not exist. Furthermore, when the hard determinist supposes that human actions are describable by laws which presuppose or embody *TD*, he is either begging the question or making a claim in the face of evidence to the contrary.

The second claim available to the libertarian at this point can be roughly stated in the following way: "The choices of men (sometimes) do not fall under *TD*, for they are made by the *person* and originate from the person, or some unit of agency that is often called *the self*. The libertarian claims that this notion presupposes nothing about the nature of this self, or the way in which it brings about actions. He also would claim that *any* metaphysical view about the nature of the self is consistent with his position. That is, he still relies on the notion of a self whether it is thought to be a collection of brain cells or a spiritual substance; for, he would argue, it is not any more difficult for a brain to choose than it is for a spirit to do so.

The important problem here, however, concerns the relation between the person and the actions he performs. When a man chooses to act and then does, how does his choice get translated into movements of limbs? When we think of one ball colliding with another it seems perfectly understandable

[20] There are many positive arguments of a different kind that are presented by philosophers, but we shall not introduce them here. One clear presentation of such arguments is to be found in Richard Taylor, *Metaphysics* (Englewood Cliffs, N.J.: Prentice-Hall, Inc., 1963), Chapter 4.

how the one causes the other to move, but what happens when we choose to move our arm and it does move? This kind of question does not belong to moral philosophy but to metaphysics proper, but let us briefly examine what R. M. Chisholm says about this problem:

> . . . If, when the agent made A happen, there was no event involved other than A itself, no event which could be described as *making* A happen, what did the agent's causation consist of? What, for example, is the difference between A's just happening, and that agent's *causing* A to happen? We cannot attribute the difference to any event that took place within the agent. And so far as the event A itself is concerned, there would seem to be no discernible difference—no discernable difference between A just happening and the agent causing A to happen. . . . Must we conclude, then, that there is no more to the man's action in causing event A than there is to the event A's happening by itself?
> . . . the difference between the man's causing A, on the one hand, and the event A just happening, on the other, lies in the fact that, in the first case but not the second, the event A was caused and was caused by the man, . . . but there was nothing that he did to cause it.[21]

Chisholm denies that every event is preceded by other, causally sufficient, events. Some human actions, he claims, are caused by the man, and that causation is not by means of an event which precedes the action. The agent does not stand in the same relation to what he has caused as an inanimate cause stands to what it has caused. In the latter case one event causes another event; in the former, an agent somehow causes an action without performing some other action to bring it about. Some will feel that this kind of causation (which Chisholm calls *immanent causation*) is mysterious and that the other kind of causation is not. This is what Chisholm says in response to such a suggestion:

> For the problem, as we put it, referring just to "immanent causation," or causation by an agent, was this: "What is the difference between saying, of an event A, that A just happened and saying that someone caused A to happen?" The analogous problem, which holds for "transeunt causation," or causation by an event, is this: "What is the difference between saying, of two events A and B, that B happened and then A happened, and saying that B's happening was the *cause* of A's happening?" And the only answer that one can give is this—that in the one case the agent was the cause of A's happening, and in the other case event B was the cause of A's happening. The nature of the transeunt causation is no more clear than is that of immanent causation. In short, as long as we talk about causation at all (and we cannot avoid it) the difficulty is one that we will have on our hands. It is not a difficulty that is peculiar, therefore, to our treatment of the problem of freedom.[22]

[21] Roderick Chisholm, "Freedom and Action," in *Freedom and Determinism*, ed. Keith Lehrer (New York: Random House, 1966), pp. 20–21.
[22] *Ibid.*, pp. 21–22.

It is true that there are many problems in describing the nature of causation, but we are inclined to agree with Chisholm that the problems that are found in the area of human causation, and particularly those concerning the self or the agent, are no more mysterious than those involved in cases of nonhuman causation.

Let us summarize briefly the points made thus far. It was argued that the evidence against *TD* weakens the case for hard determinism. The libertarian's case is strengthened as the hard determinist's is weakened. This is true because one of the main reasons for denying that men are free (in the sense indicated) is that this type of freedom conflicts with *TD*. If one can no longer assert *TD* with any degree of confidence, there is little reason to deny that men are free. When one establishes that one can make correct moral judgments about the actions of persons, one does not thereby specify the nature of those actions that must be free nor how they are brought about. We then tried to indicate the sorts of answers that can be given to these questions.

If one applies the criteria of acceptability to libertarianism and to hard determinism, it would seem that libertarianism is the better theory. There is at least one good reason in its favor: we apparently make correct moral judgments. It is not clear that there are any insuperable difficulties or objections, and it was argued, in part, that no such objections exist. Finally, the theory seems best to account for the moral phenomena we encounter from day to day. In this connection we compared the ability of the libertarian to explain the phenomena with that of the hard determinist. Once again, it seems that the libertarian fares better.

4. Fatalism. Fatalism is a position that is sometimes confused with hard determinism. The thesis of fatalism (*TF*) is the view that some (or all) events occur, no matter what else happens.

The thesis of fatalism: For some (or all) events, (e.g.) E_1 that occur, there is no possible event or set of events E_2 that precede E_1 and are causally sufficient for the nonoccurrence of E_1.

The difference betwen the thesis of fatalism (*TF*) and *TD* is that even though *TD* says that events are caused, it does not claim that the event will occur independently of those causes. For example, many soldiers in combat apparently believe that there is a bullet with "my number on it." The soldier believe that, before that particular bullet is fired, there is no need to take precaution; when that bullet is fired, there is nothing that can prevent his death.

The hard determinist would agree that it is causally impossible to prevent the death of the soldier, given the firing of the gun, the striking of the bullet, and so on; but it is not causally impossible to bring about the nonfiring of the gun. The hard determinist would claim that, if the enemy soldier were to be killed before he fired the gun (even though he is not, in fact, killed), our soldier would live.

It may not seem, at first, like much of a difference, but a contrary-to-fact conditional that the hard determinist believes is true, the fatalist believes is false. A contrary-to-fact conditional is one whose antecedent is about an event that does not occur, but specifies that if the event were to occur then another event would occur. This is the form in which many statements of physical laws are put, e.g., if one were to drop a bust of George Washington from the Statue of Liberty it would fall. Although no one has given a satisfactory explanation or analysis of the necessary and sufficient conditions of the truth of contrary-to-fact conditionals, it is usually not difficult to pick out the true statements from the false. The statement, "If a bust of George Washington were dropped from the Statue of Liberty, it would turn into a bust of Lenin," is a false statement—even though no bust of George Washington is dropped from the Statue of Liberty.

There are many true contrary-to-fact conditionals—e.g., "If the enemy soldier were killed, our soldier would not be killed"—which the fatalist believes are false. It is clear that anyone who believes that there is a science of physics is committed to saying that the contrary-to-fact conditional is true. If we ask the fatalist why he believes the contrary-to-fact conditional is false, he would say that, because the death of our soldier by that bullet at that time is fated, something else—or perhaps nothing at all—would happen to cause the pulling of the trigger. Perhaps the now-dead enemy's gun would be jarred by a shell, or the dead soldier's muscle could contract in just the right way at just the right time. This reply, however, misses the point. The fact that the conditions mentioned in the antecedent do not come about is no reason to suppose that a contrary-to-fact conditional is false. If that were so, all such conditionals would be false—which they are not.

Fatalism is possibly not only *not* supported by determinism, but actually incompatible with it. Suppose we were to try to destroy the gun that is fated to be fired; we would not be able to. Even if we threw it into a blast furnace that can melt steel, somehow or other the gun would reappear at the fated time to fire the bullet that will kill our soldier. If this is so, the fatalist denies that this event, the nonmelting of the gun, is preceded by causally sufficient events. The fatalist can claim that such causes will be present, but there is no more reason to believe there will be than to believe there will not.

We are justified in concluding that *TF* is not the same as *TD*, and that fatalism is not the same as hard determinism and is probably incompatible with *TD*. Furthermore, there does not seem to be one shred of evidence to support fatalism. There is, finally, the contrary evidence of our experience and the support of *TD*, which seems to be incompatible with *TF*.

Summary. In this chapter we posed the question, "What are the necessary and sufficient nonnormative conditions of making a correct or justified moral judgment?" We stated three positions and three different answers to our question; soft determinism, hard determinism, and libertarianism. Three conditions were thought by the soft determinist to be sufficient:

1. S was able to do A.
2. S did A intentionally or knowingly.
3a. If S had chosen otherwise, or if his character and desires had been different, S could have done otherwise.

The libertarian replaces Condition 3a with Condition 3b: "S could have done otherwise." Neither the libertarian nor the hard determinist agrees with the soft determinist. Their objections can be understood as a defense of the truth of the following premises:

1. If *TD*, then *HAD*.
2. If *HAD*, then *CDO*.
3. If *CDO*, then *NCJ*.

The soft determinist believes *TD* and *CJ* (not-*NCJ*) are compatible, whereas the hard determinist and the libertarian agree that they are not. The main argument of the soft determinist for his denial of Premise 3 was presented in detail. This argument was criticized by showing, in effect, that if one's actions are caused by factors outside one's control even when such a cause is internal, the person cannot be justifiably praised or blamed. This comes to saying that we cannot truly judge that a man's actions are right, or wrong, or obligatory if they are the causal result of factors that are not "within his power."

The hard determinist and the libertarian disagree in that the former affirms *TD* and, finally, *NCJ* by three applications of *modus ponens* to Premises 1–3; the latter denies *NCJ* and, finally, by three applications of *modus tollens*, denies *TD*. In addition to the denial of *TD* (by affirming *CJ*) the libertarian offers an argument to show that *TD* is doubtful. Thus, the hard determinist's case for *TD* is weakened while the libertarian's case for *CJ* is strengthened. The issue between these two views is not firmly resolved, and there is little doubt that more will be heard on the subject, but the weight of evidence is so far on the side of the libertarian.

Exercises

Review
1. How does the libertarian defend *CJ*?
2. What is the distinction between reasons and causes, and how does the libertarian make use of it?

3. How does the libertarian attack *TD*?
4. What is the reply of the hard determinist to these criticisms?
5. Summarize the evidence for hard determinism and libertarianism that seems to be left untouched by criticism.
6. Why is Chisholm classified as a libertarian? What contribution does he make to the problem?
7. Compare and contrast hard determinism and fatalism.

Applications

1. Argue that the following persons were, or were not, free to perform or bring about the actions and situations described:
   a. Jesus going to Jerusalem.
   b. The Romans crucifying Jesus.
   c. Socrates drinking the hemlock.
   d. Martin Luther taking the stand which led him to say, "Here I stand, I can do no other."
   e. Eichmann directing the extermination of millions of Jews.
   f. A student failing to understand the argument on p. ――――― (the reader can fill in his own favorite).
   g. Caesar crossing the Rubicon.
2. List as many different senses of 'free' as possible. Which of these are relevant to morality? Which are not? What accounts for the difference?
3. Assume that the libertarian is correct in his analysis of the problem of freedom, and that freedom is required for there to be correct moral judgments. Try to specify the "thing" which is free and how it brings about actions. What more would have to be known for the specification to be complete?
4. If you know of any reasons that are offered in support of fatalism, present and evaluate them.
5. Evaluate the following arguments.
   a. I know I am free because many times I can do what I want.
   b. Whenever anyone says he is free, he is mistaken; because every event is caused and so, therefore, are the events which are human actions.
   c. Libertarianism is correct because if people didn't believe they were free they wouldn't try to do anything.
   d. The overwhelming number of things we observe are not free (e.g., rocks, worms, and trees); so it is highly probable that men are not free.
6. Identify the position being maintained in the following. Critically evaluate the argument presented in it.

   Not only ignorance but also emotional conditions affect human responsibility. Whenever one is in such a violent emotional state that he does not see clearly what he is doing or is driven to act impulsively and without reflection, responsibility is diminished and perhaps to such an extent that it is taken away entirely and the individual is not guilty of doing what is itself a wrong and criminal act. Fear is the emotion which most often clouds consciousness and diminishes guilt.

Bibliography

*Austin, J. L. "Ifs and Cans," Proceedings of the British Academy, **42** (1956), 109–32. An attempt to refute soft determinism by an analysis of the verb 'can'.

*Brandt, Richard B. *Ethical Theory.* Englewood Cliffs, N.J.: Prentice-Hall, Inc., 1959, Chapter 20. The author attempts to show that determinism is compatible with obligation and with the nonmorally justified ascription of terms such as 'morally admirable'.

*Broad, C. D. *Five Types of Ethical Theory.* New York: Harcourt, Brace & World, Inc., 1934, pp. 192–208. A discussion of Sidgwick's indeterminism.

Campbell, C. A. "Is 'Free Will' a Pseudo-Problem?" *Mind,* **60** (1951), 441–65. A clear statement of the libertarian's position.

Carritt, E. F. *Ethical and Political Thinking.* Oxford: The Clarendon Press, 1947, Chapter 12. Carritt is a libertarian who believes that men are free in that they can obey or disobey their consciences or act contrary to their strongest desires.

Chisholm, R. M. "Freedom and Action," in *Freedom and Determinism,* ed. Keith Lehrer. New York: Random House, 1966. An attempt to explain some key libertarian notions. Chisholm argues that the man is the cause of his own actions.

Ewing, A. C. *Ethics.* New York: The Free Press, 1953. Chapter 8 contains a defense of libertarianism.

Frankena, William K. *Ethics.* Englewood Cliffs, N.J.: Prentice-Hall, Inc., 1963, pp. 57–62. A clear discussion of the various theories. The author argues that determinism is compatible with moral responsibility.

D'Holbach, Baron. *System of Nature* (1770), in *A Modern Introduction to Philosophy,* eds. P. Edwards and A. Pap. New York: The Free Press, 1965, pp. 10–19. A straightforward hard determinist position.

*Hook, Sidney (ed.). *Determinism and Freedom in the Age of Modern Science.* New York: Collier Books, 1961. An analysis of the general concept of determinism, the notion of determinism in physics, and a discussion of freedom and responsibility in law and ethics.

Moore, G. E. *Ethics.* New York: Oxford University Press, 1965, Chapter 6. Moore is an important soft determinist.

*Morgenbesser, Sidney, and James Walsh (eds.). *Free Will.* Englewood Cliffs, N.J.: Prentice-Hall, Inc., 1962. Essays on the subject of determinism by St. Augustine, Hobbes, J. S. Mill, Aristotle, Sartre, R. Taylor, and others.

*Nowell-Smith, P. H. *Ethics.* Baltimore, Md.: Penguin Books, Inc., 1954. Chapters 19 and 20 contain a carefully worked-out soft determinist theory.

*Pears, D. F. (ed.). *Freedom and the Will.* London: Macmillan & Co., Ltd.; New York: St. Martin's Press, 1963. An interesting series of debates on the topics of determinism, free will, responsibility, and actions.

*Ross, W. D. *Foundations of Ethics.* Oxford: The Clarendon Press, 1939, Chapter 10. A defense of soft determinism.

Schlick, M. *Problems of Ethics.* Englewood Cliffs, N.J.: Prentice-Hall, Inc., 1939, Chapter 7. A classical statement of soft determinism.

*SIDGWICK, H. *The Methods of Ethics.* 7th ed. London: Macmillan & Co. Ltd., 1962, Chapter 5. The author lists the evidence for hard determinism and libertarianism. However, since the author is a utilitarian, he is inclined to believe that the controversy is of no great practical importance.

*STEVENSON, C. L. *Ethics and Language.* New Haven, Conn.: Yale University Press, 1944, Chapter 14. A defense of soft determinism.

TAYLOR, RICHARD. *Metaphysics.* Englewood Cliffs, N.J.: Prentice-Hall, Inc., 1963, Chapter 4. A criticism of hard determinism and soft determinism. Taylor presents a form of libertarianism called the "theory of agency."

PART THREE

Meta-ethics

CHAPTER

IO

Meta-ethics

A. Normative Ethics and Meta-ethics

Usually people have no trouble in judging that a certain course of action is morally right or wrong, or deciding whether pleasure is preferable to pain. But sometimes people disagree in their judgments about what ought to be done, or about what is good or bad. Whether the disagreement is at a fairly specific level (over the correctness of one course of action) or at a more general level (perhaps over which of two conflicting normative theories is better), it is a normative disagreement.

Like arguments about the existence of God or the nature of the universe, normative disagreements occur on several levels of complexity and sophistication. "Bull sessions" in a college dormitory may last far into the night and the participants may emerge exhausted, but no more enlightened than when they began. A few such sessions are likely to be discouraging, and to leave the impression that such problems are insoluble, or even a matter of personal preference. We believe, however, that such conclusions would be premature. There are ways, admittedly difficult and painstaking, to reach agreement about many of the topics of universal concern.

A study of normative ethics, which begins with a consideration of such theories as hedonism and utilitarianism, inevitably leads to other problems and questions. It is possible to ask whether pleasure, for example, is good, and it is possible to argue that an action is wrong because it causes suffering —these are normative questions and arguments. But it is also possible to ask what 'good' or 'right' means, and this differs from asking what is good or bad, right or wrong, in that these are *meta-ethical* questions, questions *about* the normative judgments we are making. But, of course, not all the things we say about the normative judgments we make can be called meta-ethical statements. Thus the statement that a particular normative judgment was made by the Reverend Mister Arthur Dimmesdale on Sunday is a statement

213

about a normative judgment, but it is not a meta-ethical one. We shall restrict the term 'meta-ethical' to judgments, statements, or questions about the meaning of normative judgments, their nature, or the methods of supporting them.

The process of making a moral judgment and attempting to support it involves many things. It is impossible to separate normative, factual, and meta-ethical questions in practice, but it is possible to *discuss* them separately.

B. Some Meta-ethical Questions

There are three general types of problems in meta-ethics: those dealing with the meaning of moral judgments; those dealing with the nature of moral judgments; and those dealing with the methods of supporting, justifying, or defending moral judgments.

1. **Meaning.** After several fruitless hours of arguing about the moral rightness of capital punishment, or the intrinsic value of human life, knowledge, or pleasure, it is not uncommon to hear one disputant suggest that after all the argument is only a verbal one and that there is a need to get clear about what words like 'good' and 'right' mean. The question "What is the meaning of the word 'good'?"—though seemingly simple—is sufficiently difficult to make the wisest and most experienced moral philosopher extremely wary; and the difficulties surrounding other crucial moral terms—such as 'right', 'wrong', 'bad', 'wicked', and so on—are no less vexing.

It might be thought that no definition can be found for the word 'good', but that it is possible to give a kind of a definition of a sentence in which that word appears by providing another sentence that does the same essential job, but that does not contain that term. There will still be questions about how close such a "definition" comes to capturing the full meaning of the original expression, but it is an attempt at definition.

For example, consider the word 'and' as it appears in the following sentence: "You cannot miss all the classes and still pass the course." It might be suggested that an equivalent sentence would be, "If you miss all your classes you will not pass the course." How might such a definition work for expressions containing 'good'? One suggestion which has been given is that "X is good $=_{df}$ I approve of X, do so as well." This is to suggest that perhaps no exact verbal synonym may be found for 'good', but that the meaning of expressions containing that term can be elucidated in this way. Whether or not this is a legitimate procedure, and whether or not this particular "definition" is accurate, this is one proposal for a solution to a problem about the meaning of certain normative expressions and, as such, it falls into the domain of meta-ethics.

2. *The Nature of Moral Judgments.* It is one thing to define a moral expression and another to claim that all moral judgments are disguised commands, or objectively true or false statements about the presence or absence of a certain property. The latter claims can be said to be about the nature of moral judgments, and are related to, but distinguishable from, claims about their meaning.

3. *Justification.* In recent years, the problem of the justification of, or support for, moral judgments has received more attention than the other two questions combined. It may well be that this is the central and most important question in meta-ethics, and it certainly is the one raised by our discussion of the merits of act deontology. Must we support moral judgments by appealing to general rules, or are general rules only summary rules, derived from particular instances? Can any "ultimate" support be given to the moral judgments we make? Are the methods and techniques of ordinary deductive and inductive logic available to one who reasons about right and wrong, or is he forced to resort to some special "kind" of logic, appropriate only to those sorts of judgments, or, finally, does *any* kind of logic enter into the support of our moral judgments? These are all meta-ethical questions about the process of justifying or supporting moral judgments.

4. *The Interrelation of These Problems.* These problems are not unrelated, and sometimes an answer to one will strongly suggest, or perhaps even entail, an answer to another. The three questions, in their simplest form, are the following:

1. What is the meaning of moral terms or judgments?
2. What is the nature of moral judgments?
3. How may moral judgments be supported or defended?

a. THE RELATION OF QUESTION 1 TO QUESTION 2. If someone suggests that 'good' means 'pleasant' we can be fairly certain that when he turns to answer Question 2 he will claim that moral judgments about goodness are no different from psychological judgments about pleasure. Sometimes if an answer to Question 2 is complete enough, we are able to infer an answer to Question 1. If someone, answering Question 2, says that moral judgments express facts, then we will know the range of answers permissible to Question 1, but if he says that moral judgments are expressions about what God wills, an inference to an answer to Question 1 will at least be easier in that a large number of possible answers will be ruled out.

b. THE RELATION OF QUESTION 1 TO QUESTION 3. If it is claimed, for example, that 'right' means 'productive of the greatest good' and 'good' means 'pleasure', we know what sort of a defense to expect for the judgment "X is right." It will, or should, consist of a demonstration that a particular course of action is productive of more pleasure than any alternative course of action. Likewise, if it is claimed that 'good' cannot be defined, but stands for a simple property, somewhat as 'yellow' does, then we know not to expect a defense of the claim "X is good" to consist in scientific and psychological statements about the pleasure it produces (unless, of course, some empirical connection between the occurrence of pleasure and the occurrence of this property is established).

c. THE RELATION OF QUESTION 2 TO QUESTION 3. There is a meta-ethical theory according to which moral judgments are really disguised expressions of approval and attempts to get others to share our attitudes. It is quite clear that, if this theory were true, it would have imporant bearing on the sort of support available for our judgments. Sometimes theories of this nature are criticized on the grounds that they have no way to defend moral judgments, or at least that the usual procedures of proof and evidence are not available to them. Whether or not this is true (see Chapter 13), it is easy to see how such a criticism is suggested. If what we are doing when we say that murder is wrong is not very different from what we do when we cheer at a baseball game, or hiss at a villain, there is good reason to believe that we can no more *prove* our moral judgment that we can prove our expression of satisfaction at a successful slide—indeed it might be suggested that the concept of "proof" or of "rational" argument is as inapplicable in the former case as it is in the latter.

Exercises

Review

1. Why will it not do to say simply that a meta-ethical statement is a statement about a moral judgment?
2. To what sorts of statements is the term 'meta-ethical' restricted?
3. How might the word 'good' be defined without giving a synonym of the word 'good'?
4. In recent years, which of the three questions has come to be considered central?
5. Discuss the interrelations of Questions 1–3.

Applications

1. Discuss several normative ethical problems. At which points do meta-ethical considerations become relevant?
2. Attempt to state as clearly as possible what 'good', 'right', 'wrong' and 'duty' mean, and re-examine what you have done after each of the next three chapters.

C. A First Look at Some Meta-ethical Views

Let us attempt to isolate and classify some meta-ethical views. This task is made more difficult by the fact that meta-ethical views deal with a number of questions, and by the fact that the traditional classifications have been taken for granted for too long.

1. *Cognitivism and Noncognitivism.* Usually a distinction is made between those who hold that moral judgments are true or false, and those who deny it. The former are called *cognitivists*; the latter, *noncognitivists*. There is a good historical justification for this procedure, for most of the early noncognitivists explicitly stated that moral judgments are neither true nor false. Their view is a result of the very general philosophical theory they accepted —logical positivism, a view which holds that propositions are meaningful only if they can be verified by sense experience. This view, usually called *the verification theory of meaningfulness*, together with the belief that moral judgments are neither confirmable nor disconfirmable by experience, led these philosophers to maintain that moral judgments are not meaningful. The more careful of these philosophers talked not just about meaning *simpliciter* but about cognitive meaning. They held that a proposition is not cognitively meaningful unless it is possible to state how it might be verified. Because they believed that moral judgments cannot be verified, they argued that such judgments had no cognitive meaning. But if one says that a proposition is not cognitively meaningful, he must also say that it is neither true nor false, at least not in the way that cognitively meaningful statements, such as "the earth is round," are.

The verification principle, however, proved impossible to maintain. Nevertheless, the ethical position connected with that view continued to be held without the apparatus of logical positivism. Some noncognitivists continued to maintain that moral judgments are neither true nor false—not because they cannot be verified, but because they are entirely different in nature from factual judgments. Others (who should still be called noncognitivists maintained that, although moral judgments are different in nature from factual ones, both can be true or false. These philosophers denied that the distinction between cognitivism and noncognitivism can be made on the grounds that cognitivists believe that moral utterances are true or false and noncognitivists do not. Peter F. Strawson, for example, makes the following suggestion:

Better than asking "What is the criterion of truth?" is to ask: "What are the grounds for agreement?"—for those we see to be not less various than the subjects on which an agreed opinion can be reached. And this will perhaps also discourage us from seeking to mark the difference between one kind of utterance and another by saying, for example, "Ethical utterances are not true or false". It is correct to say that utterances of any kind are true or false, if it is correct usage to signify agreement or disagreement with such utterances by means of the *expressions* 'true' or 'false'.[1]

[1] Peter F. Strawson, "Truth," *Analysis*, 5 (1949), reprinted in *Philosophy and Analysis*, ed. Margaret Macdonald (Oxford: Basil Blackwell, 1954), p. 274.

This view has also been argued by a leading noncognitivist, P. H. Nowell-Smith:

'True' and 'false' are used in moral discourse; and this is not an accident. Their use is identical with their use in other contexts, in that they are used to endorse what someone has said or to endorse its contradictory. . . . In a moral context it is proper for Brown to say of Jones's advice 'that's true' if would be proper for him to give the same advice, which is what he is, in effect, doing; but it is not necessary that he should believe that Jones's advice corresponds to the facts, because pieces of advice are not statements and neither correspond nor fail to correspond to facts.[2]

What Nowell-Smith seems to be claiming here is that we can and do say of advice, for example, that it is true; and when we say this, no matter what our grounds for doing so, we are endorsing it. When we say that someone's advice is true we are not, according to Nowell-Smith, *saying* that we endorse the advice, but our saying that it is true is our way of endorsing it. Furthermore, when someone says a statement is true, he is not saying that the statement corresponds with the facts; he is, rather, endorsing that statement, apparently sometimes at least on the basis of its correspondence with the facts. Now whether the claims of Nowell-Smith and Strawson (and those who hold similar beliefs) are correct or not, they are *saying* that 'true' and 'false' can be applied to some moral judgments, and this makes it clear that we cannot classify noncognitivists as those who say that moral judgments are neither true nor false.

What seems to be essential to all cognitivists, however, is the belief that the relation that holds between a true nonmoral judgment and the world also holds between a true moral judgment and the world. Now, whatever else Strawson and Nowell-Smith are saying, they would seem—in common with all noncognitivists—to be denying this claim and this may provide a more satisfactory distinction between cognitivism and noncognitivism. Let us say that the cognitivist claims that all moral judgments are statements and that the noncognitivist denies this. On this point, Nowell-Smith would agree with those noncognitivists who deny that moral judgments are true or false, but he would argue that 'true' and 'false' are properly applied to some utterances that are not statements.

To clarify what we mean by the term 'statement', we shall introduce a definition of that expression which is close enough to its typical use not to be misleading, and sufficiently precise for our purposes.

p is a statement $=_{df} p$ is capable of being objectively true

[2] P. H. Nowell-Smith, *Ethics* (Middlesex: Penguin Books, Ltd., 1954), pp. 196–97. Cf. also C. L. Stevenson, *Ethics and Language* (New Haven: Yale University Press, 1944), pp. 169–73, and C. L. Stevenson, *Facts and Values* (New Haven: Yale University Press, 1963), pp. 214–20.

The all-important word here is, of course, 'objectively'; without it, we would have to classify Nowell-Smith as a cognitivist. An utterance is capable of being objectively true if, and only if, its primary function is to describe some feature of the world—a fact, a state of affairs, a situation, or a set of facts, of states of affairs, or of situations.

The cognitivist, then, can be said to be claiming that moral judgments are capable of being objectively true, because they describe some feature of the world, and the noncognitivist can be said to be denying this. Nowell-Smith would now be forced (not, we think, unwillingly) to say that moral judgments are not capable of being *objectively* true, that they are not statements, and this is the feature common to all noncognitivists. All cognitivists, on the other hand, maintain that all moral judgments are capable of being objectively true, that they all are statements. The true dispute betwen the cognitivist and the noncognitivist can now be brought into focus: the cognitivist claims that such utterances as "X is good," "X is bad," "X is right," and "X is wrong" are all capable of being objectively true; the noncognitivist would claim they are not, because (see Chapter 13) he wishes to analyze them in terms of other utterances, such as commands, commendations, and expressions of wishes, feelings, or attitudes. His claim, therefore, would be that although moral judgments sometimes have the grammatical form of statements, this is misleading, and that their true nature is something else.

Corresponding to this distinction between the cognitivist and the noncognitivist there is another—the distinction between two conflicting theories of "moral knowledge." It is a commonly accepted philosophical truth that we cannot be said to know a proposition unless it is true (and 'true' here is certainly intended to mean 'objectively true'. But because no noncognitivist would claim that moral judgments are true (i.e., objectively true), none would be willing to say that there is moral knowledge. It makes no sense at all, for example, to say that a command is true, and therefore it makes no sense to say that someone can "know" a command, though one can know what command has been given. We may also, therefore, characterize the cognitivist as one who claims that objective moral knowledge is possible, and the noncognitivist as one who denies this. For the cognitivist, therefore, the judgment "X is good" or "A is right" has exactly the same status as the judgment "the earth is round"—it is capable of being objectively true and, therefore, whether anyone actually knows it or not, it is capable of being objectively known.

Although a necessary condition of someone's objectively knowing p is that p be objectively true, and a necessary condition of someone's being capable of objectively knowing p is that it be capable of being objectively true, these conditions are obviously not sufficient. It may be objectively true that the earth is round, but no one may know this fact. In order to say that S knows p, it is necessary to add that S believes p. But even this condition is not enough to justify the claim that p is known. S may believe and assert that the earth is round, and it may be true that the earth is round, but he might not have good grounds for saying so, and this would force us to say again that he does not really know that the earth is round. The person who claims to know p must have the proper kind of evidence for p. These three conditions, stated in a general way, are accepted by most philosophers as the necessary and sufficient conditions for objective knowledge of a proposition.

1. P is objectively true.
2. S believes p.
3. S has the proper kind of evidence for p, or good grounds for believing p.[3]

It is clear that, because all noncognitivists would deny that moral judgments are objectively true (or that they are even *capable* of being objectively true), they would also deny that any moral judgment may be objectively known.

The distinction between cognitivism and noncognitivism, therefore, can thus be made in two clearly related ways. The cognitivist asserts, and the noncognitivist denies, that

1. Moral judgments are capable of being objectively true.

Also, the cognitivist asserts, and the noncognitivist denies, that

1a. There is objective moral knowledge.

Because an analysis of knowledge includes the element of objective truth, we can say that Statement 1a *includes* Statement 1. Also, 1a is more inclusive than 1, and introduces the important problem of moral reasoning.

2. **Definism and Nondefinism.** There is a second distinction among meta-ethical views—a distinction which, to some degree, cuts across that between cognitivism and noncognitivism. Consider the following claim:

2. Any moral judgment (judgment in which 'good' or 'bad', 'right' or 'wrong' is used in a moral sense) can be reduced or expanded by analysis or definition to another expression which has the same meaning or significance and contains no moral terms.

---

[3] If one holds one form of a meta-ethical position commonly called *naturalism,* one would be committed to saying that psychological evidence is the relevant and proper kind of evidence to support a moral judgment. If one holds that it is the awareness of a property, goodness itself, which justifies the claim that something is good, psychological evidence about the attitudes and feelings of humans would not provide evidence (except indirectly) for the value of something. In the following chapters we shall see that there are many different kinds of proposals for the specification of (3), and that these are often intimately connected with the stand one has taken about the truth or falsity of (1).

The essence of this claim is that moral judgments are definable nonmorally. Although this way of putting the matter (as well as the more technical way of Statement 2) is not without difficulties. If someone holds Statement 2, we shall call him a *definist*, and if he denies 2, we shall call him a *nondefinist*.[4]

We can explain what someone who accepts Statement 2 might mean by suggesting that 'wrong' in "Stealing is wrong" can be defined. Some ethical thinkers, believing that 'wrong' is equivalent in meaning to 'forbidden by God' would be inclined to say that "Stealing is wrong" means the same as "Stealing is forbidden by God." One who believes that all moral terms can be replaced either immediately or ultimately by terms designating the felings, beliefs, or volitions of God is called a *theological definist*.[5]

A second type of definist is one who believes that 'wrong' is equivalent to something like 'a cause of unhappiness'. Such a thinker would say that "Stealing is wrong" is the same as "Stealing is a cause of unhappiness." Assuming that it is possible to discover empirically whether something is, in fact, a cause of unhappiness, and assuming that our second ethical thinker believes that all moral judgments can be so defined, we may call him a *naturalist* or a *naturalistic definist*, and say that his definitions are *naturalistic*. This is the most important and most widely held definist position.

It is possible that someone may define one moral expression in terms of another. This, by itself, is not enough to permit his classification as a definist, for the definist believes all moral terms can be eliminated through definition or analysis. G. E. Moore, for example, once attempted to define 'right' in terms of 'good', but denied that any definition of 'good' could be given. For that reason, we can classify him as a nondefinist.

Whereas Moore defines 'right' in terms of 'good', A. C. Ewing, another important twentieth century ethical thinker, suggests that we might proced along exactly opposite lines:

> Once we have admitted an indefinable *ought*, we may define "good" in its specifically ethical senses by means of this notion. We can then say that to assert something to be intrinsically good is to say that it is "such that we ought to have a favourable attitude towards it, i.e., choose, desire, pursue, further, welcome or admire it, for its own sake . . ." [6]

It is, of course, possible to suggest that neither of these is definable in terms of the other, that both require separate and independent definitions—or,

[4] This terminology is due to William K. Frankena's article, "The Naturalistic Fallacy," *Mind*, 58 (October 1939), 464–77.

[5] It is conceivable that someone may define 'right' theologically but not to do this with respect to other moral terms, such as 'good'. If this happens, then it would be possible to say that 'right' is defined theologically and 'good' is defined in some other way, or not at all.

[6] A. C. Ewing, *Ethics* (New York: The Free Press, 1965), p. 93. By permission of the Macmillan Company. By permission of the English Universities Press, Limited, original publishers.

perhaps, that they can be defined relative to some third term, which is itself either definable or not.

It can be seen that the two distinctions overlap to some degree and create four possible sorts of meta-ethical theory.

1. Cognitivist definist.
2. Cognitivist nondefinist.
3. Noncognitivist definist.
4. Noncognitivist nondefinist.

In the sections that follow we shall consider these categories in a very general way. These sections are intended to be a very general survey of the ground to be covered in Chapters 11–13, in which a number of these views are discussed in detail and examined critically.

D. A Closer Look at Some Meta-ethical Views

1. *Cognitivistic Definism.* The cognitivist definist subscribes to Statements 1, 1a, and 2. Of the three main meta-ethical questions, the cognitivist definist usually places his main emphasis on the question about meaning, allowing us to infer answers to the other two questions from his answer to the one.

The cognitivist definist believes that it is possible to define moral expressions in nonmoral terms. But it is possible to distinguish among cognitivist definists on the basis of the sorts of expression they equate with moral ones.

The *naturalistic cognitivist definist,* for example, believes that moral terms can be replaced by terms from the natural or social sciences—psychology, physics, or sociology. One naturalistic definition of 'good' is 'desired by the speaker'. Samples of other naturalistic definitions are:

good $=_{df}$ pleasurable
good $=_{df}$ liked by most human beings
right $=_{df}$ approved by the sovereign
right $=_{df}$ enjoined by a law
good $=_{df}$ leads to the survival of the species

It is clear that the answer to the meta-ethical question about the *nature* of moral judgments can be deduced from such answers to questions about meaning. It is also clear that, for the naturalistic cognitivist definist, a question about the justification of a moral judgment is no different from a question about the justification of the particular sort of scientific judgments with which moral judgments have, by definition, been related.

The *nonnaturalistic cognitivist definist* holds that moral judgments are definable and that they are objectively true or false, but he denies that they can be defined by terms from the natural or social sciences. One sort of nonnaturalistic definition is theological, according to which 'good' or 'right' or perhaps both, mean 'approved of, favored, or desired by God'. A number of naturalistic and nonnaturalistic cognitivist definist positions will be discussed in Chapter 11.

2. Cognitivistic Nondefinism. The cognitivist nondefinist believes that moral judgments are capable of being objectively true, and also that there is objective moral knowledge, but he denies that all moral expressions can be defined.[7] The usual term applied to this view is 'intuitionism' but this label refers more to the way in which moral propositions are known than to the characteristics usually seized upon to distinguish meta-ethical views. Furthermore, there are different ways of accounting for the moral knowledge that the cognitivist nondefinist believes we have, and although some cognitivist nondefinists believe that we intuit moral truths, others would account for moral knowledge in other ways. Some, for example, would say that we know directly that an action is right, and this direct knowledge is not essentially different from the knowledge we have that a ball is red. It would be just as misleading to characterize these views as saying that we "intuit" the truth of moral judgments, as it would be to claim that we "intuit" the color of the ball (see Chapter 12).

The definist views we have so far considered have all stressed their answers to the meta-ethical question about meaning, but the cognitivist nondefinist quite often devotes his attention to another question, for he usually is most concerned with the way in which we know the truth of moral judgments. This is, in a way, to concentrate upon an answer to the question about the justification of moral judgments. The cognitivist nondefinist often suggests that moral judgments are known directly, and that they cannot be deduced by deductive, inductive, or any other kind of logic from more general premises. H. A. Prichard, for example, suggests that the "sense of obligation to do, or of the rightness of, an action of a particular kind is absolutely underivative or immediate." [8] No arguments, he suggests, can ever prove a moral judgment—they are self-evident.

Whereas the cognitivist definist usually stresses the question about meaning, the cognitivist nondefinist is more concerned with discussing moral knowledge, and often stresses the claim that the truth of moral judgments is known directly or that they are self-evident. This commits him to denying that moral judgments are reducible by definition or analysis to any other kind of judgment (his nondefinism), and to holding that moral judgments are essentially different in nature from scientific judgments (see Chapter 12).

[7] We have already allowed that some nondefinists believe that *some* ethical terms might be definable by other ethical terms.

[8] H. A. Prichard, "Does Moral Philosophy Rest on a Mistake?" *Mind*, **21** (1912), reprinted in H. A. Prichard, *Moral Obligation* (Oxford: The Clarendon Press, 1957), p. 7.

3. Noncognitivism. Interestingly enough, the noncognitivists can best be understood as concentrating upon Question 2, for they wish to suggest that moral judgments are not statements at all, but expressions of attitudes, commands, or something of the sort. This, in turn, dictates an answer to Question 1: either moral judgments have no meaning at all, or they have a special sort of noncognitive meaning; and an answer to Question 3: moral judgments may be supported in whatever way attitudes or commands may be supported.

It is also convenient, and perhaps necessary, to classify all noncognitivists as definists, for noncognitivists are inclined to say that moral judgments are really commands, expressions of attitudes, or the like. Thus, if moral judgments are disguised imperatives, then "X is good" might be analyzed as "Choose X!" or "Prefer X!"—neither of which contains the word 'good'.

E. Current Problems Concerning Meta-ethics

The explicit discussion of meta-ethics in recent years perhaps originates with W. K. Frankena's article, "Moral Philosophy at Mid-Century"; [9] and since then, a number of other important contributions to theoretical discussions of meta-ethics have appeared. Two questions have troubled writers on meta-ethics: First, does the acceptance of a particular meta-ethical theory logically commit one to the acceptance of a particular normative theory, and, conversely, does the acceptance of any particular normative theory logically commit one to the acceptance of a particular meta-ethical theory? And second, is the distinction between normative judgments and meta-ethical judgments really sound? The first question involves the problem of *independence*; the second, the problem of *meta-ethical neutrality*.

1. Independence. Frankena claimed that the proponents of any of the three main meta-ethical views he distinguished "might quite possibly maintain the same opinions as to what is right or good in normative ethics." This is to suggest that a particular meta-ethical analysis does not entail any normative conclusions. One might be a definist or a nondefinist, a cognitivist or a noncognitivist, and still be, for example, a utilitarian. As a matter of fact, utilitarianism has been held by proponents of the three meta-ethical views we have discussed. G. E. Moore is a cognitivist nondefinist, J. J. C. Smart is a noncognitivist, and Jeremy Bentham is a naturalistic cognitivist definist, yet all three are utilitarians.

Also, there seems to be no reason why one cannot be a deontologist, an egoist, or a utilitarian (act or rule) and still hold any of the meta-ethical positions we have discussed. These considerations are strong evidence in favor of the independence of normative ethics and meta-ethics.

Yet it would be a mistake to think that normative ethics and meta-ethics

[9] W. K. Frankena, "Moral Philosophy at Mid-Century," *The Philosophical Review*, **60** (1951), 44–55.

are totally independent. Suppose, for example, that one were not only a cognitivist definist, but a naturalistic cognitivist definist who defined 'right' as 'productive of the greatest amount of pleasure for the greatest number'. Given such an analysis of the meaning of the word 'right' we are, it seems, already committed to a teleological theory of obligation and a hedonist theory of value. It is true that such a relation can obtain only with definist positions, but this is at least one way in which a meta-ethical theory (if it is specific enough) can commit its proponents to a normative position, and one reason why it would be rash to claim that normative ethics and meta-ethics are totally independent.

But there is another side to the dependence claim. Does the adoption of a particular normative theory ever commit one to a particular meta-ethical theory? The answer to this question is more complex. One who believes that utilitarianism is correct can still be a cognitivist or a noncognitivist, a definist or a nondefinist. But if one holds that utilitarianism is correct, there are certain definist positions which he cannot consistently adopt. The utilitarian must maintain some version of the claim that right actions are those that produce the greatest good for the greatest number, and it will not be possible for one who holds this normative position to say that 'right' means 'productive of good for me'. It may be replied that a utilitarian can maintain this so long as he maintains that whatever produces good for him is also productive of the greatest good for the greatest number. But this claim is so obviously implausible that it is hardly worth mentioning. Unfortunately, however, it is the kind of ad hoc adjustment that theories often receive, and is not unlike certain desperate attempts at rationalization.

Another example will serve to show that, although the adoption of a normative position does not commit one to any particular meta-ethical position, it does eliminate the possibility of adhering to some fairly specific meta-ethical theories. A deontologist, for example, cannot claim that 'right' means 'productive of the greatest good for the greatest number', for he is committed to denying not only that this is what 'right' means but also to denying that all actions which have this effect are right. One might attempt to reconcile these views, but no serious thinker has.

The conclusion, then, is that a definist meta-ethical position will sometimes logically commit one to a normative ethical theory. Furthermore, if one holds a normative theory, he may be a definist or a nondefinist, a cognitivist or a noncognitivist, but certain specific meta-ethical views are no longer open to him.

2. Neutrality. If one believes that it is the business of a meta-ethical theory to describe what we actually mean, or intend to mean, by the moral judgments we make, or to describe the nature of the arguments we offer in support of them, it is likely that he will maintain the neutrality of meta-ethical judgments. If, on the other hand, one takes the meta-ethicist not to be describing the meaning of a moral term but, rather, to be proposing that we adopt a particular meaning for a term, then meta-ethics consists of normative propositions about how we should and should not use moral language. Whether or not this is a moral proposal depends entirely upon the case, but it could be.

Thus the answer to the question about neutrality depends upon how meta-ethics is interpreted. But because there are definists who intend their definitions to be reportive and definists who intend their definitions to be stipulative, it is better not to attempt to reach a conclusion such as "meta-ethics is descriptive" or "meta-ethics is normative." Rather, we should admit that sometimes it takes one form and sometimes another.

Exercises

Review
1. What reasons are there for and against defining noncognitivism as the view that moral judgments are neither true nor false?
2. How could a noncognitivist hold that moral judgments are capable of being true?
3. What is the difference between saying that a moral judgment is capable of being true and saying that it is capable of being objectively true? Why is this latter notion essential in a discussion of the distinction between cognitivism and noncognitivism?
4. What is the distinction between a definist and a nondefinist meta-ethical view?
5. What is the difference between a naturalistic definist and a theological definist?
6. Classify, as well as possible at this point, the meta-ethical positions of G. E. Moore and A. C. Ewing.

Applications
1. Describe some other cognitivist definist positions (perhaps after reading some of Chapter 11, if you are unsure of their nature) and show how they are related to other normative theories of obligation and of value.
2. Discuss the possibilities of giving a normative justification for the meta-ethical positions described in this chapter.
3. What reasons might there be for treating meta-ethics before discussing normative ethics in a textbook on ethics? What reasons might there be for treating normative problems first?
4. Discuss the following claim:

> Anyone who thinks that a sharp distinction can be maintained between meta-ethics and normative ethics is invited to consider the nature of such works as Aristotle's *Nicomachean Ethics*, Kant's *Grundlegung zur Metaphysik der Sitten*, or John Stuart Mill's *Utilitarianism*. Is their contents meta-ethics or normative ethics? Some, I think, would answer that the works mentioned contain elements of both types of ethics and perhaps deplore that their authors did not distinguish more sharply between the two. My own

inclination would rather be to say that the difficulties in classification here show the artificiality of the distinction. G. H. Von Wright, *The Varieties of Goodness* (London: Routledge & Kegan Paul, 1963), pp. 3–4.

Bibliography

*BLACKSTONE, W. T. "Are Meta-ethical Theories Normatively Neutral?" *Australasian Journal of Philosophy*, 39 (1961), 65–74. A discussion of neutrality in which a number of different interpretations of the question "Are meta-ethical theories normatively neutral?" are considered and answered—some affirmatively, some negatively.

*————. "On the Logical Status of Meta-ethical Theories," *Theoria*, 28 (1962), 298–303. A discussion of Wheatley's article.

*————. "On Justifying a Meta-ethical Theory," *Australasian Journal of Philosophy*, 41 (1963), 57–66. A discussion of some contemporary meta-ethical views and a relation of meta-ethics to wider issues.

FRANKENA, W. K. "Moral Philosophy at Mid-Century," *The Philosophical Review*, 60 (1951), 44–55. An analysis of the state of moral philosophy, and especially of meta-ethics, in the early 1950's. One of the first lucid discussions of meta-ethics.

GEWIRTH, A. "Meta-ethics and Normative Ethics," *Mind*, 69 (1960), 187–205. A consideration of further relations between normative ethics and meta-ethics.

*MOSHER, DAVID, "A Reply to Mr. Wheatley," *Theoria*, 28 (1962), 308–12.

*MOTHERSILL, MARY. "Moral Philosophy and Meta-ethics," *The Journal of Philosophy*, 49 (1952), 587–94. A discussion of neutrality in which it is concluded that meta-ethical theories are normative in nature.

*OLAFSON, F. A. "Meta-ethics and the Moral Life," *The Philosophical Review*, 65 (1956), 159–78. An attempt to show that the acceptance of a noncognitivist meta-ethics affects our "first order moral life." But this discussion is one in which "subjectivistic" views (See Chapter 11) are confused with noncognitivistic ones. This is pointed out by Taylor.

*TAYLOR, PAUL W. "The Normative Function of Meta-ethics," *The Philosophical Review*, 67 (1958), 16–32. A criticism of Olafson and a discussion of meta-ethical independence.

*WHEATLEY, JON. "The Logical Status of Meta-ethical Theories," *Theoria*, 26 (1960), 71–82. Actually a criticism of noncognitivistic meta-ethical views.

*WILCOX, JOHN T. "Blackstone on Meta-ethical Neutrality," *Australasian Journal of Philosophy*, 41 (1963), 89–91. A comment on Blackstone's "Are Meta-ethical Theories Normatively Neutral?" and a discussion of the question of independence.

Cognitivist
Definist Theories

In Chapter 10 we distinguished between cognitive and noncognitive, and between definist and nondefinist theories. Now we shall turn our attention to cognitivist definist views and, eventually, to the meta-ethical view usually called *naturalism* (more accurately, *naturalistic cognitivistic definism*).

A. Tenets of Cognitivistic Definism

A definist meta-ethical view, as we have said, is one according to which any moral judgment can be completely defined in nonmoral terms. If, however, someone uses the notion of goodness to define 'right', or any moral term in the definition of another moral term, he is not a definist unless he also believes that the defining term can ultimately be eliminated and replaced by a nonmoral term. We characterized the definists as maintaining 2:

2. Any moral judgment (judgment in which 'good' or 'bad', 'right' or 'wrong' is used in a moral sense) can be reduced or expanded by analysis or definition to another expression which has the same meaning or significance and which contains no moral terms.

We also mentioned the two propositions which all cognitivists would accept:

1. Moral judgments are capable of being objectively true.

and

1a. There is objective moral knowledge.

The cognitivist definist, then, is one who subscribes to 1, 1a, and 2.

B. Definitions

In order to understand the definist positions we are about to consider, it is necessary to clarify the notion of a definition. Almost all definitions take the same form:

$$p =_{df} q$$

or

p means q

This form, however, may conceal a number of crucial differences.

Definitions that tell us how a word has been used in common speech or in some particular field have come to be called *reportive definitions*. The sources for a reportive definition vary considerably. We may turn to our own knowledge of the language, we may look up the word in a dictionary, or we may proceed as F. C. Sharp did, when he attempted to find out what the "man in the street" means by the word 'right' by approaching the man in the street. The problem was, however, that Sharp did not believe that the man in the street could really *say* what he means by the word 'right':

> The subject matter of our studies is still the man on the street. It is what *he* means by "right" that interests us. And the difficulty we face is that he cannot tell us. Ask him to define the term, and he will not even understand what you are driving at. This difficulty, however, is not one peculiar to the vocabulary of ethics. John Smith cannot tell you what he means by "cause," "probable," or "now"; he cannot give a really satisfactory answer to so apparently simple a question as "What is 'money'?" . . .
>
> When we had been told that this milk was very hot, this stool very heavy, this glass very easily broken, and that we had been very naughty, the meaning of "very" dawned upon our minds, not in the sense that we could define it but that we could use it intelligently. It is in precisely this same way that we can discover what the layman means by the fundamental terms in the moral vocabulary. We watch his use of them. Thereupon, proceeding one step farther than the child, we generalize our observations and in doing so form a definition.
>
> It is indeed a curious fact that men can go through life using words with a fair degree of definiteness and consistency with no formulated definition before the mind. But it is fact, nonetheless. "I cannot define poetry," says A. E. Housman in effect, "but I know it when I see it. In the same way a terrier cannot define a rat, but he knows one when he sees it." [1]

---

[1] F. C. Sharp, *Good Will and Ill Will* (Chicago: The University of Chicago Press, 1950), p. 156.

Sharp proposed to discover what the man in the street means by 'right' by posing certain moral problems to him, and by further altering the problems slightly he hoped to see where significant differences lay. In this way Sharp was able to elicit both normative and meta-ethical theories from his informants. This type of reportive definition can be accurate or inaccurate, depending upon the skill with which the inquiry is conducted.

Sharp's method is not incompatible with looking in a dictionary—one may do both, and other things as well. Socrates, for example, used to ask a man in the street about the meanings of words and, by a dialectical process of question and answer, attempt to discover the meaning of such words as 'justice', 'friendship', or 'courage'. Although Socrates rarely got a satisfactory answer, if he had—and if he had recorded it—it would have been a reportive definition. All reportive definitions, then, share the feature of being attempts to say what a word, in fact, means. They are all either accurate or inaccurate, correct or incorrect, true or false. But also they are always attempts to report the meaning a word has in a fairly limited area. There are reportive definitions in science and in philosophy, dealing with the meanings scientists and philosophers attach to words; and there are reportive definitions which cover only United States citizens. If we were attempting, for example, to report the meaning of the word 'bonnet', or definition would be different depending on whether we were reporting English or American usage.

There are many kinds of reportive definitions for different purposes and with different kinds of support, but there are other kinds of definitions as well. In a textbook in the sciences, for example, a writer might report how a particular word is used by scientists, or he might stipulate a definition of his own. In the latter case, it does not matter whether the word has a previous meaning. A definition of this sort is a *stipulative definition*, and although a reportive definition is accurate or inaccurate, correct or incorrect, a stipulative definition cannot be evaluated in these terms. It is, rather, happily chosen, or useful. However, stipulative definitions must be used with a little caution—it is one thing to introduce a new term in a scientific textbook, for example, and another altogether to proceed like Humpty Dumpty in *Alice in Wonderland*, who stipulated that 'glory' means 'there's a nice knock down argument for you'. If one stipulates that a word will have a meaning other than its customary meaning, there had better be good reasons for doing so; for the possibility of confusion and misunderstanding is great. This possibility is made even stronger by the fact that stipulative definitions can look just like reportive ones.

There are different kinds of stipulative definitions, and the best way to distinguish among them seems to be on the basis of the sort of justification they are given. If a new term is introduced, or an old term redefined for the purpose of convenience, and if no suggestion is made that this usage should, for any reason, be continued outside the context of the work in question, *an arbitrary stipulative definition* has been given. If, on the other hand, some justification is given for stipulating a certain definition, and if it is suggested (implicitly or explicitly) that there are good reasons for accepting this stipulation into the ordinary (or technical) vocabulary, or for using an old word in a new way, then a *nonarbitrary stipulative definition* has been given.

Perhaps it will be suggested that the general adoption of a definition would have good or useful consequences. In Orwell's *1984*, for example, the word 'free' was reshaped in such a way that it was impossible to speak of political freedom. The justification for doing this was that it led to the kind of state desired. Similarly, philosophers sometimes suggest that if a word such as 'good' is given the meaning 'pleasant', definite advantages will result—we will be able to speak about value with accuracy and precision, and perhaps even to reach agreement about formerly disputed ethical questions. To take another example, one might very well give a utilitarian defense for defining 'good' to mean 'pleasant', which would be to suggest that there are good utilitarian grounds for using the word 'good' in the way suggested. A definition of this sort may be called *a defended stipulative definition*.

But there is another sort of nonarbitrary stipulative definition which must be distinguished from the rest. These definitions we can call *theoretical definitions*, and they are proposed as a consequence of a certain theory. Suppose, for example, that a philosopher believes in hedonistic psychological egoism. He might then be inclined to suggest that that 'right' means 'productive of pleasure for me', which is to say that, although he recognizes that people do not actually or always use 'right' in this way, his suggested use is understandable and consistent with the theory held. The acceptability of this suggestion depends upon several factors:

1. Is the theory actually correct?
2. Is the suggested meaning relatively close to the usual meaning of the word 'right'?
3. If this suggestion is accepted, will we need to find another word to do the job that 'right' formerly had done?

If we answer the first two questions in the negative and the third question in the affirmative, then it will not be a good idea to accept the stipulation.

A theoretical definition may be based upon a psychological theory, a sociological theory, or any other kind of theory, but the correctness of the theory should be determined before the definition is accepted; if it is not, the fact that the theory is made true by definition might be thought to show something about the world, as it certainly does not.

The definitions we have distinguished can now be listed and illustrated:

Reportive definitions
   from our own knowledge of the language
   from dictionaries
   from surveys and polls
   from dialectical discussions
Stipulative definitions
   arbitrary
   nonarbitrary
     defended definitions
     theoretical definitions
       arising from psychological theory
       arising from sociological theory
       arising from philosophical theory.
       (And so on.)

It is important to re-emphasize the fact that any of these definitions may take the same form:

$$p =_{df} q$$

The discovery of what kind of definition is being offered can come only after an examination of the circumstances under which it is offered, and whether and how it is defended. If S defines 'rump' as 'that part of the body (of an animal) from which the tail springs', he can appeal to the *Oxford English Dictionary* for support, and if he does so, he has given a reportive definition. On the other hand, Sharp, for example, finally decided that 'right' means 'that which arouses approbation under certain conditions', and his support is not a dictionary, but his surveys, his generalizations on them, and the theory he then constructed.

In his *Ethics*, Spinoza begins with the following seemingly arbitrary stipulative definition:

> By that which is *self caused*, I mean that of which the essence involves existence, or that of which the nature is only conceivable as existent.[2]

The key to the stipulative nature of this definition is the "I mean" clause, although it would not be hard to see this as a nonarbitrary stipulative definition, perhaps a theoretical one. Very often it is difficult or impossible to tell whether a term is being defined arbitrarily (for the purposes of convenience in one work only) or being at least implicitly recommended for general adoption. We shall, however, continue to call a definition arbitrary (in our

---

[2] Spinoza, *Ethics*, in *The Chief Works of Benedict de Spinoza*, Vol. II, trans. R.H.M. Lewis (New York: Dover Publications, Inc., 1951), p. 45.

sense of that word) if no explicit argument for its general adoption is offered.

The following two definitions are arbitrary:—which is not to say that they were not carefully chosen and not to say that they serve no useful function in the book in which they occur:

A *critical interpretation*, for the purposes of this book, is a statement that purports to declare the "meaning" of a work of art.

Thus when I speak of the regional qualities of a complex, I mean its perceptual regional properties.[3]

Quite different from these definitions are Beardsley's definitions of 'aesthetic value'. In the latter case he begins by considering and rejecting other possible definitions, and then says:

In order to decide about the acceptability of the Instrumentalist definition, we must be aware of the spirit in which it is offered. It does not claim to report what critics would say if asked for their definition of "good" (in an aesthetic context); but it does claim to indicate what they can, and probably must, mean, if they wish the reasons they actually give for critical evaluations to be logically relevant and persuasive. At least there is no doubt that the Instrumentalist definition fits in very well with practical criticism.[4]

Beardsley's definition of 'aesthetic value', which he calls *the instrumentalist definition*, therefore, seems to be a nonarbitrary defended definition, for he claims that its adoption is necessary in order for critics to be able to give relevant and persuasive reasons.

Theoretical definitions are supported, but they differ from what we call defended definitions in that they do not simply appeal to the advantages of adopting them but rely upon a whole theoretical framework. Newton, for example, did not say that it would be advantageous to adopt his definition

force = mass × acceleration

rather, it was a consequence of his entire theory of physics. Its correctness, that is to say, the degree to which we should feel constrained to accept it, depends in large part on the correctness and acceptability of his whole theory. What needs to be noticed here is that often definitions which seem to be arbitrary stipulative definitions are seen later actually to be theoretical definitions.

A theoretical definition, then, does not indicate what a word means in

---

[3] Monroe C. Beardsley, *Aesthetics* (New York and Burlingame: Harcourt, Brace & World, Inc., 1958), pp. 9, 83.

[4] *Ibid.*, p. 533.

ordinary speech, but rather that, given the correctness of a particular theory, it would henceforth be misleading to use the word in any other way. For example, if Newton is right, then there is little point in using 'force' in physics to stand for the amount of strength possessed by the gremlins who push things about in the world.

Exercises

Review

1. How does cognitivistic definism differ from cognitivistic nondefinism? How does it differ from noncognitive theories and in what respects does it resemble them?
2. What is a reportive definition? How may a number of different kinds of reportive definitions be distinguished?
3. Are reportive definitions true or false? Are stipulative definitions true or false? Explain your answers.
4. How may different sorts of stipulative definitions be distinguished?
5. What is a theoretical definition? How may different kinds of theoretical definitions be distinguished?
6. What kind of a definition does Sharp give?

Applications

1. Examine the following definitions, and classify them on the basis of the list of kinds of definitions on p. 232.
   a. In Greek the word 'tragedy' means 'goat song'.
   b. Truth is when someone says of what is that it is, and of what is not that it is not.
   c. "If this view of war and peace is correct, we should have been at peace since V-J Day in 1945, save for the 'police action' in Korea. But few people would assert that the past sixteen years have been a time of peace. The common idea of war and peace simply does not apply to the present period. . . . Our view of war, then, must be broadened to include both armed conflict and battles of diplomacy, economic aid, and propaganda." Mortimer Adler, *Great Ideas from the Great Books.*
   d. "Happiness is an activity of the soul in accordance with perfect virtue." Aristotle
   e. "The mutual transferring of right, is that which men call contract." Thomas Hobbes, *Leviathan.*
   f. "The third type of creator I can only call, for lack of a better name, the traditionalist type. . . . The traditionalist type of composer begins with a pattern rather than with a theme." Aaron Copland, *What to Listen for in Music.*
2. Find other attempts at giving definitions and say whether they fit into the categories we have given, and which.

C. Differences Among Cognitivist Definists

1. *Type of Definition.* One method of distinguishing different cognitivist definist views would be according to the type of definition offered. Is the definition stipulative or reportive? If it is stipulative, is it defended or theoretical? This is a reasonable suggestion because the strength of the position being considered and the relevance of the arguments against it often depend upon the answers to these questions. The major disadvantage to distinguishing among cognitivist definist views in this way is that the grouping created by such a procedure throws into the same category views which are clearly very diverse.

2. *Nature of the Definiens.* Suppose that the following definition should be offered:

good $=$ $_{df}$ pleasurable.

The '$=$$_{df}$' sign indicates that a definition is being given, and in this definition 'good' (the term to the left of the sign) is called the *definiendum*, whereas 'pleasurable' (the term to the right of the sign) is called the *definiens*. The term being defined (in this case, 'good') therefore is the definiendum, and the term used to define it (in this case, 'pleasurable') is the definiens. In any definist theory (of morals) the definiendum will always be a normative expression or term, but the definiens may be any of a number of kinds of expression. A naturalistic term or a nonnaturalistic—e.g., metaphysical or theological—term may serve as the definiens. Also, with naturalistic definitions further distinctions may be made on the basis of which naturalistic properties are used to define the normative expressions to be eliminated.

3. *Naturalistic and Nonnaturalistic Cognitivistic Definism.* We have already pointed out (see Chapter 10) the difference between naturalistic and nonnaturalistic cognitivism. The naturalistic cognitivist definist (or the naturalist for short) believes that moral terms can be replaced by terms which appear in the natural or social sciences—psychology, physics, or sociology, for example. The nonnaturalistic cognitivist definist believes that moral terms can be replaced, but not with terms which refer to properties or qualities the presence or absence of which can be determined by scientific observation. Because we shall devote the majority of this chapter to naturalism, it may be helpful to examine the most frequently discovered nonnaturalistic view.

If someone holds that

right $=$ $_{df}$ willed by God

we shall call him a *theological definist.* Such a view has been held by John Locke (1632–1714) and William Paley (1743–1805), and it is, or seems to be, one to which many modern religious thinkers would adhere. There are, however, rather serious difficulties in this position. If 'right' really means 'willed by God'—that is, if this is a correct reportive definition—then the claim that God was right to will something becomes empty and trivially true, because it simply asserts, through a substitution of equivalent expressions, that God's willing something was in accordance with his will. It would, on this view, be a contradiction to say that God acted or willed wrongly.

In a fine book on definist theories A. N. Prior discusses what he calls the classical formulation of this view, which he calls *theological naturalism:*

Paley defines virtue as 'the doing good to mankind, in obedience to the will of God, and for the sake of everlasting happiness'; 'right' as 'consistency with the will of God'; and 'obligation' as being 'urged by a violent motive resulting from the command of another'.[5]

Paley's views were objected to early in their history by Richard Whately (1787–1863) on the grounds we have already mentioned. The substance of Whately's objection is contained in the following passage, also quoted by Prior:

Whately notes, to begin with, that if a man 'attaches no meaning to the words "good", and "just", and "right", except that such is the divine command, then, to say that God is good, and his commands just, is only saying in a circuitous way, that He is what He is, and that what He wills He wills, which might be said of any Being in the universe'.[6]

Now it certainly seems that theologians would want to be able to say, in a nontrivial way, that what God does is right, or that God is good. If Whately is right, they are incapable of saying this. But the theological definist who claims to be presenting a reportive definition will encounter another rather serious difficulty, for it is quite clear that when people say an action is right, few of them mean that it is willed by God. If, on the other hand, the theological definist is presenting either a nonarbitrary stipulative definition or a theoretical definition, he is open to criticism. If he is presenting a definition he wishes us to adopt, he needs to give some reasons why we should adopt it, why it would be right to adopt it, and he can hardly argue that it is right to adopt it because God wills that we adopt it. Such an argument smacks of the grossest circularity; furthermore, there is no reason to believe that God wills any such thing. This kind of definition and theoretical definitions are only as strong as the arguments for God's existence, and philosophers are almost universally agreed that, whether or not God does exist, the arguments pur-

[5] A. N. Prior, *Logic and the Basis of Ethics* (Oxford: The Clarendon Press, 1949), p. 100.
[6] *Ibid.*, p. 101.

porting to show that he exists are beset with grave difficulties. More arguments could be given against the theological definist, but perhaps these will suffice, and when objections to other forms of cognitivistic definism are presented the reader may satisfy himself whether they also apply to this view.

Other nonnaturalistic definist views differ from the theological definist in that the definiens they offer makes no reference to any theological notion. Instead of appealing to the will of God, or some similar notion, these thinkers attempt to define 'good' or 'right' in terms of some concept which is neither natural nor theological. G. E. Moore characterizes this view in the following way:

A 'Metaphysical Ethics' is marked by the fact that it makes the assertion: That which would be perfectly good is something which exists, but is not natural; that which has some characteristic possessed by a supersensible reality. Such an assertion was made by the Stoics when they asserted that a life in accordance with Nature was perfect. For they did not mean by 'Nature,' what I have so defined, but something supersensible which they inferred to exist, and which they held to be perfectly good. . . . Such an assertion is made by Kant when he tells us that his 'Kingdom of Ends' is the ideal. And such, finally, is made by modern writers who tell us that the final and perfect end is to realise our *true* selves—a self different both from the whole and from any part of that which exists here and now in Nature.[7]

Again, it is clear that, as reportive definitions, these would fail miserably, but it is also clear that, as nonarbitrary stipulative definitions, they are only as good as the theory behind them or the reasons supporting them (reasons presupposing the existence of the metaphysical entity used in the definiens). For this reason and because we have yet to examine the general arguments against definism, we leave all the nonnaturalistic definists for an examination of some general arguments against cognitivistic definism, framed to apply to the naturalist. If the reader needs more proof that nonnaturalistic cognitivist definist theories fare very badly under criticism, let him apply whatever arguments he finds in the next section to these views, but let him also keep in mind the fact that it is important to be clear as to whether a definition is being criticized as a reportive definition or as a stipulative definition.

Exercises

Review
1. Why is it not a good idea to distinguish different cognitivist definist positions on the basis of the type of definition they offer?
2. Which term of a definition is the definiens, and which is the definiendum?

[7] G. E. Moore, *Principia Ethica* (Cambridge: Cambridge University Press, 1959), p. 113. By permission of the publishers.

3. What is the difference between naturalistic and nonnaturalistic cognitivistic definism?

4. Give some examples of nonnaturalistic cognitivist definists, and criticize their views.

Applications

1. Examine the following definitions of moral terms and state in each case what the definiens is and what the definiendum is. Then try to say whether the definitions are more plausible as reportive definitions or as some other kind.

   a. "When I recommend an action to someone as being 'good' I express the fact that I desire it."

   b. To say that something is good is to say that it is desired by the members of the critics board of assessment.

   c. "A is right" simply means that someone wants to do A.

   d. 'Right conduct' means 'telling the truth and restoring anything we have been trusted with'.

   e. To say that an action is right is to say that it is in the interest of the strongest party in the state, the party in control.

2. In your reading, discover some definitions. Determine first what the definiens and the definiendum are, and then discover, if possible, whether the definition is a reportive definition or some other kind.

D. Naturalistic Cognitivistic Definism (Naturalism)

G. E. Moore is perhaps the most widely known of the critics of naturalism. He characterizes the naturalist as holding the view that "good can be defined by reference to a *natural object.*" According to naturalism, he continues, "ethics is an empirical or positive science: Its conclusions could be all established by means of empirical observation and induction." [8] More recent thinkers are also inclined to define naturalism in similar ways, stressing that, for the naturalist, moral judgments are really factual, empirical, and scientific, testable in the way that any statement about ordinary things is testable—by observation and experiment. The naturalist is also characterized as claiming that this is true because of what moral expressions mean. For the naturalist, then, the definiens is always a naturalistic term or expression—or, as Moore would put it, a natural object. Without questioning the expression 'natural object', but assuming that pleasure and potentiality for survival are "natural objects," two naturalists might argue over whether "A is right," means "A is more pleasurable than any alternative," or "A is more likely to bring about the survival of the race than any other alternative." This seems already to indicate that distinctions among naturalistic views may be made, as between cognitivist definist views in general, according to differences found in the definiens.

[8] *Ibid.*, p. 39.

1. *Natural Properties.* One of the more serious problems the naturalist seems to face at the beginning of his work is the clarification of the notion of a "natural property." Moore, in criticizing naturalism, used the term extensively, but was forced to admit later that his suggestion as to what such properties were was "utterly silly and preposterous." [9] Ethical thinkers who have discussed this notion usually suggest that a natural property is any property the presence or absence of which can be discovered by sense observation or experience, experiment, or through any of the available means of science. There are difficulties with this definition however, for a cognitivist nondefinist might also claim that the property of goodness is discoverable by sense experience or observation (see pp. 283–84).

But even if the notion of a natural property cannot be specified, this does not really damage the philosopher who says that 'good' means 'pleasant', for he probably never talks of natural properties. It is only in a criticism of naturalism, or in an attempt to distinguish between naturalistic and nonnaturalistic definist theories, that such a concept is needed. For this reason, then, there seems to be little need to ask the man who defines 'good' as 'pleasant' to give an analysis of the notion of a natural property, for we all understand what pleasure is.

2. *Naturalistic Views.* In this section, we shall critically examine a number of the more important naturalistic meta-ethical theories. We must, however, re-emphasize the fact that we are considering theories about the meaning of normative terms and that there are many kinds of definitions. It follows from this that no naturalist theory can be adequately criticized, or even understood, unless an attempt is made to discover what sort of definition is being offered.

a. SUBJECTIVE NATURALISM. The first sort of naturalist theory we shall discuss is called *subjective naturalism.* Subjective naturalists are usually not able to give one-word definitions of evaluative terms; rather, they suggest that a definition like the following is required:

1. X is good $=_{df}$ I like X.
2. X is good $=_{df}$ S likes X.
3. X is good $=_{df}$ The members of Group G like X.

Other phrases or terms, such as 'feel a favorable attitude toward', 'approve of', and so on, may be substituted for 'like' in these definitions without altering their essential feature—their reference to an actual person or group and their claim that this person or group has a particular belief about, or feeling or attitude toward, what is being judged. If there are no such persons, the judgment cannot be true (it is either false or the question of its truth cannot

---

[9] G. E. Moore, "A Reply to My Critics," in P. A. Schilpp, *The Philosophy of G. E. Moore*, 2nd ed. (New York: Tudor, 1952), p. 582.

legitimately arise); if they exist but do not have the belief, feeling, or attitude attributed to them, the judgment is false.

Someone may be said to hold subjective naturalism, then, if he holds that, because of the meanings of expressions such as "X is good" and "A is right," the truth of these judgments is a function of the actual beliefs or feelings of a person or group. If one wishes to claim that moral judgments may be defined naturalistically, but denies that once the definition is given the truth of the judgment depends upon the way someone feels or believes, then we shall say that his definition is not subjective but *objective*.[10]

(1) *Individual Subjective Naturalism.* We may distinguish, further, two sorts of subjective naturalist theories, an individual and a general form of the view. If someone holds that a judgment such as "X is good" or "A is right" is identical in meaning with some proposition about the way one particular person believes or feels, then the theory is *individual*, for the crucial term is defined with reference to one and only one person. Thus 1 and 2 are examples of individual subjectivist definitions. It would also be possible to distinguish a "first-person" from a "third-person" form of this sort of theory. According to first-person views, when we say that "X is good," or "A is right," we are saying that we ourselves have a particular feeling or belief about X or A; according to the third-person theories, a statement to the effect that "X is good" or "A is right" is also a statement to the effect that some other person has such a feeling or belief. G. E. Moore has characterized the first-person version of subjective naturalism:

To begin with, it may be held that whenever any man asserts an action to be right or wrong, what he is asserting is merely that he *himself* has some particular feeling towards the action in question. Each of us, according to this view, is merely making an assertion about *his own* feelings: when I assert that an action is right, the *whole* of what I mean is merely that I have some particular feeling towards the action; and when *you* make the same assertion, the *whole* of what you mean is merely that *you* have the feeling in question towards the action.[11]

First-person theories, however, commit us to some rather peculiar conclusions. For example, it will follow that there are really no disagreements about what is good, for two apparently contradictory statements such as "X is good" and "X is not good" are not really contradictory; they simply express two compatible facts—namely, that one person likes X and the other does not. Furthermore, the proof of any moral judgment will only be a proof that a particular person does in fact have a feeling, belief, or attitude. A penetrating criticism of this view has been offered by A. C. Ewing:

[10] The notion of an objective definition must not be confused with the notion of objective truth, introduced in Chapter 10. One who gives a subjective definition of moral terms will still maintain that moral judgments are capable of being objectively true.

[11] G. E. Moore, *Ethics* (New York: Oxford University Press, Inc., 1965), p. 37.

Firstly, if this definition were correct, it would follow that a man could never be wrong in an ethical judgement unless he had made a mistake about his own psychology. Again, two people would never mean the same thing when they pronounced an action right or wrong, since either would just mean "It is approved (disapproved) by *me*." Indeed the same person would never mean the same thing by an ethical judgement on two different occasions, since each time he would mean "I *now* feel (or tend to feel) approval of this." Nor, if A pronounced the same action right as B pronounced wrong, would they ever really be in disagreement, for what A would mean is—I (A) feel approval, which is quite compatible with B feeling disapproval at the same time of the same act. Further, when I condemned, e.g. Stalin, I should not be talking about Stalin but only about my own feelings. These consequences would follow if the theory under discussion were true, and they surely constitute a conclusive *reductio ad absurdum* of the theory.[12]

Ewing objects to these theories on the grounds that they do not accord with certain accepted facts—for one, the obvious and undeniable fact of genuine ethical disagreement. This is nothing more than an application of the familiar third criterion for the acceptability of theories: the theory must fit or explain the range of phenomena better than other competing theories. There is one very important phenomenon, ethical disagreement, which this theory does not explain at all, and thus it is reasonable to suggest that any other theory which can account for the existence of ethical disagreement, is so far preferable.

But this theory has been criticized as a reportive definition, and we might ask if it would fare any better if it were taken as a nonarbitrary stipulation. The answer must be in the negative. Whether the definition is a report or a stipulation, it still cannot account for disagreement, and as a stipulation, it asks us to define something out of existence which there is reason to believe exists. This is very much like defining a man as a leaf-bearing perennial growth, and then declaring that men cannot think. What is wrong with that definition is that we all know that men can think, and what is wrong with the first-person views of subjective naturalism is that we all know that there is ethical disagreement, and we are, and have a right to be, much more certain of this than we are of any facts that would support the definition—as a stipulation or as a report.

According to third-person theories "X is good" means something like "S likes, approves of, or has a favorable attitude toward, X." Here relativism is escaped and disagreement is possible, for there may be genuine disagreement about whether or not a particular person does feel in a certain way. But the theory still meets with rather serious difficulties. First, it might be asked how we specify the S in question. It cannot be some individual chosen

[12] A. C. Ewing, *Ethics* (New York: The Free Press, 1965), p. 84. By permission of The Macmillan Company. By permission of The English Universities Press, Limited, Original publishers.

at random, for then there would be no reason why some other S would not do just as well. It might be suggested that S should be God, or the sovereign. The first choice, however, would produce a nonnaturalistic subjectivist theory which has already been criticized; the second would give rise to other problems: few would maintain that "The Queen of England approves of X" is correct as a report of what anyone means by "X is good," or an acceptable suggestion as to what anyone should mean by that expression even in England, let alone in other countries not in the Commonwealth. Finally, the acceptance of such a stipulation would make the expression "The Queen of England likes what is bad" a contradiction, and that, too, is quite an unacceptable consequence.

(2) *General Subjective Naturalism.* Moritz Schlick seems to waver between adopting an individual first-person form of subjective naturalism, and the general form of the same view. In one place he says, "When I recommend an action to someone as being 'good,' I express the fact that I *desire* it." [13] However, in another place he says, "The word 'good' has a moral sense when (1) it refers to human *decisions*, and (2) expresses an approbation by human *society*." [14] This second quotation illustrates the general subjectivist view. One adheres to general subjective naturalism if he believes that moral judgments are identical in meaning with some statement about the way a group of persons believes or feels.

The difficulties with this view are similar to those encountered by the various forms of limited utilitarianism. How, for example, can we select the proper group? Even if all the members of the group in question agree that the meaning of "X is good" is "We approve of X," it is not likely that outsiders will agree with it either as a report or as a stipulation—and with good reason, for it is unfair and arbitrary, seriously ambiguous and contrary to many other things most people would wish to accept.

First for the ambiguities. If we say

$$X \text{ is good} =_{\text{df}} \text{Members of my group approve of } X$$

this is little different from the first-person views, for if S, who is a member of G, says "X is good," he is saying that the members of G approve of X; if S_1, who is a member of G_1, says "X is good," he is saying that the members of G_1 approve of X. There can never be ethical disagreement between two people from different groups. But people are members of many groups at the same time, which seems to have puzzling consequences for this view. Thus we find that this view is subject to a modified and somewhat limited relativism, and entails an unacceptable limitation of the possibility of ethical disagreement:

[13] Moritz Schlick, *Problems of Ethics* (New York: Dover Publications, Inc., 1962), p. 12.
[14] *Ibid.*, pp. 82–83.

two seemingly incompatible judgments made by members of different groups are, according to this view, not really incompatible. Where disagreement is possible—within a group (whatever that means)—it turns out to be only disagreement about consensus, a most peculiar end for ethical disputes.

But perhaps most people who have defended this view do not so interpret it. It is quite possible to be "universalist" here, and to say that "X is good" means that "Everyone approves of X," but of course then nothing would be good. Another possibility is that "X is good" means, not that the members of the speaker's society approve of X, but that the members of some otherwise objectively specified group do. But this raises all the difficulties facing the individual third-person views: How shall the group be chosen? What likely candidate is there? Why should we believe, or accept as a stipulation, that the members of a certain group can never be said, without contradiction, to be wrong? The final possibility is to take all society or mankind as a group and to suggest that "X is good" means "More than half (most?) of the members approve of X." But by now the poverty of such a suggestion should be obvious, and again, we can do no better than quote the arguments of Ewing against such views:

One proposed way of definition is in terms of approval, by which is meant the unique emotion or emotional attitude that we have when our attention is called to something ethically worthy or admirable. Thus it has been suggested that to say that something is right or good is to say that it is of such a kind as to evoke the approval of most people. But this view is surely open to objections of a very obvious kind. If it were true, it would be self-contradictory to say that a minority who felt disapproval of what most people approved could ever be in the right, and this is surely not so. We cannot possibly say that the majority and not the minority are necessarily right about any particular issue unless we have first considered the issue in question. And how are we to determine what constitutes a majority? It would obviously be arbitrary to confine oneself to people alive at the present time. Why should their ethical sentiments have this supreme authority in determining what is right or good and those of their late parents or grandparents none at all? But, if we took into account everybody who has ever lived, we should have a queer ethics inded for, taking into account all ages, crude and savage far outnumber tolerably civilized men. And if we included also all future generations, which seems the only consistent course, this would make it impossible save by a miraculous prophecy to determine what is good or right at all. The Earth may continue to be inhabited by men for millions of years, and how are we to tell what the people who inhabit it in those far distant ages will approve or disapprove? Again the mere fact that people disapprove of what I do may make me feel uncomfortable, and if their sentiments are strong enough it may make it highly prudent to change my conduct provided I can do so without going against my conscience, but it could not of itself make it my moral duty to do so. The motive—Seek the approval of others—is not specifically moral: on the contrary it has been recognized by the greatest moral teachers as a major obstacle to true morality. My argument may be put like this—It is obvious that we ought to seek what is intrinsically good or right, just because it is good or right, as the only moral end-in-itself. But it is certainly not the case that we ought to seek what most people approve as the only moral end-in-itself just because they feel approval of it. Therefore "good" or "right" cannot mean the same as "approved by most people."[15]

(3) *The Interest-Theory of Ralph Barton Perry.* There is another kind of subjectivistic naturalism that does not fall conveniently in the categories of "individual" or "general" views. Consider the following three definitions:

X has value $=$ $_{df}$ interest is taken in X by S
X has value $=$ $_{df}$ interest is taken in X by the members of Group G
X has value $=$ $_{df}$ interest is taken in X by someone (i.e., anyone)

The third definition does not state that a specific person or group takes an intrest in X but, rather, that someone—i.e., anyone—does. All three views, however, share the feature that, if there are no persons, no judgment of the form "X is good" is true. The judgment is also false if the conditions set down by the definition are not met.

The third definition has been given by the American philosopher Ralph Barton Perry (1876–1957), who says:

Any object, whatever it be, acquires value when any interest, whatever it be, is taken in it; just as anything whatsoever becomes a target when anyone whosoever aims at it.[16]

This theory is really much more liberal than either of the other versions of subjective naturalism, for its acceptance increases the number of valuable things that can be said to exist in the world. It might be pointed out that Perry has given a nonarbitrary stipulative definition, and this is fortunate, for as a report, this suggestion is quite implausible, as Perry himself admits.

Perry arrives at his view by attempting to eliminate other theories. But even if Perry were successful in presenting conclusive objections to all other possible definitions and denials of definism, if there are conclusive objections to his own view he has no more reason for accepting it than he has for accepting anyone else's—and there are such objections.

One charge often leveled at Perry is that his theory entails relativistic consequences, and these do seem inescapable. Here is how Perry meets these objections:

[15] Ewing, *op. cit.*, pp. 82–83.
[16] Ralph Barton Perry, *General Theory of Value* (Cambridge, Mass.: Harvard University Press, 1926), pp. 115–16.

But is not contradiction escaped only by falling into *relativism?* Well, if one may be permitted a vulgarism, and so what? [17]

The answer to his question is that, in stipulating a definition for 'good' one must accept what is entailed by the stipulation, and Perry, in recommending his definition, is also recommending its relativistic consequences. If taken seriously, however, his recommendation would entail that, although he could say that his definition is good, he would be forced to admit that other conflicting definitions are also good because they are clearly desired by other philosophers.

Equally troublesome is the fact that his theory seems to be open to serious counterexamples. For instance, we should have to say that rape, murder, revenge, cruelty, hate, war, death, prostitution, pain, suffering, theft, adultery, blasphemy, the narcotics trade, and the end of the world were all good because there are, without doubt, people who desire these things. An even more serious problem is pointed out by Ewing:

However, in any case we may object that, if good = desired, better must = desired more, so that the degree of goodness is in proportion to the degree of desire, and this is obviously not so. We all desire the welfare and continued life of those near and dear to us much more than that of people equally worthy, of whom we have just read in a newspaper, and it is certainly not true that most people desire virtue quite as much as they ought to in comparison with other things, e.g., their own happiness or even material welfare.[18]

It is hard to see how Perry could surmount these difficulties, or why we should accept the stipulative definition he offers.[19] The subjective views we

---

[17] Ralph Barton Perry, *Realms of Value* (Cambridge, Mass.: Harvard University Press, 1954), p. 12.

[18] Ewing, *op. cit.*, pp. 85–86.

[19] There is a sense in which Perry may be thought to escape these objections. In addition to giving a subjectivist definition of 'good', he offers an objective definition of another term, 'morally good'. He says that a thing is morally good "when the interest which makes it good satisfies the requirement of harmony, that is, innocence and coöperation." *Realms of Value, op. cit.*, p. 104. This is objectivist, since whether or not a desire may harmonize with other desires is not a function of what anyone thinks or feels. But our concern here is not to examine Perry's entire theory, but rather that part of it which attempts to define the important moral concepts. To assess his definition of 'morally good', also a nonarbitrary stipulative definition, it would be necessary to ask such things as how far harmony of conflicting interests can be achieved, and isn't it the case that some interests which clearly do not harmonize with the rest ought to be satisfied and some which do ought not? If so, then even though these are, by definition, morally good, the notion does not serve us well, since it is as difficult to see how something can be said, in any sense to be both good and morally good, and yet unworthy of choice. But still, there is more to Perry's theory than we have the time or the space to treat.

have considered, then, seem to be lacking as reports of what we mean by the moral terms being defined and there are too many disadvantages with accepting them as stipulations. It is necessary, therefore, to seek a more acceptable sort of naturalism.

b. OBJECTIVE NATURALISM. The objective naturalist claims that moral judgments are not definable by appealing to what some person or group believes or feels, though he maintains that moral judgments are reducible to equivalent nonmoral ones.

(1) *Tendency and Nontendency Views.* One type of naturalist view is difficult to categorize, though it probably belongs in the objective category. At any rate, it is important not to confuse it with any of the views just discussed. Consider the following two definitions:

X is right $=_{df}$ I approve of X
X is right $=_{df}$ X has a tendency to cause me to approve of it

There is no doubt that these two definitions are different. One may be willing to admit that X has such a tendency but still not approve of it, or the tendency may be there even if one is not acquainted with X. Indeed, the tendency is there even if there are are no people at all. For this reason, then, it does not seem correct to treat these two definitions on a par. Serious confusion, therefore, could result from failing to keep the two definitions separate.

(2) *Edward Westermarck.* Problems of interpretation are usually difficult, and the case is no different when we turn to the writings of Edward Westermarck (1862–1939). It is generally believed that Westermarck was a naturalist, and this belief is easily borne out by many passages from his works. Nevertheless, Westermarck tends to adopt something like a noncognitivist meta-ethical view. He seems to believe that moral judgments are not objectively true, though he admits that, in a sense, they *are* objectively true. The classification of Westermarck's view depends upon which of these assertions we accept, or take to be more representative of his theory. The correct conclusion is probably that he would have been a noncognitivist had he seen that consistency required it, and had he pursued the implications of the following remark:

I have thus arrived at the conclusion that neither the attempts of moral philosophers or theologians to prove the objective validity of moral judgments, nor the common sense assumption to the same effect, give us any right at all to accept such validity as a fact. So far, however, I have only tried to show that it has not been proved; now I am prepared to take a step further and assert that it cannot exist. The reason for this is that in my opinion the predicates of all moral judgments, all moral concepts, are ultimately based on emotions, and that, as is very commonly admitted, no objectivity can come from an emotion.[20]

But, although many of his statements have noncognitivistic overtones, he probably should be treated as a naturalist who holds some kind of tendency view. He says, for example;

> The doing of what ought not to be done, or the omission of what ought not to be omitted, is apt to call forth moral indignation—this is the most essential fact involved in the notion of "ought."
>
> "Ought" and "duty" express only the tendency of an omission to call forth disapproval, and say nothing about the consequences of the act's performance.[21]

> The tendency in a phenomenon to arouse moral disapproval is directly expressed by the term *bad*, and closely allied to it is the term *wrong*.[22]

The truth of moral judgments (or their falsity) is then clearly a function of whether or not there is this tendency:

> It is of course true or not that we in a given moment have a certain emotion; but in no other sense can the antithesis of true and false be applied to it.[23]

But the point is that, in this sense, the antithesis of true or false does apply to moral judgments, and this, for good or ill, justifies the classification of Westermarck as a naturalist.[24]

But, although Westermarck is a naturalist, he does not hold a subjectivist theory. He says: The theory of the emotional origin of moral judgments that

---

[20] Edward Westermarck, *Ethical Relativity* (New York: Harcourt, Brace & World, Inc., 1932), p. 60.

[21] Edward Westermarck, *The Origin and Development of the Moral Ideas*, Vol. I (London: MacMillan & Co., Ltd., 1906), pp. 135, 136.

[22] Westermarck, *Ethical Relativity, op. cit.*, p. 126.

[23] *Ibid.*, p. 60. He probably should have said that it is either true or false that in a given situation a phenomenon has the tendency to arouse approval or disapproval, in order to avoid the first person subjectivist overtones of this remark, and make it consistent with his other claims.

[24] Recent philosophers have been in agreement that Westermarck is to be interpreted as a naturalist. Richard B. Brandt, for example, says "To say that an action is reprehensible, according to Westermarck, is essentially to say: 'I have a tendency to feel moral disapproval toward the agents of all acts like this'." *Ethical Theory* (Englewood Cliffs, N.J.: Prentice-Hall, Inc., 1959), p. 166. Another characterization of Westermarck's view is offered by Roderick Firth in his "Ethical Absolutism and the Ideal Observer," *Philosophy and Phenomenological Research*, 12 (1952), 320. "Westermarck believes, if I understand him, that the meaning of statements of the form 'x is wrong,' can be expressed by other statements of the form 'The speaker tends to feel towards x (i.e., *would* feel in the absence of specifiable inhibiting factors), an emotion of disinterested moral disapproval which would be experienced by him as a quality or dynamic tendency in x.'"

I am here advocating does not imply that such a judgment affirms the existence of a moral emotion in the mind of the person who utters it.[25] What it
asserts is that there is a tendency to feel approval or disapproval upon the
presentation of certain things, and this is a clear case of an objectivist
tendency view.

Westermarck does seem to present some kind of reportive definition, although, again, the matter is far from clear.

As Mr. Bertrand Russell observes, "to say that a word has a meaning is not to
say that those who use the word correctly have ever thought out what the meaning
is: the use of the word comes first, and the meaning is to be distilled out of it by
observation and analysis. . . ." And in analyzing the predicates of moral judgments,
we are guided by the fact that if we ourselves emphatically and truly mean what
we say when we pronounce such a judgment, we recognize that we are apt, or at
least think we are apt, to feel a moral emotion of approval or disapproval with
regard to that on which the judgment is pronounced.[26]

This does not sound too different from Sharp's method, although it relies
more on introspection.

Is this a plausible suggestion as to what we really do mean when we make
a moral judgment? There are several reasons for thinking that it is not. First,
the fact that an object tends to arouse a moral emotion in us does not show
that, when we declare the object good, we are thereby *saying* that it has this
tendency. Furthermore, the chief support for his reportive definition is introspection, and many naturalists and nonnaturalists have found, by introspection and other methods, that this is not what they mean when they say
that something is good. Also, his reportive definition, if correct, would mean
that it is impossible to say correctly that something is good or bad if it does
not have the tendency to make us feel the requisite moral emotion. And
finally, some objects may have a tendency to make some people feel one
thing and others another. Is this to say that the object is both good and
bad, or are we to specify some perfectly objective moral observer?

If the moral emotions of an "ideal observer" are called upon the result is
the (still naturalistic) *ideal-observer theory*. Since some such theory seems to
be called for by the shortcomings of Westermarck's theory detailed above, let
us turn to an examination of that theory.

(3) *Sharp and Firth—The Ideal-Observer Theory*. In 1728, the English
moral philosopher Francis Hutcheson suggested:

When we say one is obliged to an Action, we either mean, 1. That the Action
is necessary to attain Happiness to the Agent, or to avoid Misery: Or, 2. That

---

[25] Westermarck, *Ethical Relativity, op. cit.*, p. 116.
[26] *Ibid.*, p. 116.

every Spectator, or he himself upon Reflection, must approve his Action, and dis-approve his omitting it, if he considers fully all its Circumstances.[27]

If we concentrate upon the second suggested meaning, we can notice that Hutcheson speaks of "Reflection" and considering "fully all its circum-stances," and we can find here the seeds of an ideal-observer theory and at least some of the requirements of the ideal observer. He does not claim that, when we say that someone is obliged to do something we are saying that we approve of the action, but only that we would approve if we considered fully all the circumstances of the action. The truth of a statement, then, is not a function of our feelings or beliefs, so this position is not subjectivistic. In more recent times, versions of this theory have been offered by F. C. Sharp and Roderick Firth.

Sharp's point was that although we want to know what the man on the street means by 'right', the man on the street cannot tell us. Yet we can dis-cover what he means by observing how he uses that expression, and by generalizing from our observations. Sharp claimed to have discovered that " 'right' must be definable in terms of desire, or approbation, that is to say, in terms of 'feeling'." [28] But he was aware that there is more to saying that an action is right than simply saying that we have a certain feeling, and sug-gested that "we must define 'right', if we are to use the term in the sense in which the ordinary man uses it, as *that which arouses approbation under cer-tain conditions*." [29] Once again, however, it is not possible to discover these conditions by asking the man in the street to tell us what they are.

The man in the street does not carry about with him in his mental kit a set of formulas covering these conditions, any more than when he cuts a corner he says to himself, 'A straight line is the shortest distance between two points.' . . . When John Smith calls an action "right," he means that complete acquaintance with its results would evoke impersonal approval. Exchanging the negative term "imper-sonal" for a positive one, "right" characterizes the kind of action he would want all human beings to perform under the given conditions if he had a complete ac-quaintance with all the relevant consequences.[30]

Sharp's position is presented even more clearly in an earlier book, *Ethics*. There, in a chapter entitled "The Meaning of Right," he says that, although those actions which procure the greatest happiness for the greatest numbers

---

[27] Frances Hutcheson, "An Essay on the Nature and Conduct of the Passions, with Illustrations upon the Moral Sense," *British Moralists*, ed. L. A. Selby-Bigge (New York: Dover Publications, Inc., 1965), I, p. 408. Here Hutcheson is suggesting that the ideal observer is one possible meaning for "X is right," the other being "X promotes happiness or avoids misery," another naturalistic theory.

[28] Sharp, *op. cit.*, pp. 156–57.

[29] *Ibid.*, p. 157.

[30] *Ibid.*, p. 162.

are right, this is not true in virtue of the meaning of the word 'right'. He continues, "We might accordingly define right conduct as that which is desired when it is looked at from an impersonal point of view." [31]

Ultimately, Sharp seems to be suggesting that to say that an action is right is to say that, if it were looked at from an impersonal point of view and with a complete acquaintance of all the relevant consequences, it would be desired or approved.

Roderick Firth's view differs from Sharp's in two important respects. First, it is put forward as a nonarbitrary stipulation rather than as a reportive definition. Second, Firth suggests different conditions for an ideal observer:

1. He is omniscient with respect to nonethical facts.
2. He is omnipercipient.
3. He is disinterested.
4. He is dispassionate.
5. He is consistent.
6. He is normal in other respects.[32]

The ideal observer is said to be omniscient to *all* nonethical facts because, if we accept Sharp's suggestion that the ideal observer be aware of all the *relevant* facts, we discover an embarrassing circularity in our definition. Firth says:

But it is evident that a concept of relevance cannot be employed in *defining* an ideal observer. To say that a certain body of factual knowledge is not relevant to the rightness or wrongness of a given act, is to say, assuming that an absolutist dispositional analysis is correct, that the dispositions of an ideal observer toward the given act would be the same *whether or not* he possessed that particular body of factual knowledge or any part of it. It follows, therefore, that in order to explain what we mean by "relevant knowledge," we should have to employ the very concept of ideal observer which we are attempting to define.[33]

This seems to be correct and, as Brandt points out, there may be some "inexorable necessity for embracing this unwelcome alternative. Firth has a reason for his requirement: that there is no other practicable way of specifying which facts a person must know in order to know all the ethically relevant facts, without circularity." [34]

The ideal observer must be omnipercipient; for he must be able to imagine situations as vividly as if they were being perceived, in order that he may be

---

[31] F. C. Sharp, *Ethics* (New York: Appleton-Century-Crofts, 1928), p. 109.

[32] Roderick Firth, "Ethical Absolutism and the Ideal Observer," pp. 333–45.

[33] *Ibid.*, pp. 333–34.

[34] Richard B. Brandt, "The Definition of an 'Ideal Observer' Theory in Ethics," *Philosophy and Phenomenological Research*, 15 (March 1955), 410.

able to assess different alternatives impartially. To say that he must be disinterested is not to say that he need be *un*interested, but simply that he must be impartial. He must also be dispassionate, one who does not let his emotions affect his judgments—a condition clearly essential for an ideal observer. He must also be consistent, "a being whose ethically-significant reactions to any particular act would always be exactly similar." [35] Finally, he must be normal —he cannot "lack any of the determinable properties of human beings." [36]

This examination of the characteristics of the ideal observer leads one naturally to object that there are no such beings, so that even if we accept this definition we shall have no way of knowing what actually is right and wrong. Still, this consequence, if it is a consequence, does not seriously damage the theory, for it does not vitiate the definition—something still is right if, and only if, it *would* be approved of by an ideal observer *if* he existed. Furthermore, it is quite possible to argue that we can, at times, approach the requirements for an ideal observer.

R. B. Brandt lists the advantages in adopting this definition. He suggests that Firth could have argued that

... this theory enables us to regard as really relevant to ethics all the facts which on reflection we take to be relevant; (2) that it enables us to explain the heterogeneousness of the actions which we regard as right or wrong; (3) that it explains how ethical disagreement is possible even when there is agreement about the nature of the act being appraised, (4) that it explains why our feelings and attitudes—and especially our sympathies—are (and properly are) engaged in ethical reflection, and why moral philosophers have thought that moral experience is distinctively a union of cognition and emotion; (5) that it enables us to hold that moral opinions are subject to objective criticism and are correct or incorrect; that (6) it explains why we value the advice of knowledgeable, impartial, and consistent persons at times of moral decision, and why we reject previous moral opinions of our own which we think reflect self-interest, inconsistency, or lack of information; and that (7) it enjoys advantages over the emotive theory such as the capacity to give a satisfactory analysis of "ethical relevance", and the ability to explain why ethical judgments do not always correspond with favorable or unfavorable attitudes on the part of the judge. All this of course needs a good deal of explanation, but perhaps even this brief sketch will be of use to any who wonder why this type of analysis is attractive to some people.[37]

This is an impressive list of advantages, but they are matched by equally weighty disadvantages.

Firth objects to the ideal-observer theories of the sort defended by Sharp on the grounds that they contain a circularity in the specification of condi-

[35] Firth, *op. cit.*, p. 343.

[36] *Ibid.*, p. 344.

[37] Brandt, "The Definition of an 'Ideal Observer' Theory in Ethics," *op. cit.*, pp. 407–08.

tions for the ideal observer and, as we have seen, he introduced the notion of omniscience to avoid this difficulty. The addition, however, does not eliminate circularity for, even if we grant that the ideal observer is omniscient, he must make his judgment *on the basis of* all and only those facts which are relevant. If he does not, there is reason to believe that his judgment will be no better—and perhaps worse—than that of anyone else. Thus, although the ideal observer knows all the nonethical facts, he must also know which are relevant.

This line of argument would seem to indicate that the ideal observer must not only be defined as someone who knows all the relevant nonethical facts (a requirement which *is* taken care of by his omniscience), but also he must be defined as someone who knows that the truly relevant facts are indeed relevant. This latter requirement is not fulfilled by the omniscience claim; it must be added to that quality.

The ideal-observer theorist might avoid this criticism in one of three possible ways: (a) he might claim that the knowledge of which facts are relevant is simply an additional nonethical fact; (b) he might claim that there is no need for the ideal observer to have information about relevance, or to know which facts are relevant; or (c) he might claim that it is possible to include relevance in a noncircular way in the definition of the ideal observer.

(a) It is unlikely that anyone would claim that knowledge of which nonethical facts are relevant is simply another nonethical fact. But, even if such a claim were feasible, it would not be possible for Firth: he believes that no notion of relevance can be included in the definition of an ideal observer, because relevance can be defined only in terms of the reaction of an ideal observer. This alternative is closed to everyone until some nonethical specification of relevance can be given, and it is closed to Firth until some specification of relevance can be provided which does not involve reference to the ideal observer (Cf. c).

(b) Any argument that would justify saying that the ideal observer needs to know any facts at all, would also justify saying that he needs to know which facts are relevant. The requirement of omniscience was inserted to insure that he knows relevant facts, but the fact that relevant facts do not wear "relevance markers" was overlooked. Furthermore, any argument showing that the ideal observer does not need to know which facts are relevant, could be turned into one showing that he does not need to know any facts at all. Thus, if one should argue that the judgments of the ideal observer *constitute* rightness and wrongness, and that—because any judgment he makes is, by definition, right—he does not need any knowledge of relevance, it is possible to argue that he does not need *any* knowledge at all—he can just make an arbitrary decision. The flaw here, of course, is that there is absolutely no reason why we should accept such a definition of 'right'. Finally, if we insist that the ideal observer needs to know *any* facts, we must also insist that he know which ones are relevant, for any observer who does not know what is relevant is no better than one who knows nothing at all.

(c) Now we must deal with the possibility that the requirement of relevance can be specified noncircularly. Although relevance is not an additional nonethical fact, it may be possible to specify in some noncircular way that the ideal observer must know which facts are relevant. It is clear, however, that this line of argument is not open to Firth. We can easily paraphrase his argument which purported to show that the ideal observer cannot be required (without circularity) to know the relevant nonethical facts; showing with our paraphrase, that he cannot be required (without circularity) to know which nonethical facts are relevant. Here is the paraphrase: To say that the ideal observer knows that a particular fact is not relevant to an ethical judgment is to say, assuming that an absolutist dispositional analysis is correct, that he would know that his dispositions to make the particular judgment would be the same whether or not he possessed that particular fact.

It is now possible to present Firth with a fairly serious dilemma: either the condition that the ideal observer knows which facts are relevant must be added to his characteristics of the ideal observer, or it need not. If it must be added, the definition must be rejected as circular; if it is not added, the definition must be rejected on the grounds that an ideal observer who does not know what is, and is not, relevant, is no better than one who knows nothing at all.

Of all the naturalistic objectivist tendency views, the ideal-observer theory, treated as a nonarbitrary stipulation, seems to be the best—its advantages have been outlined by Brandt above. But because it is not possible to specify in a noncircular way the requirements for the ideal observer, the theory suffers from a serious flaw. Therefore, we are inclined to reject it.

(4) *Bentham—The Definition of 'Right'.* According to Jeremy Bentham, the truth of utilitarianism follows from the meaning of the words 'right' and 'wrong' (see Chapter 4). This provides us with an instance of someone who believes that a normative theory follows from meta-ethical considerations, and with an illustration of another sort of objective naturalism. Bentham makes this claim in the following passage:

Of an action that is conformable to the principle of utility, one may always say either that it is one that ought to be done, or at least that it is not one that ought not to be done. One may say also that it is right it should be done; at least that it is not wrong it should be done: that it is a right action; at least that it is not a wrong action. When thus interpreted, the words *ought*, and *right* and *wrong*, and others of that stamp, have a meaning: when otherwise they have none.[38]

[38] Jeremy Bentham, *Introduction to the Principles of Morals and Legislation* (New York: Hafner, 1948), p. 4.

It is worth repeating here also that Bentham's theory of value (as well as his theory of obligation) seems to have a naturalistic definition for a support:

Now, pleasure is in *itself* a good; nay, even setting aside immunity from pain, the only good: pain is in itself an evil; and, indeed, without exception, the only evil; or else the words good and evil have no meaning.[39]

Although there are those who do not think that Bentham should be treated as defining 'good' and 'right', it is difficult to see how else to understand these passages. But if he had merely defined 'right' in accordance with the principle of utility, he would be no more a naturalist than G. E. Moore, who did the same thing. It is not until 'good' is defined in terms of pleasure that the naturalism emerges.

Bentham's suggestion that 'right' and 'wrong' have a meaning when interpreted in the light of the principle of utility, but none otherwise, seems to be some kind of theoretical nonarbitrary stipulative definition. The words are given a meaning by the theory. The same would be the case with 'good' and 'bad'.

At this point, however, there is one rather serious difficulty with Bentham's view, and one serious ambiguity. If the words in question are to be given a meaning on the basis of the theory of utilitarianism, that theory is not true by definition—and no version of utilitarianism escapes serious objections. Similarly, if 'good' is to be defined as 'pleasurable', and if this is a theoretical definition, then hedonism must be acceptable, but there are fairly good reasons for thinking that it is not. Thus, to the degree acceptance of Bentham's definitions depends upon acceptance of hedonistic utilitarianism, there is little to be said in their favor.

But if we are to treat Bentham as a naturalist, we must determine what sort of definition he is giving—a subjective definition, an objective tendency definition, or some other kind. It is very difficult to tell what should be said here because of the ambiguity of the following definition:

X is good $=_{df}$ X is pleasurable

Does this mean that to say that something is good is to say that it causes pleasure, or to say that it is capable of causing pleasure, or to say that it is likely to cause pleasure? These questions have never been answered satisfactorily, but this is because Bentham does not really say enough about these questions to suggest a likely interpretation. Given the fact that Bentham's naturalism is so sketchily presented, there seems to be no justification for treating it as a serious candidate for acceptance.

(5) *Herbert Spencer—The Definition of 'Good'.* At least one example of

---

[39] *Ibid.*, p. 102.

an objectivistic naturalist view that is clearly not a tendency view can be found in the writings of Herbert Spencer (1820–1903), who is usually classified as the foremost proponent of *evolutionary ethics*. He held that 'good' must be defined by taking into account the developments of evolution, and argued that "the conduct to which we apply the name good is the relatively more evolved conduct; and that bad is the name we apply to conduct which is relatively less evolved." [40] If this is offered as a reportive definition, it is hard to accept. Even if we think very carefully about our use of these terms, or take polls as Sharp did, we could never come upon such a meaning. The best suggestion is that this, too, is a theoretical definition supported by the entire theory of evolution. But, although the truth of the theory on which it is based is a necessary condition for the acceptability of a theoretical definition, it does not seem to be sufficient. That is, our acceptance of the theory does not commit us to an acceptance of the definition.

What other reasons might be given for and against the acceptance of this definition? We can point out that moral disagreement is made possible, and some hope for an increase in objectivity is offered. After all, it might be a reasonably easy matter to discover which conduct is, in fact, more evolved. A moment's thought, however, might turn this second "advantage" against the theory, for if we seriously ask how we are to discover which conduct is more evolved, it is difficult to see what answer we will get. If 'more evolved' simply means 'older', or 'having a longer history', or 'having more antecedents', Spencer is in trouble. For it is quite possible that there may be throwbacks in evolution, in which case they would have to be said to be more evolved. Nor must Spencer be allowed to include 'moral superiority' in 'more evolved', for this would make the definition circular. Thus, it seems that, because there are throwbacks in the chain of evolution, it is not possible to say that good conduct is that which is more evolved if we cannot specify some noncircular sense of 'more evolved', and if we cannot find some way to avoid the possibility that actions analogous to evolutionary throwbacks are superior. Finally, Spencer seems to be assuming that evolution, in life and in conduct, has some definite goal—that later conduct is closer to the goal and that the goal is worthwhile. But this theory presupposes a great deal more in the line of normative ethical considerations than a meta-ethical theory (which is supposed to be neutral, in the sense discussed in the last chapter) should.

c. THE CRITICISM OF NATURALIST THEORIES. We do not feel that there is any general argument which applies to all forms of naturalism; rather, each naturalist view has to be discussed separately (or at least as a member of a fairly well specified group), and we must discover exactly what definition is being offered, and what kind of definition. Because of the many naturalist

---

[40] Herbert Spencer, *The Principles of Ethics* (New York and London: Appleton-Century-Crofts, Inc., 1895), p. 15.

theories available it is not surprising that there is no final argument against the view—but it is also not surprising that attempts have been made to construct such arguments. We believe that the best one can do is to examine the most serious and best types of naturalist theory. Then if we find a view which is relevantly similar to an earlier one, we will have criticisms at hand. If we do examine the best naturalist theories that have so far been offered, and we believe that we have done this, then there is little possibility that another theory may, like a "dark horse" spring to the front and win the day.

Exercises

Review
1. What is the difference between subjective and objective naturalistic views?
2. What is the difference between individual and general subjective naturalism? Construct examples of each view.
3. What is the difference between "first-person" and "third-person" forms of individual subjective naturalism? Construct an example of each view.
4. What are some objections which could be raised against "first-person" forms of individual subjective naturalism? Against "third-person" forms of that view?
5. Describe the naturalism of Moritz Schlick.
6. What are the criticisms that can be raised against general subjective naturalism?
7. How does the interest theory of Ralph Barton Perry differ from the other forms of naturalism discussed? How does Perry react to the claim that his view entails relativism?
8. What are Ewing's criticisms of Perry?
9. What is the difference between a tendency and a nontendency objective naturalist view? Who holds a form of the tendency view?
10. Is Westermarck a subjectivist? Why or why not?
11. What is the ideal-observer theory? Who holds it? What advantages are claimed for it and what problems can be raised against it?
12. Discuss the claim that any formulation of the requirements for the ideal observer will be circular.
13. How does Bentham's view differ from subjective naturalist views?
14. What sort of a criticism of naturalistic theories seems required by the discussion above?

Applications
1. Examine several of the naturalistic views described and attempt to evaluate them first as an attempt to provide a reportive definition and then as an attempt to provide some nonreportive definition.
2. What sort of evidence would be relevant in determining whether "X is good" *really means* the same as "I like X"?
3. How might a naturalist argue that discoveries in psychology would help us to determine what is right and wrong? Discuss and evaluate this argument.

4. Evaluate the following argument:

> The only things we can have knowledge about are the objects of science. The objects of science are natural objects. Therefore, if we want to have moral knowledge, it can only be knowledge about the objects of science.

3. General Arguments Against Naturalism. Although we do not believe there are general arguments against naturalism others do.

a. BERTRAND RUSSELL—NATURALISTS DISAGREE. One point sometimes made by opponents of naturalism is that nearly every naturalist has given a different definition of the crucial moral expressions. Bertrand Russell appeals to this fact in his criticism of naturalism:

> Some have contended that "good" means "desired," others that "good" means "pleasure," others again that it means "conformity to Nature" or "obedience to the will of God." The mere fact that so many different and incompatible definitions have been proposed is evidence against any of them being really definitions; there have never been two incompatible definitions of the word "pentagon." [41]

Russell does not maintain that the definitions are all incorrect; rather, he takes the disagreement to show that the naturalists are not giving definitions at all. According to Russell, when a naturalist claims that 'good' means 'pleasurable' he is really making a moral judgment to the effect that all pleasurable things are good.

It is clear, therefore, that Russell does not take the naturalist to be offering a reportive definition, but it is also clear that some naturalists (Sharp, for example) intend to do just that. To the degree, then, that Russell is arguing that naturalists are not giving reports, he is wrong when naturalists do report. He does not, in this work, seem to be aware of the possibility of stipulative definitions, arbitrary or nonarbitrary (at least, he does not distinguish them from moral judgments). This "objection," then, is that naturalists are not doing what they claim to be doing. But it is clear, at least in some cases, that they are trying to do what Russell says they are not doing. Perhaps, then, Russell wants to claim that they cannot do what they are trying to do, but for that conclusion he offers no arguments. Furthermore, the mere fact of disagreement does not really show that a reportive definition is wrong. What is required is an examination of the particular report, and Russell does not undertake such an examination. The same applies to a nonarbitrary stipulation, for there the question is not whether agreement has been reached, but whether the stipulation should be accepted. To determine this, one needs to expose and to criticize the reasons on which it is based, or the theory from which it is derived. The fact that there are competitors does not show that one

[41] Bertrand Russell, "The Elements of Ethics," in Sellars and Hospers, *Readings in Ethical Theory* (New York: Appleton-Century-Crofts, Inc., 1952), p. 6.

of the competitors may not be correct. Thus, the fact that naturalists disagree does not show that they are not really offering definitions, nor that their reportive and stipulative definitions are not correct.

b. THE OPEN-QUESTION ARGUMENT. But there are other, more plausible, general arguments against the naturalist. Perhaps the most popular is the "open-question argument" proposed by G. E. Moore, which purports to be a general argument that eliminates all naturalist (and, furthermore, all definist) theories. Although this argument has been used extensively by Moore and his followers, Moore was not the first philosopher to use it.[42] According to the cognitivist definist, moral judgments can be reduced or expanded by analysis or definition to other expressions which have the same meaning or significance and which contain no moral terms. It is this part of cognitivistic definism (and especially naturalistic cognitivistic definism) to which Moore objects. He does not object to the claim that moral judgments are capable of being objectively true, for Moore was a *cognitivist* nondefinist. The dispute between the naturalist (or, more generally, the definist) and Moore, then, concerns the definability of 'good'.

Moore claimed that any attempt to define 'good' was an instance of the "naturalistic fallacy," and should be avoided. He suggested that the mere fact that all things which are good have a certain "natural property" (N) provides no reason for identifying the two things. This is, of course, quite correct. It may, as a matter of fact, be the case that all good things are also pleasurable, and all pleasurable things are good, but this alone is no reason for identifying *pleasurableness* and *goodness*. This can be seen by imagining a mythical community in which everything which is against the law is pleasurable, and everything which is pleasurable is against the law. This fact does not establish the claim that 'against the law' means 'pleasurable' for, of course, it doesn't.

According to Moore, the assumption that properties belonging to all things which are good are "absolutely and entirely the same with goodness" is the naturalistic fallacy.[43] Later, he says: "If ... [a man] confuses 'good,' which is not in the same sense a natural object, with any natural object whatever, then there is a reason for calling that a naturalistic fallacy." [44] Moore, however, must show that *goodness*, and the property the naturalist asserts to be identical with it, are really two things. Moore begins his book with a quotation from Butler: "Everything is what it is and not another thing," by which he intends to convey the idea that goodness is goodness, and not pleasure or enjoyment. But the naturalist has not made a mistake here unless he has identified a property which is other than goodness with goodness. If

[42] Cf. Prior, *op. cit.*, Chap. ix.

[43] Moore, *Principia Ethica*, p. 10. Unfortunately Moore is not unambiguous about this, for in other places in the same book he characterizes the naturalistic fallacy in different ways.

[44] *Ibid.*, p. 13.

pleasure is, as a matter of fact, the same as goodness, then no fallacy has been committed. It is here that the open-question argument comes into the picture. Suppose a naturalist asserts that 'good' means 'N'. Moore would reply that with the exception of goodness itself, no matter what property 'N' stands for, it always makes sense to ask whether N is good. In the words of Moore, "whatever definition be offered, it may be always asked, with significance, of the complex so defined, whether it is itself good." [45] Because this question makes sense in a way that "Is N N?" does not, the argument continues, goodness cannot be identical with any natural property.

Moore says that it is always possible to raise the question "Is N good?" and that this question is always significant. He would also say that it always is more than a tautology to say that N is good, and this would not be the case if 'N' means 'good'. But what gives Moore the right to say that the question is always significant, and what gives him the right to say that the proposition is more than a tautology?

The naturalist can simply assert that most other naturalistic definitions can be refuted by the open-question argument because most other naturalisms are wrong. But if there is a correct naturalistic (reportive) definition, then the fact that other definitions can be criticized by the open-question argument is no evidence that this one can. A naturalist then might claim that the open-question argument will work against every definition but his own, which gives the correct meaning of 'good'. Moore will, of course, attempt to apply his argument to this definition too, but he must support his claim that it makes sense to ask whether *this* N is good. The naturalist will simply say that, in this case, it does not make sense to ask whether N is good, for the two terms do mean the same.

To defend his claim, the naturalist might suggest (as Sharp does) that, because people are not explicitly and immediately aware of the meaning of the word 'good' they will not notice that it really makes no sense to ask if the favored property is good. Or, alternatively, the naturalist might reply that he knows that 'good' usually does not mean 'N', but that it would be advisable to adopt such a definition. This sort of nonarbitrary stipulative naturalist definition is totally untouched by Moore's argument. The naturalist who makes such a suggestion must, of course, give reasons for his stipulation and defend it—and none of the naturalist views considered has done this adequately. But whether or not this is so, it is clear that the open-question argument does little to undermine naturalism.

c. An Argument From the Function of Moral Language. R. M. Hare presents another argument designed to refute all forms of naturalism. He proposes to restate Moore's argument against the naturalists "in a way which makes it clear why 'naturalism' is untenable, not only for the moral uses of

[45] *Ibid.*, p. 15.

'good' as he thought, but also for many other uses." [46] His objections are directed mainly against those who would say that an expression such as "X is a good A" means the same as "X is an A which has C (some naturalistic characteristic)." His main point is that the naturalist omits the prescriptive element from judgments of obligation and the commendatory element from judgments of value. He argues that "X is good" has a commendatory function which "X is C" does not, and so to define the former in terms of the latter is to render it incapable of commending—which is, in fact, its distinctive function. Let us examine the argument in Hare's own words:

> For example, let C mean 'Having a tendency to arouse in people who are at that time members of the Royal Academy (or any other definitely specified group of people), a definitely recognizable feeling called "admiration"'. The words 'definitely specified' and 'definitely recognizable' have to be inserted, for otherwise we might find that words in the *definiens* were being used evaluatively, and this would make the definition no longer 'naturalistic'.
>
> Now suppose that we wish to say that the members of the Royal Academy have good taste in pictures. To have good taste in pictures means to have this definitely recognizable feeling of admiration for those pictures, and only those pictures, which are good pictures. If therefore we wish to say that the members of the Royal Academy have good taste in pictures, we have, according to the definition, to say something which means the same as saying that they have this feeling of admiration for pictures which have a tendency to arouse in them this feeling.
>
> Now this is not what we wanted to say. We wanted to say that they admired good pictures; we have succeeded only in saying that they admired pictures which they admired. Thus if we accept the definition we debar ourselves from saying something that we do sometimes want to say. What this something is will become apparent later; for the moment let us say that what we wanted to do was to *commend* the pictures which the members of the Royal Academy admired. Something about our definition prevented our doing this. We could no longer commend the pictures which they admired, we could only say that they admired those pictures which they admired. Thus our definition has prevented us, in one crucial case, from commending something which we want to commend. That is what is wrong with it. [47]

Suppose one wants to give a definition of 'good'. According to Hare, the first thing that is necessary (in order for the definition to be a naturalistic one) is that the definiens contain no words used evaluatively, for if it did, he claims, the definition would no longer be naturalistic. This is, in effect, to suppose that

1. No definition that attempts to define a value term in terms of other evaluative expressions is naturalistic.

[46] R. M. Hare, *The Language of Morals* (Oxford: The Clarendon Press, 1952), p. 84. By permission of the Clarendon Press, Oxford.
   [47] *Ibid.*, pp. 84–85.

From Statement 1, it follows that

2. A naturalistic definition of 'good' will contain no evaluative terms in the definiens.

Hare's argument continues: if we give a truly naturalistic definition of 'good' we claim that 'good' is identical in meaning with some naturalistic expression 'C', but then we cannot commend an object by calling it *good*, for we only succed in saying that it has C. This abridged version of Hare's argument may help to emphasize some of its assumptions. Let us, therefore, attempt to formulate the argument again, still remaining reasonably close to Hare's formulation of it.

3. If any two expressions are to be equated by definition, we must be able to do the same things with both of them (i.e., we must be able to use them for the same purposes).

From Statement 3 we can derive

3'. If a value term (E) and a naturalistic term (C) are to be equated by definition, we must be able to do the same things with both of them (i.e., we must be able to use them for the same purposes).

Hare makes two other assumptions:

4. 'Good' (E) is always used to commend (or, when we say that something is good, we wish to commend it).
5. No naturalistic term (C) can ever be used to commend.

Again, let us rewrite these assumptions:

4'. The use of 'good' is always commendatory.
5'. The use of 'C' is never commendatory.

Now from Statements 4' and 5' it seems possible to deduce

6. No use of 'good' is ever the same as any use of 'C'.

This might be expressed in more convenient English: "No naturalistic term can ever have the same use as a value term." There is another way of saying the same thing which allows us to relate it to Statement 3':

6'. We are never able to do the same thing with a naturalistic term ('C') and a value term ('E').

Now from Statements 3′ and 6′ we are able to get

7. We cannot equate a value term ('E') and a naturalistic term ('C').

This, finally, is to say that no naturalistic definition of a value term is possible. Now Statement 6 follows from Statements 4 and 5 (via their reformulation as Statements 4′ and 5′) and Statement 7 follows from Statement 6 and Statement 3 (via their reformulations as Statement 3′ and Statement 6′). The premises that can profitably be questioned, then, are Statements 1, 3, 4, and 5.

Few naturalists would be inclined to accept Statement 1, for a naturalist can admit that 'good' is an evaluative term, and suggest that the fact that it is identical in meaning with a term such as 'pleasant' shows only that some value terms are also naturalistic terms. Thus, the naturalist would argue in the following way:

good $=$ $_{df}$ pleasant
'Pleasant' is a naturalistic term—i.e., discoverable by observation and experiment. Therefore, 'good' is a naturalistic term.

The conclusion of Hare's argument is a denial of the first premise of the previous argument—which, he feels, is generalizable to any naturalistic definition. But the conclusion of the naturalist's argument is a denial of Statement 1, and it is hard to see how Hare can escape the charge of begging the question here.

According to Statement 3, no two premises can be equated by definition unless they can be used to do the same thing, or to perform the same tasks. This assumption has been questioned frequently on the grounds that, if it were granted, it would follow that no term could ever be defined. If 'brother' for example, were defined as 'male sibling', there are things which we can do with the latter term but not the former. Just one of them is to explain what 'brother' means. For this reason, Statement 3 does not seem to have much initial plausibility, for—if taken literally—it rules out all definitions.[48]

Hare might reply that, when we say two expressions are able to "do the same thing," we do not mean that they can be used to perform exactly the same tasks but, rather, the same *kinds* of tasks. Thus, one kind of task an expression can be used to perform is description and another is commendation. Now we would have to reformulate Statement 3 to read:

3″. If any two expressions are to be equated by definition, then we must be able to do the same kind of job with both of them (i.e. we must be able to use both of them for the same kinds of tasks).

[48] In a recent article Hare's attempts to reply to this point have been examined and seriously criticized. Cf. Robert L. Holmes, "The Case against Ethical Naturalism," *Mind*, 73 (1964), 291–95.

It is not clear whether this addition will really be of any use to the critic of naturalism attempting to use Hare's argument, for (among other things) it depends upon the ability to specify clearly what *a kind of use* (or *task*) is. So far this has not been done satisfactorily.

We shall examine, and offer reasons for rejecting, Statement 4 (in Chapter 13), but here let us examine Statement 5: "No naturalistic term can ever be used to commend." If we pause, and ask what a naturalistic term is, it would seem that the following answer would be in order: A naturalistic term is one which refers to some actual or possible object in the world whose presence or absence can be discovered by the senses, or which mentions some naturalistic property. For example, 'red', 'horse', 'unicorn', and 'man' would all be naturalistic terms. If so, Statement 5 immediately becomes false, for Hare himself points out that "almost every word in our language is capable of being used on occasion as a value word (that is, for commending purposes)...."[49]

One who would use Hare's argument in criticizing the naturalist must make an adjustment somewhere. Most terms in our language can be used to commend, so perhaps we will have to reformulate Statement 5 to read:

5″. No naturalistic term is used typically or primarily to commend.

This will, of course, require a revision of Statement 4:

4″. The typical or primary use of 'good' is to commend.

Unfortunately, this will require a slight modification of Statement 3:

3″. If any two expressions are to be equated by definition, then their typical or primary use must be the same.

Let us restate the argument now, using fresh symbols for the different propositions:

A. If any two expressions are to be equated by definition, then their typical or primary use must be the same.
B. The typical or primary use of 'good' is to commend.
C. No naturalistic term is used typically or primarily to commend.
D. No naturalistic term is used typically or primarily in the way 'good' is.
E. Therefore, no naturalistic term is to be equated by definition with 'good'.

Now Statement D seems to follow from Statements B and C, and Statement E follows from Statements D and A, so the expressions to question are A, B, and C. Statement B (and its analogue 4) will be examined in Chapter 13, but a few words may be said about Statements A and C here.

[49] Hare, *op. cit.*, p. 79.

Analogous moves will have to be made in Statement A to remove the difficulties in the earlier Statement 3, for similar problems—specifications of a *kind* of use—will arise again. Until this problem is solved, the argument does not rest upon a firm foundation. Even if this were not a problem, there would be the new problem of specifying what is meant by a "typical" or "primary" use (see Chapter 13).

The naturalist, replying to this argument, would probably be inclined to deny Statement A, and one way to do this is to suggest that the meaning of an expression has nothing to do with its typical use, and that therefore even if Statements B and C were true, nothing would be established about the possibility of giving a naturalistic definition of 'good'.

Could the naturalist deny Statement C? Hare believes he could not, claiming that if the typical or primary use of a word is commendatory, the word becomes an evaluative word. In the end, therefore, Hare seems to be making Statement C true by definition. He is not saying that naturalistic terms are not used to commend; rather, he is saying that, as soon as a word is used to commend, it is not a naturalistic term at all.

A naturalist who replied to Statement 1 in the way we have suggested could simply claim that Statement C is false because 'good' means 'pleasant', 'pleasant' is a naturalistic term, and so because 'good' is used typically or primarily to commend, a naturalistic term (i.e., 'pleasant') is also used typically or primarily to commend. In order to deny this, Hare would have to offer some further argument to show that 'pleasant' is not, or cannot be, both a naturalistic term and primarily used to commend. Hare attempts to support this point by defining a naturalistic term as one which is not used to commend—but, unless some reasons are given for accepting this definition, there is no reason for the naturalist to be moved.[50] It is not clear whether Hare is actually proposing this argument, but it sems to be the strongest one of that sort available. It poses, however, serious difficulties. First, it is quite likely that Statement B is false, or at least misstated. At best, much would have to be done to establish it, and it has been frequently criticized by philosophers. Statement A, on the other hand, presupposes an entire theory of meaning—the use theory of meaning—and although many philosophers have come to accept this theory recently, many have not been satisfied by either the arguments for, or explanations of, that theory. A could not be shown to be correct until much more has been said about the use theory of meaning, and until that theory has been compared with its rivals. Furthermore, crucial notions are left unexplained, and those that are explained might well involve further difficulties. Two of these are 'kind of use or function' and 'primary or typical use'.

[50] There is another alternative open to the naturalist. He can say that C is, in fact, true, and that, although this shows that there are no "naturalists" it is still true that 'good' = $_{df}$ 'pleasant'.

The critic of naturalism who uses this argument would undoubtedly argue not only that reportive definitions which equate 'good' with some naturalistic term are wrong, but also that a nonarbitrary stipulation to the effect that 'good' shall mean 'pleasant' is unacceptable because it equates two terms which have different *kinds* of use, or which do different *kinds* of things. At this point, it becomes even more important for the critic of naturalism who reformulates Statement 3 by talking about an expression being used to do a *kind* of thing (cf. Statement 3″) to make it quite clear what he means by this. This is also intimately related to explaining the notion of a typical or primary use.

It would seem, therefore, that much explaining would have to be done (some of it has been attempted, but not enough) before this argument can be used with any confidence by the critic of naturalism. But worse, given the falsity of Statement B (see Chapter 13), and the difficulties with Statements A and C, all the explaining in the world would not make this *the* conclusive argument against naturalistic theories.

d. ANOTHER CONTEMPORARY CRITICISM. Carl Wellman presents another criticism of naturalism which makes use of some of the techniques of contemporary analytic philosophy. Wellman argues:

> We do not teach the meaning of ethical words in at all the same way that we teach the meaning of those words which stand for empirical characteristics. This difference in the ways in which the words are taught would seem to imply that the two groups of words have different kinds of meaning.[51]

We learn the meaning of words referring to "empirical characteristics" by pointing to and calling out their names, or by defining them in terms of expressions which have been taught in the former way. We do not, Wellman argues, teach ethical words in either of these two ways:

> The word "wrong" brings this out most clearly. When the child does something which we think that he ought not to do, we tell him that it is wrong. (Notice that the occasion for teaching the word is not when the child is attending to something, as is the case in ostensive definition.[52] but when he is doing something.) We tell the child that it is wrong to pull the cat's tail. We may explain that it hurts the cat. We probably frown and scold the child. Often we forceably keep the child from continuing the action. We may even punish him.[53]

The argument here is this:

[51] Carl Wellman, *The Language of Ethics* (Cambridge, Mass.: Harvard University Press, 1961), p. 37.
[52] Ostensive definition is the practice of getting someone to know what an object is by pointing to it while calling out its name.
[53] Wellman, *op. cit.*, p. 39.

1. Ethical words are taught differently from empirical words.
2. If a class of words (W_1) is taught differently from another class of words (W_2), they have different kinds of meaning.
3. If the words in a class of words (W_1) and the words in another class of words (W_2) have different kinds of meaning, then no W_1 word is synonymous with any W_2 word.
4. No ethical word is synonymous with any empirical word.
5. Naturalism is false.

Why does Wellman believe Statement 1 is true? He believes empirical words are taught by ostention or definition and ethical words are not, and even suggests that this is a Wittgensteinian approach. But Wittgenstein was one of the first to argue that not all empirical terms can be learned by ostension and by definitions using terms ostensively learned.[54] Furthermore, the notion of a "way" of learning a word is very unclear. Is 'fast' really learned in the same way as 'red' or 'snow'? It does not seem that it is, but does this mean that they have different kinds of meaning?

Even if two words have to be learned in different ways, it does not follow that they have different kinds of meaning unless Statement 2 is true, for which there seems to be little evidence. Given all this, it does not seem that one is justified in going along with Wellman's conclusion: "The obvious implication is that ethical words do not stand for empirical characteristics and that their ethical naturalism must be rejected." [55] But there are two further replies open to the naturalist: ethical words do sometimes mean the same as empirical words (the thesis of naturalism) and, therefore, they can be taught in exactly the same way—to deny this is simply to beg the question; also, the naturalistic definitions are not all reportive so that, even if ethical words are not taught in the same way as empirical words, they should be.

[54] Wittgenstein, *Philosophical Investigations* (New York: The Macmillan Company, 1953). Wittgenstein says in paragraph 43 of that book that "the *meaning* of a name is sometimes explained by pointing to its *bearer*." But this would seem to imply that sometimes it is not explained in that way, even when there are things which bear the name. He admits the possibility of various interpretations of an ostensive definition (paragraph 28) and suggests that sometimes people do make this mistake. To think that one could always be successful in guessing right which element of experience is being singled out by pointing, is to suppose that he is already master of a language. "The ostensive definition explains the use—the meaning—of the word when the over-all role of the word in language is clear." (paragraph 30) "We may say: only someone who already knows how to do something with it can significantly ask a name." (paragraph 31) To imagine that ostensive definition is sufficient for the learning of all words, even all empirical words, is to imagine that one already has a language before he begins to learn the one he is being taught. (paragraph 32) Cf. also what Wittgenstein says about the word 'game', an empirical word, and how we learn the meaning of a word ('good' for instance). Both have a family of meanings and neither can be taught by simple ostention. (paragraph 77)

[55] Wellman, *op. cit.*, p. 45.

Summary. If these four general arguments against the naturalists applied at all, it would be an easy matter to turn them against all definists; but naturalists could probably reply satisfactorily to each of these arguments, and the arguments are, at best, inconclusive. What must be done, and what we have tried to do, is to take each sort of naturalistic position (and more generally each cognitivist definist position) separately. This does not mean that we have examined all the cognitivist definist positions that exist, but we have criticized—and found wanting—the most important and most representative ones.

Exercises

Review

1. Bertrand Russell maintains that there have never been two incompatible definitions of the word 'pentagon', and uses this fact as an argument against naturalistic positions. Present and evaluate his argument.
2. If Russell is not attempting to show that all naturalists are incorrect, what is he trying to show? Evaluate his claim.
3. What is the relation between the naturalistic fallacy and the open-question argument?
4. What, according to Hare, do naturalistic definitions fail to account for? What meta-ethical theory is presupposed by this criticism?
5. Restate, as clearly as possible, Hare's criticism of naturalism and the naturalist's possible reply.
6. Why is the notion of a typical or primary use required by Hare's argument?
7. Why was it claimed that Statement A (see p. 263) presupposes a whole theory of meaning?
8. What is Wellman's criticism of the naturalist?

Applications

1. Moore argues that the fact that all X's are Y's and all Y's are X's does not show that 'X' and 'Y' mean the same thing. We gave an illustration of this claim, but provide other instances of the "coextensiveness" of two concepts which have different meanings.
2. An important discussion of the naturalistic fallacy is William K. Frankena's "The Naturalistic Fallacy," reprinted in Sellars and Hospers, *Readings in Ethical Theory*. Read this article and discuss the several possible things a man might be doing who is committing the naturalistic fallacy.
3. How might someone go about showing that pleasure and goodness are not two things, but one?
4. Why is Perry's view, for example, not touched by the open-question argument?

Bibliography

BENTHAM, JEREMY. *An Introduction to the Principles of Morals and Legislation.* New York: Hafner, 1948. A naturalistic defense of hedonistic utilitarianism.

BRANDT, RICHARD. *Ethical Theory*. Englewood Cliffs, N.J.: Prentice-Hall, 1959, Chapter 7. A criticism of ethical naturalism.

*———. "The Status of Empirical Assertion Theories in Ethics," *Mind*, 61 (1952), 458–79.

*BROAD, C. D. "Some Reflections on Moral-sense Theories in Ethics," *Proceedings of the Aristotelian Society*, 45 (1944–45), 131–66. One of the few places where Broad defends a form of naturalism.

*CAMPBELL, C. A. "Moral and Non-moral Values: A Study in the First Principles of Axiology," *Mind*, 44 (1935), 273–99. A defense of a form of subjective naturalism, and a criticism of objective views.

*EDWARDS, PAUL. *The Logic of Moral Discourse*. Glencoe, Ill.: Free Press, 1955, Chapter 2. Presentation and discussion of arguments for and against subjectivistic naturalism.

EWING, A. C. *The Definition of Good*. New York: The Macmillan Co., 1947, Chapters 1 and 2. Discussion of subjective and objective forms of definist theories.

———. *Ethics*. New York: The Free Press, 1953. Chapter 6 contains a criticism of cognitivist definist theories.

*FIELD, G. C. "The Place of Definition in Ethics," *Proceedings of the Aristotelian Society*, 32 (1931–32), 79–94.

FIRTH, RODERICK. "Ethical Absolutism and the Ideal Observer," *Philosophy and Phenomenological Research*, 12 (1952), 317–45. A form of objective naturalism.

FRANKENA, WILLIAM K. "The Naturalistic Fallacy," *Mind*, 48 (1939), 464–77. The classic discussion of Moore's argument against naturalism.

HARE, R. M. *The Language of Morals*. Oxford: The Clarendon Press, 1952, Chapter 5. A noncognitivist criticism of naturalism.

*HARRISON, JONATHAN. "Empiricism in Ethics," *The Philosophical Quarterly*, 2 (1952), 289–306. Replies to criticisms of certain cognitivist views; discusses the naturalistic fallacy.

*HOLMES, ROBERT L. "The Case Against Ethical Naturalism," *Mind*, 73 (1964), 291–95. A criticism of Hare's argument.

MOORE, G. E. *Principia Ethica*. Cambridge: Cambridge University Press, 1959. The best known attack on cognitivistic definism.

*NOWELL-SMITH, P. H. *Ethics*. Baltimore, Md.: Penguin Books, 1954, Chapter 2. Some objections to naturalism.

*PERRY, R. B. *Realms of Value*. Cambridge, Mass.: Harvard University Press, 1954. A defense of naturalism.

PRIOR, A. N. *Logic and the Basis of Ethics*. Oxford: The Clarendon Press, 1949. An attempt to clarify the dispute between naturalists and "anti-naturalists." A historical examination of the "naturalistic fallacy."

SELLARS, WILFRID, and JOHN HOSPERS (eds.). *Readings in Ethical Theory*. New York: Appleton-Century-Crofts, Inc., 1952, Sections 2 and 4. Contains articles critical of definism and articles defending that position. The most useful anthology of contemporary works on meta-ethics.

*SHARP, F. C. *Good Will and Ill Will*. Chicago: University of Chicago Press, 1950, pp. 156–62.

*————. "Voluntarism and Objectivity in Ethics," *The Philosophical Review*, **50** (1941), 253–67. Presents a form of the ideal-observer theory.

*SPENCER, HERBERT. *The Principles of Ethics*. New York and London: D. Appleton and Co., 1895. Defends a naturalist position.

*STEVENSON, C. L. "Moore's Arguments against Certain Forms of Ethical Naturalism," in *The Philosophy of G. E. Moore*, (ed.) P. Schilpp. Evanston, Ill.: Northwestern University Press, 1942.

*TOULMIN, S. *An Examination of the Place of Reason in Ethics*. Cambridge: Cambridge University Press, 1950. Chapters 2 and 3 contain a criticism of some forms of definism.

*WELLMAN, CARL. *The Language of Ethics*. Cambridge, Mass.: Harvard University Press, 1961. A criticism of naturalism drawing upon the work of Wittgenstein.

*WESTERMARCK, E. *Ethical Relativity*. New York: Harcourt, Brace & World, 1932. Presents and defends a form of subjectivism.

*ZIFF, PAUL. *Semantic Analysis*. Ithaca, N.Y.: Cornell University Press, 1960, especially Chapter 6. Ziff argues that 'good' means 'answering to certain interests'.

Cognitivist
Nondefinist Theories

The procedure in this chapter will be first to explain the tenets of cognitivist nondefinist theories. Next we shall distinguish the various cognitivist nondefinist positions from one another. Then, we shall explain how the tenets of cognitivist nondefinism are defended. Finally, we shall eliminate all the cognitivist nondefinist theories but one, to which we shall apply the criteria of acceptability of theories.

Cognitivist nondefinist positions have traditionally been called *intuitionist*. However, the latter name, although appropriate for some older theories, is today quite misleading. We shall be primarily concerned with the meta-ethical problems of moral obligation, rather than moral value. Most cognitivist nondefinists have presented similar analyses of value and obligation, so it seems safe to say that in most cases the meta-ethical treatment of the theory of value is like that of the theory of obligation. Also, many aspects of the theory of value of Ross and Moore were covered (see Chapters 6 and 7). Because both are cognitivist nondefinists, the reader is aware of the kind of value theory cognitivist nondefinists hold, and can be aware of the meta-ethical answers that would be given to meta-ethical problems of value.

A. Tenets of Cognitivist Nondefinist Theories

1. *Objective Moral Knowledge.* We have already presented (see Chapter 10) two propositions, the affirmation or denial of which determines the meta-ethical position one holds. The first proposition is really a pair:

1. Moral judgments are capable of being objectively true.
1a. There is objective moral knowledge.

Let us review the explanations of these notions. It is a well-known philosophical principle that, if one *knows* a proposition, that proposition is true. Similarly, if one has objective knowledge that p, then p is objectively true. If one has objective knowledge that the earth is roughly a sphere, then it is objectively true that the earth is roughly a sphere. In the same way, if one objectively knows that it is morally right to relieve suffering whenever possible, then the proposition or judgment "It is morally right to relieve suffering," is objectively true.

The noncognitivist denies Propositions 1 and 1a, so if one could establish either, all noncognitivist theories would be shown to be mistaken. To put it another way, the dispute between the cognitivist and the noncognitivist is really over Propositions 1 and 1a.[1]

It is easy to misunderstand this and to suppose that it is one's knowledge of p that makes p true. This is not so; rather, the truth of p is a necessary condition of one's knowledge. One cannot be said to know p unless p is true, but what makes p true is, roughly, whether it says of things that are that they are, or of things that are not that they are not. "The earth is a sphere" is true because the earth is a sphere, not because someone knows that the earth is a sphere.[2]

When the cognitivist nondefinist claims that there is objective moral knowledge, he thereby denies that when we make correct or justified moral judgments we are merely expressing an attitude or evincing an emotion, or saying we have a particular attitude or emotion. In the former case, moral judgments would not be capable of being true or false: in the latter, they would be capable of being true or false, but not objectively true or false.

If S says, "I have a favorable attitude toward X," the truth of this proposition is not dependent upon any property of X.[3] The only thing that is relevant in determining the truth of this proposition is whether S has the attitude he claims. If he has, the proposition is true. The fact, if it be one, that makes the proposition true is something internal to S. The proposition can

---

[1] The cognitivist nondefinist would be aided here to some degree by some cognitive definists. These cognitive definists who hold objectivist positions would agree that judgments such as "A is right" or "X is good" are objectively true and false, but (because they are definists) they would deny that this knowledge is characteristically moral. It is, rather, just another kind of factual knowledge. On this issue the cognitivist nondefinist and the noncognitivist join in taking issue with the naturalists and other cognitive definists.

[2] Any theory of truth can be used to explain the same point, or so it would seem. No particular theory of truth is being presupposed. One could equally well say something neutral such as "The earth is a sphere" is true if and only if the earth is a sphere. One could adopt a particular theory of truth and say that the above proposition is true if it coheres with other propositions of a certain sort; or allows one to succeed in reaching goals; or reflects objective reality. It seems clear that the theory of truth most natural to the cognitivist nondefinist is the correspondence theory, but such philosophers do not seem to be committed to that theory.

[3] Cf. the discussion of objective and subjective definist views in Chapter 11.

be known, but what is known is a subjective fact about S. If moral judgments are about attitudes or emotions (as Perry, for example, believes), although there is objective moral knowledge, it is of what is subjective only. The cognitivist nondefinist does not wish to claim that moral knowledge is subjective.

A different kind of knowledge is represented by the proposition "The earth is a sphere," the truth of which does not depend upon some fact about the internal life of the person making the judgment. Another kind of proposition the truth of which is independent of the beliefs or attitudes of the person making it is a relational proposition: e.g., the truth of "S is camping north of Sudbury, Ontario," depends, in part, on S, but not upon his beliefs or mental state. The truth of the proposition and the corresponding judgment depend upon S, but the fact it describes is not concerned with S's subjective life.

Moral judgments invariably concern human beings, and most cognitivists hold that a necessary condition for the truth of moral propositions is the existence of human beings (in a certain state). It can be admitted by most cognitivist nondefinists that moral judgments are relational. When one judges that S's doing A is right, part of the justification of that judgment concerns S, part concerns A, and part concerns the relation between the two. This fact does not throw doubt on the objective nature of moral judgments, but one must be aware of the kind of proposition by means of which moral judgments are expressed.[4]

2. **Denial of Definism.** The second proposition used to distinguish the various meta-ethical positions is the following:

2. Any moral judgment (judgment in which 'good' or 'bad', 'right' or 'wrong' is used in a moral sense) can be reduced or expanded by analysis or definition to another expression which has the same meaning or significance and contains no moral terms.

The denial of Proposition 2 entails the rejection of all definist positions. A simpler, but also less accurate way of putting the denial of Proposition 2 is to say that correct or justified moral judgments are not reducible to any kind of nonmoral judgments or expressions. If so, then the moral knowledge we are said to have (Proposition 1a) is not reducible to any kind of nonmoral knowledge.

Philosophers who claim that ethics is autonomous often deny Proposition 2. To suppose that ethics is autonomous is to suppose that there is no other discipline, such as psychology or sociology, of which ethics is a division. If (sociological) ethical relativism, for example, is correct, then one can argue that ethics is really a branch of sociology. In that case, the methods of sociology would be appropriate, and all courses in ethics should be taught

---

[4] It may be that this account of the objective nature of moral judgments is peculiar to this work, but since this is the view of this kind that is thought to be best we shall present it.

by sociologists. The denial of Proposition 2 is, in part, the denial of any such reduction of ethics and is, therefore, one way of asserting its independence or autonomy.

3. *Moral Knowledge is Sometimes Direct.* The third proposition held by all cognitivist nondefinists is the following:

3. Moral knowledge is sometimes direct.

This proposition is best explained by showing how it is a consequence of Propositions 1a and not-2. If we have (objective) moral knowledge (Proposition 1a) and this knowledge cannot be derived from any other kind of knowledge, because it is not reducible to any other kind of knowledge (not-2), it seems to follow that we must obtain this kind of knowledge directly. To explain this notion of directness, an analogy is often drawn between moral knowledge and color knowledge. Let us suppose that color knowledge (or the knowledge that objects have certain colors) is not reducible to the knowledge of properties such as size, shape, weight, molecular structure, and so on.[5] If someone knows that a ball is red, he has somehow perceived that property because no other characteristic of the object conveys this knowledge. This is direct knowledge. Someone can tell us, of course, that an object is red, or we may know that all objects of this kind are red, but that kind of knowledge is obviously derived from instances of direct knowledge.

Another way of understanding this same example is in terms of the notion of inference. One can often infer that a situation or thing has a certain property. For example, when the sound of footsteps is heard in the hall, one can infer that a person is approaching. When one sees the front of a building, one can infer that there is a rear to it. Whatever the principles of inference, we are all familiar with this kind of knowledge.

There is yet another kind of knowledge, though. Suppose, for example, that a blind man is placed in a well-lighted room and asked the color of various objects placed in his hand. This blind man, if he consistently replies correctly, is making use of some nonvisual information. For example, he might have a tiny radio receiver in his ear through which someone else transmits the answer. The blind man can be said to infer from the voice saying, "The ball in your hand is red," that the ball is red. Or the blind man might have a machine which measures light waves and, when he "reads" the braille dial, he finds it points to 'red' and infers that the object is red. The question

---

[5] The cause and explanation of our perceiving an object as being red is that the object reflects light waves of a certain length and absorbs others. We can know that, if an object reflects such-and-such wave lengths, it is red, but we know this because we have observed the color and also observed that the object reflected these light waves. Our ability to know that an object is red when it reflects such-and-such light waves is dependent, in part, on being able to recognize red things independently of our knowledge of the wave lengths of light it reflects.

now is whether the blind man can know other than by inference that the ball is red. The answer seems to be that he cannot.

In contrast with the blind man's inability, we can imagine a sighted person knowing that the ball is red. The sighted person can, of course, carry a radio receiver in his ear or a light wave measuring machine, but he need not do so. The sighted person can know the color of the ball by perceiving the color itself. The blind man must infer the color from someone else's knowledge or from its causal effects, but the sighted man can know the color of the ball without making any inference.[6]

One last example will help to clear up a point of possible misunderstanding. Suppose that the man who is transmitting the message to the blind man is himself blind. This is possible as long as we provide some means for the second blind man to know that the ball is red. The second blind man may have a receiver in his ear, through which he receives a message from a third man. We can even suppose that this third man is blind, but it is clear that sooner or later we must reach some man who is not blind and who does not rely upon the information of others—a man who can know the ball is red without inferring that it is.

The notion of noninferential, or direct, knowledge has caused a great deal of misunderstanding. Some philosophers, for example, have (mistakenly, we believe) supposed that, because color perception is used to explain direct perception, the object of moral knowledge must be very much like that of color knowledge. Analogies are useful for understanding, but they should not be mistaken for an exact description.

Cognitivistic nondefinism has traditionally been called *intuitionism* partly in order to emphasize the directness of moral knowledge. However, the term 'intuition' is somewhat misleading because it has unfortunate associations with such terms as 'mysticism', 'mystery', 'emotionalism', 'feminine intuition', and so on. Because of this and because the classification system we use is more descriptive of the various meta-ethical positions, we shall not use it.

In the statement of Proposition 3 the term 'sometimes' was included. Once again we can draw an analogy to our knowledge of colors. Even though one usually has direct knowledge of colors, on many occasions one has indirect or inferential knowledge. If a United States Army band is marching through a dusty field playing *Stars and Stripes Forever*, we can infer that the flag (which we can barely see) is red, white, and blue. Here again, however the colors must be directly perceived by some people at some time.

For those who are rule theorists, there are some principles whose truth or

---

[6] One may want to make finer distinctions among the kinds of inferences that can be made. When one is told that something is red, this is far removed from feeling a trace of clay on it which has a characteristic feeling (and is known, by other means, to be red). However, one can easily see the similarities of the two cases and contrast them with seeing the color, as it were, right off.

correctness must be directly perceived. For Ross, one such prima facie principle enjoins us not to injure others, and one can no doubt derive many other principles from the six principles that Ross lists or from any other set of principles (see p. 105).[7] From the principle that one has a prima facie duty not to injure others, we can infer the principle that one has a prima facie duty not to injure his next-door neighbor. This latter principle is known inferentially, but the former one, according to Ross, is known noninferentially, or directly. Philosophers such as Ross argue that one cannot continue to derive the principles we use in our moral reasoning from more basic principles; there must be a principle (or set of principles) from which all other principles are derived and which must be known directly.

Some ethical theorists—e.g., act deontologists—believe that principles do not play the part in moral reasoning that rule theorists suppose. It is not by virtue of principles, the act deontologist claims, that moral judgments are justified, but by virtue of the characteristics of the act or thing. Principles play a secondary role in the justification of moral judgments; they are rules of thumb or summary rules which are useful on some occasions but which can be dispensed with (although only with great practical difficulty).

The act theorist who is a cognitivist nondefinist does not maintain that we directly perceive certain principles but, rather, that the rightness, wrongness, or obligatoriness of certain specific actions, or the goodness or badness of certain objects, is known directly. Such theorists claim that we can infer general principles which work more often than not, but that these principles are not directly perceived. Furthermore, one can apply these derived principles to a specific act to justify one's judgment concerning that act. For example, one may use the principle, "Help others when they are in need," to support the judgment, "It is morally right to contribute to CARE." The principle is not that by virtue of which the judgments are justified because it is derived, as an induction, from past particular judgments.[8]

Because Proposition 3 is a consequence of Propositions 1a and not-2, one may wonder why it is discussed separately and at length. First, the introduction and explanation of the notion of direct knowledge helps immensely in the explanation of the positions we are now considering. By drawing out the consequences of the claim that there is objective moral knowledge which is not reducible to other kinds of knowledge, we can better understand these positions. Second, different explanations of the notion of direct knowledge are given by different cognitivist nondefinists, and this helps to distinguish the various versions of the general position.

Interim Summary. All cognitivist nondefinists hold Propositions 1a, not-2, and 3:

[7] W. D. Ross, *The Right and the Good* (Oxford: The Clarendon Press, 1930), p. 21.
[8] The act deontologist claims, among other things, that effective counterexamples can be raised against any such principle.

1a. There is objective moral knowledge.
2. Any moral judgment (a judgment in which 'good' or 'bad', 'right' or 'wrong' is used in a moral sense) can be reduced or expanded by analysis or definition to another expression which has the same meaning or significance and contains no moral terms.
3. Moral knowledge is sometimes direct. Proposition 1a can be taken as the thesis of cognitivism and not-2 as the thesis of nondefinism. Proposition 3 is a consequence of Propositions 1 and not-2. Direct knowledge is best understood as being a kind of noninferential knowledge. Another kind of noninferential knowledge is color knowledge. What is known directly can be either a principle (or set of principles) or the rightness (or wrongness, or obligatoriness, and so on) of a specific act, or the presence or absence of a property.

Exercises

Review
1. What is the most succinct way of describing the disagreement between the two kinds of cognitivists?
2. What accounts for the fact that, if someone knows a proposition, we can be sure that it is true?
3. Why is it necessary to add 'objective' in Proposition 1a?
4. Show how the third tenet of cognitivistic nondefinism follows from the first two.
5. Describe the various ways of explaining the notion of direct knowledge.
6. Why is it misleading to use the term 'intuitionist'?

Applications
1. Contrast the disagreement among the three main kinds of meta-ethical theories.
2. Mention an instance of nonmoral direct knowledge, and try to say what, according to the cognitivist nondefinist, are the similarities and differences between it and moral knowledge.

B. Differences Among Cognitivist Nondefinists

There are many different cognitivist nondefinist positions to be distinguished. There are two ways to distinguish these views: by the object of moral knowledge and by the mode of moral knowledge.

1. *Object of Moral Knowledge.* Some cognitivist nondefinists believe that we sometimes directly perceive the correctness of principles, some that we perceive moral properties, and some believe that we perceive the rightness of specific acts.

a. PRINCIPLES. Ross believes that what we directly know is a set of prima facie principles. Other philosophers have supposed that other principles were directly known. On one interpretation, Kant holds that the categorical imperative is directly perceived. More clearly, Sidgwick believes that the principle of utility is directly perceived. In the passage quoted below Sidgwick uses the older terms, 'intuition' and 'intuitionist'; but the reader should remember our discussion of that notion and how we preferred to use the equivalent but less misleading expressions 'direct perception', and 'cognitivist nondefinist'.

> And I had myself become, as I had to admit to myself, an Intuitionist to a certain extent. For the supreme rule of aiming at the general happiness, as I had come to see, must rest on a fundamental moral intuition, if I was to recognise it as binding at all. And in reading the writings of the earlier English Intuitionists, More and Clarke, I found the axiom I required for my Utilitarianism [That a rational agent is bound to aim at Universal Happiness], in one form or another, holding a prominent place.
> I was then a Utilitarian again, but on an Intuitional basis.
> But I could find no real opposition between Intuitionism and Utilitarianism. . . . The Utilitarianism of Mill and Bentham seemed to me to want a basis: that basis could only be supplied by a fundamental intuition; on the other hand the best examination I could make of the Morality of Common Sense showed me no clear and self-evident principles except such as were perfectly consistent with Utilitarianism.[9]

Sidgwick was a utilitarian, but he believed that the principle of utility was known directly. It is interesting to note that one of the main reasons that Sidgwick believed that an "intuition" was required was that otherwise the principle of utility had no basis. Sidgwick held that the principle was, in some way, objectively correct and so he wanted to be able to claim that he *knew* it. Apparently, Sidgwick believed in the autonomy of ethics, and so he believed that we have direct knowledge of the principle of utility.

b. Propositions Which Concern Acts. Some philosophers believe that the object of our moral knowledge is the rightness of a particular act or the goodness of a particular thing. They hold that, when we know a proposition of the form "A is right," we do not know this by virtue of knowing the truth of, say, some principle of the form "All A's are right." When such philosophers say that one knows "A is right," they do not thereby commit themselves to the existence of some kind of metaphysical property called *rightness*. When one says that a proposition is true, one is predicating truth of it, but one is not thereby committed to saying that the proposition has some strange property called *truth*. Similarly, it would seem that, when one says that some actions are right, one is not committed to a peculiar kind of nonnatural property called *rightness*. One may go on to say that there is such a property, but that would be another thing. All cognitivist nondefinists can say that there is

---

[9] Henry Sidgwick, *Methods of Ethics*, 7th ed. (London: Macmillan & Co., Ltd., 1962), pp. xix, xx, xxi.

such a property as rightness as long as it is understood that they are committed to no more than when someone says there is a property of truth.

Carritt (see Chapter 5) holds that the object of our moral knowledge is a proposition about a particular act. The man who influenced Carritt most is H. A. Prichard:

The sense of obligation to do, or of the rightness of, an action of a particular kind is absolutely underivative or immediate. The rightness of an action consists in its being the origination of something of a certain kind A in a situation of a certain kind, a situation consisting in a certain relation B of the agent to others or to his own nature. To appreciate its rightness two preliminaries may be necessary. We may have to follow out the consequences of the proposed action more fully than we have hitherto done, in order to realize that in the action we should originate A. Thus we may not appreciate the wrongness of telling a certain story until we realize that we should thereby be hurting the feelings of one of our audience. Again, we may have to take into account the relation B involved in the situation, which we had hitherto failed to notice. For instance, we may not appreciate the obligation to give X a present, until we remember that he has done us an act of kindness. But, given that by a process which is, of course, merely a process of general and not of moral thinking we come to recognize that the proposed act is one by which we shall originate A in relation B, then we appreciate the obligation immediately or directly, the appreciation being an activity of *moral* thinking. We recognize, for instance, that this performance of a service to X, who has done us a service, just in virtue of its being the performance of a service to one who has rendered a service to the would-be agent, ought to be done by us.[10]

Prichard is here denying that any moral principles are essentially involved in our moral reasoning. There are principles, but they concern nonmoral matters—e.g., we may use a principle to determine the effects of our action. For those who doubt that Prichard believes the object of our moral knowledge is that a particular act is, say, obligatory we should draw attention to his geometrical analogy. What we recognize is "that *this* three-sided figure, in virtue of its being three-sided, must have three angles." Our italicizing of the term 'this' draws attention to the fact that Prichard believes that the object of moral knowledge is the rightness of that specific act or the obligation that one has in that specific situation.

Sometimes Aristotle is interpreted as holding a similar position. He argues that the virtuous man chooses the mean between excess and deficiency in all things. In considering how to arrive at this mean, Aristotle seems to be arguing that we cannot appeal to principles or reason; rather, we must perceive what the mean is in each specific instance:

[10] H. A. Prichard, "Does Moral Philosophy Rest on a Mistake?" *Moral Obligation* (London: Oxford University Press, 1957), pp. 7–8.

But this is no doubt difficult, and especially in individual cases; for it is not easy to determine both how and with whom and on what provocation and how long one should be angry; for we too sometimes praise those who fall short and call them good-tempered, but sometimes we praise those who get angry and call them manly. The man, however, who deviates little from goodness is not blamed, whether he do so in the direction of the more or of the less, but only the man who deviates more widely; for *he* does not fail to be noticed. But up to what point and to what extent a man must deviate before he becomes blameworthy it is not easy to determine by reasoning, any more than anything else that is perceived by the senses, such things depend on particular facts, and the decision rests with perception. So much, then, is plain, that the intermediate state is in all things to be praised, but that we must incline sometimes towards the excess, sometimes towards the deficiency; for so shall we most easily hit the mean and what is right.[11]

We have set out the view that one's basic moral knowledge concerns the rightness, say, of specific acts, but there is another distinction that is profitably drawn.[12] We can get at this distinction by recalling that Prichard suggests that certain preliminaries are necessary before one can make a justified judgment. One must "follow out the consequences of the proposed action" and determine the relationships of the persons involved in the action. One could expand this by suggesting that the motives of the persons involved are sometimes morally relevant. Not all the consequences, relationships, and motives are to be taken into account, only those that are relevant for making a moral judgment.[13]

Some philosophers have supposed that cognitivist nondefinists did not hold that consequences, relationships, and motives were to be considered.[14] They supposed that the proposition describing one's moral knowledge, according to the cognitivist nondefinist, was about the action as captured by a short

[11] Aristotle, *Nicomachean Ethics*, trans. W. D. Ross (Oxford: The Clarendon Press, 1925), Book II, Chapter 9, 1109 b 14–27.

[12] The distinction that follows overlaps, in part, the distinction between an act and an action. However, more is at stake. The difference between an act and an action does not involve consequences, relationships, etc.

[13] One must be careful in specifying the notion of *relevant* not to give a circular specification which includes some moral term.

[14] Some of R. B. Brandt's criticisms in *Ethical Theory* (Englewood Cliffs, N.J.: Prentice-Hall, Inc., © 1959), make sense only if we interpret him to be considering such a view.

"Let us begin with the decisions, acts, and states of minds of *other* persons. Do we have intuitions of their ethical properties? We do not *perceive* these things; if we know about them it is because we can draw inferences from behavior that we do perceive. Since we do not perceive the decisions, acts, or events themselves, it is odd to say that we are directly aware of their qualities." (p. 190. By permission of the publisher.)

". . . we obviously know the nature and direction of our obligations not directly or, as it were, out of nowhere, but only from awareness of the situation. For instance, if we know that we have an obligation to pay $5 to A, it is because we know we have borrowed $5; we do not just suddenly become aware of an obligation to pay someone $5–" (p. 191. By permission of the publisher).

film clip. Suppose a camera man opens a door and records the following scene: a young man is directing a red-hot poker toward the flesh of an old man strapped to a table; the poker touches the old man and he screams and writhes; end of scene. The knowledge that one would have of the act as thus captured by the camera does not reflect what is to be gained from the preliminaries that Prichard suggests are relevant. No one can know, from that short film sequence, the consequences of the act, whether or not the old man and the young man were related in any morally relevant way, or what the relevant motives of the act were. All the viewer has is what we shall call a *partial-situation* view. We shall call the contrasting view a *total-situation* view.

c. PROPERTIES. Some cognitivist nondefinists apparently have held that the object of one's moral knowledge is neither a principle nor the rightness of an action, but a special kind of property of an object or action:

'Good,' then, if we mean by it that quality which we assert to belong to a thing, when we say that the thing is good, is incapable of any definition, in the most important sense of that word. The most important sense of 'definition' is that in which a definition states what are the parts which invariably compose a certain whole; and in this sense 'good' has no definition because it is simple and has no parts. It is one of those innumerable objects of thought which are themselves incapable of definition, because they are the ultimate terms by reference to which whatever *is* capable of definition must be defined. That there must be an indefinite number of such terms is obvious, on reflection; since we cannot define anything except by an analysis, which, when carried as far as it will go, refers us to something, which is simply different from anything else, and which by that ultimate difference explains the peculiarity of the whole which we are defining: for every whole contains some parts which are common to other wholes also. There is, therefore, no intrinsic difficulty in the contention that 'good' denotes a simple and indefinable quality. There are many other instances of such qualities.

Consider yellow, for example. We may try to define it, by describing its physical equivalent; we may state what kind of light-vibrations must stimulate the normal eye, in order that we may perceive it. But a moment's reflection is sufficient to shew that those light-vibrations are not themselves what we mean by yellow. *They* are not what we perceive. Indeed we should never have been able to discover their existence, unless we had first been struck by the patent difference of quality between the different colours. The most we can be entitled to say of those vibrations is that they are what corresponds in space to the yellow which we actually perceive.

Yet a mistake of this simple kind has commonly been made about 'good.' It may be true that all things which are good are *also* something else, just as it is true that all things which are yellow produce a certain kind of vibration in the light. And it is a fact, that Ethics aims at discovering what are those properties belonging to all things which are good. But far too many philosophers have thought that when they named those other properties they were actually defining good; that these properties, in fact, were simply not 'other,' but absolutely and entirely the same with goodness.[15]

G. E. Moore, then, presents what he calls the *naturalistic fallacy* (see Chapter 11). What we wish to draw attention to here is Moore's claim that good is a "simple and indefinable quality" of the sort that yellow is. The argument that Moore uses, although it is put in the context of definitions, is similar to the arguments presented in the discussion of direct perception. Moore believes that one can define a thing by stating its component properties. Some of these properties, in turn, can be defined. However, there must finally be some property or set of properties which is used to define other properties, but which is not itself definable. Non-definable properties cannot be divided into simpler elements because they are the simplest elements. Moore believes that good is such a simple moral property.

2. *Mode of Direct Knowledge.* There are two ways or modes in which moral properties are known.

a. MATHEMATICAL OF A PRIORI MODEL—RATIONALISTS. Many cognitivist nondefinists have believed that moral knowledge is like mathematical knowledge; they believe that moral knowledge is necessary. This selection from Prichard was used to emphasize the object of one's direct knowledge, but it now draws attention to the mode of such knowledge: it is known in the same way that certain geometrical truths are known.

This apprehension is immediate, in precisely the sense in which a mathematical apprehension is immediate, e.g. the apprehension that this three-sided figure, in virtue of its being three-sided, must have three angles. Both apprehensions are immediate in the sense that in both insight into the nature of the subject directly leads us to recognize its possession of the predicate, and it is only stating this fact from the other side to say that in both cases the fact apprehended is self-evident.[16]

This same explanation of the mode of knowledge can be coupled with any view concerning the object of moral knowledge. Here is Ross' view:

[15] G. E. Moore, *Principia Ethica* (Cambridge: Cambridge University Press, 1959), pp. 9–10. Once again let us stress that Prichard may hold that when we are directly aware of the obligatoriness of an action we are aware of a property of obligatoriness. It can also be that moral principles are correct or legitimate in virtue of describing moral properties and their relations. In this case the property view, on the one hand, and the act and pinciple views, on the other hand, are not exclusive. However, some philosophers wish to hold a view concerning the objects of moral knowledge without thereby committing themselves to a position in the metaphysics of morals. Everyone can admit there is a property of goodness as long as it is specified in a metaphysically neutral manner. Moore seems to be committing himself to a certain metaphysical view, but Prichard does not seem to have done that. Let us not make all the distinctions that the above will allow, but admit that they can be made. By permission of the publishers.

[16] Prichard, *op. cit.*, p. 8.

That an act, *qua* fulfilling a promise, or *qua* effecting a just distribution of good, or *qua* returning services rendered, or *qua* promoting the good of others, or *qua* promoting the virtue or insight of the agent, is *prima facie* right, is self-evident; not in the sense that it is evident from the beginning of our lives, or as soon as we attend to the proposition for the first time, but in the sense that when we have reached sufficient mental maturity and have given sufficient attention to the proposition it is evident without any need of proof, or of evidence beyond itself. It is self-evident just as a mathematical axiom, or the validity of a form in inference, is evident. The moral order expressed in these propositions is just as much part of the fundamental nature of the universe (and, we may add, of any possible universe in which there were moral agents at all) as is the spatial or numerical structure expressed in the axioms of geometry or arithmetic. In our confidence that these propositions are true there is involved the same trust in our reason that is involved in our confidence in mathematics; and we should have no justification for trusting it in the latter sphere and distrusting it in the former. In both cases we are dealing with propositions that cannot be proved, but that just as certainly need no proof.[17]

Ross believes that the object of our moral knowledge is a set of prima facie principles and Prichard does not, but both agree about the mode of such knowledge. Ross believes that certain axioms in geometry are self-evident and, in the same way, so are the six prima facie principles he lists.

When one has mathematical knowledge that, e.g., $2 + 2 = 4$, one does not have to verify this proposition by examining pairs of couples. One can justify one's knowledge of that proposition without appealing to any experience. When the verification of propositions does not depend upon experience, these propositions are said to be known a priori. This kind of knowledge is to be contrasted with the knowledge, e.g., that the earth is roughly a sphere. One must make observations of the earth in order to justify one's knowledge of that proposition. When one's knowledge is of this type, it is a posteriori knowledge.

One can obtain a priori knowledge by the use of reason alone, but this is not true of a posteriori knowledge. Because reason alone is sufficient for a priori knowledge, those who believe the mode of moral knowledge is on the mathematical model are sometimes called *rational theorists*. If we put together the object and the mode of direct awareness, we can get, for example, an a priori (rational) principle cognitivist nondefinist position.

When we discussed the view that the object of moral knowledge is a property, we quoted from Moore, but he is not the only one to hold that view. Plato apparently held that kind of view:

So here, the summit of the intelligible world is reached in philosophic discussion by one who aspires, through the discourse of reason unaided by any of the senses,

[17] W. D. Ross, *op. cit.*, pp. 29–30. By permission of The Clarendon Press, Oxford.

to make his way in every case to the essential reality and perseveres until he has grasped by pure intelligence the very nature of Goodness itself.[18]

Plato is saying that what we apprehend is goodness itself, and we do so by reason alone. This seems to be a clear case of a *rational-property theorist*.

   b. A POSTERIORI MODELS—EMPIRICAL THEORIES. There are two a posteriori theories. Moore compares the apprehension of good to that of yellow:

Let us, then, consider this position. My point is that 'good' is a simple notion, just as 'yellow' is a simple notion; that, just as you cannot, by any manner of means, explain to any one who does not already know it, what yellow is, so you cannot explain what good is.[19]

Although we do not suggest that Moore believes the apprehension of good and yellow to be of the same type, many have taken him to hold such a view. Let us try to explain that type of view without attributing it to a specific person.

   In order to perceive an object as being yellow, one must have certain experiences. One cannot determine by reason alone that an object is yellow, one must look and see. Therefore, the knowledge is a posteriori knowledge. In this case, however, the kind of knowledge is influenced by the object of that knowledge. We can, apparently, know that an object is yellow without being aware of any other properties of the object. We can know, for example, that an object is yellow without knowing that it is a tooth. The knowledge that an object is yellow does not seem to depend upon our having any other knowledge about it.

   Other cognitivist nondefinists believe that the object of one's moral knowledge is a function of many things, such as the relevant consequences, motives, and relations of those involved— The object of one's moral knowledge is a resultant of all of these relevant factors; it is, in short, a *totiresultant*.[20]

---

[18] Plato, *The Republic*, trans. F. M. Cornford (New York: Oxford University Press, Inc., 1956), p. 252.

[19] Moore, *op. cit.*, p. 7.

[20] If an object or act has a property in virtue of only some of its characteristics, then according to some there is a sense in which it also has that property in virtue of all of its characteristics. If X is a round ball in virtue of the relation of its parts to one another, then it is a round ball in virue of the relation of its parts to one another *and* its color. It is true that its color has no positive role with regard to its shape, but it doesn't prevent it from being that shape either. Similarly, there are those who can say that the value of an object or action is a function of all the properties (and perhaps relations) of the object or action even when some of those properties and relations are not relevant to the value.

   Because Ross is inclined to suppose that the relation between moral properties and non-moral properties is necessary in the way that geometric or logical relations are necessary, we can explain the above point in yet another way for him. It is a truth of logic that if p entails q, then p in conjunction with any r entails q. It is not necessary that r have anything to do

Prichard mentions these factors; he is, though, a *rational theorist*.[21] A toti-resultant empirical property that can be directly perceived is shape. One must first grant that one can directly know, or perceive, that a plane figure (drawn in black ink) is a triangle. However, in order to be able to perceive directly that a plane figure is a triangle, one must be aware of the three lines which compose it. The recognition of these lines and their relationship to one another is absolutely required to be able to know that the figure is a triangle. However, one cannot know a priori that this figure is a triangle; one must look and see—therefore, one has a posteriori knowledge.

A more interesting example is that of meaning. The meaning of "The ball is red" is a function of the meanings of the various words, and so the meaning of the whole sentence is a totiresultant of the meaning of the parts.

Similarly, if one knows that the action of burning an old man with a hot poker to test his pain threshold is wrong, he must be aware of, or know, many things. We know the motives of the doer of the action, whether he has any special relations to the old man (the old man could have been *his* torturer a few years ago), and the consequences of the action. This, however, is quite compatible with our directly perceiving or knowing that the act is wrong. Most cognitivist nondefinists have held a totiresultant model of direct knowledge, but most critics, strangely enough, have considered them to hold a simple property model.

Interim Summary. There are three tenets of cognitivist nondefinists:

1. There is objective moral knowledge.
Not-2. No moral judgment (A judgment in which 'good' or 'bad', 'right' or 'wrong', is used in a moral sense) can be reduced or expanded by analysis or definition to another expression which has the same meaning or significance and contains no moral terms.
3. Moral knowledge is sometimes direct.

---

with p at all, only that it not be inconsistent with p. It seems best to interpret the notion of totiresulant in this sort of way, because it is hard to believe, for example, that the exact shape or mass of an object has anything to do with its value; and even more difficult to suppose that it is always part of its value. We can suppose that such properties as these have no real relevance to the value of an object, and yet say that the value of the object is a resultant of these properties plus all the others. One advantage to be gained is that one does not have to specify which properties are relevant to the value of the thing (or which characteristics of the action are relevant to its rightness). The specification of relevance is difficult without circularity, and this is no small reason for holding to the inclusive sense of 'totiresultant'. However, we believe that, because not all the properties and relations of an object or act are relevant to its value properties, it is more realistic to speak of the *relevant* properties and relations. If it should turn out to be impossible to specify which properties and relations are relevant in a noncircular way those who hold such a theory can always return to the wider notion of totiresulant.

[21] We should note here that although we did not say that Prichard held a rational toti-resultant model, because he believes in what he calls "preliminaries," it might be more accurate to characterize him in that way.

There are three different theories concerning the objects of moral knowledge:

1. Principles
2. The moral rightness of acts
    A. Partial-situation view
    B. Total-situation view
3. Properties

There are two different modes of moral knowledge:

1. Rational—a priori
2. Empirical—a posteriori

All these positions are represented in Table 3.

Table 3.   Tenets of Cognitivist Nondefinists

Mode of Knowledge	Object of Knowledge				
	The Moral Rightness (or Wrongness, and So On) of Acts		Moral Principles		Moral Properties
A priori (rational)	Partial-situation view	Total-situation view	Single	Multiple	Plato
		Prichard Carritt	Sidgwick	Ross	
A posteriori (empirical)	Partial-situation view	Total-situation view	Single	Multiple	Moore
		Aristotle			

Exercises

Review

1. What is wrong with the following claim: "Prichard holds that moral reasoning never involves principles"?
2. What is the distinction between the partial- and total-situation views?
3. Give an example of each of the three kinds of objects of moral knowledge the cognitivist nondefinist might accept.
4. Describe the difference between an *object of moral knowledge* and a *mode of moral knowledge*.
5. What is the crucial difference between a cognitivist nondefinist who holds an a priori model view and one who holds an a posteriori model view?
6. With what kind of property should we contrast a totiresultant property? Describe the difference between the two kinds of properties.

Applications

1. If S directly knows some proposition *p*, why should we expect other kinds of propositions we know to throw little light on the sort of knowledge we have when we know that *p*?
2. Present one reason to support a multiple-principle empirical model cognitivist nondefinist position. Why would it be strange to say that the principles are summary principles? Are there any problems in saying that they are constitutive rules?
3. The views in this chapter are all formulated in the language of obligation. Formulate as many views as you can in the language of value. If there are any striking differences, explain why they are striking.

C. Defense of the Tenets of Cognitivistic Nondefinism

Let us determine the reasons in favor of the three tenets of cognitivistic nondefinism. The reasons we shall discuss are not, by themselves, an adequate defense of the theory. It is still necessary to show that the position best meets the criteria of acceptability of theories. The first part of that criterion is that there be reasons in favor of the theory. In this section we shall examine the attempt to fulfill that part of the criterion.

1. *There Is Objective Moral Knowledge.* We shall now examine the evidence the cognitivist non-definist offers for his first claim.

a. THE USE OF MORAL JUDGMENTS. There are said to be two positive reasons in favor of accepting the first tenet of cognitivistic nondefinism. There is a theory of meaning which asks us to determine the meaning of an expression, or a kind of expression, by observing the way in which that expression is actually used (see Chapter 13). One does not have to subscribe to the view that the way to discover the best ethical theory is to start with a theory of meaning to agree that much can be learned by observing how people use moral judgments. It is suggested that, if we ask people whether they believe their moral judgments are capable of being objectively true or not, the vast majority would say that their judgments are objectively true. It is also suggested that most people would agree, after much discussion, that, if one of their judgments is mistaken, some other judgment is correct in the way they believed their first judgment was correct. In short, most people intend their moral judgments to be objectively true and they believe them to be so.

The claim is that the majority of man's beliefs, actions, and intentions constitute some evidence that moral judgments are objectively true. It is not being claimed that this evidence is final, or that the degree of confirmation is very high.

It may be that most men are mistaken in believing their moral judgments are objectively true. It may be that they always fail to carry out their intention to be making objective moral judgments. These possibilities must not be discounted, but to establish them we require, say the cognitivist nondefinists, some positive evidence.

b. THE USE OF REASONS. The second argument offered in support of the first tenet of cognitivistic nondefinism is the use of reasons in moral discourse. Here are three different kinds of propositions.

1. Ice cream tastes good.
2. Burning an old man with a hot poker is wrong.
3. The earth is a sphere.

The first proposition does not represent objective knowledge. Its truth, if it can be said to be true, depends upon the state or condition of the person making the judgment (see Chapter 10). If someone says, "Ice cream tastes good," it is inappropriate to ask him for reasons to substantiate the judgment. Such a judgment is an expression of his tastes concerning ice cream. We do not say, "You are mistaken: ice cream does not taste good." We might point out that *we* do not like ice cream, but that is quite compatible with his liking it.

The fact that it is inappropriate to ask for reasons to substantiate a judgment of taste is quite compatible with the giving of reasons for other purposes. Someone might say that ice cream tastes good, and then go on to say that it tastes good because it is rich and creamy. We can interpret this in at least two ways: the person is explaining the factors that cause the ice cream to taste good to him, or he is describing the characteristics of ice cream that everyone knows he likes or that we all like. In the first instance, the causal explanation is not a substantiation of the original judgment of taste; it is only an explanation of how it is that this sort of creature should come to have tastes of certain kinds and, indirectly, how he could come to make the judgment that he did. If someone suggested that this kind of causal statement *justified* judgments of taste we would simply point out that

whether the causal statement is true or not, and whether the person knows
about the causal relation or not that is not a justification of his taste judgment.

It is possible that S_1 and S_2 both like the same kind of ice cream, the kind
that is rich and creamy and, because each of them knows this, they can convey the same information by saying, "This ice cream is rich and creamy," as
by saying, "This ice cream tastes good." It may also be true that S_1 likes
chocolate ice cream whether or not it is rich. If S_2 sees S_1 eating some ice
cream, he may ask if it tastes good, and then also ask why it does, because
he wants to know if he would like it. If S_1 says, "It is good because it is rich
and creamy," S_2 knows that he will like it, but if S_1 says, "It is chocolate but
not rich," then S_2 knows he will not like it. However, even in this case, S_1 is
not *substantiating* his judgment that the ice cream tastes good, but only
giving some additional information to S_2. It would still be inappropriate for
S_2 to say to S_1, "You are wrong in saying that the ice cream tastes good,
because it is not rich." When S_1 says what he does, he is not giving reasons
to support his judgment, even though what he says is informative.

The cognitivist nondefinist concludes that, whatever the reason, it is inappropriate to ask for and be given, reasons for taste judgments. A request
for an analysis of that kind of proposition is another thing. The failure to
fulfill this request does not, by itself, show that the claims are untrue or
meaningless. All of us, for example, know how to use induction in a great
variety of ways, and yet there are many unsolved problems concerning induction.

We shall suppose, then, that there is some evidence that supporting
reasons for judgments that are not objectively true, are neither required nor
(legitimately) requested. This is to be contrasted, say the cognitivist nondefinists, with judgments such as Proposition 3 (the earth is a sphere) which
is an objectively true judgment. Although most of us accept this judgment as
correct, it is appropriate to ask for, and present, reasons to support it. We
can present photographs of the earth that show its spherical shape. And we
know that it is possible to begin at one point on the earth, travel constantly in
one direction, and eventually return to the same place. This kind of evidence is our reason for making the judgment that the earth is a sphere. Furthermore, it would seem, say the cognitivist nondefinists, that whenever
reasons of this type are appropriate for supporting a judgment, the judgment
is objectively true.

We must now determine whether Proposition 2 (Burning an old man with
a hot poker is wrong) is like Proposition 1 (Ice cream tastes good) or like
Proposition 3 (The earth is a sphere). The cognitivist nondefinist says we
shall have provided evidence for showing that it is like Proposition 3 if we
can show that the requesting and giving of reasons is appropriate when moral
judgments are made. It is not difficult to establish that reasons are appropriate; this is a fact about which we are all aware. If one judges that the

burning of an old man by a young man with a hot poker is wrong, reasons are almost invariably given. We say, for example, that the old man did not do the young man any harm, or that the only motive the young man had in burning the old man was to test his pain threshold. If we fail to give such reasons, then our listener can justifiably ask for them. If we fail to provide such reasons, this seriously weakens our claim to be making a justified moral judgment.[22]

Suppose that when we request some reasons for the judgment under consideration, the person says that he likes the burning of the old man by the younger one. This sort of reason, apparently, is not acceptable and we would point this out to the person making the judgment. (Yet it is the very sort of response that we accept when nonobjective judgments such as "Ice cream tastes good" are made.)

These considerations are evidence that support the claim that Proposition 2 is like Proposition 3 rather than like Proposition 1. The cognitivist nondefinist would admit that this conclusion might be false and that the evidence is not infallible, but if someone says that the evidence is not evidence at all, he must support his own contention with reasons. The two reasons in favor of the first tenet of cognitivistic nondefinism can be said to constitute a prima facie case. The strength of the case depends upon its successful defense against criticisms and its accordance with a coherent theory which meets the criteria of acceptability of theories.

2. Nonreducibility. The second tenet of cognitivistic nondefinism (not-2) is that no judgment can be reduced or expanded by analysis or definition to another expression which has the same meaning or significance and contains no moral terms or concepts (see Chapters 10 and 11). The cognitivist definist holds Proposition 2, but there are reasons to reject all the familiar forms of this position (see Chapter 11). If it can also be shown that noncognitivistic definism is not an acceptable theory, then not-2 can be asserted (a procedure similar to that carried out in Chapter 11 would have to be completed).

The cognitivist nondefinist does not subscribe to the noncognitivist criticism of cognitivistic definism (see Chapter 11), but there is an argument which especially appeals to those cognitivistic nondefinists who hold the empirical model of the mode of moral knowledge. The cognitivist definist makes the claim that he can present a certain kind of definition of some moral terms or expressions. However, no successful definition of that type has yet been provided. This would lead those who believe in induction to

---

[22] If a judgment is a basic principle, supposing there to be such principles, then it would be inappropriate to ask for reasons. Some philosophers believe there is a great problem in specifying the point at which one can legitimately stop giving reasons to support moral judgments. This does seem to be a problem, but exactly the same problem arises with physical judgments. Whatever kind of solution can be effected in that area can be used by the moral philosopher.

conclude that the endeavor to provide such definitions is fruitless. There is no reason to suppose there are such definitions, and past failures lead us to believe that no such definition will be provided. There are at least two other competing theories that offer a total theory (the noncognitivist definist and cognitivist nondefinist). This seems to be a total failure to meet the criteria of acceptability for this part of the theory of cognitivistic definism. Therefore, the statement of not-2 receives further support. If the same procedure can be applied to noncognitivist definist positions, the support is substantially increased.

3. *Moral Knowledge is Direct.* It will be recalled that we attempted to show that Proposition 3 is a result of Propositions 1 and not-2. Many cognitivist nondefinists have presented reasons for Proposition 3 which are independent of Propositions 1 and not-2, and we shall briefly review two of those arguments.

a. SIMPLICITY. G. E. Moore believes that good is one of two basic simple moral properties. He believes that this basic property of good is not definable because it is simple. Because it is not definable, one cannot be aware of the property by being aware of some other set of properties in terms of which it is defined. Because of this, one must be aware of the property, without inferring its presence from something else. When one is in this position, one directly perceives good.

The difficulty with this argument is that one must first prove that good is a simple indefinable property, and the only method that Moore provides for doing that is the open-question technique. This technique was shown to be of doubtful value in establishing that conclusion (see Chapter 11).

b. CHAIN-OF-REASONS ARGUMENT. When one presents reasons to justify or support one's moral judgments, these reasons are themselves judgments. If one judges that it is wrong to burn the old man with a poker, one may offer the reason that, because the old man is being hurt, it is wrong to burn him. This second judgment, which is the reason for the first, may itself be supported by a reason—perhaps that hurting old men is always wrong. We shall finally reach a point, however, at which a reason is given for a judgment but no reason is required or can be given for that reason. When such a reason is presented, we know the correctness of it because of its own nature. It is sometimes said that the judgment is its own evidence, or that it is self-evident. A self-evident judgment is known directly.[23]

In order for the argument to be fully effective, one would have to determine why it is that the reasons given must run out. It does seem that they must, but why that is now seems unclear. Furthermore, if one accepted this position, he would be committed to identifying certain reasons or judgments as

---

[23] Sidgwick, in the passage quoted earlier, seems to have had this kind of argument in mind. Aristotle also held a version of this argument to be effective.

basic and others as nonbasic. For the cognitivist nondefinist, however, there seems to be no clear and effective method of identifying such judgments other than by saying that a basic judgment is one that is directly known. This answer is not acceptable because the argument is designed to show that some judgments are directly known.

Such problems are difficult to solve, and would lead us far afield. Because the cognitivist nondefinist can find support for Proposition 3 in Propositions 1 and not-2, the path of discretion should lead him to do so. The simplicity argument, then, offers little evidence for Proposition 3 and the chain of reasons argument offers some evidence but raises many problems. Therefore, we allow the cognitivist nondefinist to defend Proposition 3 by pointing out that it is a consequence of Propositions 1 and not-2.

D. Narrowing the Field

In order to compare the cognitivist nondefinist view that seems best with its noncognitivist counterpart, we must determine which cognitivist non-definist view is best. To accomplish this we shall present some criticisms of all but one cognitivist nondefinist position. We shall not present all the criticisms of these positions because there are so many and also because many criticisms do not take sufficient account of the different cognitivist nondefinist views.

1. *Criticism of the Property Views.* This view is Moore's and, perhaps, Plato's. According to this view, there is one or more moral properties of which we can be aware, and it is the presence or absence of this property that makes things good or acts right. There is a criticism of this view by R. M. Hare which is now generally accepted as being effective.[24]

The argument can be briefly summarized in the following manner: The property cognitivist nondefinist must say either that the moral property is a function of the nonmoral properties or it is not. If the moral property is a function of the nonmoral properties, then this is the naturalist position or one of the other cognitivist definist positions. That alternative cannot be accepted by the cognitivist nondefinist. If the moral property is not a function of the nonmoral properties, then it would be possible for two things (situations or actions) to have the same nonmoral properties but different moral properties. This latter situation, however, is not possible, and so property cognitivist nondefinist theories must be rejected.

The notion of *function* is important because all cognitivist nondefinists (with the possible exception of the property theorists) hold that moral knowledge, either of principles or of specific acts and things, *is* a function of

---

[24] R. M. Hare, *The Language of Morals* (Oxford: The Clarendon Press, 1952), pp. 80–81. The argument that follows is not exactly what Hare says, but is rather derived from what he says.

nonmoral knowledge and the objects of that knowledge.[25] Hare's argument in this form works only against views that claim there is no such functional relation. Therefore, we must find some reason other than that argument for rejecting any other cognitivist nondefinist positions.

2. Criticism of the A Priori or Rational Views. There are two effective arguments against the a priori views.

a. BRANDT'S ARGUMENT. There are two a priori views: the principle and the act view. According to these views, our moral knowledge of principles or acts is a priori. Against this view an argument adapted from R. B. Brandt will be presented. We shall not quote Brandt because his presentation of the argument is lengthy and the argument itself is quite complex. We are not even certain that what we are about to present is what Brandt had in mind. If it is not, we shall say that it is an argument which is inspired by what Brandt says.[26]

In his criticism Brandt uses the notion *requiredness*, which is closely related to the notion of a function. We have said that all the cognitivist nondefinists (except the property theorists) hold that moral knowledge (and its obects) are a function of nonmoral knowledge (and its objects). Brandt, when he speaks of *requiredness*, is specifying the nature of the function. Ross, for example, relates promise-keeping and obligation. Promise-keeping is (we shall suppose) a nonmoral phenomenon that is related to the moral phenomenon of having an obligation. If S promises to do A, then S has a (prima facie) obligation to do A. S's (prima facie) obligation to do A is a function, in this case, of S's promise. If we say that the promise of S to do A requires the (prima facie) obligatoriness of A, then we have partially specified the relation between the promise to do A and the obligation to do A. Because Ross holds the principle a priori model of moral knowledge, we can say that the promising requires the obligation in the way in which a plane figure's having three equal sides requires that it have three equal angles.

Brandt uses as his model of a priori knowledge not mathematical or geometrical knowledge but the knowledge of the proposition "Anything red is spread out." This proposition may represent a priori knowledge that is of a type different from mathematical or geometrical knowledge, but this latter type of knowledge does seem far removed from moral knowledge, and so his use of that model seems justified. What we take to be the essential elements of this argument now follow.

The cognitivist nondefinist (who takes the a priori model) supposes that sometimes an act or thing has a natural property which requires that that act or thing have a value property. This same point can be put in nonprop-

---

[25] Such philosophers must, of course, specify the function in such a way that they are not definists. We have seen some of the different explanations of the function involved, and others will be presented.

[26] Brandt, *op. cit.* The argument referred to is to be found on pp. 198–200.

erty terms: sometimes an act or thing has a natural (nonmoral) characteristic which requires that the act or thing be (for example) right or (for example) good.[27] The requirement—i.e., the relation between the natural property and the value property—is known directly. The statement of the requirement between the natural property is either a categorical or a prima facie principle, on the one hand, or a judgment only about a specific act, on the other.

If the principle is categorical, then it states that whenever a certain natural or nonvalue property is present, a value property is present too. An example of this might be, "It is always obligatory to tell the truth." However, as we have seen, there are always counterexamples to such principles. The counterexamples can be formulated because the value property is not a function of just one natural property but of an indefinitely large number of such properties. There are invariably some other natural properties which, if present, would change the judgment. If one can prevent a nuclear war only by lying, then one is not obliged to tell the truth. One is not obliged to tell one's wife or girl friend that she does not look pretty when she asks, "How do I look?" even when she doesn't look pretty. In both these cases there are other relevant nonmoral characteristics of the situation. Indeed, it would not be far wrong to say that any nonmoral characteristic can be morally relevant.

If so, then one can never simply say, "All things having such-and-such nonmoral characteristics have so-and-so moral characteristics." One can only say, "All things having such-and-such nonmoral characteristics have so-and-so moral characteristics *provided that there are no other morally relevant characteristics*." This statement is considerably different from "Anything red is extended" (or "Any enclosed plane figure that has three equal sides has three equal angles"). There are no characteristics of a thing which, when added to its redness, are capable of making it false that it is extended. No other property of an enclosed plane figure having three equal sides can make it false that such a figure has three equal angles. By contrast, there are, apparently, always additional discoverable characteristics of acts and things which may render moral judgments incorrect. This clearly indicates that categorical moral principles are not known a priori in the way in which we know that anything red is extended or that any enclosed plane figure which has three equal sides also has three equal angles.

Perhaps a similar criticism can be made of the a priori prima facie principle theory; the principles may be known to be true, but because other characteristics are relevant they are not known a priori. Brandt does seem to apply the argument in this way but also presents counterexamples to many of Ross' prima facie principles. We shall not mention those counterexamples

[27] In what follows we shall often use the *property* terminology because it is easier to use and because Brandt uses it. However one must remember that the use of the expression *value property* in this discussion can always be eliminated.

because there is some doubt concerning their effectiveness, and also because the relation of counterexamples to prima facie principles was discussed (see Chapter 5).

It seems that Brandt's argument applies also to the act version of the a priori model. Prichard says that we know that we have an obligation in a certain situation in the way in which we know that a particular triangle, by virtue of its having three sides, also has three angles. However, once again there is no further characteristic of this triangle that we could discover which, when conjoined with its having three sides, would show that it does *not* have three angles. In the moral sphere, however, one can find further characteristics of an act which may show that it is not obligatory. This is strong evidence that moral insight into obligations in particular cases is not the same as a priori knowledge of mathematical or geometrical properties.

b. Ross' ARGUMENT. There is another interesting argument against the a priori act model cognitivist nondefinist which Ross presents. This argument may be taken by some as an earlier version of Brandt's argument. If so, we must give Ross the credit he deserves. Here is what Ross says:

Our judgements about our actual duty in concrete situations have none of the certainty that attaches to our recognition of the general principles of duty. A statement is certain, i.e., is an expression of knowledge, only in one or other of two cases: when it is either self-evident, or a valid conclusion from self-evident premises. And our judgements about our particular duties have neither of these characters. (1) They are not self-evident. Where a possible act is seen to have two characterisics, in virtue of one of which it is *prima facie* right, and in virue of the other *prima facie* wrong, we are (I think) well aware that we are not certain whether we ought or ought not to do it; that whether we do it or not, we are taking a moral risk. We come in the long run, after consideration, to think one duty more pressing than the other, but we do not feel certain that it is so. And though we do not always recognize that a possible act has two such characteristics, and though there *may* be cases in which it has not, we are never certain that any particular possible act has not, and therefore never certain that it is right, nor certain that it is wrong. For, to go no further in the analysis, it is enough to point out that any particular act will in all probability in the course of time contribute to the bringing about of good or of evil for many human beings, and thus have a *prima facie* rightness or wrongness of which we know nothing. (2) Again, our judgements about our particular duties are not logical conclusions from self-evident premises. The only possible premises would be the general principles stating their *prima facie* rightness or wrongness *qua* having the different characteristics they do have; and even if we could (as we cannot) apprehend the extent to which an act will tend on the one hand, for example, to bring about advantages for our benefactors, and on the other hand to bring about disadvantages for fellow men who are not our benefactors, there is no principle by which we can draw the conclusion that it is on the whole right or on the whole wrong.[28]

[28] Ross, *op. cit.*, pp. 30–31.

Let us restate Ross' argument:

1. A statement (and in this case a moral judgment) is certain if, and only if, it is self-evident or follows from what is self-evident.
2. Here the argument that "A is right" is not self-evident.
    a. We judge that A is right because we judge that A is *FGH*, and there is no *J* such that if A were *FGHJ*, then A would be wrong.
    b. If it is not self-evident that A is *FGH* and not *J*, then it is not self-evident that A is right.
    c. It is never self-evident that A is *FGH* and not *J* because (just to mention two reasons) we cannot foresee all the future consequences of A, and the relevant *J* may be a mental state of someone whose mental states are difficult to determine.

From a–c it follows that

    d. It is never self-evident that A is right.
3. Here the argument that "A is right" does not follow from what is self-evident:
    a. Only premises of the form "All instances of promise keeping are prima facie right" can be used in moral arguments.
    b. Even if it is self-evident that A is an instance of promise-keeping, this only allows the conclusion that A is prima facie right.
    c. We can only conclude that A is right if we have a premise of the form "All instances of promise keeping are right." However, all such principles are false.

From a–c it follows that

    d. "A is right" does not follow from what is self-evident.

From Statement 1 and Statements 2d and 3d we are able to draw the conclusion

4. No moral judgment is certain.

Another way of stating the conclusion is that individual acts cannot be known to be right with certainty when the requirement of certainty is the same as mathematical self-evidence. If so, then we must say that the act a priori model of cognitive nondefinism is not tenable. If one has evidence short of certainty that this figure is three-sided, he is not allowed to assert with certainty that the figure has three angles. Similarly, we are not allowed to assert, "It is certain that A is right," on any grounds except, "It is certain that A is *FGH* and is not *J*"—which, Ross shows, we are never allowed to assert.

Ross' argument does not show that his own position is correct because there are alternatives to his view, and also because there are reasons against his a priori model view. Ross is concerned not only with the status of moral knowledge, but also with the object of moral knowledge. He maintains that the object of one's moral knowledge is a principle. Many who do not think that our moral knowledge is certain, or even that we have moral knowledge (of a certain sort), would agree with Ross that what basically justifies moral judgments is a set of principles.

3. *Criticism of Principle Views.* We have examined a number of arguments concerning the use of principles in moral reasoning (see Chapter 5). We examined the arguments presented by Aristotle, Carritt, Frankena, Hare, and some arguments perhaps peculiar to the authors of this work. That discussion was not really concluded because the necessary meta-ethical groundwork had not been laid. Now, however, we shall try to settle that issue. In so doing, supposing that the previous two critical sections have been successful, we shall have reduced the number of cognitivist nondefinist positions we must consider to one.

The main argument used by the principle theorist is that all particular moral judgments presuppose a general principle (see Chapter 5). There are other arguments used by the principle theorists, but the counterarguments (see Chapter 5) seem adequate. Let us briefly review the dialectical development of the disagreement with the principle theorist. The principle theorist holds that the following scheme describes all correct moral reasoning:

Scheme R

1. If A has F, G, and H, then A is right (or wrong, or obligatory).
2. A has F, G, and H.
3. A is right (or wrong, or obligatory).

Statement 1 is the statement of a principle, and it is this sort of statement that is thought to be required for justified moral reasoning.

The act theorist responds by arguing that the use of counterexamples shows that sometimes we must do our moral reasoning without the use of principles. Whenever a principle is put forward, effective counterexamples can be presented. These counterexamples are justified specific moral judgments which go counter to the principle. This fact shows that we do not always use principles in moral reasoning; that they are not basic to it.

The principle theorist's response is that the counterexample itself presupposes a principle. The argument, most clearly expressed by Frankena, is that, if someone judges that A_1 which is F, G, and H is right but that A_2 which is also F, G, and H (and is not different from A_1 in any morally relevant respects) is not right, that is sufficient grounds for judging that person irrational. This fact supposedly shows that the principle "Any A which is F, G, and H is right" (or "If A is F, G, and H, then A is right") is presupposed in our moral reasoning. It is at this point that we wish to resume the argument.

1. If S judges that X is G on the grounds that X is F (where F and G are different properties or characteristics of X), then S is committed to judge that any Y which is F (and which is similar to X in the relevant respects) is also G.
2. If S does not judge that Y is G (in the circumstances described in Statement 1) S can be justifiably judged to be irrational.
3. If Statements 1 and 2 are correct, the principle "All things which are F are G" (or "If something is F then it is G")
    a. is used in all justified reasoning which reaches the judgment that X is G;
    b. is presupposed in the justified judgment that X is G;
    c. must be assented to by S in order for us to be justified in accepting any (other) judgment of S.

The principle theorist asserts Statements 1 and 2 and then, depending on who he is, asserts one or all of Statements a, b, and c. What we shall do is throw some doubt on the truth of Statements 1 and 2, and seriously attack Statement 3.

The problem with statements such as Statement 1 is that they always presuppose that some statement is to be added at the end, such as "provided that no other circumstances arise in which S would not be committed to judge that X is G." Sometimes one can be morally justified in uttering or making a judgment which is false or completely unjustified in other ways (see Chapter 9). S may, for example, utter the judgment that some person's skin color is white and judge, on another occasion, that a different person's is brownish, even though the skins of the two are the same in all relevant color respects. The utterance of this judgment may be justified if the man judged to be white is being rescued from a lynch mob, or he is involved in some other morally relevant set of circumstances.

Those who defend Statement 1 can add the "escape clause" suggested in order to explain such cases, but the clause takes all the force out of the principle. It now seems to say that we are committed to judge similar cases similarly unless we are not. This statement, although true, is not terribly useful in moral reasoning.

The best way out of the difficulty is to add a clause that specifies that one will not be judging *truly* if one does not judge that Y is G (in the circumstances described). This addition, although welcome to the cognitivist, does not fit in very well with noncognitivist views. Perhaps the addition of a noncognitive equivalent of 'truly' can be found.

Statement 2 can be criticized in exactly the same way, but also for another reason (which would also apply to Statement 1). Suppose that we are asked to determine whether the proofs of two theorems are valid or invalid, and the method of proof in each case is the same. It might also be true that the effort to determine the validity of one proof renders it psychologically impossible (because of fatigue) to determine the validity of the second. In this case one would not be irrational if one failed to judge both to be valid or invalid.

One might be tempted to say that Statement 2 is a negative injunction—that one must not judge two similar things differently unless one is to be judged irrational. However, we can understand that a simple mistake in a complex problem, when one is tired, can lead to different judgments. That performance does not qualify one as being irrational.

Another possible reply is that the two things being judged are not the same in all relevant respects because, in one case, the person is fresh and, in the other, he is not. However, the person making the judgment is not the *object* of the judgment, and it is objects that must be similar. One can add that all the factors in the situation, including the state of mind of the person making the judgment, must be similar, but then the resulting statement will probably become as empty as the second version of Statement 1.

Statement 3 contains the important claims. There are principle theorists who make claims like those in Statement 3 but not, perhaps, identical with them. We believe, though, that the remarks concerning Statement 3 apply (in an appropriately modified form) to all similar statements.

There is one antecedent to Statement 3 and three consequents; let us examine the truth of the resulting statements by using each of the consequents with the antecedent. The first is Statement 3a: "If Statements 1 and 2 are correct, the principle 'all things which are F are G,' (or 'if something is F, then it is G') is used in all justified reasoning which reaches the judgment that X is G." This statement appears to be a claim about what actually occurs in all instances of justified moral reasoning and, as such, seems to be refuted by the facts. In many, if not most, instances of moral reasoning, no principle at all is used.

Someone might reply that, although the principle is not formulated, it is nevertheless presupposed in one's judgments. This claim, however, is Statement 3b and it does not save Statement 3a. Let us then turn to Statement 3b. One way to show that the antecedent of an "if . . . then" statement does not provide adequate support for the consequent is to present an exactly similar statement which is false. Those who claim that Statement 3b is true would replace 'G' with some value term, but let us replace it with a color term, perhaps 'green'.

1'. If S judges that X (a leaf) is G (green) on the grounds that X is F (appears to be green or is on a growing tomato plant), then S is committed to judge that any Y which is F (and which is similar to X in the relevant respects) is also G.

2'. If S does not judge that Y is G (green) (in the circumstances described in Statement 1') then S can be justifiably judged to be irrational.

3b'. If Statements 1' and 2' are correct, then the principle "All things which are

F are G" (or "If something is F, then it is G") is presupposed in the justified judgment that X is G.

The claim we wish to make is that Statement 3b′ (and thereby also Statement 3b) is either false or irrelevant to the respective kinds of reasoning.

We have already established, in effect, that, if someone claims that we must always use the principle that tomato leaves in certain situations are green in order to determine that this tomato leaf is green, he is saying what is false. We usually determine that a leaf is green by looking at it, not by appealing to principles.

If someone claims that the principle is nevertheless presupposed in our judgment, we can reply that that kind of presupposition has nothing to do with the *reasoning* that arrived at the judgment. Because we do not usually use a principle as evidence for our judgment that the leaf is green, and we do not usually use a principle as evidence for our judgment that an act is wrong, it is difficult to see how such principles have a place in our reasoning about such matters, although it may be true that principles of the sort described are presupposed. This claim, as we have seen, is compatible with admitting that summary principles are sometimes, or even often, used in moral reasoning (or color reasoning). The use of such principles, though, presupposes that we sometimes arrive at judgments without using principles. We could, for example, judge that a tomato leaf is green because it is a leaf on a growing plant. This judgment can be made because we have seen many leaves on growing plants and have seen that they were green. The (summary) rule or principle, "All leaves on growing tomato plants are green," can be known only because we (or someone else) directly perceived the color of many leaves on growing plants in the past.

The consequent c, coupled with the antecedent of Statement 3, offers no help to the principle theorist either.

3c. If Statements 1 and 2 are correct, then the principle "All things which are F are G" (or "If something is F, then it is G"), must be assented to by S in order for us to be justified in accepting any other judgment of S.

Once again we must point out that, although Statement 3c may be true, it does not show anything about moral reasoning. There are many statements to which a man must assent in order for us to be justified in accepting any judgment of his. Here are some candidates which, in the proper circumstances, fulfill the required role:

1. It is never true that today is Monday and today is not Monday.
2. I am alive.
3. I am not Napoleon.
4. China exists.

5. All enclosed plane figures having three angles have three sides.
6. All men who make judgments are alive.

These are all statements that a man, in most circumstances, must assent to before we can be justified in accepting other judgments of his. No one would want to claim that Statement 5 or 6 is relevant to our moral reasoning, and yet it is just as necessary for our acceptance of his further judgments that a man assent to those principles as that he assent to any moral principles. Thus, a statement such as 3c does not show that principles are always used in justified moral reasoning.

There are many judgments to which we must assent but which are not used in (justified) reasoning about every subject. A necessary condition of rationality seems to be the acceptance of certain principles such as "Similar cases are to be judged similarly." This does not show, however, that one of the elements in our reasoning is that necessary condition.

Interim Summary. We have reduced the number of cognitivist non-definist positions to one by offering criticisms of the others. We have criticized the property views of Moore and Plato, the a priori model as held by Ross and Prichard, and, finally, all principle views, and, thereby, the cognitivist nondefinist principle views. Because no one wants to hold a partial-situation view, the position left unscathed is the a posteriori total situation cognitivist nondefinist position. A review of this position and how well it meets the criteria of acceptability will next occupy our attention. Then, as quick as you can say 'a posteriori total situation cognitivistic nondefinism' we shall see how this position compares with its noncognitivist rival.

E. Application of the Criteria of Acceptability to the Remaining Cognitivist Nondefinist Theory

The one position that has escaped devastating criticism is the a posteriori act theory. It differs from other cognitivist nondefinist theories in its explanation of the mode of moral knowledge, the object of moral knowledge, or both. How well does this theory meet the test of a good theory, and what further must be done to make it acceptable?

1. Reasons in Its Favor. We have considered reasons in favor of the tenets of cognitivist nondefinist theories. Reasons to suppose that cognitivist nondefinist theories other than a posteriori act theory are mistaken have been presented, but that does not weaken the case for the former view. In summary, the reasons are these:

Tenet 1: There is objective moral knowledge.
Reasons: The use of moral judgments (see pp. 286–87). The use of reasons in moral discourse (see pp. 287–89).
Tenet 2: No moral judgment can be reduced or expanded by analysis or defini-

tion to another expression which has the same meaning or significance and contains no moral terms (not-2).

Reasons: The evidence against cognitivistic definism in Chapter 11. No existing linking principles and failure of attempts to discover them and the expectation of similar evidence against noncognitivistic definism (see pp. 289–90).

Tenet 3: Moral knowledge is direct.

Reasons: Simplicity (see p. 290). Chain-of-reasons argument (see pp. 290–91). Tenets 1 plus 2 are evidence (see pp. 273 and 291).

To these reasons, which support all cognitivist nondefinist positions, can be added another which supports act theories. It seems that the most acceptable normative theory is some kind of act deontology (see Chapter 5). Given that this is so, then the a posteriori act cognitivist nondefinist theory "fits in" quite well with this normative theory. This is not to say that some noncognitive or naturalist theory might not also be compatible. However, if those positions were to be weakened in relation to act cognitivistic nondefinism, then this reason would loom larger.

2. The Theory Can Answer Serious Objections. The second part of the criterion of acceptability has scarcely been mentioned, but it will become increasingly important as the position is criticized. There are, however, some common criticisms, and we can show how the cognitivist nondefinist view we have chosen as the best responds to them.

a. MORAL FACULTY. Cognitivist nondefinists often speak of a moral faculty by means of which our moral knowledge is attained. This is criticized by the claims that this is unscientific and that no one is aware of such a faculty.

The reader will no doubt first be puzzled by this criticism because the notion of a moral faculty is not essential to the statement of cognitivistic nondefinism. It is true that some cognitivist nondefinists have spoken of a moral faculty or a moral sense, but the positing of such a faculty is, or can be seen to be, a result of the rest of the theory. It has long been noted by philosophers that if one has knowledge (Tenet 1) which is not reducible to other kinds of knowledge (Tenet 2), then there is some means whereby this knowledge is gained. Such a means, whatever it is, is called a faculty. Thus the claim that there is a moral faculty is a result of the first two tenets of cognitivist nondefinist theories. If one wishes to deny that there is a moral faculty, he must find reasons for denying one or both of these tenets.

It is neither scientific nor unscientific to claim that there is objective moral knowledge. It is the job of the scientist to discover the nature of faculties and to explain how they work. It may be true that scientists discover faculties and that sometimes they show that there are no faculties of a certain type, but—given the truth of Tenets 1 and 2 and the connection between them and the claim that there is a moral faculty—it is difficult to see how any scientific evidence could show that there is no such faculty.

b. DISAGREEMENT. It is often claimed that cognitivistic nondefinism cannot account for moral disagreement. If Tenets 1–3 are true and it is also true that everyone has the same moral faculty, then, it is claimed, there would be no moral disagreement. Because there is moral disagreement, one of Tenets 1–3 is mistaken and there is no moral faculty.

The answer to this criticism will, it is feared, appear deceptively simple. It is part of the theory being considered that moral knowledge is a posteriori. It is true of a posteriori knowledge that there is, or can be, disagreement. This disagreement does not show, for example, that we do not have knowledge of the shape or color of objects, and so it is difficult to see why such disagreement should show that we do not have moral knowledge. If two persons disagree about the color of an object, we call in a third to help settle the issue. It is not that the third person can see better than the first two, but that agreement is some evidence that one has succeeded in directly perceiving the color of an object. This evidence does not always lead to correct judgments but, after all, it is not very fruitful to appeal to indirect evidence in cases of disagreement over things that are directly perceived.

It is fortunate that there are very few, if any, disagreements concerning the color of objects when we have removed the obvious sources of such disagreement. It is also fortunate that there are few, if any, disagreements concerning the moral worth of things when we have removed the obvious sources of such disagreement. In judging color, we must insure that the lighting conditions are proper and that the observers are normal. In judging moral worth we must insure that all the relevant consequences and motives are known and that those making the judgment are not abnormal in any way. When we specify the conditions of observation in judging color, we must be certain that we do not make essential use of any color terms and, similarly, we must not make any essential use of moral terms in specifying the conditions in judging moral worth. It is often said that this latter condition cannot be met in judging moral worth, but that would seem unduly pessimistic to the cognitivist nondefinist. The main task is to avoid circularity in specifying the conditions. This can be done by listing certain physiological and physical conditions which do not make reference to the property involved. A rough description of a *normal moral observer* is that he is a normal observer of nonmoral properties and that he does not hold a mistaken ethical theory to which he appeals when he makes moral judgments. It should be added that the specification of the nature of a normal moral observer does not seem more necessary to having moral knowledge than the specification of a normal color observer is to having color knowledge.

c. EMOTIVE FORCE. It is often said that cognitivists do not adequately account for the emotive force of moral judgments. In the cognitivist view we are considering, it will be said, moral judgments are just reports of a certain kind of fact, but an essential part of moral judgments is the emotive element.

Furthermore, it is said, if moral judgments are just a kind of factual judgment, then it would not be understandable why men act on such judgments or feel guilty when they do not.

The cognitivist nondefinist would claim that an emotive force is connected with all important judgments. There is a great deal of emotive force connected with the judgment to get married, or with the judgment that one's father is dead. It would be a mistake to conclude that there is an emotive element in the judgment, "My father is dead," because attendant emotion and powerful attitudes are almost invariably at work. It seems that there is emotive force attendant upon all judgments thought to be important, and moral judgments are among these. Also, the cognitivist nondefinist would say that it is difficult to see how emotive force can be an element of a judgment, which is some kind of linguistic entity, or mental entity or activity. It may be that the nature of judgments can be analyzed so that it becomes understandable how emotive force can be part of a judgment or part of the analysis of a judgment, but a satisfactory analysis of that type has yet to be made.

Furthermore, the claim that some emotive force must be part of moral judgments because men act on their moral judgments or feel guilty if they do not seems misguided. Many factual judgments move men to act, and we do not suppose that they must be, in part, emotive judgments. The judgment that one's child is in danger will move most men to act even though it is purely factual. Furthermore, the cognitivist nondefinist can say, why cannot it be a fact about human beings that they do tend to act on what they believe is right and obligatory? Why must there be some mysterious connection between a judgment and an action?

One may well wonder, as Russell did, why men prefer to act on what they believe is true. It is perhaps difficult to give an answer, but whatever answer can be given, the cognitivist can apply it. Men act on what they believe are correct moral judgments for very much the same reason that they act on any judgment they believe to be true. Some judgments are more important than others, and these would probably be more likely to be acted upon than others. Among the most important kind of judgments we make are moral judgments.

The answers presented above in the name of the cognitivist nondefinist are not meant to be final answers to the kinds of criticisms directed against that view. The defense of a theory against criticisms is a continuing activity. However, we have now made a beginning, and it is hoped that the reader will understand the activity and enter into it himself.

d. FURTHER DIFFICULTIES. There are many problems remaining in the areas mentioned, and in others. A cognitivist nondefinist needs clearly to divorce the claim that there is a moral faculty from the shadow of some strange science. The way to do this is to show that the claim that there is a moral faculty is a derived claim, not an independent one. Furthermore, the notion of a moral faculty is not needed to state the position of cognitivistic nondefinism.

The nature of moral disagreement cannot be treated adequately in such a short space as was done. The beginning of an answer has been outlined, but the complete answer has not yet been presented.

In order to give an adequate account of emotive force, we must have a more complete analysis of the nature of moral judgments. We must be able to say how they differ from, and are similar to, other types of judgments. A start was made, but much more needs to be done.

The most serious problems remaining for the cognitivist nondefinist involve direct perception and the nature of the object of that knowledge. The notion of direct perception was explained more by circumscription and contrast than by direct description. This is understandable for, if there is such a thing as direct perception one would expect that other kinds of knowledge would throw little light on it. In spite of this disclaimer, however, much more needs to be said. Many analogies and metaphors were presented, and we should strive to replace these with precise statements and accurate descriptions. Until this is done one cannot have complete confidence in any view which makes essential use of it.

When one directly perceives the color of an object, one can make many statements about his knowledge of the color. One can be justified in claiming that he knows that a ball is red. The nature and analysis of this knowledge can be given. Another kind of question concerns the metaphysical status of the property *red color*. We can say that the property exists "in the mind," or "in the object." We can also say that the color is simply the reflection of certain wave lengths of light, or of some other physical thing or process. When we describe what color is and the way it exists, we have entered the area of metaphysics. There is, similarly, an area of philosophy called *the metaphysics of morals*. In this area, the remaining cognitivist nondefinist view must specify the kind of thing that is being directly perceived. Is it a property of the thing or action alone? We are told that it is not, that what is being directly perceived is relational. This response is not, however, fully satisfying.

It seems to be true that one can present an adquate theory of moral knowledge without specifying the nature of the objects of knowledge, but it is philosophically unsatisfying—and the theory of knowledge is not even adequate until the key notion of direct perception is more fully explained.

3. Competitors. The third part of the criteria of acceptability requires that a theory account for, and explain, the moral phenomena better than its competitors. In meeting the first two parts of the criteria, one partially meets the third. One does not meet it fully until the competitors confront one another. In the next chapter we shall set the scene for this confrontation by presenting the other of the two views which we consider to be the most serious contenders for the role of best theory.

Summary. We have selected the cognitivist nondefinist view we thought best, and justified that choice. We have presented criticisms of the other cognitivist nondefinist views to reduce the number of views to be considered. We shall now attempt to reduce the number of noncognitivist definist views to one.

Exercises

Review

1. Summarize the defense of each of the tenets of cognitivistic nondefinism.
2. Why is no independent evidence required to support the claim that moral knowledge is sometimes direct? Describe two arguments sometimes used to support that claim.
3. Describe one effective reason against the property views.
4. Describe one argument used against the principle theorist.
5. What is the criticism of the a priori model views?
6. Why is the application of the criteria of acceptability only tentative?

Applications

1. Show how the argument against the principle theorists presented in Chapter 5 is augmented by what is presented in this chapter.
2. Describe some further evidence that would have to be gathered to complete the application of the criteria of acceptability to cognitivist nondefinist theories in general, and the act empirical view in particular.
3. Why is the cognitivist nondefinist not holding an ideal-observer theory when he brings in the notion of a normal moral observer?

Bibliography *

BRANDT, RICHARD B. *Ethical Theory.* Englewood Cliffs, N.J.: Prentice-Hall, Inc., 1959, Chapter 8. A very thorough, critical discussion.

BROAD, C. D. *Five Types of Ethical Theory.* New York: Harcourt, Brace & World, 1935, pp. 266–73. A discussion of the nature of ethical judgments, including several types of "intuitionism."

CARRITT, E. F. *The Theory of Morals.* New York: Oxford University Press, 1928. This is a clear statement of an act cognitivist nondefinist theory. See especially Chapters 11–14.

EDWARDS, PAUL. *The Logic of Moral Discourse.* New York: The Free Press, 1955, Chapter 4. Contains some criticisms of cognitivistic nondefinism.

EWING, A. C. *The Definition of Good.* New York: The Macmillan Company, 1947, Chapter 5. Contrasts Ross' view with that of the "ideal" utilitarians.

FRANKENA, WILLIAM K. *Ethics.* Englewood Cliffs, N.J.: Prentice-Hall, Inc., 1963, pp. 85–88. A brief statement of cognitivistic nondefinism and some criticisms of that view.

* All the items in this bibliography are somewhat advanced.

Moore, G. E. *Ethics*. New York: Oxford University Press, 1965, Chapters 3 and 4. Discusses and defends the claim that moral judgments are objectively true.

————. *Philosophical Studies*. London: Routledge and Kegan Paul, Ltd., 1948, Chapter 8. An attempt to say what is meant by "subjective" and "objective" predicates. Also a discussion of intrinsic goodness.

————. *Principia Ethica*. Cambridge: Cambridge University Press, 1959. One of the most influential statements of cognitivistic nondefinism.

Nowell-Smith, P. H. *Ethics*. Baltimore: Penguin Books, Inc., 1954. Chapters 2–4. An interesting set of criticisms of cognitivistic nondefinism.

Plato. *Republic*. Books 4–7. An apparent statement of an a priori property view.

Price, Richard. *Review of the Principal Questions of Morals*. Reprinted partly in A. Selby-Bigge, *British Moralists*. Oxford: The Clarendon Press, 1897, Chapter 2, pp. 105–14. A classical statement of an earlier cognitivist nondefinist view.

Prichard, H. A. *Moral Obligation*. New York: Oxford University Press, 1950. These essays represent the most carefully worked out a priori model act cognitivist nondefinist view.

Reid, Thomas. *Essays on the Power of the Human Mind*. Edinburgh: Bell and Bradfute, 1808. Essays on the Active Powers, Vol. 3, Part 3, Chapters 5 and 6; Essay 5, Chapter 1.

Rice, Philip Blair. *On the Knowledge of Good and Evil*. New York: Random House, 1955, Chapter 2. A survey of various cognitivist nondefinist views.

Ross, W. D. *Foundations of Ethics*. Oxford: The Clarendon Press, 1939, Chapters 1, 8, and 11. A defense of cognitivistic nondefinism against some of its critics.

————. *The Right and the Good*. Oxford: The Clarendon Press, 1930, Chapters 1, 2, and 4. A thoroughly worked-out principle cognitivist nondefinist view.

Schilpp, Paul (ed.). *The Philosophy of G. E. Moore*. Evanston, Ill.; Northwestern University Press, 1942, pp. 535–611. Moore here attempts to answer criticisms.

Sidgwick, Henry. *The Methods of Ethics*. 7th ed. London: Macmillan & Co., Ltd., 1962. In the Preface to the 6th edition, Sidgwick suggests that we must hold that the principle of utility is known directly. Chapter 13 is a penetrating discussion of "intuitionism."

Toulmin, S. *An Examination of the Place of Reason in Ethics*. Cambridge: Cambridge University Press, 1950, Chapter 2. A criticism of cognitivist nondefinist property theories.

13

Noncognitivist Theories

We have examined cognitivistic definism and cognitivistic nondefinism and discovered that of all the cognitivist positions considered, one form of cognitivistic nondefinism best met the criteria of acceptability. Now we shall examine the noncognitive views and here, too, we shall find that one sort of noncognitive view best meets the criteria. It will then be left to the reader to decide between these two views, to propose a view which meets the criteria better than either, or to show that one of the rejected views can be restored.

A. The Tenets of Noncognitivism

Noncognitive theories differ from cognitive ones in that the noncognitivist denies two propositions the cognitivist asserts:

1. Moral judgments are capable of being objectively true.
1a. There is objective moral knowledge.

It is convenient, and perhaps necessary, to classify all noncognitivists as definists; that is, we interpret all noncognitivists as affirming, in common with cognitivist definists, another proposition:

2. Any moral judgment (judgment in which 'good' or 'bad', 'right' or 'wrong' is used in a moral sense) can be reduced or expanded by analysis or definition to another expression which has the same meaning or significance and contains no moral terms.

There is some danger in this classification, for not all noncognitivists would claim that a definition, in the strict sense of that term, can be given for moral judgments. For example Stevenson, although speaking of "definitions," points out that the subtlety of moral language cannot be captured by his formula:

X is good = $_{df}$ I approve of X, do so as well

Still he would claim that, although "X is good" is a more subtle instrument, and more effective than the other expression, this is not a difference in meaning. Other, more recent noncognitivists who hold that meaning is to be identified with use might argue that two expressions have the same meaning when they can be used to perform the same linguistic task. Obviously much more will have to be said about these theories, but it does not seem incorrect to claim that they are all interested in giving an analysis or definition of moral expressions, and so we shall call those who hold these theories definists.

1. **The Denial of Cognitivism.** The noncognitivist usually believes the noncognitive aspect of his theory to be a consequence of his analysis of moral judgments. He claims that moral judgments must be identified, at least in part, with other sorts of utterances—expressions of emotion, resolutions, commands, decisions, commendations, and so on. He then argues that, because moral judgments are analyzable in this way, and because a command or a decision is not capable of being objectively true, moral judgments also are not capable of being objectively true. The noncognitivist claims that this inference is legitimate, and sees his job as one of defending his analysis, and his claim that the sort of thing with which he identifies moral judgments is not the sort of thing which is capable of being objectively true.

2. **The Definism in Noncognitivistic Definism.** The naturalistic cognitivist definist offers various sorts of definitions, stipulative or reportive; and, because we are interpreting the noncognitivist as a definist, we must be aware of the sort of definition he offers. We saw in Chapter 12 that the cognitivist nondefinist who denies proposition 2 affirms the autonomy of ethics, and this means that he does not believe that ethics is reducible to some other field, such as sociology or psychology. But the noncognitivist, who offers a definition of moral judgments, does not thereby deny the autonomy of ethics, for he is not claiming that ethics must be reduced to some other discipline but, rather, that moral judgments are not translatable into the factual statements of some other field. Thus, the cognitivist nondefinist and the noncognitivist both affirm the autonomy of ethics, even if one believes that moral judgments may be defined and the other denies this.

B. Differences Among Noncognitive Views

Just as we were able to distinguish among naturalistic views on the basis of the definiens offered, so too we can distinguish among noncognitive views on the basis of the sort of expressions with which moral judgments are equated. According to A. J. Ayer, "ethical statements" are "simply expressions which can be neither true nor false." [1]

---

[1] A. J. Ayer, *Language, Truth and Logic* (New York: Dover Publications, Inc., 1936), pp. 102–103.

The exhortations to moral virtue are not propositions at all, but ejaculations or commands which are designed to provoke the reader to action of a certain sort. . . .

In saying that a certain type of action is right or wrong, I am not making any factual statement, not even a statement about my own state of mind. I am merely expressing certain moral sentiments.[2]

Suggestions of this sort were being made as early as 1934 when W. H. F. Barnes suggested that "value judgments in their origin are not strictly judgments at all. . . . They are exclamations expressive of approval." [3]

Thus, for Ayer, moral judgments are ejaculations or commands, not factual statements; and for Barnes, they are exclamations of approval or disapproval. One consequence of such an analysis is that moral judgments lack objective truth or falsity. Notice here that, according to Ayer, at least, moral judgments have *two* functions: an expressive one, and an imperative one. According to Ayer, then, even though moral judgments are sometimes phrased as declarative sentences, they actually convey no factual information in the way that other declarative sentences do. The only way that information might be conveyed is by the inferences we might make from the fact that someone used a sentence containing, for example, 'good'; but we can, of course, make inferences from the fact that a person has sneezed—yet this does not make the sneeze true or false.

The view that moral judgments are expressions of wishes, rather than expressions of emotions or commands, has been maintained by Bertrand Russell:

If, now, a philosopher says "Beauty is good," I may interpret him as meaning either "Would that everybody loved the beautiful" . . . or "I wish that everybody loved the beautiful." . . . —The first of these makes no assertion, but expresses a wish; since it affirms nothing, it is logically impossible that there should be evidence for or against it, or for it to possess either truth or falsehood. The second sentence, instead of being merely optative, does make a statement, but it is one about the philosopher's state of mind, and it could only be refuted by evidence that he does not have the wish that he says he has. This second sentence does not belong to ethics, but to psychology or biography. The first sentence, which does belong to ethics, expresses a desire for something, but asserts nothing.[4]

The reader might object at this point that expressions such as "I wish that such and such" are indeed true and false. If this objection is correct, all it means is that Russell is a cognitivist after all, but there are rather weighty reasons for not accepting this objection. It would be inappropriate to go too

---

[2] *Ibid.*, pp. 103, 107.

[3] W. H. F. Barnes, "A Suggestion about Value," *Analysis*, 1 (1934), 45.

[4] Bertrand Russell, *Religion and Science* (New York: Holt, Rinehart & Winston, Inc., 1935), pp. 236 ff. Notice here how the autonomy of ethics is defended.

deeply into these here, but we can point out that the expression "I wish that *p*," can be treated as a report of a wish we are making or have made (in which case it *is* either true or false) or it can be treated as a verbal manifestation of a wish (in which case it probably would be wrong to classify it among expressions that can be objectively true). Russell clearly meant it to be taken in the second sense, and if this is true, it follows that value judgments do not have a truth value.

Another suggestion for the analysis of moral judgments is provided by C. L. Stevenson, in his *Ethics and Language,* the first extended development of a noncognitivist meta-ethical theory. Stevenson begins by making a distinction between a *disagreement in belief* and a *disagreement in attitude.* A disagreement in belief is a disagreement about a matter of fact (and there are no ethical facts, according to Stevenson) and a disagreement in attitude is a dispute which involves a difference of opinion not about how things are but how they should be—it is "an opposition of purposes, aspirations, wants, preferences, desires, and so on." [5]

According to Stevenson, moral disputes are ones which involve, in an essential way, disagreements in attitude, and he suggests that it is possible to construct preliminary "working models" to emphasize this important fact. He carefully notices, however, that these "definitions" (the term is his) will not be adequate to the "subtleties of common usage," but adds that they will "preserve in rough form much that is essential to ethical analysis." His definitions, then, are:

1. "This is wrong" means *I disapprove of this; do so as well.*
2. "He ought to do this" means *I disapprove of his leaving this undone; do so as well.*
3. "This is good" means *I approve of this; do so as well.*[6]

Stevenson's point is that, whenever we make a moral judgment, we are doing more than saying that something has a certain property, or that we feel a certain way. Stevenson claims that moral judgments are expressions of attitudes, and are designed to get others to share those attitudes. Two points are important here: first, the models do not adequately show the expressive nature of moral judgments, for the first part of the definition is not so much an expression of an attitude as a claim that the speaker has that attitude; second, and more important, wheras Ayer speaks of the expression of *feelings* or *emotions,* Stevenson speaks of the expression of *attitudes,* and whereas Ayer sees moral judgments as an attempt to get someone to act in a certain way, Stevenson sees them as an attempt to redirect the attitudes of others.

[5] C. L. Stevenson, *Ethics and Language* (New Haven: Yale University Press, 1944), p. 3. By permission of the publisher.

[6] *Ibid.,* p. 21.

The distinction between expressing a feeling and expressing an attitude is stressed by Stevenson in the following passage:

The term "emotion" is introduced temporarily, since the term "emotive" [in 'emotive meaning'] suggests it; but hereafter it will be convenient to replace "emotion" by "feeling or attitude"—both to preserve terminological uniformity throughout the book and to emphasize an important distinction. The term "feeling" [Ayer's term] is to be taken as designating an affective state that reveals its full nature to immediate introspection, without the use of induction. An attitude, however, is much more complicated than that.... It is, in fact, itself a complicated conjunction of dispositional properties ... marked by stimuli and responses which relate to hindering or assisting whatever it is that is called the "object" of the attitude.[7]

An attitude, therefore, is more complex than a feeling, and it is a mark of the greater sophistication of Stevenson's theory that this difference is stressed.

Stevenson also introduced a distinction between *descriptive meaning* and *emotive meaning*. We shall not discuss Stevenson's working out of this distinction at this point (cf. pp. 320–322), but we can mention that it allows for a possibility which Ayer ignored—the possibility that a moral judgment may be an expression of an attitude or emotion and may communicate factual information as well. Thus the remark "S is courageous" not only expresses approval for S and invites others to share the speaker's attitue but also conveys something about the sort of behavior to expect from S in a dangerous situation.

The noncognitivist, however, would be quick to assert that the descriptive meaning does not exhaust the meaning of a moral judgment and that, even though (with respect to its descriptive meaning alone) it is capable of being objectively true, the analysis of a moral judgment consists of two parts: a cognitive part, which is capable of being objectively true, and a noncognitive part, which is not capable of being objectively true. He then argues that the judgment taken as a whole is, therefore, not capable of being objectively true. This is because the proper analysis of a moral judgment, according to the noncognitivist, is a conjunction of two elements, and since conjunction is a truth functional relation (a truth functional relation being one where the truth of the compoud is a function of the truth of its parts) if one of those parts cannot be assigned a truth value, the whole cannot be assigned a truth value either. More recent noncognitivists have accepted some parts of Stevenson's analysis but rejected others. On the whole, more emphasis has come to be placed upon the imperative role of moral judgments than on their expressive uses. R. M. Hare, for example, suggests that the primary function of the word 'good' is to commend, and that, "when we commend ... anything, it is

---

[7] *Ibid.*, pp. 59–60.

always in order, at least indirectly, to guide choices, our own or other people's, now or in the future." [8]

In discussing words such as 'right' the imperative function naturally plays an even greater part in Hare's analysis. He says that such words as 'right' and 'ought' "are used primarily for giving advice or instruction, or in general for guiding choices." [9] Further he claims that the word 'ought' is used for "prescribing." [10]

Like Stevenson, Hare makes a distinction between two kinds of meaning a moral judgment may have, but he speaks of "descriptive" meaning and "evaluative" (rather than "emotive") meaning. We can best characterize the evaluative meaning of 'good', according to Hare, by saying that 'good' is used to commend, and we can best characterize the evaluative meaning of the word 'right' by saying that it is used to prescribe, but both of these uses have, Hare feels, a function of guiding choices.

It would be unfair to Hare's analysis to suggest that "X is good" means exactly the same as "I hereby commend X," for we would have failed to take into account the descriptive meaning, which varies from case to case. But it would be correct to say that he feels that the element of a judgment such as "X is good" which remains constant is the commendatory element, and this is the reason that Hare takes the evaluative meaning as primary and the descriptive meaning as secondary. He argues that if S says, at one time, "That is good," and later, speaking of a different kind of thing, uses the same words, he is both times using 'good' to commend, but is commending the objects being judged on the basis of their having different properties. If we know what the object is, we can sometimes figure out the descriptive meaning of 'good'; but even if we do not know what the object is, we always know the evaluative meaning of 'good'—that is, we know that it is being used to commend.

Each of these positions appeals to certain facts about the way we use moral language. But some philosophers have come to believe that a really adequate theory must take account of the vastly differing uses to which moral language can be put. The suggestion has been made, therefore, that even though there is something distinctive about moral judgments, and even though they should not be treated as objectively true or false, no account of them which mentions merely one or two functions can be accepted.

P. H. Nowell-Smith, another contemporary English philosopher, for example, has suggested a theory sometimes called *multifunctionalism*, according to which value words:

---

[8] R. M. Hare, *The Language of Morals* (Oxford: The Clarendon Press, 1952), p. 127. By permission of The Clarendon Press, Oxford.

[9] *Ibid.*, p. 155.

[10] *Ibid.*

... are used to express tastes and preferences, to express decisions and choices, to criticize, grade and evaluate, to advise, admonish, warn, persuade and dissuade, to praise, encourage and reprove, to promulgate and draw attention to rules; and doubtless for other purposes also.[11]

Yet Nowell-Smith believes that these activities fall into a family of cases, for he holds that "the central activities for which moral language is used are choosing and advising others to choose." [12]

We have, it seems, come a long way. The early noncognitivists maintained that moral judgments are to be treated as expressions of emotion or as disguised commands. Great sophistication was added to noncognitivistic meta-ethics by Stevenson, and further refinements were made by Hare and Nowell-Smith, yet all of them hold that moral judgments cannot be completely identified with statements and, therefore, are not capable of being objectively true.

Exercises

Review
1. What are the tenets of noncognitivism? How do noncognitivist views differ from cognitivist definist views?
2. What is the *autonomy of ethics* and how do the noncognitivist and the cognitivist nondefinist differ from the naturalistic definist on this matter?
3. By what methods can a number of noncognitivist views be distinguished?
4. What analysis does Ayer give of *ethical statements*? Why is this not a type of subjective naturalist theory?
5. Why is the position of Bertrand Russell discussed in this chapter properly describable as noncognitivistic?
6. How does Stevenson's view differ from Ayer's?
7. What use does Stevenson make of the distinction between descriptive meaning and emotive meaning?
8. Compare Hare's analysis with that of Stevenson.
9. What does Hare mean when he says that the descriptive meaning is secondary and the evaluative meaning is primary? What argument does he give to establish this point?
10. In what ways would Nowell-Smith agree with Hare about the nature of the judgment "X is good"? How would they disagree?

Applications
1. Consider the formula (used by the noncognitivist): "Moral judgments are really ——————————." Russell fills the blank with 'expressions of wishes', and Ayer with 'expressions of emotion'. Think of a number of other ways to fill in the blank so that a new noncognitivistic analysis is provided. E.g., "Moral judgments are really resolutions (to be distinguished from reports of resolutions)."

[11] P. H. Nowell-Smith, *Ethics* (Baltimore: Penguin Books, Inc., 1954), p. 98.
[12] *Ibid.*, p. 11.

2. To the best of your ability, apply the criteria of acceptability to the theories you have invented in answer to Question 1.
3. Consider carefully the following claims:
   a. Expressions of attitudes are not capable of being objectively true.
   b. Wishes are not capable of being objectively true.
   c. Commands are not capable of being objectively true.
   d. Promises are not capable of being objectively true.
   e. Resolutions are not capable of being objectively true.
   What is being asserted by these statements? Try to decide whether they are true or not. If necessary, review the distinction between 'true' and 'objectively true' introduced in Chapter 10.
4. What is it to "commend" something? Look up 'commend' in the *Oxford English Dictionary*. Does this help provide an answer? Why, or why not?

C. Defense of the Tenets of Noncognitivism

According to the noncognitivist, Propositions 1 and 1a are false. That is, the noncognitivist believes that moral judgments are not capable of being objectively true and that there is no objective moral knowledge. Yet this conclusion is not one which the noncognitivist sets out to establish; rather, it is one which he takes to follow from his analysis of moral judgments, and which he has come to believe he must live with. The crucial thing for the noncognitivist is his analysis of moral judgments, and noncognitivists believe that no moral judgment is a report of some actual property or object. Most recent noncognitivists would claim that there is a sense in which moral judgments do convey information, but only about natural properties or objects.

The noncognitivist very often arrives at his conclusion about Propositions 1 and 1a by the following chain of reasoning:

1. If two expressions are identical in meaning or significance, then if one of them is not capable of being objectively true, neither is the other.
2. Given any moral judgment, it is identical in meaning or significance with some expression which is not capable of being objectively true.
3. Therefore, given any moral judgment, it is not capable of being objectively true.

The noncognitivist feels confident in his affirmation of Premise 1 of this argument, and also in the argument's validity. It is Premise 2 that requires the support. Because there are many different sorts of noncognitivism, there are as many noncognitivistic proofs of Premise 2 as there are noncognitive theories. One of our main tasks in assessing noncognitive theories, therefore, is to examine carefully the arguments given for, and the interpretations placed upon, Premise 2.

A critic of noncognitivism might agree that the above argument is valid and that Premise 1 is true. But he might replace the Premise 2 with

3'. Given any moral judgment, it is capable of being objectively true.

And he would replace the conclusion with:

2′. Given any moral judgment, it is not identical in meaning or significance with some expression which is not capable of being objectively true.

Now it is clear that 3′ is simply the denial of 3, and 2′ is the denial of 2. The question is: Is 2 or 3′ more plausible? We have already had occasion to examine some of the arguments which a cognitivist nondefinist might offer for 3′. The noncognitivist's reply will have to consist in an adequate defense of 2 and a rebuttal of the opposing arguments for 3′. Therefore, it is important for the proponent of noncognitivism to discover the best type of noncognitivist analysis of moral judgments, for it is only by doing so that 2 can be made plausible. Our job, therefore, in the next section, will be to isolate the non-cognitivist analysis of the nature of moral judgments which best satisfies the criteria of acceptability. Our approach will be historical, for there has been a gradual evolution of non-cognitivist theories, a new theory arising to remedy the defects of an older, discredited, one.

Exercises

Review
1. How does the noncognitivist arrive at his claim that moral judgments are not objectively true?
2. Why may no general proof of Premise 2 of the non-cognitivist's argument be given?
3. What argument might the cognitivist offer in reply to the noncognitivist? How could it be decided which of these arguments is better?

Applications
1. Review the arguments of the cognitivist nondefinist presented in Chapter 12, and show how they can be used to support 3′.
2. Construct two arguments, one leading from 1 and 2 to 3, and one leading from 1 and 3′ to 2′, only rewrite the premises and the conclusion so that the validity of the arguments is clearly revealed.

D. Narrowing the Field

1. *Early Emotivism.* Very often, when noncognitive views are criticized, the theory presented by A. J. Ayer receives much of the criticism. According to Ayer, moral judgments must be treated as expressions of emotion and/or commands, and this view has come to be called by the (at first rather pejorative) name of *emotivism*. There are few reasons for believing that there is nothing more to a moral judgment than an expression of emotion, and many reasons for believing that, when we say of something that it is good, we are saying more than "Hurrah!"

No strong arguments have been offered in support of the earliest forms of noncognitivism. The theory probably gained acceptance because of its compatibility with logical positivism, which was very popular in the 1920s, the 1930s, and the 1940s. Other reasons for the success of Ayer's version of noncognitivism might range from the force and vivacity of his presentation to the fact that the aspect of moral judgments which he stressed had been long neglected. But the fact that we very often feel emotions when we make moral judgments does not show that moral judgments must be *identified* with the expression of emotions, and Ayer did make such an identification, even if he did not argue precisely in this way.

Perhaps the failure to have positive arguments in its favor would not seem so damaging to the early emotivists if their theory did not go counter to many of the more obvious facts of our experience, and if there were not so many seemingly effective counterexamples to their view. Let us suppose, first, that the theory is an attempt to tell us what we are really doing when we make a moral judgment. That is, let us suppose Ayer is suggesting that, when we say "X is good," we are really and in fact doing just what we do when we say something like "Hurrah for X!" The latter expression is usually taken to be the model of an overflow of strong feeling, but it is quite possible to say that something is good without feeling strongly about it. In fact, we may even say that X is good, and be rather sorry that it is so.

Similarly, if moral judgments are taken to be commands, it is difficult to see how we can account for the fact that we make moral judgments about past events. For example, we might now make the judgment that Caesar was wrong to cross the Rubicon, but we certainly cannot now command Caesar not to cross the Rubicon.[13] This difficulty is sometimes met by the claim that we are not commanding Caesar but, rather, we are commanding our contemporaries or even ourselves. But commanding them to do what? Certainly not to refrain from leading their armies across the Rubicon. And what about the silent moral judgments we make to ourselves? If the command analysis is correct, we must be commanding ourselves not to do something when we say that that thing is wrong—but this is a peculiar notion indeed, for it is unlikely that any of us need to be commanded, by anyone else or by ourselves, not to lead our armies across the Rubicon. Nor will it help to suggest that, when we say "What Caesar did was wrong," we are commanding ourselves (or others) to refrain from doing some analogous action, for example to refrain from being hasty or from disturbing the present political scene. If that were true, we would be forced to accept the totally implausible claim that our judgment about Caesar's action is really not about Caesar's action

---

[13] In fact we could not have commanded Caesar not to cross the Rubicon had we been alive in Caesar's day, for there were no people in a position to *command* Caesar to do anything: yet anyone could say that what he did, or was contemplating doing, was wrong.

at all (crossing the Rubicon) but rather about some action of our own, actual or possible.

So far we have been talking about a reportive definition or analysis; but what has been said is sufficient to show that any stipulation to the effect that 'good' and 'right' should be used in these ways would be open to simliar criticisms. Thus, if we resolve to allow "X is good" to mean "Hurrah for X!" and "A is right" to mean "Do A!," we should have to invent some other words to serve the functions that 'good' and 'right' now serve; and one may well ask what is to be gained from this. The answer, we think, is: "Nothing at all."

Another objection to early emotivism seems, by itself, to be totally effective against that view. Suppose we see some object and we feel a liking for it. Suppose we smile. Our smile might be said to be an "expression" of our favorable emotion, but it is clear that there is no way to "prove" our smile. We can perhaps explain why we smiled, but we cannot—and need not—justify it. But moral judgments are quite different from this, although it is impossible for the emotivist to say so. We can explain why we made a moral judgment, but we can also attempt to prove, to establish, or to give reasons for our moral judgments—and such a policy is not open to one who equates moral judgments with mere expressions of emotion. The conflict which arises between two people, one of whom says "That is good" and the other of whom says "That is bad" is different from the conflict between two people, one of whom cheers and the other of whom boos at a baseball game, and this difference is something for which this version of noncognitivism is utterly unable to account.

In fact, this inability to account for moral reasoning has been the major criticism leveled against all noncognitivist theories, and much of the work of the noncognitivists in recent years has been to show how moral reasoning is not inconsistent with their theories. Richard B. Brandt, for example, suggests that, for the noncognitivist like Ayer, there is no logic in arguments about moral judgments at all:

The "logic" of ethical reasoning, then, is thought to be quite different from that of reasoning in science and mathematics. Indeed there is no "logic" at all. Anything goes that works.[14]

Another critic of noncognitivism, Philip Blair Rice, tells us:

Now this aspect of the emotivist position [viz. the notion of there being not a logical relation between the premises of an argument about value and its conclusion, but only a psychological one] has led to the charge that its proponents are

[14] Richard B. Brandt, *Ethical Theory* (Englewood Cliffs, N.J.: Prentice-Hall, Inc., © 1959), p. 211. Reprinted by permission of the publisher.

opening the doors to all sorts of irrationalism, even that they provide a justification for unprincipled rhetoricians with dictatorial ambitions who make "doublethink" their stock in trade. Such conclusions the emotivists ... have repudiated with horror. But it still remains possible to ask whether they have squared their theories as so far propounded with their convictions.[15]

Stephen Toulmin criticizes what he calls the "subjective" view (by which he means noncognitivism) on identical grounds, calling this feature "the fatal weakness of the subjective approach":

> What we want to know is in which of these discussions the arguments presented were *worthy* of acceptance, and the reasons given *good* reasons; in which of them persuasion was achieved at least in part by valid reasoning, and in which agreement was obtained by means of *mere* persuasion—fine rhetoric unsupported by valid arguments or good reasons. And it is over the criteria (or rather) the complete lack of criteria) given for the validity of ethical arguments that the most telling objection to this (and any) subjective theory arise.[16]

There are two ways to interpret these criticisms. First, they may be suggesting that, because noncognitivism makes it impossible to argue about or defend moral judgments, it is itself an immoral view and ought to be rejected. We shall not be concerned with criticisms of this sort—they are similar to "proofs" of God's existence which depend upon the claim that, if men do not recognize that there is a God, they will misbehave. But there is another interpretation of these arguments which has more force. According to the third criterion for the acceptability of theories, it is important for a theory to be able to account for the phenomena, and, it might be argued, one phenomenon which any meta-ethical theory must account for is the obvious and unquestionable role of moral reasoning and argumentation. To the degree that the noncognitivist cannot account for this role, or is forced to deny it, his theory lacks plausibility.

Ayer did not believe that there is any sense in which moral judgments are subject to proof, and his is one of a few noncognitivistic theories that openly espouses this claim. Ayer claimed that moral judgments "have no objective validity whatsoever." [17] and that "it is plain that the conclusion that it is impossible to dispute about questions of value follows from our theory also." [18] Furthermore, he claimed:"... the man who is ostensibly contradicting me is merely expressing his moral sentiments. So that there is plainly no

[15] P. B. Rice, *On the Knowledge of Good and Evil* (New York: Random House, 1955), pp. 67–68.

[16] Stephen Toulmin, *The Place of Reason in Ethics* (Cambridge: Cambridge University Press, 1950), p. 38.

[17] Ayer, *op. cit.*, p. 108.

[18] *Ibid.*, p. 110.

sense in asking which of us is in the right. For neither of us is asserting a genuine proposition.[19]

But it is one thing to say that moral judgments are not objectively true (as all noncognitivists do) and another to say that it is impossible to dispute about value. Most noncognitivists would reject the latter claim, and this is well, for the fact that there are moral disputes, and that very often reasons are relevant in deciding moral questions, is one of the most important phenomena to be explained by any meta-ethical theory. A theory which claims otherwise must make a stronger case than has been made by Ayer.

Exercises

Review

1. Are there any facts of ordinary experience to which early emotivism seems to go counter? What are they?
2. Ayer's theory actually contained two elements. What are they?
3. What stand did the early emotivists take on the possibility of moral reasoning?
4. How has the emotivists' conception of moral reasoning been used as a criticism of their view?

Applications

1. There are many situations where we take ourselves to be engaging in genuine moral disputes and arguments, offering reasons for and against the moral judgments of other people. Give an emotivist explanation of this phenomenon and then apply the criteria of acceptability to this explanation.
2. Present and then give arguments for an emotivist analysis of 'good' and 'bad', and compare this with the arguments which could be given for an emotivist analysis of 'right' and 'wrong'. Are there any crucial differences? Attack both sets of arguments. Are the same counter-arguments always equally effective?

2. Stevenson's Theory. When we turn to the noncognitivistic theory proposed by C. L. Stevenson, the question is whether or not it can escape the objections raised against Ayer's view. The objections to the earliest formulations of noncognitivism were that although there were no compelling reasons to be given for the view, there were many strong reasons against it. The most important of these was that it could not account for the existence of moral reasoning, and for the rational assessment of moral judgments.

a. THEORIES OF MEANING AND NONCOGNITIVISM. Until recently, it was customary to distinguish three distinct theories of meaning: *the referential theory, the ideational theory,* and *the behavioristic theory.*[20] According to the referential theory, the meaning of a word which refers is the object to which it

---

[19] *Ibid.,* pp. 107–108.

[20] A critical discussion of these theories can be found in W. P. Alston's *Philosophy of Language* (Englewood Cliffs, N.J.: Prentice-Hall, Inc., 1964), Chapter 2.

refers. The proponents of this theory hold that the meaning of a sentence is a function of the meanings of the words in it, and if a word (with the exception of logical words such as 'or', 'if', or 'and') fails to refer, it is meaningless, and the sentence containing it is meaningless too. The ideational theorist holds that the meaning of a word is the idea it calls up in the mind of the man who is presented with it or, perhaps, with the *tendency* of that word to call up an idea. The proponent of the behavioristic theory maintains that the meaning of a word or sentence is a function of the behavior it elicits, or at least of the behavior it tends to elicit.

Ayer held a version of the referential theory of meaning, and although the form of noncognitivism he adopted is compatible with that theory of meaning, it does not seem to be necessitated by it. Stevenson held a similar meta-ethical theory, but opted for quite a different theory of meaning. One of the interesting differences between Ayer's theory and Stevenson's theory is that Stevenson employed his theory of meaning, a form of the ideational theory, in order to explain some of the crucial notions he used. For example, he made a distinction between a disagreement in belief and a disagreement in attitude, and it is largely the contrast between descriptive meaning and emotive meaning which makes this distinction intelligible. Let us see how he does this.

His theory of meaning identifies the meaning of an expression with the idea it gives rise to in the mind of a hearer. One of the earliest defenders of such a theory was John Locke (1632–1714), whose ideational theory has been characterized by William P. Alston:

> Let us see what would have to be the case for this theory to work. For each linguistic expression, or rather for each distinguishable sense of a linguistic expression, there would have to be an idea such that when any expression is used in that sense, it is used as an indication of the presence of that idea. This presumably means that whenever an expression is used in that sense, 1. the idea must be present in the mind of the speaker, and 2. the speaker must be producing the expression in order to get the audience to realize that the idea in question is in his mind at that time. Finally, 3. insofar as communication is successful, the expression would have to call up the same idea in the mind of the hearer, with analogous qualifications as to an "unthinking" grasp of what was being said that might hold on some, though not on all, occasions.[21]

Stevenson is quick to disassociate himself from this form of the view and he specifies that meaning is not a "specific psychological process," but rather a "dispositional property." Thus, Stevenson denies that one and only one idea accompanies the occurrence of a word and constitutes its meaning; he maintains, rather, that each word has a tendency to cause certain psychological processes—a tendency that constitutes the meaning of the word.

[21] *Ibid.*, pp. 23–24.

Stevenson attempts to explain his term by drawing an analogy between the dispositional property of a word and another sort of dispositional property we all understand—that of coffee to stimulate. Coffee tends to stimulate the drinker, and this disposition is relatively constant. In the same way, according to Stevenson, meaning is a disposition to cause psychological processes. Meanings, however, are limited to the dispositional properties of signs of a certain kind:

A sign's disposition to affect a hearer is to be called a "meaning" . . . only if it has been caused by, and would not have developed without, an elaborate process of conditioning which has attended the sign's use in communication.[22]

According to Stevenson, this distinguishes a generic sense of 'meaning'—a dispositional property of a sign which has developed in language. It is now possible to follow Stevenson further in distinguishing the two kinds of meaning referred to above. *Emotive meaning* is said to be "a meaning in which the response (from the hearer's point of view) or the stimulus (from the speaker's point of view) is a range of emotions." [23] Later on, 'emotion' is replaced by 'feeling' or 'attitude'.[24]

Descriptive meaning, on the other hand, is distinguished from emotive meaning by the psychological reaction that serves as the stimulus or the response. Stevenson suggests that "a sign's descriptive meaning is its disposition to produce cognitive mental processes, where 'cognitive' is to be taken as a general term designating such specific kinds of mental activity as believing, thinking, supposing, presuming, and so on." [25] As Stevenson himself admits, the notion of a dispositional property is far from clear. He suggests that in his treatment of the notion "accuracy will have to be sacrificed to simplicity." [26] This is unfortunate, for it is one of the crucial notions of his analysis. Let us suppose, however, that we understand this notion, and then consider his claim that there is a generic sense of 'meaning' with at least two species.

The descriptive meaning of a sign is said to be the disposition that sign has to cause mental states such as believing, supposing, thinking, presuming, and so on. But can the meaning of 'car' really be identified with such a "disposition," or does 'car' have that disposition because of its meaning? A word can have a meaning before having the requisite disposition, and for this reason alone it does not seem likely that meaning is to be equated with a dispositional property. Suppose that a scientist discovers a new element, and

---

[22] Stevenson, *op. cit.*, p. 57.
[23] *Ibid.*, p. 59.
[24] Cf. above fn. 7.
[25] Stevenson, *op. cit.*, p. 62.
[26] *Ibid.*, p. 46.

gives it the name 'crepton'. Now that word has a meaning, though it certainly does not have a disposition to cause any beliefs in anyone but the scientist. If the scientist goes home and forgets the name, 'crepton' will not have a disposition to cause any ideas in anyone. But it still has a meaning, for it has been recorded in the scientist's journal, and in due time people will learn its meaning.

The difficulties with the notion of emotive meaning are even more serious. There is no reason whatsoever to think that, because a word has certain effects, these effects have to be counted a part of its meaning. The word 'good' may cause others to approve, but there is no reason for saying that this causal power is part of its meaning. The word 'evil' may frighten people, or thrill them, but neither of these effects should be counted as part of its meaning.

Finally, if there is another theory of meaning which is more acceptable than Stevenson's, which accounts for more features of language, and which is open to fewer counterexamples and subject to less criticism, Stevenson's account is accordingly weakened. But if Stevenson's ideational theory of meaning fails, what becomes of his meta-ethical theory? It may well be, then, that some new theory of meaning can succeed in making Stevenson's essential distinctions; if so, a rejection of his theory of meaning does not entail a rejection of his noncognitivism. But there are other objections to the form of noncognitivism proposed by Stevenson—and these do not depend upon the rejection of his theory of meaning.

b. STEVENSON'S THEORY AND MORAL ARGUMENTS. If Stevenson's account of the nature of moral judgments is to be more acceptable, it will have to be more truly descriptive of what we do when we make moral judgments, and it will have to provide a place for, and an explanation of, moral argumentation. Stevenson seems to be attempting to give a descriptive account of what goes on when we make, and attempt to defend, moral judgments (although he has denied this). Let us here treat his account as descriptive. If it turns out to be inaccurate, then the reasons for accepting a proposal that we view moral reasoning and argumentation in the way he suggests will have to be supported by even stronger considerations.

Stevenson introduces two "patterns of analysis." Both, however, place some emotive element in the meaning of a moral judgment. The sample "definitions" we have given come from the first pattern of analysis, and the contribution of the second pattern is to introduce explicitly the descriptive meaning of a moral judgment. Because both patterns contain an emotive element, it will be sufficient for our purposes to concentrate on the first pattern. If we remember the "models" set up by Stevenson, we will remember that his analysis of "X is good" is "I approve of X, do so as well." Although the first part of this analysis (a), "I approve of X," can be said to be either true or false, the second part (b), "Do so as well," is not. In the words of Stevenson:

Sentence (a) offers no trouble. . . . Sentence (b), however, raises a question. Since it is an imperative, it is not open to proof at all. What is it like to prove a command? [27]

In a later work, Stevenson makes this point more clearly:

. . . [Reasons that are given] cannot, of course, be judged by the rules of deductive or inductive logic. That is precluded by the very notion of reasons for approving, which fall outside logic simply because they require inferences . . . from belief-expressing sentences to attitude-expressing sentences.[28]

A similar point is also made by Lars Bergstrom, who presents the argument in question in the following way:

(i) if "$A_1, \ldots A_n$, therefore B_1" is a (logically) valid inference, then $A_1, \ldots A_n$ and B_1 are either true or false. (This assumption is part of a general idea of what it means for an inference to be valid, and the negation of (i) is in fact inconsistent with many proposed definitions of "valid inference.")
(ii) Imperative sentences are neither true nor false.
(iii) Therefore, imperative sentences can be neither premisses nor conclusions in a valid inference.[29]

The argument, as Bergstrom sees it, applies to imperative sentences but may be generalized to apply to many more types of sentences. For example, expressions of emotion, commands, wishes, orders, advice, and so on all might be denied a truth value, and thus fall into the scheme presented above.

The belief that noncognitivists cannot account for the justification of moral judgments often rests upon an acceptance of some argument such as the one set down by Bergstrom. There are several ways of reacting to such a suggestion. Many contemporary noncognitivists are inclined to deny the first premise of the argument. Others, such as Ayer and Stevenson, seem willing to accept the premises and to suggest either that there is no way to argue about moral judgments or that the relation between the premises and the conclusion is merely a psychological one. The first alternative seems to be the one taken by Ayer; the latter is the one taken by Stevenson. It has also

[27] *Ibid.*, p. 26.
[28] Stevenson, "Relativism and Nonrelativism in the Theory of Value," reprinted as Essay 5 in C. L. Stevenson, *Facts and Values* (New Haven: Yale University Press, 1963), pp. 84–85.
[29] Lars Bergstrom, *Imperatives and Ethics* (Stockholm: Filosofiska Institutionen uvid Stockholms Universitet, 1962), p. 32.

been suggested that there is some kind of "evaluative" inference, different from inductive or deductive reasoning, and peculiar to ethical arguments. Let us examine Stevenson's proposal that the relation between the reasons and the judgment being defended is merely causal and psychological.

If ethical disagreement is essentially a disagreement in attitude, the point of ethical argumentation must be to secure agreement in attitude. It would seem, then, that a good reason is one which achieves this end, which causes the opponent to alter his attitudes. The reason supports the conclusion, then, when it alters the hearer's attitudes in the direction desired. Stevenson is explicit about this point. In speaking about reasons given in support of a moral judgment, he says:

> These reasons cannot be called "proofs" in any but a dangerously extended sense, nor are they demonstratively or inductively related to an imperative; but they manifestly do *support* an imperative. They "back it up," or "establish it," or "base it on concrete references to fact." . . . The *way* in which the reasons support the imperative is simply this: The imperative is used to alter the hearer's attitudes or actions. . . . The supporting reason . . . describes the situation which the imperative seeks to alter, or the new situation which the imperative seeks to bring about; and if these facts disclose that the new situation will satisfy a preponderance of the hearer's desires, he will hesitate to obey no longer. More generally, reasons support imperatives by altering such beliefs as may in turn alter an unwillingness to obey.[30]

But reasons support ethical judgments psychologically rather than logically:

> The reasons which support or attack an ethical judgment have previously been mentioned. Subject to some exceptions that will be noted as we proceed, they are related to the judgment psychologically rather than logically. They do not strictly imply the judgment in the way that axioms imply theorems; nor are they related to the judgment inductively, as statements describing observations are related to scientific laws. Rather, they support the judgment in the way that reasons support imperatives.[31]

Thus it is safe to conclude that Stevenson did not believe that the reasons we ordinarily give in support of our moral judgments can have any relation, other than a causal or a psychological one, to the conclusions we draw. What makes a reason good, then, is its ability to bring about the change in attitude we desire.

c. "EXCEPTIONS" TO STEVENSON'S CONCLUSIONS. Stevenson attempts to show that there are some exceptions to his claim that the only relation be-

---

[30] Stevenson, *Ethics and Language, op. cit.*, pp. 27–28.
[31] *Ibid.*, p. 113.

tween the premises and the conclusion of a moral argument is a psychological
or causal one. This would suggest that he was not quite satisfied with the
conclusion that effectiveness was the only criterion for a good argument. In
this section we shall show that, according to his own theory, Stevenson is
unable to allow these exceptions, and that he is indeed committed to the view
that effectiveness in reasons is all that anyone has a right to demand.

Here is one example of a purported exception, a place where ordinary
logical validity enters into an ethical argument:

Example (1) A: It would be a good thing to have a dole for the unemployed.
B: But you have just said that a dole would weaken people's sense
of independence and you have admitted that *nothing* which
has that consequence is good.[32]

If there is a logical support here, where is it? What is it, exactly, that is
being supported? And how? According to Stevenson, B has pointed out a
"formal inconsistency" in A's position. But the logic was used to deduce an
ethical conclusion (i.e., "the dole is not good") from a set of premises, one of
which is ethical. This conclusion was then set against another, conflicting,
ethical proposition. No ethical conclusions were established; all that was
shown was that A is committed to two incompatible claims and, in order
to be consistent, he must abandon one.

But, in light of what Stevenson has already said about validity, logic, and
value judgments, how can he say this? How, on his view, can the following
be a logical inference?

X has P.
Anything with P is not good.
Therefore, X is not good.

If, as Stevenson says, validity is tied to truth and falsity, and if the conclusion of this argument is a moral judgment and therefore neither true nor
false, how can it be said to follow from the premises? Yet it certainly is necessary that it follow from the premises for logic to play even the simple role it is
supposed to have played, for what we have there is (a) a statement that the
dole is good, and (b) a statement that the dole has P and nothing with P is
good. From (b) we get the claim that the dole is not good, but how do we
do this if what has been said about validity and truth and falsity by Stevenson
is allowed? We do not have the inconsistency until (a) and the conclusion
of (b) are juxtaposed, but it is difficult to see, on the theory being considered,
how we are to bring this about.

[32] *Ibid.*, pp. 115–16.

Let us consider another example:

Example (4) A: Their friends are all of them shamelessly immoral.

B: Not knowing them all, you should not generalize so sweepingly.

A: I know a great number of them, such as C and D and E . . ., and their immorality gives my judgment no little support.[33]

The judgment which is supposed to be supported by logical means here is the claim that their friends are all immoral. But if this judgment is not capable of being objectively true, and if an ethical argument must consist of premises and a conclusion which are capable of being objectively true in order to be deductively valid, the same must be the case for inductive validity. Thus, again on Stevenson's principles, it is not possible to show that there is any more to an argument than its effectiveness. This means that, although it might be possible to account for the use of logic in arguments about value, it is not possible for Stevenson to do so; therefore, his defense of non-cognitivism does not explain satisfactorily the facts of ethical argumentation.

d. WHY USE A PARTICULAR FORM OF ARGUMENT? Stevenson makes another attempt to escape the objection that the only good reason is one which works and that the best is the one which works best. He suggests that the expression 'good reason' is itself a normative notion, and that when someone says that one makes use of "good" reasons, he is making a normative judgment:

Any decision about what methods are to be used, if it cannot be made with reference to validity, is itself a normative ethical matter. . . .

To evaluate or recommend an ethical method (whenever validity can have no bearing on the case) is to moralize about the ways of moralists. . . .

There are any number of grounds for choice between methods; and if in certain cases these do not depend upon validity, it does not follow that they depend on oratorical strategy.[34]

When we ask what some of these grounds might be, the answer that we get is this:

Certain factors may incline . . . [one] to use persuasive methods. Perhaps his hearer is blinded by wishful thinking to all reasons which undermine his present attitudes, and persuasion is a necessary preliminary to making him "listen to reason." . . . On the other hand, certain factors may incline him to use rational methods. He may believe that the attitudes of the hearer, if directed to objects of whose nature and consequences he remains ignorant, will express themselves in actions of a blundering, disorganized sort. Reasons may remedy this ignorance, whereas persuasion may conceal it.[35]

[33] *Ibid.*, p. 117.
[34] *Ibid.*, pp. 158, 156.
[35] *Ibid.*, pp. 156–57.

Let us grant that sometimes we feel that one type of persuasion is called for, and that at other times we feel that some other type is required. Suppose A wants to get B to believe, to do, or to approve of something, and that he is faced with two ways to bring this about—a rational way, and a nonrational way. Even if, as is sometimes the case, the nonrational way is quicker and more efficient, A might choose the other way—and often we will agree that he has made the correct choice. From this it would seem that effectiveness is not always considered to be the only criterion in choosing a method—although it is probably necessary that any method, to be approved, must be, in some measure, effective.

But let us pause here and consider the following answer to the above argument. Perhaps the claim that effectiveness is the only criterion for a good reason could be made plausible by insisting that the end which is sought be specified more clearly than just "getting B to believe, to do, or to approve of something"; for otherwise it really would make no difference which methods we employ. It might be suggested that what is really desired from a good reason is that it gets B to believe something, for example, without making him look foolish by his submission to our nonrational persuasion, or without ourselves engaging in any type of persuasion we would not like to have tried on us. Perhaps the rational means of persuasion will, in fact, be more effective in attaining this end; and so Stevenson might be able to claim that the truly effective method is the one which satisfies the more complex set of criteria—a form of effectiveness to be clearly distinguished from persuasion at any cost and by any means.

This reply has the effect of removing some of the disturbing features from the claim, to which Stevenson seems to be committed, that effectiveness is the only criterion of a good reason, but it raises further embarrassing questions. Suppose we are faced with the task of persuading someone of something, and we have the option to engage in quick and efficient nonrational persuasion or in slower but rational argumentation. That is, according to the argument now being examined, we can choose between ends: to persuade someone or to persuade him rationally. Why, Stevenson must be asked, is one end preferable to another? It is difficult to see how this question could be answered by the theory under consideration, and furthermore, it is difficult to know why reasons in support of one end would be required to be rational reasons rather than merely effective ones.

We have interpreted Ayer as offering a description of what we do when we make a moral judgment, and we have suggested that he is wrong in describing the situation as he does. It is also tempting to treat Stevenson as offering a descriptive account (giving a reportive definition) of the meanings of moral expressions. We have criticized his account as though it were such an account, but there are reasons for believing that he is, instead, offering a nonarbitrary stipulation. For example, he says that in *Ethics and Language* he was making a "deliberately prescriptive proposal." [36] This could not be inferred from the work itself but, if he is offering a proposal, what reasons are there for accepting it? Those who proposed the ideal-observer theory at least could argue that certain advantages were to be gained from its acceptance (cf. pp. 250–51); but none of these advantages would follow the acceptance of Stevenson's proposal. If we examine the advantages listed by Brandt in accepting the ideal-observer theory, we see that one of the more important is that moral judgments are thereby made subject to objective criticism. One of the serious disadvantages of Stevenson's proposal is that it does not accomplish this. Given that later noncognitivist positions have attempted to make a place for objective criticism, and for logic in ethics, it would seem that in this most important respect they are to be preferred to Stevenson's theory.

Exercises

Review

1. Discuss the three theories of meaning mentioned at the beginning of section 2 (p. 319). What theory of meaning does Ayer hold in *Language, Truth and Logic?* How does this differ from Stevenson's theory of meaning as presented in *Ethics and Language?*
2. How does Stevenson's theory of meaning differ from the traditional ideational theories of meaning?
3. What distinction does Stevenson make between descriptive meaning and emotive meaning?
4. What criticisms were given of Stevenson's theory of meaning?
5. Does Stevenson's view of moral argumentation differ relevantly from Ayer's? If so, how does it differ?
6. What sort of support does Stevenson think we can give to moral judgments?
7. Discuss Stevenson's account of the meaning of moral judgments, first as an attempt to report what people who make moral judgments mean by what they say, and then as a deliberately prescriptive proposal.

3. *Hare's Theory.* Hare, unlike Stevenson and like Ayer, is not making a proposal about how we should view moral judgments; rather, he is presenting a description or a report of how moral language works.[37]

Hare believes that the function of moral principles is to guide conduct and, as such, moral judgments form a subclass of what he calls *prescriptive lan-*

---

[36] Cf. a passage from an interesting letter written by Stevenson in which this claim is made. This can be found in Cynthia Schuster, "Peter Glassen on Moral Judgments," *Mind,* 70 (1961), 95–98.

[37] In discussing the meaning of 'good' Hare quites from the *Oxford English Dictionary,* and in another place he says "And since what we are trying to do is to give an account of the word 'good' as it *is* used—not as it *might* be used if its meaning and usage were changed—this reference is final." *Op. cit.,* pp. 91–92.

guage. Moral judgments are most frequently phrased in the indicative mood, not the imperative, but Hare feels that the "logical behavior" of such indicative sentences is quite different from that of ordinary indicative sentences. An important difference between Stevenson's theory and Hare's is that Stevenson (as well as such other early emotivists as Carnap and Ayer) believed that moral language has a different function from other language. They believed that moral language was used to alter the attitudes, emotions, or behavior of those to whom they were addressed. Hare sees the difference between his view and theirs as that between telling someone to do something and getting him to do it:

The process of *telling* someone to do something, and *getting* him to do it, are quite distinct, logically, from each other. The distinction may be elucidated by considering a parallel one in the case of statements. To tell someone that something is the case is logically distinct from getting (or trying to get) him to believe it. Having told someone that something is the case we may, if he is not disposed to believe what we say, start on a quite different process of trying to get him to believe it (trying to persuade or convince him that what we have said is true). No one, in seeking to explain the function of indicative sentences, would say that they were attempts to persuade someone that something is the case. And there is no more reason for saying that commands are attempts to persuade or get someone to do something; here, too, we first tell someone what he is to do, and then, if he is not disposed to do what we say, we may start on the wholly different process of trying to get him to do it.[38]

Contained in the above passage is Hare's main disagreement with Stevenson and those who emphasize the persuasive nature of moral judgments. He does not believe that such judgments are attempts to alter attitudes or to get people to do something—for, if they were, he argues, we would indeed be forced to admit that there is no difference between reasoning and propaganda. The success of an attempt at persuasion is judged solely by its effects, which is to repeat the objection that, for Stevenson, the only criterion of a good reason is effectiveness.

Recent noncognitivists have not felt compelled to prove that moral judgments are not capable of being objectively true, but we have shown this is indeed a consequence of their theory. We suggested that this conclusion could be arrived at by the following argument:

1. If two expressions are identical in meaning or significance, then if one of them is not capable of being objectively true, neither is the other.
2. Given any moral judgment, it is identical in meaning or significance with some expression which is not capable of being objectively true.

[38] *Ibid.*, pp. 13–14. Cf. also in this respect an article by W. D. Falk, "Goading and Guiding," *Mind*, 62 (1953), 145–71, where the same criticism is made of theories like Stevenson's.

3. Therefore, given any moral judgment, it is not capable of being objectively true.

The job for the noncognitivist, of course, is to establish Premise 2, by establishing that his particular analysis of the meaning of a moral judgment is correct.

Hare suggests that 'good' has an "evaluative" meaning and a "descriptive" meaning. The evaluative meaning of 'good' is discovered by examining how the word is used. And, according to Hare, 'good' is used to commend. He believes that, when we say that x is good, we are commending it.[39] Hare suggests that commendations are always related to choice. In fact, he says, "When we commend or condemn anything, it is always in order, at least indirectly, to guide choices, our own or other people's, now or in the future." [40] The "evaluative" meaning of the word 'good', according to Hare, is given when we point out its commending function; although that word may also have a "descriptive meaning," this changes from occasion to occasion. 'Good', however, in its typical use, is always used to commend—which is to say that its evaluative meaning remains constant.

There are several problems connected with this which Hare does not discuss. It might well be asked by the cognitivist why the fact that 'good' is always used to commend (granting for the moment that it is) should have anything to do with the meaning of "X is good." After all, the argument might continue, Premise 2 has to do with meaning or significance, not use, and just as Stevenson was wrong to think that the fact that moral judgments may be used to express emotions had anything to do with their cognitive status, so Hare is wrong to think that the fact that moral judgments are used to commend (or to tell people what to do) has anything to do with their meaning (and, hence, with their cognitive status).

Behind Hare's claims there seems to lie an assumption of a particular theory of meaning, the use theory of meaning. It is only by adopting this theory that the use to which an expression is put can be significantly related to its meaning. Hare rarely, if ever, makes this assumption explicit in *The Language of Morals*,[41] but, in a more recent book, he does:

Without attempting to give a complete account of meaning in general, I may perhaps be allowed to say that meaning of any kind (so far as it is words that are said to have meaning) is or involves the use of an expression in accordance with certain rules; the *kind* of meaning is determined by the *kind* of rules.[42]

[39] There are exceptions to this which Hare discusses (pp. 124–26), but he believes that these uses are not typical or characteristic, and calls them *the inverted-commas use, the ironic use,* and *the conventional use.*

[40] *Ibid.*, p. 127.

[41] But cf. pp. 91–92.

[42] R. M. Hare, *Freedom and Reason* (Oxford: The Clarendon Press, 1963), p. 7.

Because this theory of meaning is presupposed by Hare, and because it is explicitly appealed to by other contemporary ethical thinkers who should be called noncognitivists, it may be of some help to examine it in detail.

a. THE USE THEORY OF MEANING. Difficulties with the referential theory, the ideational theory, and the behavioral theory of meaning have led some philosophers to suggest that we either identify meaning with use, or replace questions about meaning with questions about use. Ludwig Wittgenstein was one of the first thinkers to suggest that we make this transition:

> For a *large* class of cases—though not for all—in which we employ the word "meaning" it can be defined thus: the meaning of a word is its use in the language.[43]

This is echoed in a number of equally dark sayings—for example: "The question 'What is a word really?' is analogous to 'What is a piece in chess?' "[44] Of course, one tells what a chess piece is by saying how it is used, what role it has in the game of chess. It is reasonable, perhaps, to interpret Wittgenstein as telling us that to know what a particular word is, what its *meaning* is, is to know how it functions in the language. There are grave problems surrounding the notion of the use of an expression, and—though we cannot delve very deeply into them—we must examine this notion a little further.

The suggestions quoted above were quickly developed—and sometimes misunderstood—by contemporary philosophers. Let us notice how these ideas recur in the writings of some of the leading noncognitivists. P. H. Nowell-Smith, for example, suggests that, "if someone asks what the meaning of a word is, he is usually asking for an explanation of the way in which it is used." [45] Furthermore he suggests:

> Elucidating the meaning of a word is explaining how the word is used, and it is only in the exceptional case in which a word is the name of something, either a proper name which is used to refer to just one thing, or a 'general' or 'common' name that is used to refer indifferently to a number of things, that explaining how it is used can be identified with saying or showing what it refers to. . . .

> For the question 'What does the word . . . mean?' I shall therefore substitute the two questions 'For what job is the word . . . used?' and 'Under what conditions is it proper to use this word for that job?' [46]

From the writings of Hare, it is plain that he believes that the meaning of 'good' has much to do with its typical commendatory function or use, and

[43] Ludwig Wittgenstein, *Philosophical Investigations* (New York: The Macmillan Company, 1953), ¶43.

[44] *Ibid.*, ¶ 108.

[45] Nowell-Smith, *op. cit.*, p. 66.

[46] *Ibid.*, pp. 67, 69.

his criticisms of naturalism depend upon taking this function as a part of the meaning of 'good'.

The prevalence of this use theory of meaning is also noticeable among philosophers who do not write primarily in ethics. For example, Gilbert Ryle suggests that "to know what an expression means is to know how it may and may not be employed," [47] and G. J. Warnock tells us that "to know the meaning of a sentence is to know how to use it, to know in what circumstances its use is correct or incorrect." [48]

Finally, some students of language, who are not philosophers, have also found the use theory of meaning attractive. A recent linguistics text has the following to say:

The meaning of a word, therefore, may be considered as the way it is used as a part of different sentences; what the dictionary does is to try and summarize for each word the way or ways it is used in the sort of sentences in which it is found in the language.[49]

b. THE USE THEORY AND HARE's POSITION. Now we have seen that Hare claims that 'good' is used to commend and that when we commend something we always are interested in guiding choices, and he claims that 'right' also has a "prescriptive" function. Hare further argues that the commending use of 'good' is "primary"—that is, although there is a descriptive use of 'good', that use varies as we apply the term to different objects. Only the commendatory use remains constant. Let us not criticize this claim for the moment, and attempt to see how this fact (if it is a fact) might be used to establish a noncognitivistic theory of the meaning of value judgments.

Hare might argue in the following way:

1. If two expressions have the same (primary) use, they have the same meaning.
2. "X is good" and "I hereby commend X" have the same primary use (namely, commending X).
3. Therefore, "X is good" and "I hereby commend X" have the same meaning.

But the argument will continue:

4. If two expressions are identical in meaning or significance, then if one of them is not capable of being objectively true, neither is the other. (cf. the argument on pp. 260–65.
5. "I hereby commend X" is not capable of being objectively true.
6. Therefore, "X is good" is not capable of being objectively true.

---

[47] Gilbert Ryle, "The Theory of Meaning," in *British Philosophy in the Mid-Century*, ed. C. A. Mace (London: George Allen & Unwin, Ltd., 1957), p. 255.

[48] G. J. Warnock, "Verification and the Use of Language," *Revue internationale de philosophie*, 5 (1951), 318.

[49] R. H. Robins, *General Linguistics* (Bloomington, Ind.: Indiana University Press, 1964), pp. 21–22.

Premise 1 is merely a statement of the use theory of meaning, and Premise 2 contains Hare's claim that 'good' is used primarily to commend.

The cognitivist could reply to this argument in several ways. He could, of course, deny the use theory of meaning, but other effective replies are open to him. For example, he might agree that "X is good" has both a descriptive use and a commendatory use, but argue that neither is primary. The argument Hare uses to show that the primary use of 'good' is commendatory depends upon the claim that the descriptive use varies while the commendatory remains constant. He argues, for example, that the descriptive use of 'good' in 'a good knife' is different from the descriptive use of 'good' in 'a good car'. But the cognitivist may deny this and suggest that the descriptive use of 'good' is always to be analyzed as 'answering to some interest', or (if he is a cognitivist nondefinist) that 'good' is always used to refer to some totiresultant (or partiresultant) property. If this is true (and Hare has not really shown that it is not), the commendatory and descriptive uses of 'good' are on a par, and neither is primary.

The cognitivist could also argue that, in fact, 'good' is not always used to commend, and that, therefore, there is no way to go from the claim that the commendatory use is constant to the conclusion that that use is primary. If the cognitivist could show that the commendatory use is not constant, two alternatives are open to him: he can claim that the descriptive use *is* constant, thus turning Hare's argument back upon Hare; or he can argue that neither use is constant, thereby accepting a stalemate in which Hare has not proved his point.

Here, then, are the three alternative replies open to the cognitivist: (1) He can grant that the commendatory use of 'good' is constant, but argue that its descriptive use is also constant. If that were true, then the argument Hare uses to show the commending use is primary would fail. (2) He could also deny that the commending use is constant and argue that the descriptive use is. In that case he would (if his arguments were successful) be able to turn Hare's arguments to his own advantage. (3) Finally he could argue that neither is constant, in which case nothing is established on these grounds about which use (if any) is primary. Let us illustrate these possibilities by a table:

	Descriptive Use	Evaluative Use
1.	Constant	Constant
2.	Constant	Not constant
3.	Not constant	Constant
4.	Not constant	Not constant

Hare claims that Row 3 describes the way things are, but the cognitivist has only to show that one of the other rows more accurately describes the situation in order to refute that claim. In the next section we shall argue that the cognitivist is on firm ground here, for there are good reasons for believing that the evaluative use is not constant (or at least that, in any sense in which it is constant, the descriptive use can also be said to be constant).

c. Is 'Good' Always Used to Commend? When we considered Hare's rejection of naturalism (see Chapter 11), we noted his claim that 'good' is always (or primarily) used to commend. We suggested there that this claim is questionable, and it is now time to defend our remarks. Hare says that, "When we commend or condemn anything, it is always in order, at least indirectly, to guide choices, our own or other peoples, now or in the future." It seems, therefore, that he is suggesting that there is an intimate connection between commending and guiding choices—indeed, that to commend *is* to guide choices.

If this is what it is to commend, then it is obviously false that when we say that something is good we are always commending it. Counterexamples come readily to mind. When S says to his impoverished friend, "The Rolls Royce is a good car," there is no sense at all in which he could be said to be telling his friend what to do or attempting to guide his choice. We say of things that no longer exist (yesterday's dinner, for example) that they are good and of actions in the past that they were right. Can anyone seriously maintain that we are attempting to guide someone to choose the meal we have eaten or to do what has already been done? Suppose S is about to die, and we say to him that he has had a good life and that his insurance policy is a good one because it will take care of his wife and family (who also, we might add, are good). We know he is about to die, so are we to be said to be guiding a choice we know will never be made? This is no more plausible than the claim that on such occasions we are guiding our own choices, telling ourselves to have a life like S's, to take out his kind of insurance, to take up with his wife and family. Finally, let us suppose that S has been an alcoholic for seventeen years, but has finally cured himself. We know this, and would not for the world advise him to have a drink, but we might well say to him "Gin and tonic is a good drink. It's too bad you can't have one, but here's a Coke." We are not guiding S's choices here, nor are we guiding our own. For these reasons, and many more like them, it is completely implausible to say that whenever we use 'good' we are always commending something, *if to commend something is to guide someone's choices.*

But it may be replied that we can commend something without guiding choices, that Hare is right in claiming that 'good' is always used to commend although he is wrong to link commendation to the guiding of choices. The suggestion here would be that 'commending' is a generic name for a family of activities or performances. When we commend, we sometimes guide choices, we sometimes praise, we sometimes rank, we sometimes evaluate favorably, and so on. With this suggestion, however, the commendatory invariance of 'good' slips away. The cognitivist can argue that, in this sense of 'invariance' the descriptive use is also invariant, for the descriptive use of 'good' is always to "describe" or to state something which is true of the object being judged.

There are many more replies open to the noncognitivist who would defend Hare's analysis, and many counterreplies the cognitivist might make—depending, of course, upon what kind of a cognitivist he happens to be. The debate on this point continues. It is reasonable to conclude, however, that Hare's analysis of moral judgments has not been established, and that none of the noncognitivistic analyses of value judgments we have yet considered has succeeded in escaping serious objections and in establishing noncognitivism as a correct meta-ethical theory.

d. HARE'S THEORY AND MORAL ARGUMENTS. In our discussion of Ayer and Stevenson, we stressed the fact that neither could account for the fact that we reason about our moral judgments and seemingly apply the rules of logic to them. This phenomenon is so pervasive that any theory which cannot account for it seems doomed to failure.

Although he does not reduce moral judgments to imperatives, Hare believes that moral language is "prescriptive" in nature, and that moral judgments fall under the general heading of prescriptions. He also adds that moral judgments are distinguishable from other prescriptive judgments in that they are *universalizable*.[50]

In his earlier book Hare claimed that all sentences containing 'ought' (when they are being used evaluatively) entail imperatives. He would also claim that when we say "X is good," this, too, has some relation to prescriptive judgments. In his later book, *Freedom and Reason*, he again claims that there can be logical relations among prescriptive judgments, even among commands, which are "extreme cases" of prescriptive judgments. Therefore, it is necessary for him to show, rather than to assume, that such logical relations are possible—and much of *The Language of Morals* is directed toward this end.

In order to account for moral reasoning and logical relations among prescriptions, Hare makes a distinction between the *phrastic* and the *neustic* of a sentence. The phrastic is the "content," and the neustic is a sort of

[50] Much has been made recently of the universalizability of moral judgments. Hare goes into this feature of moral judgments in *The Language of Morals*, but more thoroughly in his later book *Freedom and Reason*. When Hare says that moral judgments are universalizable he means that "the meaning of the word 'ought' and other moral words is such that a person who uses them commits himself thereby to a universal rule." *Freedom and Reason, op. cit.*, p. 30. He argues that this is not itself a moral principle but a logical one. His point is (highly oversimplified) that if someone says "I ought to do A," and allows that S is in relevantly similar circumstances but has no obligation to do A," he is making some sort of logical error. Cf. also, Marcus Singer, *Generalization in Ethics* (New York: Alfred A. Knopf, Inc., 1961), and cf. above pp. 296–300.

modifier, indicating how the content is to be interpreted—as a statement of fact, a command, a question, a request, and so on. He then argues that all logical words, such as 'if', 'and' and 'or' appear in the phrastics of sentences, and that the same is true of the logical quantifiers.[51] Furthermore:

The imperative and the indicative moods also have in common, because of their common phrastic element, everything to do with their reference to actual or possible states of affairs.[52]

Now if this is the case there is no reason, it is argued, why there cannot be logical deductions among commands, inasmuch as we need only deal with the phrastics. And perhaps this argument will do, as long as we are dealing with expressions with similar neustics. For example, we might have two commands, and deduce from these a third command. If we do this, it is because we have to deal only with the phrastic. Consider the following syllogism:

> Close either the door or the window.
> Do not close the door.
> ∴ Close the window.

Translated into neustic and phrastic language, this would become:

> Your closing either the door or the window, please.
> Your not closing the door, please.
> ∴ Your closing the window, please.

Because, for the purposes of logical deduction, the neustics (according to Hare) are irrelevant, this inference differs in no way from the following:

> Your closing either the door or the window, yes.
> Your not closing the door, yes.
> ∴ Your not closing the window, yes.

And this argument, Hare feels, is an analysis of one containing premises in the indicative mood:

> You close either the door or the window.
> You do not close the door.
> ∴ You close the window.

This illustration is overly simple, for it deals with arguments in which the neustics are all the same. If the premises and the conclusion are "mixed," the

[51] Hare, *The Language of Morals, op. cit.*, p. 21.
[52] R. M. Hare, *The Language of Morals*, p. 22. By permission of The Clarendon Press, Oxford.

situation becomes more complex, for we need to know how to modify the conclusion. Consider the following argument:

> Take all the boxes to the station.
> This is one of the boxes.
> ∴. Take this to the station.

Assuming that we can separate this into phrastic and neustic language, and assuming that we can carry our inferences among the phrastics, we need some rule to tell us that the conclusion must be in the imperative mood rather than the indicative mood. That is, how do we know that the above argument is valid and that the one immediately below is not?

> Take all the boxes to the station.
> This is one of the boxes.
> ∴. This is something you are going to take to the station.

To deal with this problem, Hare introduces two rules, the adequacy of which must be established for the success of his theory:

(1) *No indicative conclusion can be validly drawn from a set of premisses which cannot be validly drawn from the indicatives among them alone.*

(2) *No imperative conclusion can be validly drawn from a set of premisses which does not contain at least one imperative.*[53]

The obviously invalid argument would be ruled out by Rule 1. Given that this set of rules is supposed to account for the neustic elements in inferences, let us consider the number of possible combinations of imperative and indicative neustics. Let 'C' stand for an imperative neustic sign (a command-indicator); let 'S' stand for an indicative neustic sign (a statement-indicator). The following combinations are possible:

	p	q	r
1.	C	C	C
2.	C	C	S
3.	C	S	C
4.	C	S	S
5.	S	C	C
6.	S	C	S
7.	S	S	C
8.	S	S	S

Given any combination of Premises p and q, there are two possibilities for Conclusion r: it has either a C or an S.[54] (Assume for the purposes of expo-

---

[53] *Ibid.*, p. 28.

[54] We are, of course, assuming that if the conclusion is indicative it is different from the indicative premise.

sition that we are concerned only with two kinds of sentence: imperatives and indicatives.) According to Hare's second rule, Number 7 is ruled out, for it draws an imperative conclusion from premises which do not contain an imperative. The first rule, on the other hand, would eliminate Numbers 2, 4, and 6, because the conclusions of these three rows are indicatives. That conclusion, however, cannot be drawn from the one indicative premise; it needs the phrastic of the imperative as well. This would seem to allow only four possible valid inferences: Numbers 1, 3, 5, and 8. And we can generalize to say that if the premises contain an imperative, the conclusion must be imperative; if not, the conclusion must be indicative.

The question to be raised now is: "Are Hare's rules adequate, or can counterexamples to them be discovered?" If there are counterexamples, they will be of three possible types: Type I will show that premises which are all imperative entail an indicative conclusion; Type II will show that premises which contain both imperatives and indicatives entail an indicative conclusion; Type III will show that premises which are completely indicative entail an imperative conclusion.

Type I counterexamples are relatively easy to discover. P. T. Geach offers two:

Imagine a king knighting a subject of doubtful loyalty and saying: "If you are a faithful subject, then rise up, Sir George!—but do not rise; stay on your knees, fellow!" The conclusion of this *modus tollens* is obvious; moreover, it is one to which the king is logically committed; his two imperatives are reconcilable only on the assumption that George is no true subject.

The use of a ritual imperative as an example may look like cheating, so let me take another example. The games master says to the cricket captain at 12.45: "If the 12.55 weather forecast says it will be showery, cancel the afternoon's match." At 1.15 he sees him again and says: "Don't cancel the match." Here again, the games master is logically committed to the assertion that the 12.55 weather forecast did not say it would be showery.[55]

Another example, not from Geach, and in Hare's form, would be:

> Kill only members of the nobility.
> Kill that man with the long beard.
> ∴ That man with the long beard is a member of the nobility.

Type II counterexamples might be suggested by the following:

> Only members of the nobility are to be executed.
> Execute that man with the long beard.
> ∴ That man with the long beard is a member of the nobility.

[55] P. T. Geach, "Imperative and Deontic Logic," *Analysis*, 18 (1958), 52.

This would seem to be a counterexample to Hare's own theory, and the fact that it is can be shown on Hare's own grounds. We can say that the two premises entail the conclusion in just the sense of 'entailment' which Hare accepts, for Hare says:

A sentence P entails a sentence Q if and only if the fact that a person assents to P but dissents from Q is a sufficient criterion for saying that he has misunderstood one or other of the sentences.[56]

It is easy to see that, with this version of entailment, the premises of this argument entail the conclusion. It might be suggested that the first premise is really a disguised imperative, and can also be expressed as "Execute only members of the nobility!" If this were so, we would merely have another instance of a Type I counterexample.

It would seem that these counterexamples are sufficient to show that Hare's rules are not acceptable, and that there are logical relations among imperatives which seem intuitively valid and yet which seem to violate the rules.[57] Thus, even though we agree with Hare that there must be some way to account for the logical relations between moral judgments (even if it be only between summary rules and particular judgments), we must conclude that the attempt to explain such reasoning in *The Language of Morals* is not satisfactory. Thus, despite the fact that Hare comes to grips with problems avoided, or dealt with unsuccessfully by earlier noncognitivists, and despite the fact that his theory is an improvement over theirs, it is still beset by unresolved questions and unestablished claims.

Unfortunately, these questions and claims are crucial. Hare has not satisfactorily established his claim that the primary use of judgments using 'good' is to commend, and he has not really shown, with his separation of the phrastics from the neustics and his rules for the manipulation of the neustics, how moral arguments can be valid. Therefore, in order to find the best noncognitivist theory, it is necessary to look further.

---

[56] Hare, *The Language of Morals, op. cit.*, p. 25.

[57] A counterexample of Type III would be interesting, for that would be a case of going from a set of statements which are purely descriptive to an imperative, which is not descriptive. This would be to cross "Hume's gap," or to go from what philosophers call an "is" to an "ought" judgment. Hume is usually interpreted as claiming that this is impossible and contemporary philosophers have tended to agree with him. However, for one interesting attempt to make the crossing cf. John Searle, "How to Derive 'Ought' from 'Is'," *The Philosophical Review*, 73 (1964), 43–58. There are many interesting replies to this article scattered through recent philosophical journals.

Exercises

Review

1. What reasons are there for believing that Hare, unlike Stevenson, is attempting to give a descriptive account of the meaning of moral terms and expressions?

2. What does Hare take the function of moral judgments and principles to be?

3. What, according to Hare, is the distinction between telling someone what to do and getting someone to do something?

4. What argument could be given, using Hare's analysis of the meaning of moral expressions, to establish the claim that moral judgments are not capable of being objectively true? Criticize this argument.

5. What is the "use theory of meaning?" Discuss some of its earlier presentations. How might it be used by a defender of Hare's theory?

6. What reason does Hare give for claiming that the descriptive meaning of a moral judgment is always secondary? Criticize this position.

7. Discuss the truth of the claim that 'good' is always used to commend.

8. How does Hare's theory of moral argumentation differ from Ayer's and from Stevenson's?

9. Explain Hare's notion of the phrastic and the neustic. What part does this distinction play in his discussion of moral reasoning? Criticize this theory in light of the objections discussed above.

4. *Another Theory.* The noncognitivist theory we are about to discuss is, we believe, the one that best satisfies the criteria for acceptability of theories. It makes use of suggestions of two English philosophers, J. L. Austin and P. H. Nowell-Smith, and so we shall first have to say something about the contributions of each of these men. Then we shall explain the theory we call the *multifunctionalist performative theory.*

a. Nowell-Smith. P. H. Nowell-Smith suggests that "the central activities for which moral language is used are choosing and advising others to choose," [58] and maintains that ethics is a practical, rather than theoretical, discipline.

Because Nowell-Smith openly and explicitly adopts the use theory of meaning, when he gives a "definition" of an expression it will be an account of its use, and he would say that two expressions mean the same thing if they have the same use.

Hare's account of the use of moral judgments is similar to, but less complex than, that of Nowell-Smith. Hare claims that moral language is used to guide choices and, thereby, to guide conduct. Nowell-Smith, although he insists that the guiding of choices (our own and others') is the *central* use of moral language, argues that moral language is not *always* used in this way:

[58] Nowell-Smith, *op. cit.*, p. 11.

"The commonest practical words do not have just one use. They have many uses and can be used to do more than one job on any given occasion." [59]

In perhaps the most well-known passage from his book, Nowell-Smith tells us that moral judgments

...are used to express tastes and preferences, to express decisions and choices, to criticize, grade, and evaluate, to advise, admonish, warn, persuade and dissuade, to praise, encourage and reprove, to promulgate and draw attention to rules; and doubtless for other purposes also.[60]

He admits that *one* of the uses of 'good' is to commend, and his analysis of commending is very like Hare's: "To commend something to someone is to advise him to choose it." [61] But we do not, he claims, always commend something when we say that it is good, for sometimes when we say that something is good no choice is involved. (cf. pp. 334–35).

In discussing 'right' and 'ought' Nowell-Smith points out that "the main purpose for which these words are used is to tell someone to do something, but they have subsidiary uses not unlike the subsidiary uses of 'good'." [62] The cognitivist, as we have seen, would undoubtedly be happy with these points, for he can admit the correctness of the use theory of meaning, and agree that such words as 'good' and 'right' have a number of uses. Indeed, one of the criticisms the cognitivist is likely to make is that Hare has restricted his analysis of the use of 'good'. The point of contention between the cogniti- vist and the noncognitivist (here represented by both Hare and Nowell- Smith) is whether 'right' and 'good' have another use—that of predicating properties (of any sort) of actions and objects. The cognitivist definist main- tains that they do, and that these properties are to be identified with the properties studied by the natural sciences (e.g., pleasantness and conducive- ness to survival). The cognitivist nondefinist, too, often claims that 'good' and 'right' refer to properties (of different sorts), and that "X is good," for example, is used to say of things which are, in fact, good (or, as Moore would put it, of things which have goodness) that they are good, or of things which are right that they are right.[63]

The job for both Nowell-Smith and Hare (and for any noncognitivist) is to show that this is not the case, and this cannot be done by showing that those words are used to commend, to rank, to grade, to evaluate, to praise, and so on. It is quite possible for the cognitivist to admit this and to argue

[59] *Ibid.*, p. 95.
[60] *Ibid.*, p. 98.
[61] *Ibid.*, p. 163.
[62] *Ibid.*, p. 185.
[63] In order to be fair to the version of cognitivistic nondefinism defended in Chapter 12, one must not assume that it is being claimed that 'right' and 'good' are the names of simple nonnatural properties, as some proponents of cognitivistic nondefinism have held.

that they are also used for the purpose of truly predicating rightness of actions and goodness of things. Hare had attempted to show that the *primary* job of moral language is to guide choices, and we saw how it might be thought to follow from this that moral judgments are not capable of being objectively true. But the cognitivist seems to have adequate replies to this claim. Nowell-Smith attempts to prove his point more directly, arguing that moral judgments cannot be used as the cognitivist definist says they are, and appealing to Moore's argument:

> Ethical sentences are not, as Moore so clearly shows, psychological or metaphysical or theological sentences. Almost all earlier theories had tended to reduce ethical concepts and sentences to those of some other subject, usually psychology; they tried to define such words as 'good' and 'ought' in terms, for example, of the satisfaction of desire or of pleasure and pain. Against all such attempts the intuitionists produce a crushing argument. . . . [64]

We have already had occasion to consider Moore's "crushing" argument against the definist, and we are not alone in feeling that the open-question argument and the naturalistic fallacy fail to provide a conclusive answer to all kinds of cognitivistic definism. But even if cognitivistic definism could be defeated by Moore's argument, by some other general argument, or in the way we have suggested, there would still be cognitivists left to engage with Nowell-Smith.

Nowell-Smith is aware of this and attempts to present arguments against the cognitivist nondefinist. He argues that, even if we know directly that an action has a characteristic of rightness (whether it is a simple characteristic, a totiresultant or a partiresultant characteristic), nothing follows about what ought to be done. Nowell-Smith believes that, when one says that an action is obligatory, this is just another way of saying that it ought to be done, but he claims that the cognitivist nondefinist has created a gap between what is obligatory and what ought to be done. If we now recall the formulation of cognitivistic nondefinism (see Chapter 12), we should be able to see that, whether or not this argument applies to other cognitivist nondefinist views, it does not apply to the view defended there. The cognitivist nondefinist argues that we know directly that an action is right, and claims that this is just to say that we know directly that we ought to do it. There is no gap—and, therefore, no criticism on these grounds will work.

Nowell-Smith attempts to fortify his claim that moral terms do not apply to properties (natural or nonnatural) by arguing that it is a mistake to believe that all adjectives stand for properties. Although this can be granted, he has no effective argument to show that 'good' is one of those adjectives that do *not* stand for properties. One argument he offers to show that 'good'

[64] Nowell-Smith, *op. cit.*, p. 36.

is not a property-referring adjective is that we know what 'standing for a property' means because we know how typical property-referring adjectives behave. He then argues, "To say that goodness is a property commits us to the very debatable assertion that the logic of 'good' is like that of 'blue', 'loud', and 'round'." [65] But, again, there is no reason to draw this conclusion, for there are different sorts of "properties," not all of which must fit into the same category as color terms.

b. J. L. AUSTIN. Nowell-Smith has called such activities as praising, recommending, advising, and commending *performances*. A performance is an activity which we do, and one of the major contributions of the late J. L. Austin is the development of a theory about these kinds of linguistic activities.[66] Very often we do things with words—we promise, bet, warn, frighten, insult, and convince, to mention only a few of the actions which can be performed with words. In order to chart this relatively unexplored territory, Austin introduced the notion of a *performative utterance*. For example, S can report to someone the fact that he promised to do a certain thing, or he can actually make the promise. Often, when one promises to do something, a certain form of words (e.g., "I promise to do A") is used. There is a great difference between telling someone that a promise was made and actually making the promise. The same difference applies to betting, grading, ranking, commanding, commending, requesting, advising, approving, and other similar activities. Austin's initial suggestion is that, when we (successfully) utter such performative verbs, we are *doing* something as opposed to merely *saying* something, and that such utterances are "happy" or "unhappy" rather than true or false.[67] He contrasts performative utterances with statements, which are claimed to be either true or false and merely to say something.

But Austin saw certain difficulties in this view. He was aware, for example, of the "irritating" fact that, in the case of the performatives he called *expositives*, truth and falsity began to enter the picture:

And when we come to pure explicit performatives such as 'state' or 'maintain', surely the whole thing is true or false even though the uttering of it is the performing of the action of stating or maintaining.[68]

Therefore, he made a fresh start and distinguished three kinds of acts performed with words. When we utter a sentence (whatever kind of sentence

[65] *Ibid.*, p. 64.

[66] J. L. Austin, *How to Do Things with Words* (Cambridge, Mass.: Harvard University Press, 1962).

[67] A promise is "happy" if it is a successful promise. Much has to be true before the words "I promise to attend the World Fair" results in the actual performance of a promise. There are many ways such actions can go wrong, or fail to "come off." When they do fail, the utterance is said by Austin to be unhappy. Cf. Austin, *op. cit.*, Lectures ii–iv.

[68] *Ibid.*, p. 90.

and whether we mean it or not), we have performed *a locutionary act*. But when we utter sentences, we usually can be said to have done more than merely utter sentences—we have stated something, we have made a bet, a promise, an appeal, and so on. One who makes a promise does not "do" any more than one who says "I promise"—at least in one sense of 'do'. But, in another sense, he has done something more than the person who merely utters those words to see how they sound—he has made a promise. The act of making a promise, and similar acts, are called, by Austin, *illocutionary acts*. Our locutionary and illocutionary acts often have consequences—we frighten, persuade, or insult people by uttering certain words, or by making certain statements or requests, or by giving certain orders. The actions of doing these things (which are consequences of locutionary and illocutionary acts) are called *perlocutionary acts*.

Thus, a report of a locutionary act would be: "He uttered the words (i.e., said) 'Never darken my door again.'" A report of an illocutionary act would be: "He ordered him never to darken his door again." Finally, a report of a perlocutionary act would be: "He got him to leave his house and never to return." One clue to whether or not a verb is illocutionary is the fact that illocutionary verbs, but not perlocutionary verbs, fit into the formula "I hereby _____." It is possible, for example, to say "I hereby promise to do A," but not "I hereby lead you to believe that I will do A." Again, one can say, "I hereby order you to do A," or "I hereby advise you to do A," but not "I hereby persuade you to do A," or "I hereby annoy you." Part of the reason for this, according to Austin, is that the use of language for performing illocutionary acts is "conventional," which is not the case with the use of language for performing perlocutionary acts. "Strictly speaking, there cannot be an illocutionary act unless the means employed are conventional. . . ." [69]

There are many discussions of Austin's theory of illocutionary acts. William P. Alston, for example, employs Austin's distinctions in order to restate the use theory of meaning:

> . . . The fact that two sentences are commonly used to perform the same illocutionary act (have the same illocutionary act potential) is sufficient to give them the same meaning. [70]

If the use theory of meaning is not stated in some similar way, it will, of course, be subject to immediate and obvious counterexamples. S may use the

[69] *Ibid.*, p. 118.

[70] Alston, *op. cit.*, p. 36. The careful reader of Austin will discover that this account of the use theory given by Alston, although making use of Austin's distinctions, is not derived from Austin. Austin identifies meaning with *sense* and *reference* (cf. p. 100) and distinguishes it from *force* which is how the utterance is to be taken, but he never expands his remarks about sense and reference. It is far from clear how much of this dispute is verbal.

sentence "It's bedtime" in order to get his no-longer-welcome visitor to leave, but "It's bedtime" certainly does not mean anything like "I get (am getting) you to leave." In escaping such objections, the illocutionary-perlocutionary distinction is of great use. But S may use that same sentence to perform the same illocutionary act one would perform if one said, "I must ask you to leave," or (in radically different circumstances) he might use that sentence to perform the same illocutionary act typically performed by "The attack will be at dawn." This does not mean, of course, that "It's bedtime," means either "I must ask you to leave," or "The attack will be at dawn," and given the way Alston has stated the theory, those consequences are not entailed, for the two sentences have to be *commonly* used to perform the same illocutionary act.

c. A PERFORMATIVE THEORY OF MORAL JUDGMENTS. Alston has suggested that the term

> ... 'moral judgment' is a blanket term, covering a loosely organized group of illocutionary acts—reprimands, behests, injunctions, exhortations, imputations of obligation, etc.[71]

And Austin, who did not write about normative ethics or meta-ethics, suggests that "You ought to shut it" resembles (not "means") "I advise you to shut it." [72] If these suggestions (backed by the theory of meaning presented by Alston) are coupled with Nowell-Smith's insights into the plurality of uses of 'good' and 'right', it is possible to formulate a meta-ethical theory about the meaning of moral judgments which, although still classifiable as noncognitivistic, escapes many of the objections raised against the earlier forms of that theory.

Austin was not satisfied with his initial performative/statement contrast on the grounds that some performatives are true or false (and also on the grounds that some statements are not).[73] But Austin was not clear or consistent about what he meant by a performative.[74] Therefore, the noncognitivist theory we are presenting will be served by some further distinctions. The word 'statement' is ambiguous, for it may refer to the act of stating or to the statement made. The acts of stating, or of betting, or of promising are performed with words and, like the act of running, jumping, or flying, they are

---

[71] *Ibid.*, p. 49.

[72] Austin, *op. cit.*, p. 74.

[73] Cf. *ibid.*, pp. 141–46.

[74] In some places he distinguishes between sentences and statements (p. 1) and then speaks of "utterances" which look like "statements," (p. 2) but are not. In other places he proposes to use the word 'performative' to mean "a *performative sentence* or a performative utterance" (does he mean to equate the two here?) (p. 6). Again (p. 11) he identifies the utterance with an act.

not capable of being true or false. When using 'statement' or 'bet' or 'promise' to refer to the act, we shall say that it is being used in the *act sense*. When we want to speak of the statement, the bet, or the promise that is made, we shall say that we are using 'statement', 'bet' or 'promise' in the *object sense*. There are illocutionary acts, therefore, and none of them—because they are acts—is capable of being objectively true. This is why Alston's remark (see p. 345) is misleading. A moral judgment, in the most usual sense of that term, is not an illocutionary act at all, but an illocutionary object.

The noncognitivist who takes this approach will suggest that the difficulties with the views of Stevenson and Ayer are that they fail to make the distinction between illocutionary acts and perlocutionary acts, and confuse the meaning of moral judgments with their consequences or their intended consequences. He will then argue that the problem with Hare's view is that it narrowly selects just one illocutionary act—commending—and assimilates all the uses of 'good' to the performance of that act and all the uses of 'right' to the illocutionary act of advising.

d. MORAL REASONING. The difficulties in the older forms of noncognitivism were twofold: they did not adequately recognize the nature of moral judgments, and they were unable to account for moral reasoning. The theory presented here claims to have provided techniques for overcoming the first difficulty—but what about the second?

One of the most serious objections raised against Ayer's theory was that it did not allow for the use of reasons and logic in moral arguments. Stevenson's theory had the objectionable consequence that the only relation between the reasons and the conclusion of an argument about what is good or bad, right or wrong, is a causal or psychological one.[75] Hare attempted to overcome this difficulty by separating the neustics of sentences from the phrastics, and by suggesting that there were special rules applying to the neustics, but we have already examined the reasons for believing that this solution is not acceptable.

It might be suggested that the noncognitivist act deontologist does not need to explain this notion, for he does not subscribe to the view that we need always appeal to a general principle and then deduce our particular moral judgments from it. But he does admit the use of summary rules, and even if, as a noncognitivist, he wants to deny that these summary rules and the particular judgments which follow from them (in conjunction with factual statements) are capable of being objectively true, he still must explain how we are able to derive particular judgments from the summary rules. He must explain this because it is more than obvious that this is one of the things

---

[75] He also seems to be committed to the claim that any statement at all is a reason for any moral judgment, and that this "reason" supports the moral judgment if the person to whom it is addressed believes it and if it actually makes a difference to his attitudes. Cf. *Ethics and Language, op. cit.*, pp. 114–15.

we do, and not infrequently. (This is not incompatible with the claim that we *need not* do this every time we make a moral judgment.)

In discussing the way that the noncognitivist encounters this difficulty, we quoted an argument framed by Lars Bergstrom (see p. 323). In effect, he argued that, because logically valid inferences must consist of premises and conclusions which are capable of being objectively true, and because (according to the noncognitivist) moral judgments are not capable of being objectively true, it follows that moral judgments can play no role in valid inferences. We mentioned that one of the ways noncognitivists might escape this difficulty is to deny the first premise of the argument. (Hare chose that way, but Stevenson and Ayer did not.) Another way is to introduce a special form of inference (see Chapter 5, fn. 9), but we shall not discuss that alternative here. Hare's attempt to provide for normal deductive relations between premises and conclusions of evaluative arguments consisted in the attempt to provide rules for the manipulation of neustics. But another approach open to the noncognitivist seems to be both more simple and more promising.

In Chapter 2 we accepted the following definition of a deductively valid argument: "An argument is valid if, and only if, the form of that argument is a valid argument form." We then explained the invalidity of an argument form:

We may define the term 'invalid' as applied to argument forms as follows: an argument form is invalid if, and only if, it has a substitution instance with true premises and a false conclusion.

A deductively valid argument form, then, is one which is not invalid. Given these two definitions, the noncognitivist may claim that moral judgments may be substituted in valid argument forms, and that there may be deductively valid arguments with moral judgments in the premises and the conclusion. Given these definitions one can show that *modus ponens*, for example, is a valid argument form. The noncognitivist will then ask why it is not possible to say that the following argument is valid by virtue of the fact that it has a valid argument form: [76]

> If you borrowed the gin, you should replace it.
> You borrowed the gin.
> ∴ You should replace it.[76]

[76] Indeed he might even want to claim that the following argument is deductively valid for the same reason:

> If you borrowed the gin, return it.
> You borrowed the gin.
> ∴ Return it.

The noncognitivist who espouses the theory we have been discussing wants to maintain that utterances such as "X is good" and "A is right" have the same meaning as certain other illocutionary objects. But the identity of meaning works both ways and, if this is so, and if there is nothing about the form of "X is good" or "A is right" that prevents them from playing a role in valid deductions, he will claim that it is possible for them to play the same role as the cognitivist has them play. Thus it is not even necessary to introduce elements into arguments which are not in the form of declarative sentences. For example, if, on a particular occasion, "A is right" is being used in the way that "Do A!" is being used, then—for the purpose of argumentation—all the inferring may be done with the former expression.

e. A DIFFICULTY FOR THE PERFORMATIVE THEORY. The cognitivist may be unimpressed by this theory, and may suggest that, even if it accurately describes many of the things we do when we make moral judgments, it does not tell the whole story. As Austin says, making a statement is an illocutionary act, and nothing has yet been done to show that one of the illocutionary acts we perform when we make a moral judgment is not the act of making a statement. This objection is not different from the objection the cognitivist definist might make to Hare's theory (see p. 264).

What sort of reply is open to the noncognitivist who is confronted by such an argument? There seem to be two possibilities: he can attempt to discover reasons for believing that moral judgments are not typically used to make objectively true statements, or he can allow that—even when they are so used, this does not affect their cognitive status. He could, of course, also argue that, although moral judgments are not typically used to make factual statements, such a use would not affect their cognitive status.

Both the cognitivist definist and the cognitivist nondefinist believe that moral judgments—whatever other uses they have—are used to make statements. We have given reasons (see Chapter 11) for believing that, if moral judgments are used to make statements, they are not used for making the sorts of statements the cognitivist definist believes. (This claim is not incompatible with the claim that they might sometimes be used in that way, for the noncognitivist definist need only hold that this is not their typical use.) On this, the noncognitivist and the cognitivist nondefinist agree.

It is also reasonably clear that moral judgments are not used for ascribing simple properties to objects and actions (see Chapter 12). It remains only for the noncognitivist who would support his view by appealing to the use of moral judgments to show that they are not used in the way claimed by the

---

Certain limitations will have to be placed upon what can replace the variables in the argument form, but there seem to be no conclusive reasons why any phrase which when inserted preserves the well-formed sentential status of the premise or the conclusion should be excluded. We could not, however, allow substitutions which would yield sentences like "If take the book to the store you are going to be sorry."

a posteriori total-situation cognitivist nondefinist. This debate will not be entered here, but the reader is invited to join it. In such a debate the arguments for Tenet 1 of cognitivistic nondefinism (see pp. 270–72) would have to be examined and either rejected or answered by stronger ones. The arguments could be met by showing that the claims about what people believe about their moral judgments is incorrect, and by showing that the fact that it is appropriate to give reasons in support of moral judgments does less than is claimed to establish the similarity between moral judgments and shape judgments. Stronger arguments could be provided for the noncognitivistic analysis if an analysis of the illocutionary act of making a statement were given which demonstrated that moral judgments are not statements. No such analysis, however, has appeared and it is beyond the aspirations of this book to provide one.

But the noncognitivist will, perhaps, be able to mitigate the charge of "unfinished work" by pointing out that cognitivist definists who claim that a definition of moral judgments may be given in terms of naturalistic or metaphysical properties have not succeeded in providing one that is free from objections, and that the cognitivist nondefinists who are his most formidable rivals (by their own admission) have yet to work out a theory of direct perception and an explanation of the object of our (purported) moral knowledge. The conclusion, then, is that there is work to be done in both camps, but the prospects are promising and considerable progress has been made in the last few years.

Let us suppose that, when all the arguments are considered, it is established that, when someone makes a moral judgment, he is also typically (or even always) performing the illocutionary act of making a statement. (It does not matter what kind of statement here—the kind suggested by the cognitivist definist or that favored by the cognitivist nondefinist will do.) Is this sufficient to justify the claim that moral judgments are capable of being objectively true? One way to argue that it is not would be to point to the countless other illocutionary acts that moral judgments are used to perform. Then it might be suggested that any moral judgment, M, will have at least two "components"—a cognitive component and a noncognitive component. Furthermore, the noncognitivist definist (being a definist) will suggest that M must therefore be identical in meaning (because it is identical in use) with the following pseudoconjunction: "X has characteristics A, B and C *and* I hereby commend (or praise, or approve, or _____) X." [77] He then might argue (much as Stevenson argued—see p. 311) that, for that reason, even

---

[77] The noncognitivist would be forced to call this a *pseudoconjunction* because conjunction is a truth-functional relation and it is not clear what a conjunction with a non-truth-functional component would be. It is conceivable, however, that the noncognitivist who would take this approach might again give a formalistic account of conjunction, which would be in keeping with his formalist account of validity.

though one of the components is capable of being objectively true, the "conjunction" as a whole is not.

E. Application of the Criteria of Acceptability to the Remaining Noncognitivist Theory

One noncognitivist position has emerged as the best contender from the noncognitivist camp: the *multifunctionalist performative theory*. It differs from the other noncognitivist views in two respects: its analysis of moral judgments is more complex than that of its noncognitivist opponents and makes use of the notion of an illocutionary act and of the distinction between an illocutionary act and an illocutionary object; and it offers a formalist definition of *validity* (and, perhaps, *conjunction*) to explain the role ot deductive logic in arguments. This latter need must be fulfilled even if rules are thought to be merely summary rules. Let us see how well this theory meets the test of a good theory, and what more must be done.

1. Reasons in Its Favor. It has to be shown, first, that there are reasons in favor of this theory as a noncognitivist theory, after which it can be asked whether there are reasons in favor of noncognitivism (as presented by this theory) and which may be used in arguments—not with other noncognitivists, but with cognitivist definists and cognitivist nondefinists.

All noncognitivist theories hold that moral judgments must be analyzable in terms of other expressions which are not capable of being objectively true. If so, it can be claimed that the theory being defended has much merit (as a noncognitivist theory), for it reflects the actual uses to which moral judgments are put, and that—unlike other noncognitivist theories—it does not confuse illocutionary and perlocutionary acts or oversimplify the function of moral judgments. These facts (if they are facts), coupled with the use theory of meaning, lend much support to the multifunctionalist performative theory.

The reasons which could be given to support this form of noncognitivism against its cognitivist rivals consist of criticisms of those views on the basis of the claim that either moral judgments are not used to make statements, or that, even if they are, the total moral judgment (consisting of a statement plus some non-truth-functional illocutionary object) is not capable of being objectively true.

These are not arguments but, rather, descriptions of arguments that must be produced. Whether or not they can be fully elaborated and defended is an open question.

Just as the cognitivist nondefinist theory favored in Chapter 12 mentioned the compatibility of this theory with act deontology, the best normative theory of obligation, so, too, the noncognitivist who holds the theory favored in this chapter can argue that it, too, is quite compatible with that normative theory. The arguments against the rule theorists presented in Chapter 12, will be, on the whole, acceptable to him.

The theory depends, crucially, upon the acceptance of the use theory of meaning, and this theory, too, has not been shown to be correct, nor is the truth of this position entailed by that theory. It is true, however, that the truth of the use theory is a necessary condition for the truth of the multi-functionalist performative theory. The use theory must be perfected and explained, but there seems to be no obvious reason why progress cannot be made along these lines.

The use theory of meaning is also crucial in the defense of the definist aspect of the particular noncognitivist position favored here. But more important is the description of the actual use of moral judgments. All that can be claimed at this point is accuracy, but—given the reportive element in this theory—this claim seems decidable, and there is much evidence to support the claim that moral judgments are used for a variety of purposes.

2. *The Theory Can Answer Serious Objections.* The most serious objection raised against noncognitivist theories is that they cannot account for moral reasoning and argumentation. There are three sorts of difficulty of this nature facing the theory proposed here. One kind of difficulty rests upon the claim that, if moral judgments are not capable of being objectively true, they can play no part in deductive reasoning from summary rules and statements of fact to a moral judgment. The noncognitivist definist's answer to this objection (in the form of a formalist account of validity) has been presented. Another kind of difficulty is the problem of how the act deontologist who adopts this noncognitivistic theory can arrive at general summary rules. It is likely that the proponent of this theory would suggest that the analysis of deductive reasoning can be supplemented by a formalist analysis of inductive reasoning, and that summary rules are arrived at by induction.

The third, and perhaps the most serious, problem concerns the relation between reasons and particular judgments when particular judgments are not derived from, but conflict with, summary rules. It might be objected that, at such times, moral judgments are arbitrary, and therefore the inductively arrived at summary rules—and all the particular judgments deduced from the summary rules—are arbitrary too. This serious objection can be answered in two ways: by an appeal to the arguments which have been offered against the rule theorists, and by the claim that the particular judgments made are supported by reasons in a way that obviously arbitrary judgments are not. It is one thing to say, "That is wrong," and to have no reasons at all, and another altogether to say, "That is wrong," and to add that it is wrong "because it is a case of X, Y and Z." The fact that all cases of X, Y, and Z are not wrong does not change this, for the difference remains.

The likely reply to this is that no judgment which does not appeal to absolutely unalterable first principles can ever be justified, but to say this is merely to repeat the thesis of the rule theorist. It can also be suggested that no theory has ever been able to establish (by definition or by fiat) unquestionable first principles and that, if the choice is actually between making an "arbitrary" judgment at the particular level and making one at the general level, the safer alternative is the first. There are two reasons for this: first, exceptions can be found to all general principles, second, if we rely on particular "arbitrary" judgments, the possibility of error is thereby lessened. An error one makes about a general principle is likely to affect every moral judgment he makes, but an error about a particular judgment goes no farther, and although it may possibly be used in an induction to a general rule, there are a great many other particular judgments which may be correct and which are likely to correct the error before it enters a person's moral code.

3. **Competitors.** According to the third part of the criterion of acceptability of theories, a theory must account for and explain the moral phenomena better than its competitors do. The scene has been set for the confrontation between the two theories we consider best, and a little has been said about what each must do to fortify its position.

One of the general characteristics of a good theory is simplicity. The fact that the heliocentric theory is a simpler theory than the geocentric theory is considered to be a mark in its favor. The noncognitivist may be wrong about this, but he would undoubtedly suggest that his theory does explain the phenomena of moral experience in a more simple way than do the theories of his competitors. He would also argue that the theory makes possible a simple explanation of *all* evaluative language (judgments of value, judgments of obligation, even aesthetic judgments), because all of these are analyzable in terms of illocutionary acts and objects. If a competitor cannot match this comprehensiveness with equally satisfactory simplicity, the noncognitivist would claim victory here.

It is not clear how various cognitivists would react to this claim, but it is likely that many of those we have already found reason to criticize (e.g., the simple-property cognitivist nondefinist and the theological definist) would find it difficult to construct a theory of equal simplicity and comprehensiveness. At any rate, until the noncognitivist actually produces a completed version of the multifunctionalist performative theory, covering all evaluative utterances, he does not have the right to claim a victory on this count alone. But, at this point, he can argue that this gives his theory the advantage over many of the cognitivist theories, for the outlines of the theory he would construct have been drawn.

Exercises

Review

1. What does Nowell-Smith mean when he says that ethics is a practical, rather than a theoretical discipline?
2. Contrast Hare's meta-ethical theory with that of Nowell-Smith.
3. How does Nowell-Smith attempt to establish his noncognitivism?
4. What, according to J. L. Austin, is a performative utterance?
5. What distinction was made in this chapter between an illocutionary action and an illocutionary object? How was this distinction used in the construction of a meta-ethical theory?
6. What theory of moral reasoning is presented in the preceding section? How does this differ from Hare's theory? Why is such a theory necessary for the noncognitivist?
7. What reasons are there for and against the claim that the primary function of moral judgments is to make a statement?

F. A Final Word

In the field of normative ethics, we feel that we have been able to reach some positive conclusions. There are serious objections to all teleological theories and to all rule theories, and the normative theory of act deontology seems to satisfy the criteria of acceptability better than any of its competitors.

In the field of meta-ethics, the situation is more difficult. No one theory has emerged victorious, but two have been singled out as the most likely candidates. Suggestions have been made in this chapter and in Chapter 12 about the sort of inquiries and investigations that must be carried on to bring this debate to a close. Progress has been made toward that end by an immense narrowing of the field. Some may feel that it has been narrowed too hastily, and this may be true. But at this stage of the argument, the task of one who would make such a claim is clear: he will be obliged to say why the theory he favors should be accepted, and why the theories we find most acceptable should be abandoned. If he succeeds, his theory will have been established. We do not feel that this is likely to happen, but the task (we might even say the moral obligation) of a philosopher (or a student or teacher of philosophy) is to remain open to new arguments and suggestions. A man who would, through the desire to seem right or through the fear of admitting he is wrong, adhere to his former opinions when conclusive reasons have been presented against them deserves whatever fruits his irrationality bears.

Exercise

Describe and defend to the best of your ability the best total ethical theory— both normative and meta-ethical.

Bibliography

*AIKEN, HENRY. "Emotive 'Meanings' and Ethical Terms," *Journal of Philosophy*, 61 (1944), 456–70. A discussion of Stevenson's "The Emotive Meaning of Ethical Terms."

AUSTIN, J. L. *How to Do Things with Words*. Cambridge, Mass.: Harvard University Press, 1962.

AYER, A. J. *Language, Truth and Logic*. New York: Dover Publications, Inc., 1936, Chapter 6. A classical presentation of noncognitivism.

*BARNES, W. H. F. "Ethics Without Propositions," *The Aristotelian Society Supplementary Volume*, 22 (1948), 1–30. A defense of the claim that the emotive theory of the meaning of moral terms does not preclude rational discourse in ethics.

———. "A Suggestion About Value," *Analysis*, 1 (1936), 45–46.

*BRANDT, RICHARD B. "The Emotive Theory of Ethics," *The Philosophical Review*, 59 (1950), 305–18. A criticism of the emotive theory as it is presented by C. L. Stevenson.

———. *Ethical Theory*. Englewood Cliffs, N.J.: Prentice-Hall, Inc., 1959. Chapter 9 contains a discussion and criticism of the emotive theory and includes brief discussions of Hare and Nowell-Smith.

*———. "Stevenson's Defense of the Emotive Theory," *The Philosophical Review*, 59 (1950), 535–40. A reply to Stevenson's article "Brandt's Questions about the Emotive Theory."

*CAMPBELL, C. A. "Ethics Without Propositions," *Mind*, 59 (1950), 88–93. A criticism of the Barnes article of the same title.

*CASTAÑEDA, H. N. "Imperative Reasonings," *Philosophy and Phenomenological Research*, 21 (1960), 21–49. An argument that there are legitimate imperative inferences, but different from Hare's at important points.

*———. "A Note on Imperative Logic," *Philosophical Studies*, 6 (1955), 1–4.

*———. "Outline of a Theory on the General Logical Structure of the Language of Action," *Theoria*, 26 (1960), 151–82. A discussion of the logical structure of imperative sentences. Castañeda tries to show how imperative inferences may be valid.

*EDWARDS, PAUL. *The Logic of Moral Discourse*. New York: The Free Press, 1955. In Chapter 6 Edwards defends the claim that if moral judgments are imperatives, it does not follow that they cannot be supported with reasons, nor that they can never follow from factual judgments.

EWING, A. C. *Ethics*. New York: The Free Press, 1953, Chapter 7. A criticism of some forms of noncognitivism.

FALK, W. D. "Goading and Guiding," *Mind*, 62 (1953), 145–69. A criticism of earlier noncognitivistic views which make no distinction between getting someone to do something (goading—a perlocutionary action) and telling someone what to do or giving advice (guiding—an illocutionary action).

*GEWIRTH, ALAN. "Meanings and Criteria in Ethics," *Philosophy*, 38 (1963), 329–45. A discussion and criticism of the argument from the commendatory invariance of 'good'.

*Hancock, R. "A Note on Hare's *The Language of Morals*," *The Philosophical Quarterly*, 13 (1963), 56–63. A criticism of Hare's claims that moral judgments are primarily used to guide choices, and that judgments which guide choices entail imperatives.

*Hare, R. M. *Freedom and Reason*. Oxford: The Clarendon Press, 1963.

———. *The Language of Morals*. Oxford: The Clarendon Press, 1952.

*Harrison, Jonathan. "Can Ethics Do Without Propositions?" Mind, 59 (1950), 358–71. A consideration of some objections to early emotive theories.

*Hofstadter, A., and J. C. C. McKinsey. "On the Logic of Imperatives," *Philosophy of Science*, 6 (1939), 446–57. One of the first attempts to provide formal rules for the logical manipulation of imperative sentences.

*Kaplan, A. "Are Moral Judgments Assertions?" *Philosophical Review*, 51 (1942), 280–303. Kaplan claims that moral expressions are not assertions, but rather serve to express the speaker's emotions and to commit him to a certain course of action.

*Kerner, George C. *The Revolution in Ethical Theory*. New York and Oxford: Oxford University Press, 1966. A recent discussion of the views of Moore, Stevenson, Toulmin, and Hare. Makes use of some of the ideas introduced by J. L. Austin.

*Nielsen, Kai. "On Looking Back at the Emotive Theory," *Methodos*, 14 (1962), 3–20. Attempts to examine the emotive theory (as presented by Ayer in "On the Analysis of Moral Judgments," *Horizon*, September 1949) and yet preserve its major insights.

Nowell-Smith, P. H. *Ethics*. Baltimore, Md.: Penguin Books, Inc., 1954.

*Stevenson, C. L. "Brandt's Questions about Emotive Ethics," *The Philosophical Review*, 59 (1950), 528–34. A reply to Brandt's article "The Emotive Theory of Ethics."

———. *Ethics and Language*. New Haven, Conn.: Yale University Press, 1944.

———. *Facts and Values*. New Haven, Conn.: Yale University Press, 1963. A collection of earlier writings on ethics and a new essay containing his present ideas and reactions to criticisms of *Ethics and Language*.

*Stroll, Avrum. "The Emotive Theory of Ethics," *University of California Publications in Philosophy*, 28 (1954), 1–92. A criticism of the emotive theory of Ayer and Stevenson.

*Tomas, Vincent. "Ethical Disagreement and the Emotive Theory of Values," Mind, 40 (1951), 205–22. Tomas discusses and emphasizes similarities between disagreements in belief and disagreements in attitude.

Urmson, J. O. "On Grading," *Mind*, 59 (1950), 145–69.

*von Wright, G. H. "Deontic Logic," *Mind*, 60 (1951), 1–15. Deontic logic is the study of logical relations among judgments of obligation. This paper provides an elementary formal logic of these judgments.

INDEX

Index

359